SHAKEN AUTHORITY

SHAKEN AUTHORITY

China's Communist Party and
the 2008 Sichuan Earthquake

Christian P. Sorace

CORNELL UNIVERSITY PRESS   ITHACA AND LONDON

Cornell University Press gratefully acknowledges support from the First Book Subvention Program of the Association for Asian Studies and receipt of a Subsidy for Publication grant from the Chiang Ching-kuo Foundation for International Scholarly Exchange (USA), both of which aided in the publication of this book.

First published 2017 by Cornell University Press

Printed in the United States of America

Library of Congress Cataloging-in-Publication Data

Names: Sorace, Christian P., 1981– author.
Title: Shaken authority : China's Communist Party and the 2008 Sichuan
    earthquake / Christian P. Sorace.
Description: Ithaca : Cornell University Press, 2017. | Includes bibliographical
    references and index.
Identifiers: LCCN 2016048273 (print) | LCCN 2016049201 (ebook) |
    ISBN 9781501707537 (cloth : alk. paper) | ISBN 9781501708497
    (epub/mobi) | ISBN 9781501708503 (pdf)
Subjects: LCSH: Earthquake relief—China—Wenchuan Xian (Sichuan Sheng) |
    Emergency management—China—Wenchuan Xian (Sichuan Sheng) |
    Wenchuan Earthquake, China, 2008. | Zhongguo gong chan dang.
Classification: LCC HV600 2008.W46 S67 2017 (print) | LCC HV600 2008.W46
    (ebook) | DDC 363.34/958095138—dc23
LC record available at https://lccn.loc.gov/2016048273

Photographs are by the author.

To my parents, Phillip and Faustina

Contents

Acknowledgments   ix

Maps   xi

Introduction   1

1. The Communist Party's Miracle   17

2. Party Spirit Made Flesh   40

3. Blood Transfusion, Generation, and Anemia   59

4. The Utopia of Urban Planning: Dujiangyan Municipality   81

5. The Mirage of Development: Yingxiu Township   105

6. The Ideological Pursuit of Ecology: Qingchuan County   124

Conclusion   148

Notes   157

Glossary of Terms and Phrases   195

Bibliography   199

Index   223

Acknowledgments

In writing this book, I have accumulated many intellectual debts, only a few of which I can mention here. I must begin by thanking William Hurst, who has played several significant roles in my life as teacher, adviser, coauthor, intellectual companion, and friend. Since I met him several years ago at a conference, Andy Mertha has been a constant source of intellectual generosity, inspiration, and encouragement. I am grateful to Geremie R. Barmé for the refreshing candor of his friendship and for the red ink he has donated to various portions of this manuscript. I would also like to thank Geremie for suggesting the title of this book. I am deeply thankful to Gloria Davies for inestimably improving my manuscript with her detailed and thoughtful comments. Many thanks are due to Luigi Tomba for his critical commentary and helpful suggestions on how to revise and sharpen several key concepts and ideas in this book and the project I am working on now.

For insightful feedback on earlier versions and chapters of this project as it has evolved over several years, I thank Elizabeth Perry, Catherine Boone, Jonathan Unger, Anita Chan, Jonathan Kinkel, Edwin Schmitt, Jane Golley, and the two anonymous readers for Cornell University Press. Especially deserving of thanks is my editor Roger Haydon for his confidence, guidance, and patience in responding to my anxious e-mail queries. Bingyi also deserves many thanks for generously allowing me to reproduce a section of her breathtaking ink-on-silk scroll painting *Apocalypse* as the book cover.

I am particularly fortunate to have been supported by wonderful institutions and networks while researching and writing this book. I thank the University of Texas at Austin, Department of Government, in particular Robert Moser and Tom Pangle for generously funding my preliminary trips to China; the Fulbright-Hays Doctoral Research Fellowship for enabling me to have ample time in the field; Sichuan Academy of Social Sciences for hosting me and allowing me to follow my hunches; the Universities Service Centre for China Studies at the Chinese University of Hong Kong for its treasure troves; participants in the 2014 Association for Asian Studies–Social Science Research Council (AAS-SSRC) Dissertation Workshop "Dispossession, Capital and the State" for their critical feedback on an early version of chapter 4; the Cornell Contemporary China Initiative for inviting me to present a lecture that would become the basis of chapter 2; the Political Science Department at Hobart and William Smith Colleges for the opportunity to be a visiting professor and learn from the process of teaching; ANU College of Asia and the Pacific CartoGIS for the beautiful maps at the front of the book; and my current institutional home, the Australian National University's Centre on China in the World (ANU-CIW), for the invaluable gifts of time and intellectual nourishment needed to bring this book to fruition.

This book includes excerpts from the author's following articles, reprinted with permission. Chapter 2 is a slightly altered version of my article "Party Spirit Made Flesh: The Production of Legitimacy in the Aftermath of the 2008 Sichuan Earthquake," published in the *China Journal*. Chapter 3 contains revised sections from "The Communist Party's Miracle? The Alchemy of Turning Post-Disaster Reconstruction into Great Leap Development," published in *Comparative Politics*.

I thank the mentors, friends, interlocutors, and comrades who have influenced my life over the years, including but not limited to Eric Santner, Lauren Berlant, Erik Vogt, Drew Hyland, George Higgins, the late Kenneth Lloyd-Jones, Jodi Dean, Stacey Philbrick Yadav, David Ost, Joseph Mink, Stefanie Fishel, Benjamin Farrer, Kamran Ali, Benjamin Gregg, Patricia Maclachlan, Henry Dietz, Wendy Hunter, Paula Newberg, Fiona Jenkins, Haun Saussy, Mark Frazier, Kjeld Erik Brødsgaard, Bin Xu, Jean Hong, Guo Hong, Zhang Xiangrong, Li Yongdong, Guan Kai, Peng Dapeng, Todd Altschul, Mark Gutzmer, Ceschi Ramos, Caleb Ford, Joshua Mandell, Nicholas Loubere, Ying Qian, Olivier Krischer, Ivan Franceschini, Maria Repnikova, Marie-Ève Reny, Suzanne Scoggins, John Wagner Givens, James Joshua Hudson, Regina Goodnow, Peter Mohanty, and Elise Giuliano.

I am forever grateful to my parents for instilling in me a love for books and learning that made me the masochistic academic I am today. They are the pillars of my faith that there is kindness in the world.

Finally, I would like to thank my source of light and happiness, I-Ling Liu. Our life together is what keeps my world vibrant, dreamlike, and hopeful.

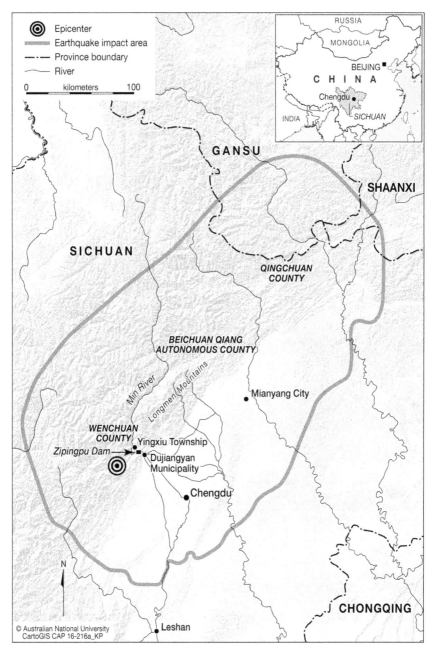

MAP 1: Map of 2008 Sichuan earthquake impact area

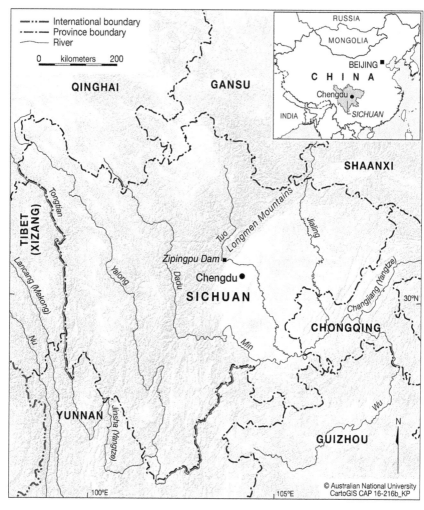

MAP 2: Map of Sichuan Province

SHAKEN AUTHORITY

Introduction

Whenever a man speaks to others, he is doing propaganda work. . . .
It is therefore imperative that our comrades should all study language.

—Mao Zedong, 1942

As St. Paul admirably put it, it is in the "Logos," meaning in ideology,
that we "live, move, and have our being."

—Louis Althusser, 1970

On May 12, 2008, a 7.9 magnitude earthquake struck the Wenchuan region of Sichuan Province. Over eighty-five thousand people died and five million were left homeless. The overall economic damage was estimated to range from $9.7 billion to $1.2 trillion. The devastation continued as multiple aftershocks hit the region. During the reconstruction effort, mudslides destroyed several newly reconstructed villages. A BBC report gives some idea of the scale of the disaster: "More than five million rooms (around 1.5 million houses) were destroyed, and over 21 million rooms were damaged (around 6 million houses). This is more than the number of houses that are in the entire country of Australia."[1]

Although the Chinese authorities earned plaudits from international media for the rapid response to the emergency and the media access they allowed to the disaster site, the tenor of public opinion changed when it was reported that over seven thousand classrooms in shoddily constructed schools had collapsed. The killer buildings were dubbed "tofu-dregs schoolhouses" (*doufuzha xiaoshe*) (tofu-dregs are soft and mushy remnants from the process of making tofu—former premier Zhu Rongji coined this metaphor for shoddy construction during an inspection visit in 1998 to the site of a newly built dam that collapsed). In Sichuan's schools, at least five thousand children died. Grieving parents staged protests and called for an official investigation into why the schools collapsed and to punish the officials and building contractors found responsible for the tragedy.

The official definition of what had transpired on May 12, 2008, focused not on the manmade disaster (*renhuo*) leading to the deaths of trapped schoolchildren, but rather on the scale of the natural disaster (*tianzai*) that was the earthquake.

1

Internally, however, the Party was telling a different story. A month after the earthquake, an article in the restricted circulation Party journal *Leadership Reference* cautioned its readers about the developing public opinion that "superficially, it was a *natural disaster*; in reality, this was a *manmade catastrophe*" (emphasis added).[2]

These are not benign, descriptive terms. In China, the distinction between "natural disaster" and "manmade catastrophe" is historically associated with the Great Leap Famine (1959–62) in which it is estimated over thirty million people starved to death.[3] During China's Great Leap Forward campaign to simultaneously collectivize agriculture and accelerate industrialization through the mobilization of society, the famine resulted from a confluence of factors, including unrealistic production targets, fabricated reports of record-breaking harvests, excessive grain requisition, failure of the political system to transmit accurate information, and a series of natural disasters. On May 31, 1961, Liu Shaoqi gave a verbal report to the Central Work Conference addressing whether the country's economic turmoil was "caused by a natural disaster or if it was a manmade catastrophe."[4] Based on investigations he conducted in Hunan Province and discussions with local peasants, Liu suggested that in certain areas, the famine was "30 percent natural disaster, 70 percent manmade catastrophe" (*san fen tianzai, qi fen renhuo*). At the Beidahe Work Conference in 1962, Mao criticized this position as "all darkness" and "no light," meaning that it one-sidedly focused on the disaster and not on the achievements. As a result, the description of the Great Leap Famine as "three years of economic difficulty" (*san nian jingji kunnan*) was removed from circulation and replaced by the explanation "three years of natural disaster" (*san nian ziran zaihai*).[5]

In China today, the term for "emergency" (*tufa shijian*), literally a "sudden occurrence," encompasses any event (natural or accidental, real or imagined) that the authorities deem *might* threaten social stability. In article 3 of the Emergency Response Law of the People's Republic of China (2007) an "emergency incident . . . shall refer to a natural disaster, accidental disaster, public health incident, or social safety incident, which takes place by accident, has caused or might cause serious social damage and needs the adoption of emergency response measures."[6] Although the fluid legal classification of "emergency" and Party discourse of "crisis" (*weiji*) blur the distinctions between qualitatively different events by grouping them together as a threat to social stability, their malleability also places ultimate control over how they are defined in the hands of the Party.[7]

Official media outlets were banned from reporting on collapsed schools and protesting parents.[8] The censorship of information, however, is only one aspect of the broader ideological goals of discursive production. Party authorities were tireless in asserting that the Sichuan earthquake was "beyond any doubt a natural disaster"; "it was an act of nature that could not be prevented."[9] Internal directives were issued to the local Party bureaucracies to "increase propaganda education efforts in order to instill in peasants a deep awareness that their houses collapsed or were damaged because of *natural disaster* and not because of *manmade catastrophe*" (emphasis added).[10]

The Communist Party not only led the mammoth post-earthquake rescue and reconstruction efforts; it was also the source of happiness and life itself. On a billboard on a highway linking Dujiangyan to Wenchuan County constructed after the earthquake was the slogan "When drinking water, remember the well-digger. We rely on the Communist Party for happiness" (*chishui bu wang wa jing ren, xingfu quan kao gongchandang*). (The origin of this phrase is from a story in which Mao witnessed an elderly man strenuously carrying buckets of muddy water attached to a shoulder pole. From talking to the man, Mao realized that the village was suffering from a water shortage and was said to have rolled up his sleeves and trouser legs and set about digging a new well. The villagers were effusively grateful.) Other slogans that appeared in the earthquake zone exhorted readers to "be grateful to the mighty Communist Party for our new roads, new bridges, and new houses" (*gan'en weida gongchandang, xin lu, xin qiao, xin zhufang*) and "An earthquake doesn't care, the Party does" (*dizhen wuqing, dang youqing*). In official media reports, local residents declared, "Without the Party organization, I would not be alive" (*meiyou dang zuzhi, jiu meiyou wo de shengming*). When earthquake survivors expressed different opinions, local Party authorities initiated a "gratitude education" (*gan'en jiaoyu*) campaign to pull them into line.[11]

FIGURE 1. "Reconstructing the homeland in the aftermath of disaster. When you drink water, remember its source: be grateful to the Party." Wenchuan County, Du-Wen Highway, March 2012

FIGURE 2. "Grateful to the Communist Party." Wenchuan County, March 2012

For the few who rejected the Party's generosity, insisting that the earthquake was a "manmade catastrophe," the state's repressive apparatus was at the ready.

Tan Zuoren, a schoolteacher with a history of activism, undertook an independent investigation into the tofu-dregs schoolhouses. He was arrested for "inciting the subversion of state power" (*shandong dianfu guojia zhengquan*).[12] In August 2009, the noted Beijing-based artist Ai Weiwei was to appear as a witness at Tan's trial in Chengdu. Even though Ai did not know the activist personally, Ai himself was pursuing a citizen's investigation aimed at collecting the names and biographical data of the dead schoolchildren and went to Sichuan as a gesture of solidarity with Tan. In the early hours of August 12, 2009 (the day of Tan's trial), police accosted Ai in his hotel room. He suffered a cerebral hemorrhage and was forced to seek treatment overseas.[13] Huang Qi, another Sichuan human rights advocate, was also arrested in 2009 but on charges of "possessing state secrets" unrelated to the earthquake.[14] His interrogators, however, focused on his post-earthquake assistance to parents of dead children who were petitioning for justice. Huang's chief jailor told his lawyer: "I have a written order forbidding any visitors for the prisoner signed by Zhou Yongkang, Chairman of the CCP Political and Legal Committee."[15]

To assuage the bereaved and irate parents, the Party employed a mix of material incentives, including undisclosed compensation fees along with policing techniques such as surveillance and arrests. Internal memoranda make it clear that the strategy was to divide the parents into "good people" who accepted the Party's view that the earthquake was a natural disaster and "bad elements" who insisted it was a manmade catastrophe that required investigation into its causes and the punishment of those responsible.[16] One memorandum advised local cadres in Dujiangyan who had been organized into Party work teams whose mandate was to manage the crisis to "listen attentively to [popular] demands" and "establish a consultation mechanism and begin dialogue"; for "individual parents who are emotionally out of control and engage in physical conflict" it would be necessary to "carry out a public security conversation,"[17] which entailed repression. According to a leaked memo from the U.S. consulate in China, "Dujiangyan authorities detained 50–60 of the parents involved. Of those, two groups of 7–8 parents were placed on the flatbeds of two trucks with their hands bound behind their backs, and then paraded through the streets of the city—a brutal message to other parents not to inquire or protest further."[18]

After the Great Leap Famine in 1962, Mao said, "Writing novels is popular these days, isn't it? The use of novels for antiparty activity is a great invention. Anyone wanting to overthrow a political regime must create public opinion and do some preparatory ideological work. This applies to counterrevolutionary as well as to revolutionary classes."[19] Although the parents in Sichuan were not penning revolutionary manifestos or subversive novels, they were challenging the Party's control of the narrative of the earthquake as a natural disaster. For the Party, control over discourse is key to political longevity.

The Discursive State

In recent years, international studies of Chinese politics have tended to favor topical specialization and integration with disciplinary norms, research questions, and methodological conventions of U.S.-centric political science. As Kevin O'Brien points out, although these changes have provided high-resolution images of specific issues, they have also "led to a certain hollowing out of the field of Chinese politics" in which big-picture questions about "how the political system operates" are no longer asked.[20]

This book addresses the political mechanisms at work in the shadow of the 2008 Sichuan earthquake and the broader ideological energies that drove these mechanisms. I propose an interpretive approach that takes Communist Party ideas and discourse as being central to how that organization formulates policies, defines legitimacy, and exerts its power. My basis for this claim is that Party discourse permeates, conditions, and filters each aspect of Chinese politics. As Michael Schoenhals commented, formal Party language is a kind of power "managed and manipulated by the state"; it "thus has a bearing upon all aspects of Chinese politics."[21] This introduction is an attempt to attune our ears to Communist Party discourse as a source of knowledge and insight into Chinese politics.

The term "discourse," however, carries a pejorative connotation associated with a caricature of postmodern thought once fashionable in U.S. academia. Vivien Schmidt, a proponent of "discursive institutionalism" in political science, observes how "'discourse' conjures up exaggerated visions of postmodernists and post-structuralists who are assumed (often unfairly) to interpret 'texts' without contexts and to understand reality as all words, whatever the deeds."[22] Recent trends and Cold War legacies in the study of Chinese politics further banish "discourse" to the realm of Communist Party "propaganda," which is considered "obsolete and far-fetched"[23] and therefore of little value in analyzing how power in China actually works. Party writing is also not particularly enjoyable to read, an experience perhaps best described by Simon Leys as analogous to "swallowing sawdust by the bucketful."[24]

As a result of these disciplinary trends, methodological assumptions, and political biases, Communist Party ideology and discourse have been relegated to the margins of serious international scholarship on the politics of China. As Frank

Pieke observed, "it has now become a 'habit of the heart' among China scholars to reject Maoism and its successor ideologies (Deng Xiaoping Theory, the 'Three Represents' and the 'harmonious society') as blatant lies that merely serve to coat the CCP's rule in a thin veneer of legitimacy, rather than as serious attempts to define socialism or the CCP's vision."[25] In the words of Anne-Marie Brady, "Many China specialists seem to have taken it as an article of faith that the CCP government is doomed and the propaganda state is dead."[26]

I believe that in both traditional and modern Chinese political theories and practices of statecraft, language has played a central role in the articulation and maintenance of political order. For the Chinese state, official discourse and terminology are not merely descriptive; they are also meant to be exemplary and normative, authoritative and binding. Intellectual historian Timothy Cheek describes a tradition that begins with the Confucian dictum that "if names were not correct and realities did not conform to correct names, then the moral state would be an impossibility" and continues with the Communist Party that "exhibits a faith in the power of names similar to that attributed to Confucius."[27] Although it is beyond the scope of this book to offer a conceptual history of language in Chinese politics, one can still identify some ideas that demonstrate how the Party-state controls the narrative context in which words assume their meaning.

In the *Analects*, Confucius says that if he were a ruler, the first thing he would do is "rectify the names" (*zhengming*) in order to bring the chaotic reality of politics in line with the cosmological order and the Way (*dao*) from which it had strayed. This passage is worth quoting in full:

> Zilu asked: "If the ruler of Wei were to entrust you with the government of the country, what would be your first initiative?" The Master said: "It would certainly be to rectify the names." Zilu said: "Really? Isn't this a little farfetched? What is this rectification for?" The Master said: "How boorish can you get! Whereupon a gentleman is incompetent, thereupon he should remain silent. If the names are not correct, language is without an object. When language is without an object, no affair can be effected. When no affair can be effected, rites and music wither. When rites and music wither, punishments and penalties miss their target. When punishments and penalties miss their target, the people do not know where they stand. Therefore, whatever a gentleman conceives of, he must be able to say; and whatever he says, he must be able to do. In the matter of language, a gentleman leaves nothing to chance."[28]

The state is not only an apparatus of control and extraction; it is also the source of meanings and moral center of Chinese society. State discourse is invested with the power of shaping reality in accordance with broader cosmological-ideological visions and normative models of behavior.[29]

In 1939, Mao's commentary on Chen Boda's report denouncing Confucian philosophy as idealism (*weixinzhuyi*) reveals intriguing similarities and marked differences between the Communist and Confucian approaches to language.[30] In agreement with Chen, Mao faults Confucius for believing that the political solution to social dislocation is the restoration of an idealized past, specifically the recovery of the rites of Zhou (*zhou li*). For Mao, the Confucian doctrine of the "rectification of names" is politically conservative because it privileges an invariant structure of "names" (*ming*) over a dynamic social "reality" (*shi*); and yet, in contrast with Chen's blanket dismissal of Confucianism, Mao suggests that the rectification of names retains epistemological value insofar as it is subordinated to a theory of practice (*shijian*) (elaborated two years earlier in Mao's essay "On Practice"). As long as the names are derived from and conform to the changing circumstances of reality, they can play an "active role" (*nengdongxing*) in guiding revolutionary transformation. Mao concludes that the Confucian doctrine is an inverted form of Lenin's dictum "Without revolutionary theory there can be no revolutionary movement"[31] and that the Communist Party's mission is to "rectify the revolutionary order of names" (*zheng geming zhixu zhi ming*). Over twenty years later, Mao referred to China's ideological war with Soviet revisionism as a struggle over "proper names." On May 11, 1963, at the Hangzhou Work Conference, Mao attacked Khrushchev's revisionism by quoting Confucius: "A single word may rejuvenate a country [*yi yan xing bang*], a single word may bring disaster to a country [*yi yan sang bang*]" and adding his theoretical signature, "This is the spiritual [*jingshen*] changing the material [*wuzhi*]."[32]

As China's heirs to Lenin's revolution, the CCP regarded discourse as a political instrument to destroy the old world and create a new one. The struggle for an emancipatory future would take place in the construction of "vigorous, lively, fresh, and forceful"[33] discursive frames, vocabularies, and speaking habits, which were to enact the Party's ideological vision.[34] As a complex and ongoing process of "exegetical bonding,"[35] Communist Party discourse was transmitted via political campaigns and mobilizations, embedded in the Party's organizational structures and reinforced by disciplinary practices. Louis Althusser once quipped that without power to enforce it, ideology is little more than the ranting of an "unarmed prophet."[36] I suggest that among the reasons for the political resilience of the CCP is its ability to weave together ideology, organization, and daily life.[37] Political technologies that originated in the Soviet Union were adapted, elaborated, and honed in the Mao era. As Yu Liu points out,

All communist states shared a similar macro-discourse, but China was the only one, or at least the most successful one, to develop a systematic method of having this discourse digested at the micro-level. In Mao's China, every person was supposed, through small-group meetings, confession-writing, and so on, to internalize the collective discourse by reproducing it in individual stories.[38]

One of the Communist Party's insights into the workings of power is that ideology takes root in people's lives through the repetition of discourse. During the Party's land reform campaign (*tudi gaige*) (1947–52), the CCP did not simply redistribute land; it dispatched work-teams of cadres to villages to enlist the peasantry in "speaking bitterness" (*suku*) sessions. According to Ann Anagnost, the goal of these sessions was to engineer "a new frame for the reworking of consciousness in which the speaker comes to recognize himself or herself as a victim of an immoral system rather than a bearer of bad fate or personal shortcoming. In other words, one had to recognize one's conditions of existence in terms of class antagonism."[39] A recurrent theme throughout this book is the CCP's ingrained belief in the dialectical transformation of economic, social, and ideological structures.

As the Party under the Great Helmsman, as Mao was called, steered China to a bright future, it was also managing crises that were often the result of its own policy failures. One of its tools for engineering public sentiment was the practice of *yiku sitian*, a Chinese expression meaning to recall the bitterness of the old society and to savor the sweetness of the present. When people were upset with their present circumstances, they were encouraged to remember how much worse it was before the Communist Party ran the country. In the shadow of the Great Leap Famine (1959–62) and as part of the Socialist Education Movement (1962–65) in 1964, a *yiku sitian* campaign was launched, which according to Ralph Thaxton was "an explicit attempt of the party-state to manipulate popular memory in ways that would help the party cast the Great Leap Forward as an episode in the continuing party-championed struggle to improve popular livelihood and save the nation."[40] I suggest that the "gratitude education" (*gan'en jiaoyu*) campaign after the Sichuan earthquake, mentioned above and discussed in detail in chapter 1, is a result of the same political narrative.

During the Cultural Revolution, Mao's pronouncements, especially those selected in the *Quotations from Chairman Mao Zedong* (in English popularly known as the "Little Red Book"), obtained a "scriptural authority" that required practices of "religious hermeneutics and catechism."[41] As kings in medieval France and England were believed to have a "royal touch" that could heal scrofula, Chairman Mao's words were imbued with sacred power.[42] Even the disposal and large-scale pulping of the Little Red Book after Mao's death in 1976 had to be handled with caution and done in secret.[43]

For many international scholars of China, the reform era is defined as a narrative of disenchantment. Freed from the shackles of ideology and the grip of the dictatorship of the proletariat, China's citizens were "liberated" (*jiefang*) to earn money, pursue their dreams, and in doing so, modernize the nation.

The view that China's economic reform is the product of naturalized historical forces with no ideological dimension has led to a tendency to treat Communist Party ideology as a mere formality and window dressing. I suggest, rather, that China's economic reform is a profoundly ideological undertaking that builds on and transforms the Maoist legacy. Economic reform is not a simple rupture with the Maoist past but the result of a continued struggle of ideas, values, and practices. This is why, for example, current Party leader Xi Jinping and his coterie of thinkers have argued that there is no fundamental rift between the first thirty years of the People's Republic of China (1949–78) and the second (1979–2008). Indeed, the Communist Party has never relinquished its belief in the power of discourse to shape the world and the people who inhabit it.[44] In the words of Li Shulei, secretary of the Party's powerful Discipline Inspection Committee in Beijing and confidant of Party leader Xi Jinping, "Language never only reflects reality; it moulds reality. . . . Language is not a political instrument; it is politics itself."[45]

Breathing the Air of Ideology

It is frequently assumed in both international media and scholarship that even if ideology still matters to the Communist Party, ordinary citizens do not actually believe in the Party's political slogans and entreaties for gratitude. Communist Party propaganda seems increasingly out of touch with the daily concerns of ordinary citizens who are more interested in purchasing a home than in the correct political line.[46] I argue that framing the problem of ideology as a question of belief misses how it functions as an assemblage of practices that shape people's everyday habits of speech and dispositions. My argument is based on the work of French philosopher Louis Althusser.

Althusser argues that ideology operates in the material world and not in the recesses of individual belief. In his analysis of Christian ideology, he focuses directly on religious practices such as "going to mass, of kneeling down, of the gesture of the sign of the cross, or of the *mea culpa*, of a sentence, of a prayer, of an act of contrition, of a penitence, of a gaze, of a hand-shake, of an external verbal discourse or an 'internal' verbal discourse."[47] According to Althusser's theory, belief is the effect of acting as if one believes, even if one does not: "kneel down, move your lips in prayer, and you will believe."[48] Discourse is also material. Prayer is not an empty act. The church's ceremonies and skein of ideas transform the physical gesture of kneeling down into a religious act of significance.[49] From the Althusserian perspective, the quest to find the smoking gun indicating direct causality between belief and action, intention and outcome, preference and political behavior is like attempting to understand the world in the reflection of a brackish pond.

Althusser speaks of "interpellation" as the process by which ideology takes a hold of and constitutes the individual as a recognizable and socialized subject. He illustrates this point with the scene of an individual walking down the street who turns around when he hears a police officer shout "Hey you!"[50] One explanation holds that the turn is a result of the individual's "passionate complicity with the law."[51] "Although there would be no turning around without first having been hailed, neither would there be a turning around without some readiness to turn."[52] In China, social groups long accustomed to life under Party rule adopt, internalize, and elaborate dominant discourses in order "to define themselves as legitimate subjects within the existing system of power relations rather than producing alternative or revolutionary worldviews."[53]

To continue with this metaphor, running from the hail of the police officer is an even deeper recognition of guilt before the law. The person who runs will be chased and arrested, perhaps shot at or beaten. Commenting on Althusser's claim that "nine times out of ten, individuals respond to the hail that was meant for them, proving themselves good subjects," Banu Bargu points out that "this means that in one out of ten cases, interpellation fails; for those, the repressive apparatus of the state is always ready."[54] According to Étienne Balibar, a person's refusal of ideology is done "at the risk, in fact, of their lives or their mental integrity."[55]

I suggest that Althusser's definition of ideology as that which guarantees identity is a salutary corrective to the tendency among scholars to view political behavior in China in instrumental terms. Take, for example, the following two sentences: People join the Party to improve their career opportunities, not because they believe in Party ideology. Protestors manipulate the language of the law to advance their own interests.[56] These kinds of narratives are both appealing and misleading for the same reason; according to Timothy Mitchell, this mode of thinking "obliges us to imagine the exercise of power as an external process that can coerce the behavior of the body without necessarily penetrating and controlling the mind."[57] What such stylized snapshots of Chinese politics miss is that people do not *stand outside* of discourse even when they manipulate it. A peasant who strategically deploys Party discourse to advance his own material interests is still thinking in, assessing from, citing, and reproducing Party discourse.

A savvy college graduate who ridicules Party ideology but nonetheless joins the Party to improve her career prospects is not somehow protected from ideology by a cloak of cynical opportunism.

Even regime dissidents are cut from the same ideological cloth as the Party they are challenging.[58] According to Geremie Barmé, "Modes of criticism in Mainland Chinese culture still readily fall back on the habits of mind and language inculcated by decades of party rule. Even in an environment of free speech and media openness the rhetorical style of totalitarianism . . . maintains its appeal."[59] The documentary film *The Gate of Heavenly Peace* (produced and directed by Carma Hinton and Richard Gordon with screenplay by Barmé) portrays how the 1989 Tiananmen student protesters borrowed Maoist idioms of blood and self-sacrifice and reproduced among themselves some of the authoritarian hierarchies and pathologies they decried in the Communist Party.[60]

Althusser's definition of ideology is conveyed in a cartoon published in the *New Yorker* of a giant squid wearing a chef's hat behind a sushi bar with the caption "He feels he can do more good working within the system." Althusser's lesson is that either way the squid gets eaten, only in the cartoon scenario the squid is complicit with its own dismemberment.

For a brief interval of time after the earthquake, it seemed as if the Party's moral authority was badly shaken. The view that the real catastrophe of the Sichuan earthquake was not the quake but the shoddy construction of schools and the death of innocent children threatened the Party's carefully managed narrative that held that the earthquake was a tragic but ultimately unavoidable natural disaster.

The reconstruction would transform Sichuan into a showcase of Party benevolence and state capacity.[61] Prominently displayed on billboards in Beichuan County, the slogans "Bid farewell to sorrow and face the future" (*gaobie chuangtong, mianxiang weilai*) and "From tragedy to heroism" (*cong beizhuang xiang haomai*) interpellated the earthquake survivors to leave behind their grief and embrace the new lives offered to them by the Party. When asked if the local villagers were unhappy with any aspect of the reconstruction, a Party secretary from a small village in Beichuan County firmly responded, "They cannot have any demands because the government has already provided them with excellent help." Many villagers I spoke with admitted that they do not dare express their grievances out of fear that others will label them as selfish and greedy and socially ostracize them. After recounting a litany of complaints with the reconstruction and behavior of local Party cadres, an elderly woman added that she nevertheless "swallows her unhappiness" because she is terrified of appearing "ungrateful." This internalization of powerlessness is an example of the Althusserian moment in which the individual turns toward the voice of authority emanating from within. The disaster victims, human rights activists, and lawyers who refuse to comply are monitored, harassed, detained, beaten, and in some cases arrested—a situation that continues to this day.[62] Viewed from the Party's perspective, the censorship of a few "emotionally unbalanced" (*xinli shiheng*) parents is perhaps regrettable but ultimately necessary as it protects the narrative of Party benevolence.[63]

Methods

During my eighteen months of fieldwork from January 2012 through August 2013 in over five municipalities, seven county-level seats, six townships, and seven villages affected by Sichuan's 2008 earthquake,[64] I conducted ethnographic observations and open-ended interviews with over one hundred villagers, government officials, nongovernmental organization (NGO) leaders, and scholars and read over one thousand pages of internal Party reports.

To capture the Party's discursive logic, I draw from a significant body of Chinese textual material ranging from mass media accounts to published Party materials, reconstruction plans, and internally circulated Party work reports and documents. In the field, I conducted interviews with local cadres administratively ranked at the village, township, and county levels. For the majority of interviews, I was introduced to cadres through networks of friends, scholars, NGOs, and the cadres I had previously interviewed. Interviews varied in both duration and location, ranging from impromptu dinners and informal car trips to formal discussions conducted in an office setting. I also draw on interview transcripts conducted by local researchers.

During my time in the field, I was affiliated with the Sichuan Academy of Social Sciences (SiASS) as a visiting researcher. As part of the Chengdu academic community, I interviewed over a dozen professors from different universities, many who played advisory roles to the Party at different stages in the reconstruction process corresponding to their field of expertise. As a general observation, academic discourse in China on the Sichuan earthquake, even in private conversations with nuanced and critical inflections, still reproduced Party discourse and rationality. I also interviewed several newly formed NGO leaders and volunteers who were drawn to the earthquake zone out of a sense of compassion, patriotic duty, and youthful idealism. My time spent with NGOs attuned me to the necessity of appropriating Party discourse to justify one's existence. To summarize my interactions with academic and NGO communities in China, my main observation was how the Party's ideological apparatuses flexibly envelop critical positions and energies as part of its own discourse.[65]

Finally, I spent considerable time in cities and villages throughout the earthquake zone and lived for over a year in a residential complex built for earthquake survivors in Dujiangyan. In my various daily encounters, observations, and sem-istructured interviews with neighbors and villagers, I listened to how Party discourse permeated their accounts of Party legitimacy and satisfaction level with the reconstruction, especially so in the case of people who were livid with the Party for its failure to serve their needs. To be clear, I am arguing not that people do not have their own ideas, opinions, voices, and desires, but that these are inaccessible without some familiarity with the discourses in which they are articulated.

Interpretive methodology functions like a seismograph that measures the sometimes subtle, sometimes dramatic movements within Chinese political life.

Overview

The post-2008 Sichuan earthquake reconstruction provides a rare window into Communist Party rationality, discourse, and governance across a range of research topics and issues. In the words of an article from a restricted access Party publication,

> Ultimately, [the reconstruction] will be used to evaluate the sustainability of China's current political, economic, and social system; it will be used to verify and measure the governing capacity of the Communist Party and the leadership ability of the social elite. The process of post-disaster reconstruction is like a prism, reflecting both the superior advantages and profound abuses of China's current political system. . . . Everyone expects the earthquake area to become a model example for the future of China's economic, social, cultural, political and ecological construction.[66]

In chapter 1, I provide a new perspective on Party legitimacy based on Mao-era norms, expectations, and discourse that contour how the Party and masses (state-society in political science terminology) view and interact with each other. During fieldwork, I was surprised by people's unrealistically high expectations and demands on the Party. Many of the earthquake survivors I interviewed held a view that the Party ought to guarantee their post-quake livelihoods and were disappointed when they felt that their lives were only marginally improved, if at all, by the reconstruction. I develop the concept of *discursive path dependence* in order to capture the ways in which the Party's narrative of legitimacy predisposed it to transform the reconstruction into a utopian promise of "great leap development" (*kuayueshi fazhan*).

In chapter 2, I analyze the discourse of "Party spirit" (*dangxing*) as a set of Leninist and Maoist ethical norms and expectations that differentiate the cadre (*ganbu*) from a generic state official or Weberian bureaucrat. I believe that the Party revitalizes its legitimacy through demonstrations of benevolence and glory, which depend on the willingness of cadres to suffer and sacrifice themselves on behalf of the people. In the aftermath of the Sichuan earthquake, these norms and expectations were implemented in concrete policy directives and work pressures. As a result, local cadres, who were also earthquake survivors, suffered from exhaustion, insomnia, and depression and in a few extreme cases committed suicide.

Chapter 3 argues that discourse is a productive factor in political economic arrangements. I apply Timothy Mitchell's proposition that "economics should be approached not as a form of knowledge that pictures the world but as a performative activity"[67] to how Communist Party discourse and understanding of the economy shape and interact with China's political economy. I also argue that the Communist Party's planning (*guihua*) apparatus continues to play a crucial role in engineering China's economy and market construction especially in the countryside. Although the Chinese language is without grammatical tenses, planning discourse evokes a future perfect tense in which its vision of future is superimposed on reality. The Party's plans are more than merely technocratic documents but circulate as utopian pronouncements of the future to come.

In the context of post-earthquake reconstruction, chapter 3 investigates how the metaphor of "blood transfusion" (*shuxue*) and "blood generation" (*zaoxue*) established the coordinates for the Party's reconstruction plan to economically develop the Sichuan countryside. The Party planned to transfer capital, technology, and skill from affluent provinces to the Sichuan countryside, which would convert these resources into a self-reliant (*ziligengsheng*) and sustainable local economy. In place of a robust, self-reliant, and blood-generating economy engineered by the mobilization of Party spirit, the economy of the disaster zones is lifeless and anemic (*pinxue*). The Party planned for the reconstruction as if the economy corresponded to a jigsaw puzzle whose pieces only needed to be put into the right place—without taking account of the possibility that some pieces were missing, misshapen, or resistant to being moved.

The first three chapters provide different conceptual lenses that bring into view some of the macroeconomic processes, patterns, and trajectories of the post-earthquake reconstruction. In the remaining three chapters, I turn to my case studies, which provide a granular perspective on the lived outcomes of Communist Party plans, rationalities, and discourses in the earthquake zone.

I chose my three cases on the grounds that they represent different types of reconstruction and local political economic models of development, namely, urban-rural integration, tourism, and ecological civilization. The Party exhortation that cadres "use methods that accord with local circumstances" (*yin di zhi yi*) authorized local cadres to determine the reconstruction plans on the basis of prior and ongoing developmental plans and considerations of local market advantages as well as constraining factors.

Chapter 4 provides an in-depth study of Dujiangyan Municipality's "urban-rural integration" (*chengxiang yitihua*) plan and the Party's obsession with urban form and ideology as the solution to rural underdevelopment. The strategy was to urbanize peasants in Dujiangyan's surrounding villages, provide them with nonagricultural employment and higher incomes, and lease the land to modernized agricultural enterprises. When sufficient industrialization, employment opportunity, and investment in agriculture did not materialize as planned, newly urbanized residents found themselves pinched between higher living costs and lack of income, and as a result, increasingly dependent on Party subsidies for economic survival.[68]

Chapter 5 is a study of Yingxiu Township, the earthquake epicenter. Yingxiu was reconstructed both as a showcase of state capacity and as a tourist destination. The state's desire to present a positive image and create an "earthquake tourist brand"[69] resulted in a situation in which local residents barely make ends meet. Relying on tourism as a form of economic salvation was common throughout the earthquake zone, even in areas where the tourist attraction remains far from evident. Local residents accused the state of wasting resources on "face projects" (*mianzi gongcheng*) that did not benefit their lives. Chapter 5 explores the contradictions of what I call the political aesthetics of development.

Chapter 6 introduces a relatively new concept in the CCP's political vocabulary. "Ecological civilization" (*shengtai wenming*) is the most intriguing and promising model because it offers a new metric of development apart from growth. Among the most remote and impoverished counties in the earthquake zone, Qingchuan County designed a reconstruction plan that would capitalize on environmental protection, forest conservation, and green modes of production. Chapter 6 demonstrates the continued salience of ideological thought work (*sixiang gongzuo*) as a catalyst for economic transformation. In doing so, it also calls to attention the tremendous obstacles for recasting not only production practices but also the very definition of economic development.

THE COMMUNIST PARTY'S MIRACLE

If I gave you a present, but it didn't suit you, you didn't need it, and you didn't even want it, but I was adamant about giving it to you, would it still count as a present?

—A municipal vice-secretary from the earthquake zone, 2012

The Party's initial response to the 2008 Sichuan earthquake seemed to reflect sea changes in Chinese politics, society, and media. The authorities granted journalists unprecedented access in the disaster zone, and volunteers poured into the countryside. Many observers expressed hope in the rescue and relief effort's potential to "create a model of local state–civil society co-operation that could be followed again in the future."[1] In hindsight, the momentary loosening of control appears to have been a mirage rather than a permanent reconfiguration of the relationship between the Party and the people.

As scholars shifted their focus from the emergency rescue period to the long-term process of reconstruction, it became clear that the rebuilding of Sichuan would be a showcase of Party legitimacy and not a platform for expanded civic participation.[2] As Bin Xu notes, "The Sichuan earthquake set the stage for another display of the compassionate nature of the state. Every detail of the government's response became a moral and emotional enactment."[3] Charlene Makley describes the process in which "state leaders attempt to maintain legitimacy in the fact of massive suffering" as one of "spectacular compassion."[4] Shifting perspective to the global stage, Yi Kang argues that the reconstruction process was planned and implemented on the basis of "the intangible aspects of nondemocratic incentive: reputation."[5]

The performance of Party benevolence, compassion, and reputation was not empty propaganda; it required a top-down process of political control over each phase of the reconstruction process. As academics inside China observed early on, "the earthquake reconstruction contains the possibility of a concealed tendency: the unlimited expansion of the scope of state power to represent public authority and control allocation of resources."[6] The "unlimited expansion" of state power also meant increased pressure on the Party to perform "miracles" (qiji) in the earthquake zone. Why, however, would the Party stake its reputation, image, and legitimacy on a utopian promise to engineer "great leaps of development" (kuayueshi fazhan) in two years of breakneck reconstruction activity?

The Communist Party's *discursive path dependence* predisposes it to make and implement policies to narrowly accord with specific norms and precedents, regardless of the drawbacks of such dependency.[7] In effect, this imperative to maintain legitimating narratives constrains the Party's ability to flexibly adapt and respond to the needs of society. As long as the Party is trapped in its own logic of legitimation, institutional reform will also be stuck in the same quagmire of contradictions. Ideology and discourse are not separate from China's political institutions but are enmeshed in their operational logic and daily functioning.

For these reasons, I propose that reading Mao offers an indispensable guide to China's political system. Building on the framework of Sebastian Heilmann and Elizabeth Perry's edited volume *Mao's Invisible Hand*, I shift focus from governance practices to their underlying political discourses and epistemologies. In what follows, I treat Mao's writing as a field of contradictions and crisscrossing grooves and ruts that Communist Party governance follows to this day.[8]

Making the Impossible Possible

The official narrative refers to the post-2008 Sichuan earthquake reconstruction as a miracle (qiji).[9] An editorial published on the third anniversary of the earthquake by Ren Zhongping, the pseudonym of the *People's Daily* collective writing team, defines the miraculous nature of the reconstruction by asking, "How long does it take after an 8.0 earthquake that swallowed nearly 90,000 lives and smashed over 100,000 square kilometers [author's note: an area the equivalent of 1/3 the size of Italy] of mountains and rivers to rebuild a peaceful and happy homeland?"[10] Following a crescendo of rhetorical questions emphasizing the massive scale of the disaster, the answer given is "Three years." In fact, the official target of three years to complete reconstruction work was further accelerated by Prime Minister Wen Jiabao, who suggested that it could be accomplished in "under two years."[11] The reconstruction was celebrated as an example of how "hard work for two to three years can leap across [kuayue] twenty years of monumental change."[12] A report by a professor from the Sichuan Academy of Social Sciences described the reconstruction as a "miracle" that "two arduous years of work" were able to "transform the entire appearance of the disaster area and leap across [*kuayue*] twenty years of development."[13]

After recounting the miraculous achievements of the reconstruction, Ren Zhongping asks, "Who is capable of this kind of faith?" The editorial answers its own question: the Communist Party's "faith" (*xinyang*) is what differentiates China's rapid and comprehensive response to the Sichuan earthquake from the protracted duration of time squandered on post-disaster reconstruction in liberal democracies. The Kobe earthquake in Japan and Hurricane Katrina in New Orleans are cited as examples.[14] The editorial claims that although the U.S. government can boast of strong state capacity, it lacks the political will to "serve the people" (*wei renmin fuwu*). In essence, Ren Zhongping's message is that China's Communist government has always possessed a socialist political will, but it took considerable time and effort for it to develop and align its economic and technological power with its ideology. The influence of this narrative on mainland academic discourse is evident. Several professors I interviewed, although often critical of certain aspects of the reconstruction, argued that the "Sichuan miracle" was possible because of the combination of reform-era economic development and state capacity with the political will, mobilizational ethos, and "faith" of the Mao era.

The Communist Party views its own history as a learning process based on the accumulation of experience and collective wisdom.[15] The Sichuan miracle was not a sudden or surprise occurrence; according to Ren Zhongping, the three years of reconstruction distilled sixty years of Party rule, ninety years of Party history, and five thousand years of China's national spiritual and material development.[16] The editorial suggests that the reconstruction of Sichuan allows people to "peer into" the "mystery of the Communist Party's ability" and decipher the "political secret of China's flourishing socialist system." At the heart of this mystery is the "Chinese people's spirit and faith."[17]

In Chinese, the word for miracle means the "trace" and "impression" (*ji*) of the "unusual" and "rare" (*qi*). According to the official narrative of the post-quake reconstruction, the new and modern schools, hospitals, roads, and houses are "evidence" (*jianzheng*) that bears "witness" (*zuozheng*) to the Party's effective governance. The reconstruction manifests the Communist Party's organizational strength, political ethics, and state capacity; offers a window into the superiority of the socialist system; and is "evidence of national faith" (*jianzheng guojia xinnian*) in Communist Party rule.[18]

Despite the florid prose, Ren Zhongping's editorial provides a cogent account of the Communist Party's legitimacy. Unlike the short-term temporality of election cycles in democracies, the Communist Party's monopoly of political power is rooted in the inheritance and continuity of tradition. This inheritance, how-ever, needs to be periodically affirmed in the production of miracles.

This raises an interesting question: What is a miracle that cannot be an act of God? A secular miracle must both have a scientific explanation and retain an aura of transcendence. According to the web-based encyclopedia Baidu Baike (the Chinese equivalent of Wikipedia), a "miracle" is possible because of the removal of an epistemological blockage of "what previous generations could not even imagine as possible" (*qianren wufa qu xiangxiang de shi*) or through a change in attitude toward something deemed "impossible to achieve" (*bu neng zuodao de shi*) by the dogma of convention and expertise. Miracles in Communist Party discourse are not inexplicable supernatural or divine occurrences. Instead, they are successful shifts of cognition, attitude, and practice, ways of realigning how people understand their society and the role of government. When the "faith" and "persistent struggle" that are required to remove "the tradition of all dead generations" which in the words of Marx "weighs like a nightmare on the brains of the living" are internalized by a large sector of the population, a miracle can be said to have occurred.[19]

A canonical text of Communist Party faith is Mao's essay "The Foolish Old Man Who Removed the Mountains" (*yu gong yi shan*) written in 1945, which was also one of the three required readings (*lao san pian*) during the Cultural Revolution. The essay recounts the fable of a Foolish Old Man who was determined to dig up two mountains in front of his house. Despite the impossibility of the task and derision of wise neighbors who knew better, the Foolish Old Man remained "unshaken in his conviction" and relentlessly kept at his mission. Moved by the old man's commitment, God sent down two angels to remove the mountains. In Mao's interpretation, the Communist Party is cast as the Foolish Old Man and the Chinese people as the power of God. "We must persevere and work unceasingly, and we, too, will touch God's heart. Our God is none other than the masses of the Chinese people. If they stand and dig together with us, why can't these two mountains [author's note: Mao is referring to the mountains of "imperialism" and "feudalism"] be cleared away?"[20]

This idea continues to find life in China's massive infrastructure projects, such as the post–Sichuan earthquake reconstruction; Three Gorges Dam; South-North Water Transfer Project (*nanshui beidiao gongcheng*); Beijing, Tianjin, Hebei (Jingjin-ji) mega-region; and construction of the "Lanzhou New Area," which will require the flattening of seven hundred mountains (over five hundred square miles of land).[21]

The pursuit of gargantuan infrastructural projects does not mean that the Party neglects the infra-individual level of ideological cultivation and attitudinal recalibration. According to the Party's dialectical rationality, macro-level changes are rooted in the governance of thoughts, attitudes, and emotions. For the Party, miracles occur at the molecular level of tiny, imperceptible shifts in cognition and behavior.[22]

Instructive in this regard is *The Miracles of Chairman Mao*, a collection of devotional literature from 1968 to 1970 edited by George Urban. In this anthology, Mao does not personally perform miracles.[23] Instead, the stories consist of ordinary people who invoke Mao's thought and recite his quotations to help them find solutions to problems everyone else (those who lack faith) regards as insurmountable. A popular theme is the story of a medical team that finds a cure for "a disease or condition considered to be incurable by experts and authorities"[24] after reading Mao at their moment of desperation. In this story, Mao does not "cure" the "incurable" through his divine touch but sustains the medical team in their faith, courage, and perseverance to find a cure. Mao's quotations never actually provide concrete solutions because they are aimed at fostering the correct attitude to receiving Party instructions. The Cultural Revolution belief that "Mao Tse-tung's thought . . . can transform consciousness into material force and perform any miracle"[25] when stripped of the invocation of Mao reveals the core of the Communist Party's epistemology.

The Chinese Communist Party's (CCP) logic of the miracle, however, bifurcates along epistemological and narrative pathways. To put it differently, miracles need to be announced before they happen. The symbolic value of miracles for Party legitimacy is prioritized to the detriment of the epistemological processes designed to facilitate them. As a result, miracles are produced by discursive fiat rather than through the "strong and slow boring of hard boards" that Max Weber defined as the laborious work of politics.[26]

The Miracles of Chairman Mao addresses "disasters" including floods, earthquakes, tornadoes, fishing boat accidents, and collapsed coalmines. This theme is not surprising given that China suffers from a high frequency of both natural disasters and manmade catastrophes. Crises are also occasions to remind people why their survival depends on the Communist Party remaining in power (even if the Party was responsible for threatening their survival to begin with). In its "miraculous" response to disasters, the Party demonstrates its awe-inspiring power and benevolence.

Emergency mobilization is an integral feature of the Party's founding narrative and on which its moral authority, and hence political legitimacy, is dependent. Today's Party organization, with a membership of over eighty-two million people (larger than Germany's population), should not obscure the fact that the early Communists belonged to a marginal political organization which operated under considerable threat from the Nationalist government led by the Kuomintang Party (KMT) under Chiang Kai-shek. Beginning with the White Terror in

1927, when the KMT massacred the Communists living in China's cities, the survival of the CCP was far from certain. The Communists who embarked on the Long March in October 1934 traversed over eight thousand miles of inhospitable mountains and rivers. When they arrived in the Yan'an base camp, an estimated seven thousand of the original one hundred thousand marchers remained alive. "Indeed for the Yan'anites, the Long March was as much a miracle as the crossing of the Red Sea was for the Jews."[27] This miracle, however, did not result from an intervention of God but from the force of ideological conviction and organizational discipline. According to David Apter and Tony Saich, Communist Party discourse played an indispensable role in maintaining optimism in dark times. "Mao's stories converted every defeat, retreat, crisis point, into a victory of some sort for the communists. Disasters became magical occasions, and failures superhuman accomplishments."[28] Each victory over a natural disaster is an affirmation of the Party's resilience and of the values it holds sacred.

On May 23, 2008, after giving a speech to the students of Beichuan Middle School, Prime Minister Wen Jiabao wrote on the blackboard a line from the classic *Zuozhuan*: "Calamity prompts renewal and awakens a nation" (*duo nan xing bang*).[29] Used in this context, the expression signifies more than abstract unity and humanitarian compassion; *xing*, which means to thrive and prosper, is a word widely used in the official phrase, "great rejuvenation of the Chinese nation" (*zhonghua minzu weida fuxing*) under the leadership of the Communist Party.[30]

The timing of the May 2008 Sichuan earthquake was a source of acute anxiety for the Party leadership given its proximity to the August 2008 Beijing Olympics. In restricted access publications, the Party warned that discontent in the earthquake zone could mar the national celebration of the Olympics.[31] Under the assumption that affective energies are malleable and can be redirected at will, the Party opted to "transform the public enthusiasm [*minzhong reqing*] for disaster relief into preparation for the Olympics."[32] Party slogans broadcast throughout the earthquake zone issued emotionally manipulative injunctions to "overcome disaster and welcome glory" (*chuanyue zainan, yingjie guangrong*) with the implication that the expression of individual grief, as negative affect, would be an affront to national pride. To many, it might seem difficult to reconcile what Makley describes as the "impossibly stark juxtaposition of ecstatic nationalist triumph and traumatic natural and social disaster."[33] According to the Party's dialectical rationality, however, linking them makes intuitive sense. "China can proudly say that the Great Sichuan earthquake did not influence the success of the Beijing Olympics and the Beijing Olympics did not slacken the efforts of disaster relief work."[34]

Far from empty propaganda, these phrases contain the message that without the Communist Party to organize the response, disaster victims would be helpless, scattered, and exposed to the devastating power of nature. For the individual, nature is terrifying and deadly, but through the collective strength organized under Party leadership, nature can be defeated. In the words of Mao, "Natural calamities are like paper tigers. If you are afraid of them, they will conquer you; if you fight them, you will find them not so powerful."[35] This militant discourse shapes and normalizes expectations that the proper response to a natural disaster is combat mobilization, courage, and sacrifice. It also morally condemns melancholic attachment to loss, in order to curb unguided "reflection" (*fansi*) on what caused the disaster.[36] I would even suggest that the friendly advice one frequently hears in China to "not think too much" (*bie xiang tai duo*) is a defense mechanism against the danger of attracting unwanted attention from the authorities.

The orchestration of national solidarity and cohesion may temporarily ameliorate the tensions, rifts, and hierarchies that striate the Party's relationship with the people. In official discourse, the Party and people find unity in their common struggle against the "enemy" of disaster; everyone is in "the same boat under wind and rain" (*feng yu tong zhou*). Official metaphors are not for decoration. Instead, they indicate the type of attitude the Party expects from the people. The Party's exhortation to "convert sorrow into heroism" and "welcome the future," for instance, excludes people who are unable or unwilling to rise above their grief. To develop the same boat metaphor to its logical conclusion, only those who are willing to submit to the direction provided by the Party will be given a place on the boat. Despite its egalitarian suggestiveness, the metaphor establishes who is the captain and who are the passengers. During an interview, a professor and leading cadre from a university in Sichuan in fact used the related metaphor of a "captainless boat sputtering in the waves" to describe how democracies respond to disasters.[37]

The professor's comment reveals another important dimension of the Party's self-representation. The ability to command and mobilize resources and to unify the people (under threat of censorship and more severe penalties) is presented as a demonstration of the superiority of China's one-party socialist system over the fragmentation, indecision, and paralysis of multiparty democracies. The Communist Party does not need to be elected because it is free of the flaws of electoral politics. Although the CCP admits to having faults, nonetheless it also claims to have an unerring ability to learn from its mistakes. "Marxists should not be afraid of criticism from any quarter. . . . Fighting against wrong ideas is like being vaccinated—a man develops greater immunity from disease as a result of vaccination."[38] Mao thus presents Party ideology as the necessary medicine for survival under Chinese Communist rule. In the less Draconian post-Maoist period, Party ideology continues to mark the boundaries of permissible speech.

In lieu of electoral legitimacy, the Communist Party's legitimacy is based on a narrative of progress in which it is the main protagonist. According to this logic, "miracles" are necessary demonstrations of progress; what was impossible in the past (or remains impossible for other political systems) is possible under the leadership of the Communist Party. After the devastating Tangshan earthquake in 1976, the official narrative stresses the comparative progress made by the Communist Party:

> Many strong earthquakes occurred in old China, laying waste the land, bringing pestilence and causing death and destruction to the labouring people. . . . Today, in the socialist new China, the situation is completely different. When a disaster strikes, help pours in from all over the country. The people unite, get organized and conquer nature. Our socialist system has fully demonstrated its superiority.[39]

Not surprisingly, this account conspicuously omits the complex history of Qing Dynasty practices of state benevolence and disaster relief. According to Kathryn Edgerton-Tarpley's study of the North China Famine (1876–79), "Qing officials and commoners" both believed that it was the responsibility of "the state to provide substantive relief"; in response, the "beleaguered" state attempted to "distribute significant, though far from sufficient, amounts of cash and grain relief."[40] Accounts of Qing benevolence, as opposed to exploitation, were incompatible with the Mao-era narrative that 1949 marked a decisive historical break with the "feudal" past. Since the 1980s, the Party has actively sought to reconnect with this same feudal past, so as to selectively incorporate Neo-Confucian ideas, phrases, and governance rationality into socialism with Chinese characteristics.

The facility with which the Party has accommodated Neo-Confucian vocabulary in its discourse has also enabled it to transpose disasters into opportunities for developmental leaps. The resulting overblown rhetoric sets an unrealistic standard of success which, in turn, poses enormous difficulties for the local government tasked with achieving the "impossible." Importantly, there is very little room in the official discourse for the articulation of modest and achievable objectives. The Sichuan disaster zone was to become a model of development on the basis of the belief that "grasping reconstruction is identical to grasping development."[41] According to a restricted access publication from the Development Research Center of the State Council, "the earthquake destroyed the residential structure, public infrastructure and industrial infrastructure of the disaster areas. We must use the reconstruction opportunity and scientific development concepts . . . to comprehensively plan for industrialization, urbanization and new countryside construction."[42] A report from the Sichuan Academy of Social Sciences describes the reconstruction in terms of national-level policy and campaign objectives: "the Sichuan model demonstrates that disaster reconstruction is no longer only reconstruction, but rather is imbued with the enriched meanings of 'expanding domestic demand,' 'developing the west,' 'comprehensive urban–rural development,' and 'construction of the new countryside' policies."[43] In the same spirit, a restricted access report published by the Dujiangyan Municipal Communist Party School in 2009 urged cadres to "tightly grasp the three opportunities of post-disaster reconstruction, expanding domestic demand, and comprehensive urban-rural development."[44]

These euphoric visions of Sichuan's future were not without detractors. On July 3, 2008, at the Post-Disaster Planning Mutual Support Work Conference, the deputy minister of the Ministry of Urban Development and Housing, Qiu Baoxing, warned of "excessively attaching importance to the short-term production of images," "blindly pursuing the new," and naively hoping to "relieve poverty in one step" via reconstruction work.[45] Research on the legal system in the aftermath of the earthquake conducted by legal scholar Chen Guaming outlines a similar set of problems:

> First, the reconstruction planning is *confused* with long-term development planning. To properly combine post-disaster reconstruction planning with local long-term development planning is certainly reasonable to some extent. But in making reconstruction plans, some regions in Mianzhu unrealistically emphasize promoting urbanization, industrialization and construction of socialist new villages, and attempt to "reach the goal with one stride," which has increased the burden of post-disaster reconstruction and aroused social dissatisfaction.[46]

A problem with "great leap" development is that it skips over the steps necessary for sustainable economic growth.

The earthquake survivors had to try to get through life despite the ephemeral bubbles of Party miracles. Party slogans promised each household in the earthquake zone a home, at least one family member with full-time nonagricultural employment, and welfare provisions (*jia jia you zhu fang, hu hu you jiuye, ren ren you baozhang*).[47] As a result, people placed high expectations and demands on the Party to provide immediate relief, housing, and long-term economic security. The propaganda directive to make the masses "deeply feel and experience the Party and state's limitless solicitude [*wuxian de guanhuai*]"[48] meant that any limitation, shortcoming, or disappointment threatened Party legitimacy.

Written into the CCP's constitution is the declaration that the Party has no interests other than those of the people. This declaration is structured like a promise, which transforms everyday problems into challenges to political commitments and complaints into breaches of political legitimacy. My interviewees did not complain that the Party was too invasive but that it was not invasive in a beneficial way (Chinese citizens are not state-phobic like many in the United States). A newspaper editor from Chengdu posted the following joke on China's popular social media platform WeChat: "Many people actually view the government as their boyfriend: (1) Why don't you pay attention to me? (2) Who needs you to pay attention to me? (3) You owe me an explanation! (4) I don't need to hear your explanations. They are all lies!"[49] We can add to the list the deceptive lover's protestations of devotion, which wound the beloved all the more when the promises prove empty.

According to a report published by the Sichuan Academy of Social Sciences, earthquake survivors "frequently believe that the government can do anything" (*wan neng*) resulting in a contradiction between "expectations that are higher than the state's limited capacity."[50] A restricted circulation research report from the Sichuan Party School based on a survey of five thousand disaster victims conducted between July 7 and July 19, 2008, voiced nearly identical concerns:

> Our investigation discovered that disaster-area residents are intensely dependent on the government in each aspect of reconstruction work. . . . Seventy percent of residents hope and feel that the government ought to improve their residential environment and offer housing subsidies, especially to those whose homes were damaged as a result of the earthquake. This indicates that the disaster victims have faith in the party and government. On the other hand, policy makers ought to be aware that a synonym for dependence is high expectation and high hopes.[51]

When people are disappointed because the Party has failed to meet their needs, the Party promptly absolves itself from all responsibility. As I will discuss in detail in chapter 4, in response to popular discontent over the reconstruction's failure to improve local residents' standard of living, Party cadres from Dujiangyan blamed the "unreasonable expectations," "collective irrationality," and "lingering feudal mentalities" of society.[52]

No Investigation, No Right to Speak

The widened rift between the Party and the people since the 1980s is, in one sense, a structural problem. First and foremost, the CCP's policy-making apparatus depends on "investigation" (*diaocha*) into local circumstances. The priority of investigation was set by Mao, who figured the activity as follows:

"Investigation may be likened to the long months of pregnancy, and solving a problem to the day of birth. To investigate a problem is, indeed, to solve it."[53] It is within this context that Mao warned cadres: "unless you have investigated a problem, you will be deprived of the right to speak on it."[54] Investigation commences an epistemological process in which facts are gathered, analyzed, debated, and synthesized into policy directions. Communist Party policy-making follows an epistemological cycle in which cadres "discover the truth through practice, and again through practice verify and develop the truth."[55] The People's Republic of China's (PRC) political system is built around an epistemological framework of policy-making and implementation.

In Mao's words, "communist Party cadres should set an example of seeking truth from facts [shishiqiushi]." Although the phrase "to seek truth from facts" is commonly associated with Deng Xiaoping Theory and its deployment at the Third Plenary Session of the Eleventh Central Committee in 1978 to repudiate the Cultural Revolution, the idiom is from the Maoist glossary. It first appeared in Mao's 1938 essay "The Role of the Chinese Communist Party in the National War" as an attribute of cadre work methods and attitudes necessary to mobilize the nation and defeat the Japanese.[56] In "Reform Our Study" published in 1941, Mao criticized cadres who "have no intention of seeking truth from facts" and because of which are "flashy without substance, brittle without solidity."[57] The phrase appears again in Mao's 1942 text "Oppose Stereotyped Party Writing" as a scientific doctrine. "The Communist Party lives by the truth of Marxism-Leninism, by seeking truth from facts, by science, and not by intimidating people."[58] The Communist Party's vanguard status and monopoly of political power are derived from its privileged access to the truth, which is based on its abilities to combine theoretical superiority and practical investigation.[59]

The Communist Party's epistemological method also depends on "intimacy" (qin) between cadres and the people. If cadres do not live among the people, it follows that the Party is unable to make policies responsive to people's actual living conditions. For Mao, the "mass line" (qunzhong luxian) is the basic method of "Marxist epistemology" (makesizhuyi renshilun) in which knowledge of local circumstances and popular opinion circulates "from the masses" to the Party and returns "to the masses" in the form of policy and instruction.[60] For information to travel back and forth between the Party and society, a relationship of intimacy and physical proximity between them is required. Mao's exhortation in 1945 that "we communists are like seeds and the people are like the soil. Wherever we go, we must unite with the people, take root and blossom among them" reverberates in Xi Jinping's warning given in 2013 that without intimacy with the people, the Party is "without root, lifeblood and power."[61]

Investigation reports also need to flow along the vertical and horizontal lines of authority reticulating China's state and Party apparatuses. Given that each Party cadre is a critical node within a massive communication network, epistemological method entails rigorous cadre cultivation and attitude training. In his March 1949 essay "The Work Method of Party Committees," Mao writes, "We should never pretend to know what we don't know, we should 'not feel ashamed to ask and learn from people below' and we should listen to the views of cadres at the lower levels. Be a pupil before you become a teacher; learn from the cadres at lower levels before you issue orders."[62] Cadres are required to act democratically during the investigation and decision-making phases and follow orders once a decision is made. China's political system of "democratic centralism" (*minzhu jizhong zhidu*) places inordinate pressure on cadres to combine contradictory attitudes of democratic responsiveness and organizational discipline. Cadre democratic work style, work method, cultivation, self-discipline, and attitude are not personal attributes (an idea I develop in chapter 2) but are embodied institutional mechanisms. Xi Jinping's annotation of an offprint of Mao's essay "Methods of Work Party Committees" published in February 2016 by the People's Publishing House attests to the congenital flaws in the design of China's political system.[63] Xi's warning that cadre work style is a "matter of life and death" is his way of reading the Communist Party's vital signs.

The final stage in the epistemological process is "verification." After policies are implemented, their consequences need to be investigated. The "discovery of unforeseen circumstances in the course of practice"[64] requires continual modification and adjustment of policies, plans, and programs. The verification phase requires a commitment among cadres to transparently expose and acknowledge their mistakes through the techniques of "criticism" (*piping*) and "self-criticism" (*ziwopiping*).

When investigations are conducted superficially, reports are manipulated to fit political needs, and information flow is obstructed, the Party becomes unresponsive to social realities. To repair its relationship with society, the Party pursues two concurrent and yet mutually incompatible strategies. The first strategy is to rely on the propaganda and security apparatuses to control the narrative context that regulates the circulation of information. The second strategy is institutional reform such as promises to increase transparency, promote democratic participation, and ensure cadre accountability.

China's political institutions are not independent from Communist Party ideology and discourse. For this reason, I suggest that proposals for institutional reform inevitably capitulate to the Party's preoccupation with safeguarding its discursive authority.

The Absence of Participation

China's political system was designed to combine centralized power with democratic participation. In particular, the mass line was intended to be a mechanism of political vitality, democratic responsiveness, and intimacy between the leaders and the led.[65] Although the mass line often became a conduit for destructive campaign mobilizations in the Mao era, it still held open the conceptual space and practical possibility for democratic interaction, theoretical debate, and the fluidity of power relations. According to Wang Hui, without the mass line, "politics have degenerated into the category of management, a politics of depoliticization."[66] For Wang Hui, the absence of the mass line deprives society of a crucial venue of interaction with and representation in the Party and cuts the Party off from society.

China's recent and much-vaunted experiments with popular consultation, participation, and deliberation are attempts to fill the void of representation. This historical understanding is missed by the current conceptual paradigm and interest in "consultative Leninism," "authoritarian deliberation," "deliberative dictatorship," and "deliberative institutions."[67] He Baogang and Mark Warren's puzzle, "why would an authoritarian regime resort to deliberative politics," depends on a historical obfuscation and ideological dismissal of the twentieth-century communist experiments in "democratic centralism" (*minzhu jizhong zhidu*). It also ignores the fact that China still regards itself to be democratic centralist. Only by not taking seriously China's twentieth-century revolutionary history can one be "surprised to learn" that "an authoritarian regime would even consider forms of deliberative democracy."[68] The popularity of this literature is perhaps due to the fact that consultation, deliberation, and participation are familiar concepts, discourses, and "best practices" in a world of transnational nongovernmental organizations (NGOs) and developmental aid projects; at least they are less alienating than exploring the conceptual and historical legacies of "people's democratic dictatorship" and the mass line. There is also something ideologically reassuring and appealing about discovering the seeds of democratic practices and civil society in authoritarian regimes. This new trend in scholarship not only overestimates the level of social participation in contemporary policymaking but also mistakenly views these participatory measures as an "innovation" rather than as a *symptom* of a systemic "crisis of representation."[69]

The solicitation of ideas and participation from different members of society is less of an innovative response to changing social conditions and demands than it is an updated and de-politicized version of the mass line (without the unpredictability and messiness of mass politics). From a historical vantage point, instead of the exciting discovery of emergent forms of popular representation and voice within an authoritarian state, one finds layers of contradictions between top-down planning and bottom-up participation, the Party's claim to scientific knowledge and reliance on investigation into local conditions, and the divergence between its practical and symbolic obligations.

As noted at the beginning of this chapter, the spontaneous outpouring of compassion, volunteerism, and nongovernmental organization formed the basis for claims that the Sichuan earthquake was a watershed moment for civil society in China. The central state also encouraged popular participation and consultation in the post-quake planning process. According to Regulation 31 of the State Council's Post-Wenchuan Earthquake Reconstruction Regulations, "in drawing up reconstruction plans, we must absorb the ideas of related government departments [and] expert participation and fully listen to the opinions of the disaster victims."[70]

At the same time, it was clear to many of the cadres, professors, and even ordinary citizens I interviewed in Sichuan that popular participation would only lead to the fragmentation of interests, paralyze initiative, and undermine the state's coordination ability. Under the imperative to transform the reconstruction into a miracle of economic development, there was neither the time nor the need, insofar as the Party defines the general interest, for popular participation. As noted by Guangzhou-based scholars Zhu Jiangang and Hu Ming,

> Despite the fact that the Post-Wenchuan Earthquake Disaster Reconstruction Regulations required the drafting of post-earthquake reconstruction plans to "absorb the ideas of related governmental departments [and] expert participation and fully listen to the opinions of the disaster victims," the fact that reconstruction plans were drafted within three months simplified many complicated issues, which were left by the wayside, or disappeared under the bird's eye view of higher-level officials. It was nearly impossible for the people to participate in the planning process.[71]

The Sichuan Communist Party School conducted a one thousand–person survey in the earthquake zone that also found abysmally low levels of participation. According to the report, "65 percent of respondents reported to have never or only very few times participated in village or community meetings, 23.1 percent reported occasional participation, and only 11.8 percent of people frequently participate."[72] The main reason 60 percent of respondents did not participate in local meetings is because they did not know such meetings existed—if the meetings did exist at all. In the words of a local professor involved in the reconstruction, "There were no institutional mechanisms for soliciting the opinions of ordinary residents. The planning bureau held meetings with different state agencies but never made these open to the public. There was an official 'request' for participation but no procedures to do it."[73] In the words of the head of an NGO from Guangdong Province, who was also involved in the Partner Assistance Program in Wenchuan County, "The government never asked villagers what they wanted or to participate in the reconstruction. So, most villagers had the attitude 'since it is not up to us, what business is it of ours?' and would sit idly and complain."[74]

I could go on with a long list of examples of how participation and investigation were stymied at the grassroots level. My purpose, however, is not to wring my hands over China's lack of democratic practices as abstract values but to articulate what their absence means in terms of China's policy implementation and political system.

Fruitless Flowers

Among the earthquake victims I interviewed, there was a common sentiment that the reconstruction improved the Party's image more than it did their own living standards. From their perspective, the "miracle" was nothing more than "formalism" (*xingshizhuyi*), the term used in mainland public culture to mean hollow rhetoric. Although largely ignored in the English-speaking literature on China's political system, the Communist Party's understanding of formalism is useful for exploring the processes that, in my view, have been responsible for the enervation of China's political system. Moreover, as a key term in the narratives of discontent told by the earthquake survivors, "formalism" merits an explanation here.

It was Mao who made "formalism" a popular negative word. He described formalism as a "contagious disease infecting the Communist Party" and as a "poison" whose "spread would wreck the country and ruin the people."[75] He even compared fighting it to the process of "cutting chives": no matter how much one cuts, it always grows back.[76] During Xi Jinping's recent campaign against formalism, it was joked that even the attempts to eradicate it are themselves products of formalism.

The theory section of the *People's Daily* defines formalism as the separation of "form" (*xingshi*) from "content" (*neirong*).[77] Formalism consists of "rushing around everywhere" (*mantianfei*) to appear busy, "mountains of paperwork and a sea of meetings" (*wen shan hui hai*), "perfunctory work attitudes" (*zou guo chang*), and "lip-service to Party slogans" (*gua zai zuiba shang*). In its most basic meaning, formalism is a bureaucratic pathology.

Formalism, in short, erodes the Party from within. Cadres who conduct superficial investigations are described as "looking at flowers from horseback" (*zou ma guan hua*) and "a dragonfly touching water lightly" (*qingting dianshui*). According to Mao, cadres who fail to engage in serious investigations resemble people who "catch sparrows blindfolded" (*bise yanjing zhuo maque*) operating in "pitch black" and whose policies will "come to nothing" (*luo kong*).

In this context, formalism describes the adverse policy-making outcomes that arise from bad bureaucratic habits. "The result is that, lost in a fog, they are unable to get to the heart of a problem and naturally cannot find a way to resolve its contradiction."[78] The label of formalism reveals that what was previously considered an achievement is nothing more than a "fruitless flower" (*hua er bu shi*), an "empty shell" (*xing tong xu she*), and a "hollow display" (*hua jiazi*)—words that circulate in most descriptions of formalism. These empty displays are fed back into the Party's epistemological circuitry, effectively paralyzing the ability to discern genuine achievements from their simulacra. The term translated as "empty shell" from the previous sentence literally means an "identical form" (*xing tong*) that is a "false display" (*xu she*). The disease of formalism impairs the Communist Party's ability to process information.

Empty displays are also described as "face projects" (*mianzi gongcheng*), "image projects" (*xingxiang gongcheng*), and "performance projects" (*zhengji gongcheng*) in both official discourse and popular vernacular.[79] Cai Yongshun defines a "face project" as a project of "impressive appearance, the practical aspects or the actual outcomes [of which] . . . are not their major concern."[80] The examples he gives include the construction of a factory without consideration or concern for its profitability, useless infrastructural expansion, and scenes staged by lower-level officials to impress higher-level officials on inspection visits. Each of my case studies contains several examples of face projects from the earthquake zone.

For now, one example will suffice to illustrate the "large gap between government relief and the needs of the victims."[81] When I was chatting with an elderly woman living in a newly urbanized township (that was an agricultural village prior to the earthquake), I commented that the new houses are beautiful. She responded angrily: "What do I care about beauty? It is totally useless. If you think it is so beautiful, why don't *you* come live in it?"[82] In the words of a professor from Chengdu involved in the reconstruction process, "who wants to live in a villa if they can't afford a bowl of rice?"[83]

As Mao once said, "it is the mischief done by this formalism which explains why the line and tactics of the Party do not take deeper root among the masses."[84] For the Communist Party to defeat formalism, it would need to be democratically responsive to discourses other than its own—a risk the Communist Party is most likely not willing to take *again* given the deluge of criticism during the One Hundred Flowers Campaign in May 1956 when authorities encouraged intellectuals and ordinary citizens to freely criticize and write big character posters pointing out flaws in the government. Further confirmation of the need to maintain a grip over ideology and discourse came from the centrifugal forces unleashed by glasnost in the final decade of the Soviet Union. Conversely, the Soviet Union is also an example of the dangers of the discursive petrification that occurs from not opening up.

In her study from the late 1980s, Françoise Thom defines Soviet *langue du bois* (wooden discourse) as "a unique and vivid example of a language which has cut itself off from thought, but has not died of the split."[85] According to Thom, "Communist Newspeak" is the ritualized repetition and incantation of phrases from the original scriptures of Marx, Lenin, and Stalin. It is a closed referential system that bars access to external facts and inhibits creative thought processes. All interpretations are based on "a prior system of ready-made interpretations; they rest, in other words, not on reality itself, but on a fixed commentary on reality."[86]

Under these conditions, investigation is reduced to the process of "reflection" of underlying essences, dynamics, and processes already identified in theory.[87] Thom's point is that Soviet "science" arrives at answers prefabricated by ideology, in the language of ideology. Whether there is a massive earthquake, factory strike, or chemical explosion, the Communist Party has a ready-made causal explanation, villain to blame, and policy response in which the outcome is known in advance. As a result, "thought is imprisoned in a cyclical movement which leads nowhere"[88] but still generates "the intoxicating illusion of discovery of having understood something new . . . a promise of discovering the truth, the feeling of a knowledge which is gradually being unraveled."[89] In Thom's description, formalism resembles a virus whose self-replication is undetectable as it insidiously mimics thought.[90]

Alexei Yurchak criticizes Thom's account for its reproduction of Cold War ideology and suggestion that ordinary people in the Soviet Union lacked agency.[91] According to Yurchak, during the late Soviet Period, official language underwent a "performative shift" in which "the form of ideological representations became fixed and replicated" and as a result "discourse no longer functioned at the level of meaning" which had become "increasingly unanchored, indeterminate, and often irrelevant."[92] Unlike Thom, Yurchak argues that the ritualization, rigidity, and meaninglessness of authoritative discourse opened "creative and unpredictable possibilities" for meaning throughout society, which cannot be reduced to the paradigm of civil society, opposition, and resistance.[93] Despite the different implications and conclusions they draw, both Thom and Yurchak view authoritative discourse as so rigidly self-referential as to be capable only of generating very specific forms of coded meaning.

The Communist Party in China has managed to survive the debilitating effects of formalism without curing itself of the disease. Among the main factors behind the Party's resilience is its control over the narrative context in which meanings are negotiated, even if the monopoly over the meaning, usage, and effect of words is only a fantasy of control.

Mandatory Gratitude

Coded as a gift from the Party, the post-earthquake reconstruction demanded reciprocity and political compliance from the disaster victims in the form of public displays of gratitude. As Jacques Derrida once noted, a gift that is conditional on expectations is no longer a gift but becomes a circle of debt and exchange. "As soon as a gift is identified as a gift, with the meaning of a gift, then it is cancelled as a gift. It is reintroduced into the circle of exchange and destroyed as a gift."[94] The Chinese phrase "to confer a favor and seek reciprocity" (*shi'en wang bao*) elegantly captures the political logic of exchange coded and performed as gift-giving.

Debt, however, exceeds this logic of exchange. In contrast to the Confucian praise of "benevolence" as a form of ethics, legalist scholar Han Fei argued that benevolence was a gift that indebts the recipient to the giver. "A physician will often suck men's wounds clean and hold the bad blood in his mouth, not because he is bound to them by any tie of kinship, but because he knows there is profit in it."[95] The physician's act transcends the terms of the accrual of interest and profit and reveals the power dynamics through which indebtedness and gratitude generate political submission and loyalty. No amount of money is commensurate to the gift of life. The resulting indebtedness is a structure that does not follow an economic logic of exchange but one of "infinite *amortization*"—it is a debt that cannot be repaid in full.[96]

As a relationship of power, gift giving is not a unilateral act. The recipient must want to recognize the gift as a gift. When I asked a municipal vice-secretary from the earthquake zone why the disaster victims were unhappy with the reconstruction, he provided the response, which is the epigraph to this chapter: a gift that "didn't suit you, you didn't need it, and you didn't even want it" is hardly a gift. The problem is that when the giver is the Party-state, the recipient people are obliged to reciprocate with expressions of gratitude acceptable to the giver. According to Lauren Berlant, when expectations of reciprocity are violated, "people often thrash around like monsters . . . not having skills for maintaining composure amidst the deflation of their fantasy about how their world is organized."[97] To repair the breached fantasy, the gift giver might boast about how much effort and thoughtfulness went into the gift, attempt to convince the recipient of the value of the gift, throw a tantrum until the giver's generosity is acknowledged, demonize the recipient as rude and unappreciative, or perhaps some combination of the above. An unwanted gift, however, cannot be magically transformed into something that the recipient wants.

In the post-earthquake period, the Party's gift of "miraculous" reconstruction was not reciprocated with spontaneous gratitude. This threatened the Party sufficiently for it to launch a "gratitude education" (gan'en jiaoyu) campaign in the earthquake zone.

This took the form of the "Notification to Launch a Gratitude Education Campaign in the Elementary Schools in the Disaster Zone," issued in July 2009 by the Sichuan Provincial Education Department, which was also sponsored and promoted by the Sichuan Provincial Propaganda Department and Spiritual Civilization General Office. From its origins in schools, the target audience and activities associated with the resulting "gratitude culture" (gan'en wenhua) spread to state-controlled work units and were reported to even have been included in cadre political evaluations.

A report from the Sichuan Academy of Social Sciences calls for the "use of gratitude culture to remove negative feelings among the disaster masses."[98] This statement can be read several ways. As therapy, "removing negative feelings" could be understood as an attempt to help disaster victims deal with their psychological trauma. Several cadres I spoke with also referred to gratitude education as a form of traditional moral pedagogy in which one learns how to "be a person" (zuoren). A professor from the Dujiangyan Party School referred to the purpose of gratitude education with the word shudao meaning to remove obstructions, dredge, open a path, and provide enlightenment. When emotional distress poses the danger of causing social "disturbance" (nao shi), the Party turns to therapeutic discourse to maintain social control. Overall, post-earthquake "gratitude culture" is best understood as the Party's way of securing the fantasy of intimacy between itself and "the people" at the core of its founding narrative.

In December 2010, a middle school in Wangcang County launched a gratitude education campaign scheduled to last until March 2014. Its website explains the campaign as follows: "First, we need to start from the reality in front of us and allow students to personally experience the 700,000 helping hands extended by Party members from the entire country in helping us repair our school. We should use our actions to repay the Party's kindness."[99] In Shifang Municipality, school activities included "letter writing to Grandpa Wen," exchanging "short stories of gratitude," gratitude essay writing contests, and activities to "sing songs of gratitude" that will "engrave in one's memory the Party's kindness" (mingji dang'en) and "inspire people to strive for self-improvement" (fenfa ziqiang).[100]

The provincial propaganda department also organized writing competitions for adults. In addition to earning a monetary prize, the best essays were published in various anthologies. At cultural events, people sang songs and recited poetry as expressions of their gratitude.[101] The fact that the Party orchestrated these celebrations and that even the people who participated in them mainly viewed them as entertainment rather than ideology (a local villager who was a vocal critic of the Party proudly gave me a CD of folk songs praising the Party's benevolence) does not negate their effectiveness as a governmental strategy.

These events served as reminders that without the Party, there would only be darkness. In the words of a professor from the Dujiangyan Party School,

> The Party will collect stories of events that happened during the earthquake and then disseminate them as a way of reminding people of the trauma they experienced and how the Party helped them recover. It is a cruel example, but if your partner died during the earthquake but you were rescued, the Party will remind you of this as a way of teaching you to be grateful for the fact that you are alive, while others are not. If the Party was not there to help pull you out, you would probably be dead too. This process is then repeated again and again until it sinks in.[102]

The prevalent assumption discussed in the introduction that "no one in China believes in Party propaganda" restricts language and its effects to the narrow category of propositional sentences. People do not have to believe what the Party preaches. The Party's discourse gets under their skin as an integral part of their everyday language. The official post-earthquake public discourse took root in feelings of guilt, debt, and anxiety.

In a speech addressed to a meeting of the Wenchuan County–level Chinese People's Political Consultative Conference, Party Secretary Qing Lidong argued that gratitude cultivation was necessary to ensure "social stability" and alleviate the social contradictions that arose during the reconstruction process:

> Deeply layered contradictions are becoming more prominent. We confront new contradictions, problems, and challenges. The people's awareness is not completely unified to the extent of perhaps being opposite. At this time, we need to promote a culture of gratitude and use this culture of gratitude to eliminate socially unharmonious elements [*xiaochu shehui bu hexie de yuansu*] and increase members of society's sense of happiness by making people's agitated, blind, and impractical attitudes return to reason. We must use a culture of gratitude to increase people's affective interactions and promote harmonious contact between people thereby progressively unifying the thinking at each level of society.[103]

Commanded gratitude and harmonious society can be sustained only through violent operations and excisions of "unharmonious elements." The line between political speech and private affect is blurred, if not entirely erased, on the grounds that emotional agitation is a latent form (Party discourse frequently refers to them as "seeds" [*miaotou*] and "sprouts" [*mengya*]) of social disturbance. People who challenge the Party narrative are not rational interlocutors with different viewpoints but emotionally unhinged threats to be contained. Those who express "gratitude" are considered to have "returned to reason."

The power relations established by the discourses of the Communist Party's "gift," expectation of "gratitude," and demand for political compliance are not limited to post-disaster contexts but permeate state-society relations and reappear in different contexts.

In her research on the urbanization and development of the Tibetan Autonomous Region, Emily Yeh observes,

> The PRC legitimation of its sovereignty over Tibet has always rested heavily on the presumption of Tibetan gratitude, first for liberation from the cruel, barbaric, and feudal pre-1950s "old society" and then, starting in the 1980s, for the bestowal of the gift of development, through the skills brought by Han migrants as well as the provision of large-scale infrastructure and massive subsidies from the government. In this narrative, all but a few radical separatists are grateful for this largesse.[104]

Far from empty rhetoric and propaganda, the Party's discourse of the "gift of development" not only frames Party and state approaches to Tibet but also bears on ethnic relations in the region. According to Yeh, in response to Tibetan complaints and discontent, Han residents living in Tibet "express bewilderment and resentment at the apparently inexplicable ingratitude of the Tibetans" who receive preferential treatment, "benevolence and generosity of the state."[105] The official discourse of "gift" and expectation of "gratitude" produces a discursive frame, reinforced by popular narratives, anxieties, and prejudices, through which Tibetan discontent is delegitimized and viewed as a threat to national cohesion. This discursive framing also determines a narrow range of possible responses including the militarization of the region coupled with the demand for displays of gratitude. Predictably, "after 2008 [author's note: when the Tibetan Autonomous Region and many predominantly Tibetan areas in Sichuan, Qinghai, and Gansu experienced violent protests and riots], many Tibetan areas were targeted by a Gratitude Education campaign, in which households receiving everything from posters of CCP leaders to new houses and tents were asked to show gratitude to the state and Party by opposing separatism, criticizing the Dalai Lama, and strengthening national integrity."[106]

Jie Yang demonstrates in the dramatically different context of deindustrialized Beijing how the logic of "gratitude" and traditional ideological "thought work" can be blended with psychological therapy in order to motivate laid-off workers to seek new employment and develop their untapped potentials. The objectives of reemployment training are about not only developing skills but also "nurturing attitudes of gratitude" among the unemployed that cultivate "an indebtedness to the life and society offered (or governed) by the ruling Party."[107] The discourse of gratitude is a powerful governance mechanism when it is addressed to marginalized and dispossessed populations who depend on the Party's mercy for their survival.

Conclusion: A Temporal Infirmity

Yan Lianke's novel *Lenin's Kisses* (*shou huo*), written in 2004 and translated into English by Carlos Rojas in 2012, vividly illustrates the formalism of gratitude culture, which has replaced the cultivation of intimacy between the Party and people.[108] It is also safe to imagine that the theme of formalism is quite familiar to Yan, who graduated from the People's Liberation Art Institute and formerly served as a propaganda writer for the People's Liberation Army (PLA).[109] Although the switch to fiction might seem abrupt and strange for a book on the Sichuan earthquake, I have chosen to end this chapter with Yan's novel, as it captures with greater verve than is possible in a political science exposition the Communist Party's governance mechanisms as deeply ingrained in cultural and social practices that constitute a way of life.

The plot of *Lenin's Kisses* is organized around the plan of Party Secretary Chief Liu Yingque of Shuanghuai County to raise enough funds to buy Lenin's corpse from Moscow and display it as a tourist attraction in his remote and impoverished county in the fictional Balou Mountains of Henan Province. The story begins with a "temporal infirmity"[110] of a blizzard during a sweltering summer in the small village of Liven. This natural disaster destroys Liven's harvest for the year. After the village canceled its annual postharvest "livening festival" because of the disaster, Party Secretary Chief Liu Yingque, whose county is administratively superior to the village of Liven, decided to organize the festival as a celebration of the Party's disaster relief effort. Before the relief goods were distributed, Liu instructed his secretary to "write about how the entire township dedicated its efforts to disaster relief and send the report to the district and provincial seat. After the disaster relief has concluded, I'll have Liven convene a several-day-long livening festival to express their gratitude to the government for its efforts on their behalf."[111] This passage captures the future perfect temporality of formalism according to which the historical record precedes the event. It also shows the resources that Party propaganda and discourse have at their disposal to organize society.

All of Liven's villagers suffer from a disability of some kind. Over generations, the villagers have developed special skills on the basis of their disability. Liven's geographical and cultural isolation allows the villagers to live tranquil and abundant lives but also leaves them unprepared for later interactions with the wider political world. After ascending the stage to commence the festival,

> Chief Liu and the villagers found themselves at a stalemate, as Chief Liu waited for the villagers to applaud, while the villagers waited for him to begin speaking. . . . A sparrow fluttered over the field, and the sound of its wings echoed over the crowd. Chief Liu became increasingly anxious, and cleared his throat to remind the crowd of what was expected of them. The crowd heard him clear his throat and assumed that he was about to speak, and therefore, they became even quieter than before.[112]

The lack of applause from the villagers withheld the recognition Chief Liu required to perform his role as their leader. As a result, "time itself had come to a standstill" until Chief Liu's subordinate Shi recognized what was happening and instructed the villagers to applaud.[113] After receiving their applause, Chief Liu paternally advised the villagers to refrain from applauding too vigorously so as not to hurt their hands.

Next, the famous regional singer Cao'er took the stage and performed a heartwrenching opera in which a disabled woman refuses to be cured of her disabilities in her next life, as she could not bear to abandon her disabled family members. After the performance, the audience was "sobbing inconsolably" and "thunderously applauded" Cao'er.[114] Feeling upstaged, Chief Liu vindictively ordered Cao'er to depart the premises and immediately commenced distribution of the disaster relief. The villagers again conspicuously failed to play their roles as grateful subjects. As one villager accepted the money, "she didn't say a word—not thanking the government, or even nodding to Chief Liu—but rather continued staring reverently in the direction in which the costumed Cao'er had departed. Chief Liu was furious."[115] Deflated, Chief Liu retreated to his room, unable to muster the appetite to eat the delicious and exotic dishes prepared for him by the villagers. "Chief Liu stared at a couple of flies buzzing around in front of him. He watched as one landed on a dish and nibbled, then flew to another dish and nibbled some more."[116] The perspicacious Shi rushed to the rescue by leading dozens of villagers into Chief Liu's room to prostrate themselves in gratitude before him. With "his face flushed bright red," Chief Liu reprimanded the villagers for their unnecessary show of servility. Revitalized by this exchange of submission and benevolence, he "wolfed down his food" and elatedly rejoined the festivities.[117]

PARTY SPIRIT MADE FLESH

> **At no time and in no circumstances should a Communist place his personal interests first; he should subordinate them to the interests of the nation and of the masses. Hence selfishness, slacking, corruption, seeking the limelight, and so on, are most contemptible, while selflessness, working with all one's energy, whole-hearted devotion to public duty, and quiet hard work will command respect.**
>
> —Mao Zedong, 1938

In electoral democracies, legitimacy is sustained through the procedural fairness of elections. As Lisa Wedeen points out, "the criterion of political success becomes, rather than governance as such, the ability to capture elections."[1] The legitimacy of the electoral process insulates democratic political systems from the bad decisions and ineptitude of individual politicians and governments. Parties and politicians may pay the price at the ballot box for them, but poor economic performance and corruption scandals usually do not become a referendum on democracy as such. As Dan Slater observes, even endemically unstable democracies that careen between oligarchy and populism have managed to avoid the arrant "restoration and consolidation of authoritarian rule."[2]

In China, political legitimacy is not concentrated in fixed-term electoral cycles but is dispersed throughout the body politic in the relationship between the Party and the people. As the bridge between the Party and the people, the role of the Communist Party cadre (*ganbu*) is fundamentally different from the role of an elected official or a bureaucrat in other political systems. While the Party cadre is responsible for state administration and economic growth, the cadre is also an embodiment and conduit of Party legitimacy.

In an essay published in March 2008 when Xi Jinping was head of the Central Party School, he argued that a cadre's "work style" (*zuofeng*) impacts the "Party's image" (*dang de xingxiang*) and "popular sentiment and support" (*renxin xiangbei*) and ultimately determines the "survival of the Party and nation" (*dang he guojia shengsicunwang*).[3] As Xi has made clear since assuming power, the legitimacy of

Communist Party rule depends less on its institutionalization and more on the "cultivation" (*xiuyang*) and work style of its cadres.

The ideological demands placed on the cadre in China's political system sharply contrast with Max Weber's influential typology of the professional bureaucrat. According to Weber, "in the place of the old-type ruler who is moved by sympathy, favor, grace, and gratitude, modern culture requires for its sustaining external apparatus the emotionally detached, and hence rigorously 'professional' expert."[4] Antithetical to Max Weber's definition of institutions as that which remove embodiment from governance, in China, cadres are Party legitimacy made flesh. As flesh, they can be called on to suffer.

In chapter 1, I explained that Party ideology and discourse insistently remind China's citizens that their well-being is the result of the Party's benevolence. The Party's claim to benevolence in turn depends on the willingness of Communist Party cadres to sacrifice themselves for the Party and the people. The discursive logic of sacrifice, debt, and gratitude is the modular blueprint of Party legitimacy. In place of "earthquake," one can insert "class enemy," "American imperialism," "SARS," "poverty," or whatever plays the role of antagonist at the time.

In this chapter, I demonstrate how the Party engineered "glory" in the aftermath of the 2008 Sichuan earthquake by mobilizing the discourse of Party spirit. The term "Party spirit" (*dangxing*) is wielded to demand from relevant cadres at such times a style of work premised on a lifelong commitment of submission to the Party. I suggest that this discourse of Party spirit exerts a gridlike network of norms, expectations, prohibitions, and pressures on such Communist Party cadres. The first section of this chapter provides an overview of the conceptual history of the discourse of Party spirit. The second section provides examples of propaganda narratives of model cadres who reportedly were so dedicated to their reconstruction work at Wenchuan that they neglected their health, resulting in their untimely deaths. They follow a formula that stretches back to the Party vision of Maoist times, in which "whatever smacks too much of the human creature—appetite, feeling, sensibility, sensuality, imagination, fear, passion, lust, self-interest, etc.—is purged and repressed so that the all-too-human is sublimated with violence into the superhuman and even inhuman realm" of Party spirit.[5] In the aftermath of the earthquake, the creaturely frailties of "human nature" (*renxing*) were to be overcome, such as concern for personal safety and depression over the deaths of friends and family.

The chapter's third section demonstrates how the norms and expectations of Party spirit were conveyed in discourses, policy directives, work pressures, and punitive sanctions. The fourth and fifth sections trace how the discourse of Party spirit inscribed itself on the bodies of cadres, regardless of their individual convictions and moral dispositions. Local cadres who were also earthquake survivors started to exhibit symptoms of exhaustion, depression, and post-traumatic stress disorder. The chapter discusses why, after several cadres committed suicide, Party leaders partially changed course and responded with policy measures based on a therapeutic discourse of self-care targeting the cadre as an individual.

I do not claim that all cadres were saintly or pure. I frequently heard colorful rumors about cadre corruption and, on occasion, even witnessed villagers hurling abuse at cadres who in their eyes misappropriated funds and fiendishly profited from the reconstruction. The purpose of this chapter is not to vindicate or disprove such allegations but to show how the mechanics of Party legitimacy and the discourse of Party spirit continue to operate whether or not cadres are corrupt.

The Discourse of Party Spirit

In his 1924 eulogy for Lenin, Stalin said, "Comrades, we Communists are people of a special mold. We are made of a special stuff."[6] In the Soviet Union, the official term for this "special stuff" was *partinost* or "Party spirit," a term translated into Chinese as *dangxing*, literally the character or nature of the Party.

The Communist Party employs the discourse of Party spirit to establish the proper relationship between the individual cadre and the Party organization.[7] Admission into the Communist Party requires candidates to swear an oath in front of the Party flag in which they declare that they are willing to "be ready at all times to sacrifice . . . all for the Party and the people, and never betray the Party."[8] In Article 3, Clause 3, of the Party constitution, Party members are required to "subordinate their personal interests to the interests of the Party and the people" and in doing so be "the first to bear hardships and the last to enjoy comforts."[9] The Communist Party Standards on Integrity and Self-Restraint, adopted on October 12, 2015, exhort Party members to "uphold the distinction between public and private; the public comes first, the private comes next; sacrificing yourself for the public."[10] According to legal scholar Flora Sapio, "a person's decision to bind himself or herself to the Party"[11] is a voluntary subjection to a particular set of political, moral, and behavioral standards. The commitments an individual Party member makes are not mere formalities. They require embodied reinforcement as well as displays of loyalty.

At the core of how the Party understands and legitimates itself is the differentiation between "Party spirit" (*dangxing*) and "human nature" (*renxing*). To put it simply, it is the collective over the individual, the politically engineered over the personally motivated. According to Liu Shaoqi's classic 1939 handbook *How to Be a Good Communist*,

> Unhesitating readiness to sacrifice personal interests and even one's life for the Party and for the proletariat and for the emancipation of the nation and of all mankind—this is one expression of what we usually describe as "Party spirit," "Party sense" or "sense of organization." It is the highest expression of communist morality, of the principled nature of the party of the proletariat and of the purest proletarian class-consciousness.[12]

From the perspective of historical materialism, communist morality does not arise from an innate goodness in human nature; it has to be learned.[13] A cadre's Party spirit is the product of submission to Party discipline, management, and molding.[14] After a cadre is inducted into the Party, the cadre's life belongs to the Party similar to how St. Augustine conceptualized the body as a vessel of the Lord. For Augustine, God is the ultimate and only reference point through which human life is meaningful: "For just as that which gives life to the flesh is not something derived from the flesh, but something above it, so that which makes the life of man blessed is not something derived from him, but something above him." On this basis, Augustine argues that a Christian should not seek praise and flattery for his or her good deeds, "for you are not anything at all in yourself."[15] Similarly, under Communist Party rule, according to organizational principles, cadres are not permitted to act in their own name and enrich themselves. A cadre's purpose is to manifest the glory of the Party.

If Party spirit is the Word, it is engraved on the flesh through a network of organizational power, training sessions, rituals, confessional practices, exhortations, media hype, promotion incentives, and punishments.[16] This point is rendered quite vividly in the etymology of the Chinese word for responsibility (*fuze*) which means to "take the burden of criticism on the back." The Party's ideological and organizational apparatuses are designed to produce, cultivate, and maintain the special stuff of Party spirit in the body of the cadre.[17]

This lifelong cultivation of the individual cadre is not primarily for personal career advancement; it is for the glory of the Party, what Ken Jowitt, a Soviet specialist, referred to as the signature "charismatic impersonality" of the Party organization in Leninist regimes.[18] Through the mechanism of cadre sacrifice in particular, Party spirit is transferred from the individual to the organization in the form of glory. In lieu of an electoral mandate to rule, Party legitimacy requires the constant production, exaltation, and acclamation of glory.[19]

Consequently, Party legitimacy can benefit from natural disasters, which provide opportunities for the mobilization of Party spirit and display of benevolence.[20]

Party propagandists are indeed quite candid about the "utilization of natural disasters as a focus for central and local government propaganda work. CCP propaganda specialists recommend this as a particularly useful means of raising governmental approval ratings."[21] Although the Party's legitimacy benefits from high approval ratings, it does not require this (otherwise, how can we explain the Party's seemingly stubborn commitment to narratives and models that are no longer appealing or believable in the eyes of many Chinese citizens?). Instead of a hazy notion of public approval, the real locus of Party legitimacy is the production of its benevolence and glory.

Party Spirit in the Words of the Dying

Confucius declared, "When a bird is about to die, his song is sad; when a man is about to die, his words are true."[22] But the poignant aura of last words is diminished if these are ventriloquized, fabricated, or clichéd. How then to explain Party propaganda in which a model cadre's last words are slogans that express gratitude for the life granted by the Party?

One answer comes from Haiyan Lee's description of hagiographical accounts of People's Liberation Army (PLA) martyrs as a propaganda genre. "The moment of death is always formulaically stylized and saturated with ideological signification. Invariably Mao's instruction or the Party's bounty would flash across the hero's mind as he (sometimes she) lies dying and, whenever possible, the last breath is expended on revolutionary slogans. There is absolutely no room to question the motivation for the sacrifice or the meaning of death."[23] Lee argues that the "aestheticization and de-individualization of death" produces the effects of what she calls the "military sublime."[24] A nearly identical narrative structure and repertoire of tropes are used in propaganda accounts of the model Party cadre, which alongside the PLA martyr contribute to the Communist Party's "charisma of power."[25]

A second answer is that the purpose of Communist Party propaganda is not the authenticity and accuracy of its representation of reality; it is supposed to be idealized. According to Børge Bakken, in traditional Chinese culture, authority is represented in models and normative ideals that are to be studied and emulated. The Party continues this tradition by elevating model cadres, soldiers, workers, work units, urban communities, and whomever or whatever it regards as useful for exemplifying both its authority and the wisdom of its policies. However, Bakken also suggests that "the fading power of the model is linked to the general crisis of power and problems of legitimacy for the present regime."[26] Whereas models instilled devotion during the Mao era, what is their role in an age of political disenchantment, public cynicism, and Party corruption? What becomes of a political system based on moral exemplarity and emulation when the authority of models is no longer believed in?[27]

The rational response would seem to be, "If the models are no longer working, stop using them." However, such a seemingly practical suggestion is insensitive to what Geertz referred to as the "inherent sacredness of sovereign power"[28] and the need for whoever is in power to maintain it. For all of the Communist Party's adaptability, fluidity, and ruthless pragmatism, it cannot divest itself of propaganda models without losing the symbolic support of its authority. Xi Jinping seems to intuitively grasp the indispensability of the appearance of faith especially in an age of rampant corruption and disbelief.

One such model cadre whom Xi Jinping has cited as an inspiration was a county-level Party secretary half a century ago named Jiao Yulu, whose life and death became famous as a model throughout China during the 1960s. Jiao had been assigned to serve as county Party secretary of Lankao County in Henan Province in 1962, during the aftermath of the Great Leap Forward. Agriculture in parts of the county were endangered by spreading sand dunes, and Jiao's love for the people motivated him to forgo rest despite severe pain he felt in his side, while he led the masses to remove the dunes. According to Charles Laughlin, "Consumed by his work, Jiao Yulu is not even aware of the nature and seriousness of his illness and seeks no medical attention until he is incapacitated."[29] In the moments before his death, Jiao can only think of the Party and the suffering people of Lankao. His last recorded words are "I only have one request after I'm gone; I want the Party to send me back to Lankao and bury me in one of the sand dunes. I might be dead, but I want to make sure you get those dunes under control."[30]

The Jiao Yulu story has been propagated at various critical political junctures in the past few decades. In the wake of the armed suppression of the Tiananmen protests, then Standing Committee member of the Politburo Li Ruihuan launched a campaign in the early 1990s to study the "spirit of Jiao Yulu." According to Geremie Barmé, "[Jiao Yulu] was an icon aimed at reconciling the masses with the party by convincing them that there are—or at least were—good and incorruptible cadres."[31] A 1991 film about Jiao Yulu was a box-office success in China and reportedly moved people to tears.

In 1990 Xi Jinping composed a classical-style poem called "Recovering the Memory of Jiao Yulu"[32] in which he praised Jiao as a model and kindred political spirit. One verse reads, "As I yearn for you one night after another / Your heart and mine are cleansed together."[33] Later, as Party general secretary, Xi exhorted county-level cadres to "compare [themselves] to and emulate the virtuous" model of Jiao Yulu. Xi has also conducted multiple trips to Lankao County and has remarked that "each time I step onto the soil of Lankao, I become emotional."[34]

After the Sichuan earthquake, propaganda groups were organized to collect stories of "progressive model cadres" who sacrificed themselves like Jiao Yulu.[35] Each story conforms to a standard story line in which the cadre prioritizes the reconstruction mission above any personal considerations. Party spirit defeats the human tendency to grieve and feel self-pity. With tremendous fortitude, the cadre does not spend time openly mourning dead relatives or consoling those who survived. Dedicated to work, the cadre compromises his or her health, ignores medical advice, falls ill, ignores the doctor's advice to rest, checks out of the hospital, returns to work, and exacerbates the illness to the point of death. The deathbed scene provides a denouement in which the cadre's last words are work instructions to fellow comrades or an expression of gratitude to the Party.

Such stories are supposed to be constructed out of real characters. One week before the earthquake, Yu Zhaorong, chair of the Wenchuan County People's Consultative Conference, was diagnosed with pulmonary heart disease and high blood pressure. When the earthquake struck, he reportedly canceled his planned medical treatment in order to devote himself to relief and reconstruction work. According to a report of the Wenchuan County Party Organization Department, Yu Zhaorong explained his decision to forgo medical treatment in the language of Party spirit: "I am a Communist Party member; I am a cadre the Party has cultivated for many years; during the moment of calamity, I must not escape right before the battle."[36] The implication is that the cadre no longer has a selfhood to preserve outside of the one cultivated by the Party. In the weeks following the earthquake, the narrative was that Yu worked overtime, slept nights in his car, and ate only sparse rations. Even after he collapsed at his post and was forced to check into a hospital, he returned to work while sick. The report also depicts Yu's stoic internalization of grief over the death of his son-in-law. "He could only allow his tears to fall toward his heart, and did not ask anything from the organization."[37]

Wang Jihong, former Wenchuan County Party Standing Committee member and head of the Wenchuan County Discipline Inspection Committee, was reported to have followed a similar pattern. When the earthquake struck, he was in the hospital because of intestinal hemorrhaging. Immediately after the quake, according to the narrative, he discharged himself so he could participate in emergency evacuation work throughout Wenchuan's remote and scattered localities.

> He was still concerned with work in his heart; his left hand inserted his intravenous drip into his arm, while his right hand clasped his cell-phone to his ear, and in a feeble voice he exhorted his comrades in the Discipline Inspection Commission office: "My illness is not serious. You must not allow comrades to visit me in Chengdu. In the next two days, there will be bids for the reconstruction projects. We must send specialists to

supervise. There can be absolutely no mistakes. We must organize a study session of the Party Center's four important documents on fighting corruption. We must make sure everything arrives at its place." Two minutes after hanging up the phone, his breath became hurried and his complexion pale as his pulse disappeared, without time to utter one sentence to his family before he passed away.[38]

The theme of self-sacrifice is not limited to death. Huang Shunquan, head of a village located in Pengzhou, was helping villagers transport cement needed for reconstruction of people's houses when his vehicle collided with a truck on a mountain road. According to a report from his Party branch, while attempting to "ensure the cement did not spill," Huang's left leg was crushed underneath a wheel of the truck and required amputation. In the hospital, Huang's daughter allegedly complained that even after the accident, "our family issues are not as important as helping villagers. Even right now, he is eager to leave the hospital and return to work."[39]

These exemplary stories were also strategically deployed for "stability maintenance" (wei wen) work—a Party keyword that designates the importance of maintaining social order and preventing public protests above all else.[40] In Qingchuan County, the Muyu Middle School collapsed, causing several dozen injuries and deaths. According to a work report of the county Mass Work Bureau, parents mourning the deaths of their children started to demand that county officials investigate the allegedly substandard construction quality of the schools that collapsed on their children. In order to placate their outrage, Bureau Chief Wang Shikun reportedly conveyed to the protesters that even though many members from his own family died, he did not abandon his post. A small work-team was organized and dispatched to each of the victims' families in order to carry out thought work and calm the situation. According to the report, "no cadre had requested a leave of absence or left their post due to the death of family members or personal injuries. . . . Because of the long period on the road under the scorching sun without a change of clothing and nowhere to shower, one after another, to different degrees, everyone fell ill, but no one shrank from the task."[41] The clear message was that the disaster victims should be grateful for the Party's sacrifice on their behalf, while indirectly delegitimizing their basis for complaint. At the same time, another message was sent to the bureau's administrative superiors that the county bureau's cadres had spared no personal cost in preventing a mass protest.

During the Xi era, model examples of post-quake cadre self-sacrifice continue to be referred to in national-level cadre training. In a 2013 mass-line campaign meeting, Liu Yunshan, member of the Standing Committee of the Politburo, promoted the exemplary life of Lan Hui, deputy head of Beichuan County, who fell off a cliff while inspecting a rural road. In the words of Liu Yunshan: "People said he was like a fire in the winter, warming where he went. . . . Lan is a mirror who could reflect other Communist Party of China (CPC) members' deficiencies and let them know in what way to improve themselves."[42] The Central Party School released a circular to organizational departments "urging all Party members to learn from Lan Hui."

"Eating Bitterness" in the Aftermath of the Earthquake

The implausibility of these propaganda models would seem to confirm that the propaganda apparatus no longer is effective and suggests why people no longer pay serious attention to Party propaganda. The Party leadership nevertheless habitually turns to this modus operandi. And in addition to seeking to bolster legitimacy (no matter how clumsily), this propaganda exerts pressure on the lives of cadres, regardless of their personal convictions. Especially during political campaigns and emergency mobilizations, the discourse of Party spirit defines the parameters in which cadre political performance is evaluated, praised, or punished.

In the aftermath of the 2008 Sichuan earthquake, local Party cadres were required to put their Party spirit into practice when engaging in rescue-and-relief efforts alongside the military. Their tasks involved the relocation of survivors into temporary shelters, the distribution of relief goods, epidemic prevention, and the recovery and removal of bodies. In addition, in order to initiate post-quake reconstruction, local cadres in tandem with "provincial partners" (duikouzhiyuan) formulated and implemented reconstruction plans. This involved a range of tasks from housing reconstruction to medium- to long-term economic planning. At each stage of this process cadres were expected to manifest the Party spirit of "tireless struggle" and to "fear no sacrifice."[43] They were expected to do so even though many of these cadres were earthquake survivors who had lost their houses and loved ones.

In a speech delivered a year and a half after the earthquake, in early 2010, Wenchuan County Party secretary Qing Lidong praised local cadres as people who were willing to "engage in work an ordinary person would not be willing to take on and to eat bitterness that ordinary people are not capable of eating."[44] A capacity to endure suffering is, in the Party's narrative, a distinguishing characteristic of the Communist Party cadre.

Party spirit requires the suppression of human nature. Restricted access Party documents and department work reports unambiguously stipulated that during disaster rescue operations "cadres must always first rescue others" before family members and friends.[45] Likewise, when dispensing relief materials, "cadres must first think of the broad masses" before considering their own needs. According to an interview with a leading Wenchuan County cadre, "Our cadre evaluation standards for post-earthquake work were extremely strict. They were first and foremost to remain side-by-side with the masses. If the masses still lived in tents, you had to live in a tent. If the masses didn't have tents, you couldn't have a tent. If the masses didn't have relief supplies, such as bottled water and dried goods, you could not have any relief supplies."[46] A professor from Dujiangyan Municipality Communist Party School explained that if cadres complained about "eating bitterness" such as exhaustion, work pressure, and low wages, their superiors would admonish them: "Why did you join the Party if you wanted comfort or money?"[47]

For cadres who failed to display Party spirit, the Party availed itself of disciplinary measures and rhetorical denunciations. Organizational sanctions such as demotions or expulsion from the Party were meted out to cadres caught "leaving their work-post without permission," "getting cold feet," and "shirking responsibilities."[48] A grassroots cadre from Qingchuan explained: "Decisions to fire errant cadres were ordered by higher-level officials. Any cadres not at their work posts would be fired; if a cadre first went to check on his children, he would be fired." When I asked him if he thought that the policy was extreme, he argued that these political sacrificial objects were necessary to reinforce positive models of behavior. When I asked the Dujiangyan Party School professor about these punishments, he responded, "While it is totally understandable from the perspective of human nature to be afraid of rockslides and aftershocks, and to want to make sure your loved ones are okay, Party spirit demands that you put your job before everything else."[49]

The discourse of Party spirit also underpinned the decision to transform post-disaster reconstruction into what planning documents described as a model of "great leap development." That is to say, the Party's goal was to accomplish twenty to thirty years of development within two to three years of reconstruction, a policy that rested totally on the mobilization and self-sacrifice of cadres. The ambitious post-quake goals and time frames required cadres to expend themselves in the project of reconstruction. As a consequence, cadres were expected to work on little sleep. The constant work pressures and lack of rest were reinforced with slogans such as "white plus black" (*bai jia hei*) (day and night) and "five plus two" (*wu jia er*) (weekday and weekend), which in current vernacular translates to

24/7 dedication and availability. The idea that development would be paid for with the flesh of individual cadres was explicitly rendered in the following Party slogan: "Shed blood and sweat but not tears; shed skin, shed flesh, but do not fall behind!" (*liuxue liuhan bu liulei, diaopi diaorou bu diaodui*).[50]

The Fragility of Human Nature

The campaign-style mobilization of Party cadres who were earthquake survivors quickly resulted in symptoms of stress, exhaustion, and depression. A survey conducted in 2009 by the Dujiangyan Municipal Party School of three thousand grassroots cadres revealed that in the aftermath of the earthquake 86 percent of respondents suffered from insomnia; 78 percent frequently experienced dread and restless anxiety; 73 percent were afraid of aftershocks and found it difficult to concentrate; 78 percent felt downcast, sorrowful, and depressed; and 77 percent reported that they were irritable and quicker to lose their temper. Overall, the report concluded that the majority of local grassroots cadres were in a state of "physical and emotional exhaustion" that compares to what Arthur Kleinman referred to as the "somatic idioms of distress" in a political culture reluctant to acknowledge psychological vulnerability.[51]

Research by Chen Qiu and Yan Qianmin reported that the deteriorating psychological conditions of these local grassroots cadres were invisible within a system that took for granted their structural role and expected their self-sacrifice.[52] The report was based on a survey conducted from November through December 2008, in which a majority of respondents described themselves as suffering from depression, obsessive compulsive symptoms, anxiety, panic, somatoform disorders, and other nervous disorders. They reported symptoms of forgetfulness, lack of energy, inability to control temper, and lack of hope for the future. An estimated 15 percent reported entertaining the thought of suicide.

The same report cites excessive work pressure as a central cause of psychological discomfort and stress. Interestingly, the researchers found that the cadres suffered not only from excessive amounts of work but also from the type of work that exceeded their capabilities and training. "Cadres whose work requires them to frequently interact with the masses suffered from comparatively high amounts of pressure." One cadre from Qingchuan County described to me feeling exhausted from "negotiating with the masses."[53] When I interviewed a Party secretary in his late fifties from a village in Mao County, he spent most of the interview describing his fatigue: "Being a Party secretary is exhausting. There are too many problems. Every day there is something new. At my age, I don't have patience to deal with all of this; I am tired; I don't want to do it any longer."[54] He enumerated a list of examples of villager dependence on him to solve problems ranging from the flooding of fields, housing quality, and internal disputes to basic subsidies. "When someone comes to find me, I feel the pressure immediately and have discomfort in my heart, head, and soul. I try not to let them know, but inside, I am uncomfortable." What is missed in accounts of Chinese governance that ignore ideology and discourse is the role of cadres as custodians of Party legitimacy.

After the earthquake, work pressure did not allow cadres to spend time with their families, which contributed to an increased sense of isolation and guilt. According to the above-mentioned report, "because of the intensity of work it's difficult for cadres to show concern for their own families and close relatives; many cadres experience guilt and blame themselves for neglecting their families."[55] These unresolved tensions between Party spirit and human nature were felt in pangs of guilt and psychological torment.

To overcome their depression, according to official publications, local cadres reportedly relied on the language of Party spirit and demanded from themselves "willpower to overcome difficulties in order not to fail to live up to the nation and people's expectations and compassion and not let down the earthquake survivors who lost loved ones."[56] Some cadres did seek to live up to the Party's image. A township Party secretary whose daughter had died when the local school collapsed told me, "At first I was numb and didn't want to do anything. Then, I thought to myself it is a natural disaster, many people suffered the same fate, and we have received the country's support, so I need to excel at my work and pull myself together. I've kept working, but sometimes in the middle of the night I think of these things and can't fall back asleep."[57] When I asked him whether he was angry over the shoddy construction materials used in the school building that collapsed on his daughter, he stared into the distance and shook his head. His role as a Party cadre prohibited public articulation of grief (especially to a foreign researcher) that might contradict the Party line.

In the summer of 2008, the head of the Mianyang Municipal Party School and Administrative Management School conducted a series of interviews with township-level Party secretaries from Beichuan County to record their experiences during the earthquake. In June 2008, he interviewed a township-level cadre whom the interview transcript describes as ill at ease, compulsively smoking, and lapsing into inaudible mumbles and long silences. The cadre recounted personal traumas, including how he identified the corpse of his wife by her hair because her face was unrecognizable,[58] and the moment he heard his mother calling for help from beneath a collapsed building but realized that he could not rescue her without the proper machinery. He did not elaborate on the death of his daughter. Disregarding his personal tragedy, he was assigned to emergency patrols between the Beichuan county seat and administratively subordinate local townships.[59] His interview responses oscillated between intense self-hatred and blame for the death of his family and Party language that "personal matters are insignificant compared to those of the country."[60] At one point, he recounted the story of another local Party secretary who fortunately was sitting next to a water cooler when the building collapsed and thus managed to stay alive for days until he was rescued. "After the military police pulled him from the rubble, he immediately threw himself back into work." The interview transcript concludes with an update from January 2009 when the cadre was visited at a mental health clinic where he had been admitted for depression. A month later he returned to work, and his demeanor at work was described by a fellow cadre as silent for hours, head in hands, only occasionally looking up to say, "My wife, daughter, and mother are gone. At night I can't sleep . . ."[61]

This was not an anomalous case. I obtained an internal Party organization Excel spreadsheet that lists the post-earthquake situation of over 2,300 cadres from Beichuan County and its subordinate townships and villages.[62] For each entry, details are provided regarding the individual cadre's personal status, the status of family members, and urgent problems in need of attention. The spreadsheet records that over 1,200 cadres had lost their homes (this estimate is based only on the categories "without home," "homeless," and "collapsed house" and excludes categories such as "damaged" and "dangerous housing"). Under the "urgent problems in need of attention" section, "no money" and an inability to afford their child's school fees were listed almost ubiquitously. One cadre's situation is described as "no home, and wife currently in hospital with no one to look after her."

Cadres throughout the earthquake zone suffered from a combination of work pressure and personal tragedy. According to a social worker in Wenchuan County, "cadres confessed to me that they hoped to be dismissed from their jobs to relieve them of the pressure of working in the post-earthquake areas."[63] The social worker cited "too much work pressure and not enough time to grieve" as the most common complaints. It was also common among cadres to feel that their sacrifices were unappreciated by their intended beneficiaries. In the words of one cadre, "I've devoted myself totally to working on providing relief since the earthquake occurred. I haven't gone home for two weeks and I don't know when I can take a proper rest. We just work and work but many people still do not understand how hard it has been for us and they do not care either. They are simply being difficult."[64]

A national spotlight was cast on the psychological conditions of local cadres in the earthquake zone after several of them committed suicide. The first case was the suicide of Dong Yufei, the director of Beichuan County's Agricultural Office.[65] His son had died when Qushan Elementary School collapsed, and although his wife survived, she was severely injured. In the account of a local witness, when Dong Yufei pulled the body of his son from the wreckage, he "held his son's life-less body in his arms, faced the sky and wept bitterly, calling out his son's name and repeating over and over, 'Please forgive Daddy; please forgive me.' "[66] With-out time to mourn the death of his child or to recover from his own injuries, Dong Yufei was immediately dispatched to work. It was reported that his suicide note described the exhaustion he suffered from the burdensome tasks of reconstruc-tion and the lack of any vacation or time to rest. Grieving over Dong Yufei, a fellow cadre posted online, "No one is made of steel."

Almost a year after Dong Yufei's death, Feng Xiang, Beichuan County's Pro-paganda Department assistant, similarly committed suicide.[67] Feng Xiang's son had also died when his elementary school collapsed. Feng was a cadre in the Pro-paganda Department, and among his post-earthquake tasks was to host higher-level officials and guide their tour of the earthquake zone, including the ruins under which his son was buried. He told his brother that "each time he had to repeat these facts, he felt tremendous pain."[68]

To assuage the spirit of his son, he wrote a poem that he posted online called "Child, There Are No Earthquakes in Heaven." In the poem, he addressed his son: "You lie in the ice-cold ground and I don't know if you are cold or not. Each day before dark, I worry that you are all alone, lying there, afraid."[69]

Feng Xiang's poem challenges the official discourse of converting pain into per-sonal character, grief into national solidarity, and hardship into Party spirit.[70] The redemptive sentiment of Hu Jintao's slogan "No difficulties can defeat the heroism of the Chinese people" (renhe kunnan dou nan bu dao yingxiong de zhongguo renmin) displayed on a billboard in Beichuan and the official descrip-tion of the national response as a process of moving "from tragedy to heroism" (cong beizhuang xiang haomai) are lost in Feng Xiang's inconsolable grief.

For a time, these deaths undermined the certitudes of Party spirit with the in-sistence of the human need for care, relaxation, and medical attention. In the words of a local Qingchuan county cadre, "They [central-level Party officials] fi-nally recognized the problem of grassroots cadre pressure—they finally under-stood that cadres are also people" (ganbu ye shi ren).[71]

Taking Care of the Self

In the Mao era, complaints about mental or emotional problems were regarded as class based and in need of ideological correction.[72] The ideology of Party spirit and organizational discipline are intentionally designed to suppress individ-ual psychological needs and considerations. But in response to the high-profile suicides, the Party took an unprecedented step by applying psychological categories, explanations, and techniques to earthquake zone cadres.

At the organizational level, Party branches throughout the earthquake zone promoted and transferred grassroots cadres to new positions as a way of relieving work burdens and mitigating psychological stress. In a speech delivered on September 5, 2008, Wenchuan County Party secretary Wang Bin detailed a plan to establish an incentive system based on performance results. The underlying rationale was to generate a sense of accomplishment for cadres who excelled in the face of adversity. Conversely, it was hoped that the threat of punishment would instill in mediocre cadres a sense of crisis. Cadres with excellent abilities were praised with commendations and rewards; cadres with average implementation received feedback that analyzed the reasons for their difficulty and demarcated areas for improvement; cadres with poor performance evaluations were handled severely, which often meant being referred to the local disciplinary inspection and supervision department.[73]

Cadres showing signs of distress were allowed to go to a sanitarium to convalesce. In Beichuan County, the "Notice Concerning the Adjustment of Cadre Rest Schedules" stipulated that cadres should sleep in an extra hour Monday mornings, enjoy two-day weekends, and leave work half an hour earlier every day. Additionally, a "compulsory holiday roster"[74] was established to guarantee mandatory vacation times.

Similar policies can be found in Wenchuan County's Organization Department 2010 End of Year Report. The section "Pay Attention and Care about Cadres' Physical and Mental Health" stipulated that work must not encroach on mandatory rest periods and alternating vacation shifts. The authorities in Abazhou Prefecture organized a trip for thirty prefectural-level cadres who received commendations to Sichuan's Jiuzhaigou nature preserve for convalescence. Wenchuan County also established an annual vacation rotation system and regularized work schedules for grassroots cadres engaged in reconstruction projects. Cadres who received commendations from the county Party and county government committees were rewarded with a week-long vacation. Township-level cadres, especially those who had lost family members during the earthquake, were to be transferred to county-level bureaus or relocated to townships near the county seat.[75]

Many cadres complained that in spite of the benevolent official policies, they were not able to take advantage of the two-day weekends, not to mention vacation time, because of their onerous work burdens. A common refrain was that "work cannot be put down." In the weeks and months following the earthquake, the high frequency of severe aftershocks and mudslides prolonged the duration of the ongoing disaster. Cadres were responsible for relocating the displaced earthquake survivors into temporary housing before winter, which is brutally cold in this mountainous area of Sichuan. As was noted earlier, even after people's basic safety and needs were provided for, cadres were ordered to begin the building reconstruction process and complete it in less than two years. According to a leading cadre from Wenchuan County, "We continuously worked until 2011. Even though it was mandated to take a vacation, our cadres didn't have time to rest because our work wasn't finished."[76]

At the provincial level, the Party school in tandem with the Party organization department held "psychological training classes" (xinli peixun ke) for over two hundred cadres from villages in the earthquake zone. During these classes, Dong Yufei's suicide was examined and discussed as a model case of exhaustion from overwork and untreated post-traumatic stress. A psychologist from a hospital attached to Sichuan University warned, "Don't mistakenly believe that you can throw yourself into the most difficult work and challenging circumstances in order to leave behind the past and forget it."[77]

During the same training session, cadres were asked to "write down their strong points" and were encouraged to "study how to view their real selves as acceptable."[78] The punitive superego language of Party spirit was supplemented with a nurturing discourse of self-acceptance: "even though everyone has flaws and is lacking in some way, we must optimistically improve ourselves." Before the training session concluded, cadres were urged to form conversation groups, pen pals, and support networks in keeping with their special identity as both Party cadres and disaster victims. This self-help discourse was supposed to encourage cadres to deal with their emotions in psychological rather than political terms.[79]

At the Wenchuan County level, special training classes were designed to improve cadre quality as well as to help cadres "relax mind and body."[80] Wenchuan also required cadres to undergo mandatory health checkups, diagnosis, treatment, and recuperation—a program that cost an estimated total of 447,720 RMB (Renminbi; the official Chinese currency), according to the Wenchuan County organization department's 2010 work report. The organization department also dispatched teams to at least two hundred cadres' homes to conduct sympathy visits and mental health crisis interventions by engaging cadres in heart-to-heart conversations. The same work report stresses the need to pay specific attention to old or retired cadres by visiting them, helping with medical reimbursements, and preparing funeral arrangements when necessary.

Beyond the earthquake zone, a sense of psychological vulnerability has emerged among cadres across China. According to a national survey conducted online in 2010 by sociologist Sun Liping, a majority of cadre respondents perceived themselves as belonging to a "marginalized and vulnerable group" (ruoshi qunti)—an official sociological category typically applied to laid-off workers, migrant workers, and other disadvantaged groups.[81] Cadres described a feeling of being squeezed between top-down pressure to display political achievements for their superiors and bottom-up demands to satisfy the needs of the people. Because of their constant exposure to scrutiny, respondents described themselves as easily frightened (figuratively described as a bird startled by the twang of a bow, *jing gong zhi niao*), anxious, and mentally and physically exhausted.

There has also been growing concern among Party leaders that cadre suicides are becoming a national problem. To understand better the psychological stress of lower-level cadres, Party leaders invited Peng Kaiping, a professor of psychology from the University of California at Berkeley, to the leadership compound in Zhongnanhai to give a course on psychology. In a later interview, Peng argued that the majority of cadre suicides are related to their position in the political system. In the words of Peng, it is a system of "cruel competition for promotion" that isolates cadres from broader affective communities and networks of support: "There is no one to whom they can vent and say what is on their mind. There are some things they cannot say, some things they do not dare to say, and some things they are not willing to say. This creates feelings of depression and helplessness and the sense of being out of options." Peng also points to an enduring political culture and Maoist legacy within the Party, though he does not mention Mao or Maoism directly: "For a long time, we have looked at psychological problems [*xinli wenti*] as attitudinal problems [*taidu wenti*], ideological problems [*yishixingtai wenti*] and [political] consciousness problems [*juewu de wenti*]." In this passage, Peng tactfully recycles key terms from a Maoist vocabulary as antecedent conditions for the creation of a political ecology in which cadres "refuse to admit they suffer from depression," afraid it will be viewed as being "weak willed."[82]

Conclusion

In 1968, when surveying the damage to Party authority being caused by the Cultural Revolution, Benjamin Schwartz asked, "Have the Maoists attacked the Party? What indeed is the Party as such?. . . . To any genuine Marxist-Leninist, it is, of course more than its cell and anatomy. It is a metaphysical organism which is more than the sum of its parts."[83] Inspired by Schwartz's willingness to reflexively question the fundamental political categories of Chinese politics, in this chapter, I have attempted to address the question, what is a Communist Party cadre? The Communist Party cultivates and invests the life of the individual cadre with its authority. Whereas the question of mandatory political education and indoctrination for leaders is not a feature of liberal democratic governance, in China's political system the cadre is a vital target of governance, training, and intervention. For these reasons, the ideal typology of the Communist Party cadre should not be conflated with the generic and vague categories of Weberian bureaucrats, experts, economic actors, or administrators.[84] Although cadres are responsible for state administration and economic growth, as Party cadres they are also subject to a lifelong process of ideological training and organizational discipline.

The Party's organizational ethos of subordination and sacrifice is perfectly expressed in Liu Shaoqi's *How to Be a Good Communist*:

> A Party member has interests of his own, which may be inconsistent with or even run counter to the interests of the Party in certain circumstances. Should this happen, it is incumbent on him to sacrifice his personal interests and unconditionally subordinate them to the interests of the Party; under no pretence or excuse may he sacrifice the Party's interests by clinging to his own. . . . Hence a Party member can and must completely merge his personal interests with those of the Party. . . . It is all the more necessary for each cadre and leader of the Party to be a living embodiment of the general interests of the Party and the proletariat.

Liu argues that Party spirit requires the endurance of "humiliations without bitterness if the occasion so demands"—which is the ultimate test of faith and devotion.[85]

In a China that has long since abandoned its revolutionary mission and ethos of class struggle, Liu's words seem to be from a bygone age. The stereotypical image of today's cadre is most likely a corrupt official wearing Louis Vuitton and certainly not an austere communist engaged in revolutionary struggle from a cave in Yan'an in the 1930s. Liu Shaoqi's words remain relevant, however, for the simple reason that the CCP is still a Leninist party governed by ideology and organization. In quotidian circumstances, this point fades into the background only to reemerge during emergency situations, such as the Sichuan earthquake, and anticorruption campaigns in which targeted cadres appear in humiliating televised confessions (a formula in which the disgraced cadre apologizes to the Party for letting it down). In both cases, the individual cadre is sacrificed for the glory of the Party.

My argument that cadres are Party spirit made flesh does not mean that the flesh is healthy or saintly. As we have seen, in the aftermath of the earthquake, local cadres experienced physical exhaustion, anxieties, and nightmares. After several cadres took their own lives, the Party responded with a new therapeutic discourse addressing the psychological needs of the cadre as an individual. However, psychological individualization of cadres can only be a temporary measure. The Party's logic of legitimation and discursive apparatus necessitates the exploitation of individual cadres in the name of Party spirit. The contradiction between the general needs of the Party and the individual needs of the cadre will always be resolved in favor of the former. Xi Jinping's anticorruption campaign is only the latest iteration of this logic.

Xi Jinping's goal is to revive the flesh of the Party—flesh that would not be inaccurately described as necrotic, considering that the Chinese word for corruption, *fubai*, is etymologically associated with "rotten meat." There is nothing new or shocking about Xi's objective or the tools he is using to pursue it. It is entirely consistent with the Party's discursive tradition of describing anticorruption and Party rectification as a hygienic and medical procedure. In the words of Liu Shaoqi, "As comrade Mao Zedong puts it, we must constantly 'sweep the floor and wash our faces' so as to prevent political dust and germs from clouding the minds of our comrades and decaying the body of our party."[86] Mao himself repeatedly extolled criticism and self-criticism as processes of "treating the disease to save the patient" (*zhi bing jiu ren*)—a phrase that remains a Party axiom today. In a recent publication from the Central Party School, Xi's anticorruption campaign was compared to an "excision of evil, malignant tumors" in the organism of the Party.[87]

Although it is prudent for scholars to refrain from making grim or glowing prognostications about the fate of Communist Party, we can at least listen to how it is diagnosing itself. The source of the Communist Party's vitality is Party spirit, and it will employ whatever measures necessary to preserve it.

BLOOD TRANSFUSION, GENERATION, AND ANEMIA

Political work is the life-blood of all economic work. This is particularly true at a time when the social and economic system is undergoing fundamental change.

—Mao Zedong, 1955

Before the Xi Jinping era began in 2012, the prevailing wisdom among international scholars, journalists, and China observers had long been: politics and ideology are dead, long live the economy! As Vivienne Shue notes,

> Among the social scientists in our field, there are not a few who would give us to believe that, whatever degree of political saturation may or may not actually have been achieved in Chinese society under Mao, in the present day anyway, the ideals and values associated with putting politics in command are well and truly dead. In Chinese hearts and minds today it is economics, and only economics, in command, so they say.[1]

Under Xi Jinping's leadership, China has appeared to reverse direction. For many international observers, the Communist Party's use of state power to tame stock market volatility,[2] increase of coerced televised confessions (and their expansion from the purely political into economic-related territory),[3] and the renewed commitment to study Marx and strengthen ideological discipline[4] all indicate that China is backsliding into the dark age of ideology.[5] Against this kind of linear understanding of Chinese history, in which the Party moves either forward (toward economic liberalization) or backward (toward ideology), this chapter advocates a critical reappraisal of political economy based on an interpretation of Communist Party ideology and discourse.

My goal is to challenge the notion that there is a mythical switch that can be flipped between politics and ideology on the one side, and economy and development on the other. I adopt a two-step approach that begins by questioning the premises of the dominant paradigm of economic performance legitimacy and concludes with a discursive analysis of China's post-2008 Sichuan earthquake reconstruction plans.

Performance Legitimacy

Performance legitimacy is the idea that "a state's right to rule is justified by its economic and/or moral performance."[6] According to the pioneer of the paradigm, Zhao Dingxin, statecraft as a kind of performance legitimacy began in the western Zhou Dynasty (1045–771 BCE) with the creation of the "mandate of heaven" (*tianming*), which meant that the right to rule could be revoked or forfeited if a ruler did not perform rituals and engage in exemplary virtuous behavior. Although its meaning and practices were constantly shifting and evolving, Zhao argues that performance legitimacy essentially defined the art of Chinese statecraft until 1949 when the Communist Party seized state power. At this crucial historical juncture and conceptual transition in his argument, Zhao devotes *one paragraph* to the Mao era, explaining that "the Maoist regime was largely founded on communist ideology and charismatic legitimacy" which induced "blind faith" among the people that led to "tragedy" and mass "suffering."[7] In Zhao's account, the Mao era is reduced to an ideological fever from which China barely recovered. In the wake of the social upheaval of the Cultural Revolution and Mao's death, "the old propaganda that claimed the superiority of state socialism was no longer persuasive." The 1980s are characterized as a period of divergence between Communist Party leaders stuck in the inertia of ideology and conservatism, and a society fitfully becoming conscious of itself, as it sheds its illusions. These dynamics culminated in the student and worker protests and June 4 massacre. As Zhao explains, "the military repression in 1989 saved the regime but shattered the confidence of the Chinese toward the government."[8] It was only after the ideological crackdown and patriotic education campaign following 1989 that Chinese officials began to abandon ideology and shift to "performance as the primary basis of state legitimacy."[9] From his observation that "top officials in China all know that economic development is now most crucial for maintaining the state's power," Zhao extrapolates that "government performance stands alone as the sole source of legitimacy in China" (although he includes morality and national strength as two dimensions of performance-based legitimacy, economic performance remains primary).[10] Finally, Zhao warns that the (inevitable) failure to maintain high levels of economic growth will (eventually) imperil the regime's political stability.

The assumption that Communist Party ideology and discourse are bankrupt logically implies that the Party-state's resilience depends on high levels of economic growth.[11] This argument underlies the belief, held by China experts of various denominations, that the Communist Party will be unable to survive a massive economic downturn, which would result in a cascade effect of elite defection, worker unrest, and social upheaval. The theory is, compared to electoral democracies in which economic crises may result in voting the incumbent government from office but do not imperil the system, authoritarian regimes that are dependent on performance-based legitimacy for survival are more directly exposed to the political risks of economic volatility. Although that theory is plausible, I would like to add that this chain of events is by no means historically inevitable.

When examined closely, the idea that the Communist Party's legitimacy depends on continued high levels of economic performance actually explains rather little. It does not provide access to how people experience the economy in their daily lives and the political, historical, and semantic contexts through which performance is evaluated. It also overlooks the Communist Party's reliance on ideological and discursive claims to authority. As I have argued in chapters 1 and 2, economic growth is only one dimension of the Communist Party's distinctive logic of legitimation. The belief that performance legitimacy exists apart from ideology and discourse, which are dismissed as relics of a bygone era, restricts the concept's explanatory range and usefulness.

The performance legitimacy argument is based on the assumption that economy and ideology are incompatible, and that the end of Maoist politics and ideology ushered in the eventual abandonment of politics and ideology in general. As the standard historical account goes, in the Mao era, the ideology of class struggle and constant political campaign mobilizations impeded China's economic development by diverting resources into political and ideological deadends; after Mao's death, the Communist Party "liberates its thinking" (*jiefang sixiang*) from the shackles of ideology to pursue economic modernization and development. In my view, this narrative ignores the fact that state-led capitalist development is also a form of politics and ideology. As Slavoj Žižek has repeatedly argued, the belief that we are living in a postideological world is the quintessential ideological claim.[12] It is also not applicable to China.

In the post-Mao era, for the Party, the official move away from the ideology of radical class-struggle and upheaval did not entail a departure from ideology. In his 1979 speech on the "Four Cardinal Principles" of ideology and politics that were regarded as indispensable for economic modernization and development, Deng Xiaoping argued,

> Without the Chinese Communist Party there would be no socialist new China. . . . It is precisely because the entire nation pins all its hopes for

the future on leadership by the Party. . . . In reality, without the Chinese Communist Party, who would organize the socialist economy, politics, military affairs and culture of China, and who would organize the four modernizations? . . . Under these circumstances, it would be all the more intolerable to the masses of our people to demand the liquidation or even the weakening of leadership by the Party. In fact, bowing to this demand would only lead to anarchism and the disruption and ruin of the socialist cause.[13]

In Deng's formulation, economic growth and modernization are dependent on the Communist Party's political leadership and organizational nucleus, which is different from the performance legitimacy argument in which the Communist Party's legitimacy is dependent on economic growth. The counterargument that a lack of economic growth invalidates the Communist Party's claim to reflexive superiority is not primarily an economic one, but shifts to the terrain of ideology, discourse, and control over definitions and narratives.

In the present, Communist Party ideology and discourse continue to suffuse the expectations and indicators of economic performance. The debates inside and outside the Party over the pernicious effects of "GDP worship" address the political decisions and belief structure that privilege certain values and outcomes over others. Xi Jinping's recent discourse of the "new normal" (*xin changtai*) of lower growth targets is only the latest attempt to redraw the political and social coordinates of economic performance indicators.[14]

Although there is no guarantee that the Communist Party will successfully navigate an economic slowdown, I find no empirical basis for making the vertiginous causal leaps between economic crisis, social unrest, and political upheaval that predict China's "coming collapse."[15] Even if China's economy declines sharply, I am not convinced by the mantra that "once the genie of middle class consumer desire is out of the bottle, there is no putting it back in." This kind of soft socioeconomic determinism does not consider the Communist Party's ability to manage the available narratives and perceptions via its control over the media, censorship of alternative arguments, and selective repression of protests.[16] It also discounts the human ability to survive in conditions of diminished expectations. There is nothing inherently Chinese about the power of ideology and discourse to make economic suffering meaningful and bearable. For decades in the United States, the culture of state-phobia and economic ideology that "someday I might be rich" has convinced a majority of America's poor to vote against their material interests.

In addition to generating predictions of questionable scientific merit, the paradigm of performance legitimacy also blocks intellectual access to how Communist Party leaders conceptualize the relationship between politics, ideology, and economy. The dismissal of Communist Party discourse and ideology as hollow limits our understanding of the rationalities, motivations, and incentives driving political decisions and behaviors in China; as Hannah Pitkin points out, "what they [political agents] do and how they do it depends upon how they see themselves and their world, and this in turn depends on the concepts through which they see."[17]

Communist Party officials problem-solve from a dialectical perspective in which "economic, social, political and cultural transformation" are to be "carried out simultaneously."[18] In practice, Party cadres govern across multiple spheres and relationships at the same time (in the field, I met cadres from the tourism bureau who were frequently assigned to "social stability maintenance" duty, and required to attend ideological training meetings).

The fundamental interrelatedness of political, economic, cultural, and social phenomena is displayed in the language, design, and structure of Chinese Communist Party (CCP) plans (*guihua*). The CCP's plans are "comprehensive" (*tongchou*) blueprints that entail "combinations" (*jiehe*) of dynamic factors which are "at once in conflict and in interdependence."[19] In many ways, this is an elaboration of my argument in chapter 1 that the Communist Party's political rationality is inherited from Mao's epistemological framework in which development proceeds through the resolution of contradictions. Problems are not resolved one at a time, but as clusters of entangled contradictions, including general interest/local interest, long-term horizon/short-term goals, city/countryside, coastal regions/interior, central authorities/local agents, and export production/domestic consumption.[20] As historical circumstances change, new contradictions emerge, and with them, new plans are developed.

The Communist Party's Planning Apparatus

China's reliance on plans to engineer capitalist growth is a marked departure from the conventional wisdom that the planning apparatus was rendered obsolete in post-Mao China. According to Barry Naughton, "Reforms [of the 1980s] were not clearly foreseen or designed in advance. . . . Reforming without a blueprint, neither the process nor the ultimate objective was clearly envisaged beforehand. . . . Such an approach might be admired as the strategy of not having a strategy."[21] Naughton's emphasis on the unplanned and piecemeal evolution of China's economic reforms in the 1980s and early 1990s is no longer adequate to explain today's state-led political economic transformations.

The return of the planning apparatus also challenges rosier accounts of China as already on the other side of the transition to a capitalist market economy. "Once the basic building blocks of institutional infrastructure for the market economy are in place, the age of tinkering has arrived."[22] In vast areas of rural China, the basic building blocks of institutional and economic infrastructures are stuck in ongoing processes of "construction" (*jianshe*) and "transition" (*zhuanbian*).[23] When shifting focus from China's coastal regions and megacities to the hollowed-out countryside, the salient problem becomes how to circulate capital and distribute economic opportunity in a way that will turn peasants into employed urban residents and consumers.[24] To accomplish these goals, intensive planning is required.

In a recent special issue of *Modern China*, Sebastian Heilmann and Oliver Melton persuasively claim that "the demise of the plan has not taken place in China."[25] They propose that the PRC's five-year plans have evolved into a form of "public policy coordination and oversight . . . geared to identify and support the growth potential offered by domestic and global markets."[26] Introducing Heilmann and Melton's article, Tsinghua University School of Public Policy and Management professor and adviser to the government Hu Angang explains China's new style of planning as the distinctive key to its miraculous economic growth, also challenging the mainstream view of China's transition from a planned economy to a market economy as overly simplistic. "China's economic reform does not involve simply replacing the traditional planned economy with a market economy, that is, replacing 'one hand' (the plan) with 'another hand' (the market); instead, it involves replacing 'one hand' (the plan) with 'two hands' (both the plan and market)."[27]

I agree with this new emphasis on the importance of planning and suggest the need to disaggregate plans according to national, regional, and local levels and type. Heilmann and Melton's claim that the planning apparatus has been "redirected to give macro-guidance to the transformation of the economic structure along with market-oriented industrial policies" does not track how the conceptualization and practical application of "guidance" changes in different contexts.[28] In affluent areas, guidance might simply mean foresight, strategy, and administrative nudging, whereas in remote counties, it might resemble extensive control over all production decisions. Because of China's uneven regional development, plans often grapple with structural crises, such as how to "construct" (*jianshe*) and "engineer" (*gongcheng*) factors of production in areas in which profitability is not immediately obvious.[29]

Planning documents are not merely technical blueprints for macroeconomic guidance and adjustment but are experimental and provisional attempts to reconcile underlying structural contradictions. As written documents, plans are textual artifacts that can be read, interpreted, deconstructed, and mined for their underlying historical and political commitments.

For this reason, linguistic tropes, and metaphors in particular, play productive roles in generating and modeling political economic relationships. If state actors controlling the strategic levers of the state's decision-making apparatus conceptualize the state's role as an acupuncturist balancing the "health" of the economy, it will delicately navigate cartographic zones and pressure points. Consider, however, viewing the state as a surgeon, invasively targeting and repairing the internal components of the economy, in which organs are analogous to specific industrial, business, commercial, and service sectors.[30] In Chinese, the term "prescription" (*yaofang*) is also frequently used to describe state macroeconomic planning as a form of administering the right dosage of medicine. Each metaphor entails different tools and operating procedures.

In the aftermath of the 2008 Sichuan earthquake, the political economic revitalization of the Sichuan countryside was envisioned as a process of "blood transfusion" (*shu xue*) from wealthy provinces to the disaster localities, which would result in "blood generation" (*zao xue*). The overarching reconstruction plan was drawn according to this metaphor. It is also worth mentioning that in Sichuan dialect "spending money" (*chu qian*) is colloquially referred to as "losing blood" (*chu xue*).[31]

The blood transfusion metaphor structured the Communist Party's macroeconomic approach to post-earthquake reconstruction, culminating in the large-scale mobilization campaign of Provincial Partner Assistance (*duikouzhiyuan*), explained in detail below. By scrutinizing the metaphorical coordinates of the reconstruction as a process of "blood transfusion" and "generation," it is possible to uncover flaws within the plan at the level of its conceptual articulation. The metaphorical description of blood transfusion dialectically transforming into blood generation conceals an unfounded assumption that external investment would stimulate the local economy. This claim rests on a further assumption that the patient receiving the blood has a working circulatory system through which blood can flow into sinews and muscles. It assumed that remote villages were already equipped with economic infrastructures through which capital could circulate in a way productive for people's livelihoods (capital always flows but seldom oxygenates the extremities). When the blood transfusions were cut off and the provincial assistance ended, it resulted in an "anemic" (*pin xue*) local economy in the Sichuan countryside. These metaphors are not superfluous descriptions of external processes, but the forms in which economic processes were envisioned and acted on.

In a complex world, ideologies and discourses unpredictably interact with political institutions, market mechanisms, material limits, and desires. The

Party's dialectical imagination of transfused blood priming the conditions for its self-generation did not account for potential disruptions, blockages, or systemic failures.

When One Place Is in Trouble, Help Comes from All Sides

The post-2008 Sichuan earthquake reconstruction effort was a political mobilization campaign authorized by administrative decrees, regulations, and planning documents rather than law. The use of a mobilization campaign that circumvented legal procedures followed the path dependence of deeply engrained Maoist political traditions and practices.[32] At the heart of the Party's reconstruction strategy was the Partner Assistance Program (*duikouzhiyuan*), in which relatively affluent coastal provinces and municipalities were assigned to severely damaged counties in the earthquake zone.[33]

On June 4, 2008, the State Council promulgated the "Regulations on Post-Wenchuan Earthquake Restoration and Reconstruction" (Order No. 526). The "Regulations" laid out guiding principles, general provisions, and an overall framework for the reconstruction, including the idea of partner assistance, without identifying reconstruction partners. A few weeks later, on June 18, 2008, the State Council Office assigned partnerships in the "Notification of the Post-Wenchuan Earthquake Partner Assistance" (Order No. 53). Based on the National Earthquake Bureau's assessment of earthquake intensity and damage, severely damaged counties were ranked and assigned assisting partners. Each assisting partner was politically responsible for the success or failure of the reconstruction process in its assigned county and mandated to earmark at minimum 1 percent of their annual GDP of the preceding year, for each year of the three-year reconstruction period (see tables 1 and 2).

The post-earthquake slogan "When one place is in trouble, help comes from all sides" (*yifangyounan, bafangzhiyuan*) described partner assistance as the culmination of national solidarity, neo-Confucian morality, and state-led socialist construction.[34] This slogan was officially interpreted as a fulfillment of Deng Xiaoping's vision of a phased path toward common prosperity epitomized by the statement, "Those people and regions who become rich first will bring along those who lag behind" (*xianfu dai houfu*). The program was widely regarded as a cornerstone of the "miracle" of the post-Sichuan earthquake reconstruction, and embodiment of the superiority of China's one-party socialist system.[35] In theory, partner assistance provided an elegant dialectical solution that comprehensively targeted a national emergency, regional disparity, and rural underdevelopment.

TABLE 1. Assisting/receiving partnerships

ASSISTING PROVINCE/MUNICIPALITY	RECEIVING COUNTY/MUNICIPALITY
Anhui Province	Songpan County
Beijing Municipality	Shifang Municipality
Chongqing Municipality	Chongzhou Municipality
Fujian Province	Pengzhou Municipality
Guangdong Province	Wenchuan County
Guangdong Province (Shenzhen Municipality)	Gansu Province Affected Disaster Areas
Heilongjiang Province	Jiange County
Henan Province	Jiangyou Municipality
Hubei Province	Hanyuan County
Hunan Province	Li County
Jiangsu Province	Mianzhu Municipality
Jiangxi Province	Xiaojin County
Jilin Province	Heishui County
Liaoning Province	An County
Shandong Province	Beichuan County
Shanghai Municipality	Dujiangyan Municipality
Shanxi Province	Mao County
Tianjin Municipality	Shaanxi Province Affected Disaster Areas
Zhejiang Province	Qingchuan County

Source: Liu Tie, *Duikouzhiyuan de yunxing jizhi jiqi fazhihua: Jiyu Wenchuan dizhen zaihou huifu chongjian de shizheng fenxi* [On the operation and legalization of partner assistance: An empirical study based on the post-disaster reconstruction of Wenchuan earthquake] (Falü chubanshe, 2010): 34.

The language of the "Regulations" provides insight into the Party leadership's vision of how the reconstruction ought to have unfolded. The third clause stipulates, "Disaster areas will combine self-reliance and self-help with national support and provincial partner assistance." The central state in tandem with designated provincial and municipal governments was responsible for supplying the lion's share of capital investment, material resources, planning, and skills. Central-level leaders were concerned, however, that excessive dependence on external capital and assistance from the coastal provinces might cripple local developmental initiative and resourcefulness. Many local governments worried how they would maintain and shoulder the costs of the new infrastructures once the assisting province withdrew. Hence, the language in the third clause called for "self-help" (*shengchan zijiu*) and "self-reliance" (*ziligengsheng*) to prevent the local disaster areas from becoming passive recipients of aid. Local governments were encouraged by top-down institutional and discursive pressures to play an active role in rebuilding their economies, and local disaster victims were exhorted through propaganda to develop an entrepreneurial spirit and shed the so-called

TABLE 2. Annual GDP and percent appropriated for reconstruction (in 100 million RMB)

ASSISTING PROVINCE	2007 ANNUAL GDP	2008 ANNUAL GDP	2009 ANNUAL GDP	APPROPRIATION BASED ON 1% MEASUREMENT
Anhui Province	543.69	724.61	863.90	21.32
Beijing Municipality	1,492.64	1,837.32	2,026.80	53.57
Chongqing Municipality	442.70	577.57	681.83	17.02
Fujian Province	699.45	833.40	932.30	24.65
Guangdong Province	2,785.80	3,310.32	3,649.00	97.45
Hebei Province	789.12	947.59	1,066.20	28.03
Heilongjiang Province	440.46	579.27	641.60	16.60
Henan Province	862.08	1,008.90	1,126.10	29.97
Hubei Province	590.35	710.84	814.78	21.16
Hunan Province	606.55	722.71	845.00	21.74
Jiangsu Province	2,237.72	2,731.40	3,228.80	81.89
Jiangxi Province	389.85	488.64	581.20	14.59
Jilin Province	320.68	422.79	487.08	12.31
Liaoning Province	1,082.69	1,356.08	1,591.00	40.29
Shandong Province	1,675.39	1,957.05	2,198.50	58.31
Shanghai Municipality	2,074.47	2,358.74	2,540.30	69.74
Shanxi Province	597.88	748.00	805.80	21.52
Zhejiang Province	1,649.49	1,933.38	2,142.00	57.25
TOTAL				687.50

Source: Liu Tie, *Duikouzhiyuan de yunxing jizhi jiqi fazhihua: Jiyu Wenchuan dizhen zaihou huifu chongjian de shizheng fenxi* [On the operation and legalization of partner assistance: An empirical study based on the post-disaster reconstruction of Wenchuan earthquake] (Falü chubanshe, 2010): 48–49.

peasant mentality of "waiting, depending, and demanding" (*deng, kao, yao*). The specific terms used in the "Regulations" were not self-contained economic categories but thoroughly imbued with political, moral, and historical significance. The first term, *shengchan zijiu*, translated for the sake of convenience as "self-help," literally means "saving oneself through production," as the character *jiu* is etymologically associated with assistance, crying out for help, life-saving rescue, and redemption. Reconstructing one's home and livelihood was considered an expression of reconstructing one's homeland (*jiayuan*) and a path to national redemption. The term *ziligengsheng*, translated as "self-regeneration," signifies rebirth through one's own efforts. Both Sun Zhongshan and Mao Zedong used the expression, in different moments of national crisis, as a solution to securing China's independence on the world stage and repairing its wounded national identity. After the earthquake, the small-scale, individual activities of rebuilding one's home and finding employment were suffused with political urgency, moral duty, and national fantasy.

The metaphor of blood transfusion and blood generation accrues added significance when set in the context of national self-regeneration. According to a report from Sichuan Academy of Social Sciences, "When helping the recovery of production equal stress must be laid on blood transfusion and blood making; industrial development and reconstruction of the disaster areas must be organically combined."[36] The transfusion of blood (representing anything that extensively flows across space, such as capital, infrastructure, technology, and expertise) catalyzes its local production and future expenditure in consumption, creating a macro-level dynamic of circulation. The circulation of blood between affluent provinces and the earthquake zones regenerates the nation as an organic totality.

Based on this preliminary analysis of planning discourse, it is worth emphasizing the multiple roles of partner assistance as an indispensable solution for financing and implementing post-disaster reconstruction, a long-term strategy for macroeconomic adjustment, an attempt to fulfill the Party's socialist promises and moral obligations, and a loosely institutionalized political mobilization campaign in the tradition of Maoism. The Partner Assistance program conformed to the epistemological view of the "entire nation as a chessboard" (quanguo yipanqi) on which pieces can be moved according to a grand strategy.[37]

Industrial Transfusions

To revitalize the rural economy, blood transfusion took the form of the construction of industrial parks and long-term agreements between the assisting and receiving governments. Only one month before the earthquake in April 2008, the Sichuan provincial government published a strategy titled "Opinions on Work Regarding the Acceleration of Receiving Industrial Relocation" (chanye zhuanyi), giving the post-earthquake demand for blood transfusion a ready-made channel to construct industrial parks and relocate coastal enterprises. The rationale underpinning this decision was that industrial parks would generate blood and become the basis for regionally "sustainable development" (kechixu fazhan). "The construction of industrial parks projects is blood transfusion engineering but is even more blood generation engineering,"[38] which made the industrial park the spatialized convergence of blood transfusion and generation processes. The industrial parks were designed to attract enterprises from the wealthier coastal areas with which local enterprises could form industrial linkages, build regional markets, provide employment opportunities, and stimulate consumption.

As of January 2010, it was reported that construction was already underway on eighteen special industrial parks, including over four hundred signed investment agreements, worth an estimated total of 537 hundred million RMB ($86.4 billion) of investment capital.[39] Among them, the most interesting example is Shifang Municipality. The initial plan for the Shifang-Beijing Industrial Park covered a surface area of 3.1 square kilometers and was designed to support petrochemical facilities along with other heavy and light industries. At the centerpiece of the plan was the Hongda copper and molybdenum smelting plant totaling $1.7 billion. The perceived environmental and health repercussions of the plant's construction sparked massive street protests initiated by students, which were met by riot police and turned violent. Because of the protest's scale, intensity, and generation of negative publicity for the local state, the plant's construction was terminated. According to Kenneth Bradsher of the *New York Times*, "The smelter was supposed to be the centerpiece of a planned economic revitalization of an area devastated by the 2008 Sichuan earthquake, through the creation of thousands of construction jobs at a time when the overall Chinese economy is suffering a sharp slowdown."[40] The municipal government's plea to consider the plan's centrality for "post-earthquake development"[41] was challenged from within society by a compelling counterdiscourse enumerating potential health problems and the specter of Shifang becoming the next "cancer town." In the Shifang example, the host rejected the transfused blood as a potential carrier of contamination, pollution, and disease.

Although Shifang was perhaps the most attention-grabbing example of failed blood transfusion, there were deeper underlying structural problems. Liu Tie identifies an "extremely large contradiction" between the "central role" played by assisting partners and the State Council's ultimate goal of "marketization" (*shichanghua yunzuo*).[42] The political and administratively planned *means* of engineering market *ends*, as the definition of command capitalism, have no intrinsic relationship with each other. Post-earthquake economic revitalization based on state planning, administrative orders, and policies follows a different logic than enterprises making decisions informed by market considerations and profitability. To borrow an instructive comparison, the administrative creation of the booming metropolis of Shenzhen was successful because of its geographical proximity to Hong Kong among other factors enhancing its attractiveness as a center of production; by contrast, administratively engineering a sprawling urban capital in the middle of the desert in Inner Mongolia is unlikely to be accompanied by the same economic flourishing, not to mention population flows, as evidenced in the desolate emptiness of the ghost city of Kangbashi.[43]

The Party's plans to revitalize the Sichuan countryside were based on logical inferences and assumed outcomes pertaining to inherently unstable and less than rational economic processes. The primary contradiction of China's command capitalism is that although the Party is capable of mobilizing the state apparatus to administratively relocate enterprises, it cannot guarantee their success, profitability, or impact on the local economy. Regarding the specific strategy of building industrial parks, it is also unclear if they are actual engines of economic growth or merely replicating the form of economic growth. The obsessive enthusiasm of local governments for building industrial parks and their copycat-like design is reason enough for skepticism. These risks, however, are hidden in the seamless language of dialectical combination.

Blockages

The promised transfusions of capital did not substantially improve the livelihoods of local disaster victims but instead were channeled and diverted along serpentine institutional pathways to serve different political ends. The post-Sichuan earthquake reconstruction in many ways exemplifies the defining characteristics of China's fragmented authoritarian system, including conflicting goals and interests between the sending and receiving partners, lack of institutional standardization and legal framework, and murky definitions and measurements of success.[44] The fantasy of blood smoothly circulating between regions and bureaucracies in reality resembled a web of varicose veins and clogged arteries. Rather than a seamless connection, there were multiple points of tension and blockages between assisting and receiving partners.

A persistent cause of tension was the dual authority structure. "The regions and departments of one-to-one assistance cannot coordinate and cooperate well with each other, which leads to low efficiency of reconstruction work."[45] The reasons for poor coordination include different administrative customs, work styles, and personality clashes to asymmetrical organizational incentives and objectives. The assisting partners approached the reconstruction as an opportunity to create "business cards illustrating assistance achievement" and sought to accomplish political achievements in record times to avoid being upstaged by other partnerships.[46] In the words of former Zhejiang provincial Party secretary Zhao Hongzhu, partnerships were a "political assignment of honor and glory."[47] Conversely, local governments in the disaster zone viewed the reconstruction as a rare opportunity to acquire needed funds and modernize the appearance of their localities. The result was a political ecology of "invidious comparisons and emulations."[48]

The idealized relationship of transfusion was to consist in a circulation of knowledge, planning, approval, implementation, and verification. Local Party and state officials collected damage assessments and information based on local conditions, which they provided to the assisting partner's command center. On the basis of these reports, the assisting partner's planning department formulated reconstruction objectives and plans, which then were submitted to local departments for "solicitation of suggestions and opinions."[49] Finally, the revised plans were submitted to the relevant, local departments for administrative approval. At each stage of the process, assisting partners were required to obtain administrative approvals from different branches of the local government, such as land-use permits, environmental impact assessments, and construction permits.[50]

In reality, the fluidly established dual administrative structure between assisting and receiving partners resulted in a seesaw of competing interests and power struggles. A local Qingchuan government official complained that "the main problem with the reconstruction is localization [respecting local knowledge, customs, and interests]. Zhejiang cannot come here and do everything according to their ideas and practices; they must adopt the perspective of the local situation."[51] A good example is New Beichuan. The initial reconstruction plan did not incorporate disabled accessibility in a city of disaster survivors—a problem now being addressed through costly renovations. Moreover, houses were designed and assembled by construction teams from Shandong Province. These teams built structures with flat roofs—perfect for the temperate and dry conditions of north China, but completely unsuited to Sichuan's wet and rainy climate, where roofs traditionally incorporate broad eaves to facilitate drainage. The duress of having to complete the reconstruction process within two years precluded the ability to solicit and integrate local viewpoints and design approaches that may have been able to prevent such regrettable mistakes.[52] Throughout the earthquake zone, it was rather common for local government officials to complain about designs foisted on them by assisting partners.

Assisting partners were frustrated by what they perceived to be the localism of their receiving partners. According to a cadre from one of Zhejiang's municipal reconstruction teams, several of the demands of the local Qingchuan government were irrational.[53] This cadre was baffled by the demand to construct public infrastructure for remote mountain villages when the cost-efficient and practical solution would be to relocate the villagers. Whereas the Zhejiang team wanted to find expedient technical solutions, such as how to supply drinking water to a mountain village, the local government had to consider the social and economic ramifications of relocation. These disputes intensified when they involved determining whether or not the requested projects were necessary or wasteful.

The monopoly over local knowledge combined with administrative veto/approval power supplied local state agents with substantial leverage over assisting partners. During the initial reporting stage, it was not uncommon for local officials to "over-report the extent of the damage to a certain area and ask for more money for a project than was necessary."[54] As a result of the assisting partners' unfamiliarity with local conditions, they had no other option than to rely on the accuracy of the reports provided by local state officials. The power hierarchies organized around the control and manipulation of local knowledge are a congenital birth defect of Leninist political systems.

At the project approval stage, local state agents threatened to withhold administrative approval for the assisting partners' projects unless their own requests for funds and projects were granted. Local officials cannily applied administrative leverage to channel resources toward their own projects. The threat of obstruction and work stoppages was powerful as a result of the political importance of completing reconstruction on time. Assisting cadres, who viewed local requests as a wasteful diversion of funds, a breach in planning protocol, or unscrupulous behavior, had no other choice than to turn a blind eye. According to one Zhejiang official,

> We wanted to complete the project and return home as soon as possible. The local governments wanted to increase their access to reconstruction funds. If we interfered with their projects, they would obstruct our efforts to complete our mission. We turned a blind eye to what local officials were doing. They used our money, but we had no authority to supervise them.[55]

The potential for productive exchanges was squandered in the quid pro quo of business as usual.

For their part, local officials complained of suffering from "political hosting fatigue"—the need to constantly procure resources and manage the visits of leading cadres from the sending partnerships (see chapter 5 for an expanded discussion of the political aesthetics of inspection visits). In a tone of exasperation, a Qingchuan County cadre described these events as "beyond [his] control" and a sheer "waste of money."[56] Another local cadre recalled how he sprained his ankle on a mission to deliver "pork, fresh vegetables, and liquor" to the assisting team in a remote location.[57] To put into perspective the unrelenting procession of visitors, within less than two years, Zhejiang conducted 412 leadership-level (*lingdao ji*) visits to Qingchuan a total of 5,968 times, including twenty-seven leaders from the deputy provincial level (*fu sheng ji*) or above and 546 at the departmental level (*ting ji*) or above.[58]

Institutional pressures for rapid project completion created an archipelago of wasteful vanity projects that did not stimulate the local economy in ways conducive to improving people's livelihoods. "In reality, due to the tremendous burdens and short project completion schedule, some partner assistance projects did not adequately *demonstrate their validity* [*lunzheng*] before starting construction resulting in their inability to satisfy the *normal needs* [*zhengchang xuqiu*] of local residents."[59] In this passage, the use of the term *lunzheng* indicates a political process through which a policy is defended on the basis of rational argumentation and demonstration of its validity; in other words, it is a process of convincing the masses that a policy is in their best interests. Without this step, even beneficial Party policies can appear as coercive impositions. The author's emphasis on how the demands of disaster victims were normal ones that any reasonable person would make is a discursive strategy to counter the Party's tendency to dismiss criticism as excessive, irrational, or ungrateful.

In a study of post-earthquake poverty alleviation, Wang Hongxin and He Lijun found strikingly similar evidence of a "misalignment between supply and demand" caused by the partner assistance. According to the authors, partner assistance gravitated toward projects that were "visible," "tangible," and produced "fast results," while neglecting remote, impoverished villages and failing to provide poor farmers a pathway to sustainable development.[60]

In restricted circulation documents and leadership speeches, Party leaders cautiously acknowledged a dangerous tendency during the reconstruction to skip the basic steps in securing an economic foundation. According to one research article, "If the public investment projects in the disaster areas lack mechanisms to promote employment and entrepreneurship for the disaster victims, commercial and construction enterprises will be the real beneficiaries and not the disaster masses that urgently need it." The article warns that this outcome would invalidate the proclaimed "social benefits of reconstruction."[61] The underlying message is that blood transfusion, if not conducted through the right channels, would lead to an anemic economy.

Partner assistance also unintentionally produced a set of contradictions between disaster localities. As a result of decentralized policy implementation and differences in the levels and types of assistance supplied by the partners, the reconstruction process lacked uniform legal standards and institutionalized mechanisms. The design of partner assistance made different outcomes inevitable. According to a report published on the legal aspects of the reconstruction,

> What's more, due to the difference in financial and effort [*sic*] aspects of assisting provinces, the assistance fund invested to various assisted regions is different. Though there is a standard of 1 percent of the financial revenue in the last year, it will still lead to the gap between the living standards of the victims in similar disaster-stricken areas with different levels of assistance [See table 2 for the differences in financial transfers based on the 1 percent of annual provincial revenue].[62]

Even in ideal conditions under which all cadres acted homogenously, the reconstruction would have produced inconsistent outcomes by virtue of its design.

To demonstrate this point, I will compare Guangdong and Jiangxi. One percent of Guangdong's 2007 budgetary income of 2,785 hundred million RMB ($448.2 billion) amounts to 27 hundred million RMB ($4.3 billion) devoted to the first year of reconstruction. By comparison, Jiangxi's 2007 budgetary income was 389.85 hundred million RMB ($62.7 billion), one percent of which amounts to 3.9 hundred million RMB ($632 million) devoted to the first year of reconstruction. Guangdong's fiscal investment alone was *six times greater* than that of Jiangxi, without yet taking into consideration different levels of technology transfers, personnel training, and production capabilities of relocated enterprises tethered to the assistance package. On the basis of these numbers, a report from the Sichuan Academy of Social Sciences suggested that the heterogeneity of assistance would inevitably result in uneven recourse allocations, subsidies, standards of construction, and levels of development, potentially triggering "negative mass sentiments" (*quntixing fumian qingxu*).[63] Partner assistance was both an absolutely essential political mobilization and transfer of resources, as well as a recipe for perceptions of unfairness and a loss of Party legitimacy.

These dynamics manifested in comparisons between the urban residents of Dujiangyan (chapter 4) and Yingxiu Township (chapter 5). In Dujiangyan Municipality, urban residents whose homes were destroyed by the earthquake were allowed to relinquish their previous land-use rights in exchange for new housing provided by the Shanghai Provincial Partnership, whereas in Yingxiu Township (twenty minutes away from Dujiangyan by car), local residents were required to pay 80,000 RMB ($12,880.78) to purchase new housing provided by the Dongguan Provincial Partnership. Despite the fact that central government subsidies and Macau Red Cross donations for households below the poverty line covered a fraction of the housing costs, villagers had to borrow money averaging 40,000 RMB ($6,440.39) either from family or from rural credit institutions in order to make up the shortfall. Yingxiu township residents were painfully aware of the beneficial terms enjoyed by their Dujiangyan neighbors, leading to widespread speculation that the township government pocketed the money. While it would be impossible to confirm the rumor of illicit activity, on a certain level it does not matter because the perception of unfairness already caused enormous damage to Party legitimacy.

These differences were also magnified in "celebrity disaster zones"[64] (*mingxing zaiqu*), which refer to areas that received comparatively more media attention, state support, and resources. Increased visibility and attention meant increased economic support. Visits from higher-level Party officials were a surefire guarantee that roads would be paved and buildings would be erected (mockingly referred to as an "inspection economy").[65] Areas visible from highways and major roads were often given aesthetic allowances to upgrade the appearance of homes, and localities that had good political connections with higher-level officials often received preferential treatment. According to a restricted access Party publication,

> The residents of "noncelebrity disaster zones" expect to receive fair treatment, attention, and support from the state and society. Our investigation discovered that the allocation of disaster relief and reconstruction resources was not entirely fair. "Celebrity disaster zones" with convenient transportation, ample resources, and media attention received distinctly more state resources and social support than remote, resource deficient disaster zones who needed help the most. . . . Cadres and residents of noncelebrity disaster zones feel that they have been treated unfairly.[66]

During my fieldwork, local residents frequently took me on tours of their miniature Potemkin villages and pointed out where a paved road petered into gravel, explaining that the road was only paved in preparation for a high-profile visit from a Party leader.

The political emotions of unfairness, neglect, and resentment were palpable in many of my interviews with disaster victims. Although these differences might seem benign or unavoidable to an outside observer, within the context of village life, they were perceived as violations of the Party's socialist commitment to equality.[67] The sense of equality and the fragility of human life in the face of death and the earthquake's indiscriminate destruction might also have heightened sensitivities to the venal political hierarchies and social relations that governed the distribution of relief goods and reconstruction aid.

Transplanted Development

The idea that uneven regional development can be solved through a process of "blood transfusion" and "generation" is not limited to the 2008 Sichuan earthquake. In fact, partner assistance is a modular governance strategy that has been applied in different contexts for decades. The main conceptual attributes of partner assistance are "nonformularized, nonlegalized transfer payments between different provinces and regions encouraged and arranged by the central government" that occur within mobilization campaigns designed to achieve official policy targets.[68] These strategic partnerships are temporary arrangements that are designed to disband when no longer needed.

Given its important role in combining China's macroeconomic and social objectives, it is puzzling that partner assistance has not been included in comparative discussions of China's political system and its mechanisms. To remedy this, I will provide a selective history of partner assistance programs in order to highlight differences in their configuration and application. My hope is that these preliminary explorations will encourage future research and conceptual refinement.

Staying with disasters, partner assistance underwent distinctive modifications in the reconstruction following the April 14, 2010 earthquake in Qinghai Province, Yushu Prefecture. These were indeed flexible adjustments to the unique conditions of the Yushu earthquake and reconstruction requirements. Because of the harsh winters in this remote and mountainous part of the Tibetan Plateau, reconstruction work could only be carried out during a few months per year.[69] The impact radius of the earthquake was relatively concentrated and therefore did not require multiple partnerships.

Instead, an agile partnership team of 102 "excellent cadres" was assembled from the central leadership, provincial and municipal levels (predominantly from Beijing and Shanghai), and State-Owned Enterprises (SOEs). The smallness of the team highlighted their advanced educational skills and political fortitude. A reported 42.2 percent of assisting cadres had graduate degrees. They were poetically described as becoming "New Qinghai Residents" (*xin qinghai ren*).[70] The core organizational innovation was the leading role given to SOEs for their ability to combine political control with technical efficiency.

Despite these improvements, the post–Yushu earthquake partner program did not avoid falling into similar contradictions as those of its predecessor. According to a restricted access report by the Yushu Prefectural Party School, "the goals pursued by the local government and assisting enterprises were not completely identical."[71] The report argues that the fragmentation of interests both slowed down the pace and hindered the efficiency of the reconstruction. Appointed by the central government, SOE partners viewed themselves as endowed with the "plenipotentiary power of the imperial sword," whose political mission was to bring the glory of the center to the hinterlands. More importantly, SOE projects were funded by the central government, provincial government, and social donations, which meant that their budget was "free of financial pressure." On the other hand, the local government aimed to modernize local infrastructure within narrow budget constraints. The report concludes that the inability to communicate and coordinate triggered frequent disputes that exerted a detrimental impact on the reconstruction process. It is worth noting that the author of this report is a task group from the Yushu Prefectural Party School who might have a vested interest in overdrawing the contrast between profligate SOEs and frugal local government. Even so, the fact that such a report was written indicates the severity of the problem.

Unlike the post–Sichuan earthquake partners, in Yushu the SOEs did not bring their own work teams. Instead, they relied on contracting and subcontracting to the extent that some construction projects were subcontracted five or six times. The fragmentation within the state apparatus and the dense layers of subcontracting significantly harmed the Party's ability to ensure construction quality, prevent corruption, and maintain accountability. In Yushu, many local residents brought to my attention the poor quality of the steel rebar being used during the reconstruction. It was alleged that construction companies from Fujian and Guangdong Provinces were flooding the market with shoddy construction materials at astronomically high prices to take advantage of local Tibetans who "did not know any better."[72]

In addition to post-disaster rescue and reconstruction, partner assistance has been and continues to be used extensively in the development of border areas and areas inhabited by China's ethnic minorities. As a remedy for underdevelopment, partner assistance is designed for the state-led transfer of capital, technology, and personnel, especially those dealing with infrastructural development and public services such as education and health care. It is also a preferred technique because it flexibly morphs into policing and social stability management when needed. Based on the following examples, it is impossible to neatly separate the categories of development from policing in their practical applications.

The Tibet Assistance partner program includes the modernization of medical treatment facilities and training of local medical personnel in the Tibetan Autonomous Region (TAR). From 2004 to 2009, Beijing and Jiangsu cumulatively donated over 20,000,000 RMB in direct financial aid and in the form of sophisticated medical equipment, such as off-road ambulances, mobile surgery units, and X-ray machines. The limitation of this approach is that technology does not operate or maintain itself. According to a restricted access report published by the Development Research Center (DRC) of the State Council in 2009, "due to a severe shortage of trained personnel, the phenomenon of providing advanced technology that no one is able to use is widespread."[73]

This pattern is not limited to hospitals but pertains to any form of technology or infrastructure that requires trained personnel for operation, management, and continued use. A central flaw of the partnership model is that once the partnerships end, the external financing dries up, and technicians return home, administrative and financial responsibility shifts to the local state. Local states in underdeveloped disaster, ethnic, or border regions typically have neither the financial nor the human resources to adequately support the projects inherited from the assisting partner.

Beyond their debatable practical effects, partnerships also serve a distinct political purpose. The Communist Party unabashedly views Tibetan Assistance as a form of instrumental humanitarianism to achieve the political ends of social stability and national unity. Its instrumentality does not negate the genuine intention to improve people's circumstances but embeds it in the dual logics of state sovereignty and national unity. What scholars may deride as hypocrisy, the Party would directly acknowledge and endorse as a part of its strategy.

In the partnership developed for the purpose of strengthening the court system in the Xinjiang Autonomous Region, home to China's Muslim Uighur population, security goals take priority over development, even though they are wedged into the same discourse. President of the Supreme People's Court Zhou Qiang's speech during a conference on December 18, 2014 emphasized the explicit connection between "Court System Xinjiang Partner Assistance Work" and the maintenance of social stability in the Xinjiang Autonomous Region. The program enables financial transfers, legal personnel transfers, and educational training between sending courts from developed provinces and receiving courts in Xinjiang. More important, court partners work together in expediting case handling and trial work guidance in cases that "endanger national security," "destroy national unity," and "influence social stability."[74] This partnership strengthens and extends the reach of the state's legal apparatus as a bulwark against terrorism and ethnic unrest.

Conclusion

The examples in this chapter indicate the conceptual and practical difficulties of demarcating where politics and ideology end and where the economy begins. It is also unclear to me what gains are to be had from parsimoniously isolating and abstracting economic performance from the political, ideological, and discursive relationships in which it is embedded. As Anne Norton has argued with regard to culture, "economic practices occur in the most ordinary and pervasive cultural contexts, inseparable in practice from the cultural matrix in which they are embedded. Yet the discourse of economics too often proceeds as if 'economic forces' operated independently, unconstrained by the cultures in which they occur."[75] Norton further points out how this "willful blindness" in economics is imitated in political science.[76] Especially when it comes to China, the desire to wrest the autonomy of the economy from the workings of politics and ideology depends on the disavowal of Communist Party discourse, in which all things are interconnected.

My claim that economic processes are shaped by political understandings and discourse, however, does not guarantee that those processes can be fully understood, controlled, or commanded into producing specific results—quite the opposite, in fact, as revealed by the failed lessons of command capitalism in the Sichuan countryside.

In the three empirical studies of localities that follow, we will see how Party discourses and ideas interact with local conditions to produce different political economic strategies and outcomes. In each case, the Party's planning apparatus sketches an anatomical blueprint, in which the state, society, and economy are designated with specific functions. They are supposed to work harmoniously as a healthy organism. When this organism's vital functions fail, the Party is the doctor who keeps the patient alive through continuous transfusions, emergency interventions, diagnoses, and experimental treatments.

4

THE UTOPIA OF URBAN PLANNING
Dujiangyan Municipality

> Traditionally, Chinese scholars, men of letters, artists would give an inspiring name to their residences, hermitages, libraries and studios. Sometimes they did not actually possess residences, hermitages, libraries or studios—not even a roof over their heads—but the existence or non-existence of a material support for a Name never appeared to them a very relevant issue. And I wonder if one of the deepest seductions of Chinese culture is not related to this conjuring power with which it vests the Written Word.
>
> —Simon Leys, 2011

In contemporary China, the name of the city is a magical incantation that produces real material consequences, transformations, and dislocations. In Communist Party ideology and discourse, the expansion of urban space is perceived, invoked, and disseminated as the solution to regional disparity, rural underdevelopment, creation of local state wealth, poverty alleviation, and modernization.[1]

The official Chinese dream is imagined as a civilized, urban one that takes the form of *utopian urbanism*—the placeless imagination of a future perfect state.[2] This idyllic vision is the antidote to what in China are referred to as "urban pathologies" (*chengshibing*) of overcrowding, pollution, ecological destruction, deteriorating infrastructures, overburdened public services, crime, and the potential for social unrest.[3] Utopian urbanism is the notional promise of a rational order of differently sized cities, townships, and urbanized villages that are economically integrated, self-sustaining, and offer high quality of living to their residents.

The Communist Party's plan for urbanization prioritizes the rationalization and ideal ordering of urban space as the parameters in which rural-to-urban migration and economic development are to take place. The administrative planning of urban construction is articulated in the policy of "urban-rural integration" (*chengxiang yitihua*), which entails the managed expansion of urban administration, space, governance practices, economic opportunities, public welfare, infrastructure, consumption, and civilized habits into the countryside.[4] Generally speaking, the goal of urban-rural integration is to resolve the disparities between the city and the surrounding countryside and transform the countryside into a more desirable place in which to reside and earn a living. In urban planning discourse, "small townships are to serve as the key 'combination point' between cities and the countryside."[5] Ideally, migration would be rendered unnecessary by the attractiveness of life in a space that would offer a combination of romanticized aspects of rural life (clean air and a sense of communal belonging) with urban amenities (social welfare, schools, and markets). According to Daniel Abramson and Yu Qi, urban-rural integration is based on the belief that "an essentially urban life style has become the model for village development."[6]

The ideology and discourse of urban utopianism gave shape to the post–Sichuan earthquake reconstruction plans and was responsible for generating "the frenetic physicality of the reconstruction effort, which is transforming the lives of isolated communities with dizzying speed."[7] The earthquake was a crisis that weakened traditional structural resistances (stubborn peasantry, vested interests, localism) and provided an opportunity to accelerate reforms that were already underway. In private conversations, local Party cadres and state officials described the natural demolition of homes caused by the earthquake as a political blessing in disguise that paved the way for the urbanization of the countryside.

Disaster areas in close proximity to the Chengdu metropole in which urbanization trends were already underway prior to the earthquake, such as Dujiangyan and Pengzhou, and villages subordinate to major cities like Deyang, Mianzhu, and Mianyang witnessed dramatic expansions in the urbanization of land, accompanied by administrative restructuring and nominal changes in status from rural village (*nongcun*) to urban community (*shequ*). In particular, Dujiangyan was targeted as a model example and experimental laboratory for urban-rural integration.[8] On a lesser scale, reconstruction "extended the periurban zone deep into what were quite recently remote and inaccessible valleys" mainly in the form of urban spatial arrangements, such as concentrated apartment buildings accompanied by administratively relocated peasants (*nongmin*).[9]

This chapter is based on the year 2012–13, when I lived in an apartment complex located on Dujiangyan's periphery that was built in the aftermath of the earthquake for the purpose of relocating and housing rural residents. In addition to my own residential complex, I also engaged in ethnographic observation and conducted interviews with Party cadres and local residents in four similar apartment complexes in Dujiangyan and two in neighboring Pi County. While living in Dujiangyan, I paid several visits to the Dujiangyan Planning Exhibition Pavilion, discussed in the conclusion to this chapter, and frequently met with workers in nongovernmental organizations (NGOs) who were responsible for helping peasants make the transition to urban citizens.

I selected Dujiangyan as a case because of its likelihood of being a successful example of urban-rural integration relative to other, more considerably marginalized areas in the earthquake zone. As I will discuss shortly, before the earthquake Dujiangyan was already a model laboratory for experiments in urban-rural integration that were accelerated and expanded during the reconstruction process. Dujiangyan's proximity to Chengdu, the capital of Sichuan Province, integrates Dujiangyan into a larger urban region. After the earthquake, the construction of a high-speed rail reduced travel time between Chengdu and Dujiangyan to less than thirty minutes. In terms of transportation logistics, Dujiangyan was more likely to attract investment capital and economic activity than peripheral areas in the Sichuan countryside. Further, Dujiangyan was already a well-known tourist attraction famous for two UNESCO world heritage sites: an irrigation system that was built during the Warring States period in 256 BCE and Qingcheng Mountain, which was the birthplace of Taoism and home to ancient temples. In contrast with Chengdu's increasing levels of pollution and urban congestion, Dujiangyan also boasts of being a city with relatively pristine skies and a clean environment.

Dujiangyan reveals the planning flaws, structural vulnerabilities, and limited feasibility of urban-rural integration, namely, that it functions as a theoretical solution that does not work in practice. As discussed in chapter 3, Communist Party plans combine social, economic, cultural, and ideological transformations on the basis of a comprehensive vision. The success of urban-rural integration depends on the ability of local officials to develop the economy, marketize land-use rights, attract investment in agriculture, solicit industrial transfer, create mechanisms for legal regulation and mediation, and stimulate nonagricultural employment. For most peripheral rural areas in China, it is extremely difficult to engineer the conditions required to create a prosperous local economy; doing so in an earthquake zone that continues to be seismically active would indeed be a miracle.

When these interlocking conditions necessary to generate economic vitality are not met, urbanization becomes a process William Hurst and I have described as the "proliferation of urban forms divorced from urban practices and uses."[10] In Dujiangyan, urbanized peasants found themselves in the precarious situation of being without agricultural land (in most cases, the rights to which were exchanged for urban housing or the land itself was physically destroyed during the earthquake) and without employment while living in urban conditions in which basic goods and services are monetized. Many had the feeling of being dispossessed twice: first by the earthquake, second by the reconstruction plan.

Utopian urbanism is development by theoretical fiat, in which the viability of a plan and the conditions required for its successful realization are asserted rather than realistically assessed and firmly in place prior to implementation. Urban planning dissolves structural crises and contradictions in an idealized future into which people are interpellated to imagine their new lives. Urban plans are more than technical policy documents to be implemented; they are also objects of desire that circulate in official propaganda, commercial advertisements, and popular imaginaries of the good life.[11] The promise of the future is sustained by the frenzied activity of state-led urbanization, the destruction and creation of landscapes, and the upheaval of countless lives. The contradictions hidden in the seamless logic and rationalization of the plan are revealed only once the dust settles.

For political scientists who like the harder edges of science but have accompanied me this far, I admit that it is hard to pin down "utopia" into an observable and independent variable whose causality can be measured. However, as I demonstrate in this chapter, it is indeed possible to engage in "process tracing" and track the effects of the ideology of urban utopianism on the conditions of Dujiangyan residents' everyday lives, economic struggles, and encounters with local Party and state agents.

Background

After the 2008 Sichuan earthquake damaged a vast area of Dujiangyan's countryside and urban space, both the Chengdu and Dujiangyan municipal governments and Party committees decided to use the earthquake as an opportunity to accelerate urban-rural integration already underway prior to the earthquake. Party discourse encouraged officials to "use the innovative spirit of overall-planning of urban-rural development to explore post-disaster reconstruction" and "tightly grasp the three opportunities of post-disaster reconstruction, expanding domestic demand, and comprehensive urban-rural development."[12]

The urban-rural integration plan for the greater Chengdu municipal area, including Dujiangyan Municipality, was organized around the implementation of "three concentrations" (san ge jizhong).[13] The plan concentrates land for large-scale agricultural investment, enterprises in industrial parks, and peasants in new urban townships. The concentration of land is intended to rationalize agricultural land-use from small, fragmented individual plots to a modernized scale in order to attract capital to the countryside (ziben xiaxiang) providing rent to peasants relocated to concentrated urban settlements.[14] The concentration of industrial clusters is designed to create industrial advantages and linkages to attract outside investment, facilitate industrial transfer, and provide employment and increased wages to the now landless peasants. The relocation of peasants to new urban communities or concentrated settlements (jizhong anzhi dian) initiated a process of identity transformation from peasant to urban citizen—alternatively phrased by the Party as "new urban citizen construction" (xin shimin jianshe).[15] The first two

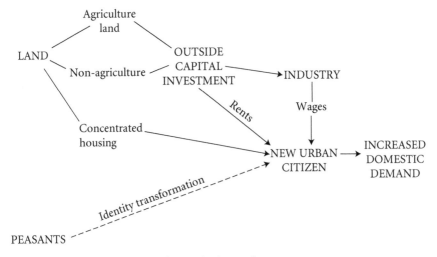

FIGURE 3. How to increase domestic demand

concentrations converge in the production of revenue streams for the new urban citizen and a "liberation of the peasantry's consumption power."[16] The macroeconomic goal is to "increase domestic demand" (*kuoda neixu*) to replace excessive reliance on exports as the main pillar of the economy, especially in light of the 2008 global financial crisis and sinking global demand for Chinese exports.[17] Figure 3 diagrams the mechanisms that will be unpacked in this chapter.

The following sections trace how the three concentrations were supposed to work in theory and how they produced less than desirable results in practice. Despite Communist Party discourse that theory must conform to practice, it is often the case, as it was during the reconstruction of Dujiangyan, that conceptual elegance is disconnected from practical consideration. Although the plan diagrammed in figure 3 is entirely logical and makes intuitive sense, in reality, each part has to interlock in a precise fashion for the plan to work. A plan is a series of processes dependent on the other processes. If key processes underperform or do not materialize, the plan falls apart.

The implementation of Dujiangyan's urban-rural integration plan for postearthquake reconstruction struggled in its attempt to achieve the first two (land, industry) out of the three concentrations. The strategy of capitalizing rural assets through the consolidation and marketization of land-use rights proved to be an overwhelming disappointment. More perniciously, industrialization attempts have sputtered without increasing employment opportunities, depriving the newly urbanized peasantry of badly needed income in light of its rise in living expenses. Without agricultural land and nonagricultural employment, the transformation of peasants into urban citizens has ironically become a process of proletariatization,

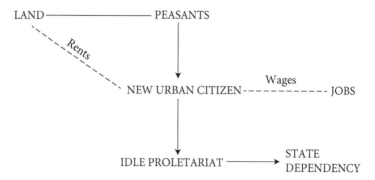

FIGURE 4. Production of the idle proletariat

although much different from the one Marx envisioned. In figure 4, the dotted lines represent the absence of what should have been income sources. Because of the pervasive "idleness" (*xianzhe*) of the residents in these hollow urban shells, I have labeled this phenomenon the creation of an *idle proletariat*. To be sure, I mean "idleness" not as a moral judgment about the vices of unemployment (hopefully that much should be clear from my writing at this point) but as a phenomenological description of a structurally imposed condition of boredom at the edges of capitalism. Peripheral cities in China's interior, like Dujiangyan, cannot generate enough employment opportunities to absorb newly urbanized citizens into the market economy. Instead, local residents are increasingly dependent on the Party even though their trust and approval of the Party has declined.

"The Three Concentrations"
Land

This section describes the first component of the urban-rural integration plan: the concentration and efficient rationalization of land use. To attract investment from industrial-scale agricultural enterprises, individual peasant plots would need to be spatially consolidated and their collective land tenures legally converted into fungible assets, which would provide farmers with a continuous source of rent or a onetime relocation compensation fee. In theory, this newly available cash would give peasants the start-up capital needed to begin their new lives as urban consumers living in apartment complexes. In reality, the plan failed to attract investors because of political, economic, and legal conditions, which resulted in a trickle of capital flowing to the countryside and an even smaller drop making its way into the hands of farmers. As a result of the inability of this economic transformation to sustain itself, the municipal government was forced to prop up local village economies with money it did not have.

This attempt at rural transformation did not happen overnight. In 2003, Chengdu "became a pilot city for the revision of its municipal master plan and land-use master plan to incorporate urban-rural integration."[18] One year before the earthquake in June 2007, China's State Council designated both Chengdu and Chongqing as the nation's first experimental zones for urban-rural integration reform. Dujiangyan Municipality was incorporated in the 2003 pilot program and in 2007 was granted status as an experimental model for the "reform of villager property rights system" (*nongcun chanquan gaige*).[19] On the day of the earthquake, Chengdu Party secretary Li Chuncheng (who has since been placed under investigation for corruption charges) was in fact en route to Dujiangyan to convene a meeting on the "pilot experiment for comprehensive urban-rural integration."[20]

Before the earthquake, the reforms proceeded at a slow pace. According to a Dujiangyan Party School professor, "Under normal conditions, it is difficult for the government to accomplish this goal of relocating farmers into apartments. Most of them are unwilling to give up their land or demand higher compensation than the government is willing to offer. During the earthquake, their homes collapsed. This provided the Party a perfect opportunity to transform the countryside."[21] After the earthquake, a torrent of documents, policies, and opinions were published calling for the transformation of post-disaster recovery into an opportunity to accelerate reform. The Dujiangyan Municipality Overall Urban-Rural Planning Work Bureau's Document No. 55 encouraged "the organic combination of village property-rights system reform and post-disaster village housing reconstruction."[22] This combination both met national-level policy targets and was tasked to "break the constraint of post-disaster reconstruction capital bottlenecks" by attracting outside investment into the locality through the capitalization of land on the property market.[23] In the words of Liu Junlin, Dujiangyan municipal Party secretary at the time, "After earnest consideration, we decided that even after the earthquake, not only we will not halt the village property right system reform, we will accelerate it. Why? By incorporating the reform of the village property rights system into the core of reconstruction, we can resolve the problem of where the money for reconstruction is going to come from."[24]

To accomplish these goals, a new planning system was created for the township and village levels. This was innovative because planning is traditionally under the jurisdiction of the national, provincial, and municipal levels. The goal was to rationalize land use through a series of property-rights reforms. Reform stipulated the clarification, demarcation, and registration of village land according to three basic ownership structures: agricultural collectives, village committees, and the township government. The border between village land and state-owned land also required clarification and legal definition.[25] Land was reserved for concentrated multistory housing, combined for intensive agriculture, and expropriated for central or provincial state-level projects such as railway construction, and the remainder was devoted to attracting investment through the building of commercial or tourist facilities. The designated uses of land also needed to conform to the regulatory indexes promulgated by the National Land Bureau at the municipal administrative level. These reforms were defended as a necessary precondition for profit sharing derived from "the capitalization of village resources" (*nongcun ziyuan bian ziben*).[26] According to Document No. 7 published by the specially created office called the Dujiangyan Village Property-Rights System Reform Leadership Working Small Group, "village property rights system reform is the most effective path for . . . advancing the liberation and development of rural productive forces."[27]

The next step was the free circulation of land contracting and operating rights through rent, subcontract, transfer, exchange, or jointly held stocks in rural cooperatives.[28] This circulation was designed to "import key enterprises for the industrialization of agriculture" based on the model of "company + village cooperative + peasant household."[29] The plan aimed at catalyzing a transition from small-scale subsistence farming on scattered, individual land plots to large-scale industrial farming with higher productivity and profitability—achieving the dream of agricultural modernization.[30] The promised outcome subtending the plan was an end to the paradox of asset-rich but cash-deprived villages and the creation of liquidity.

According to the plan, nonagricultural land would become available for commercial investment, tourism, and entertainment. Additionally, any land that was returned to farmland in surplus of the agricultural land quota could be sold or transferred to Chengdu, allowing the latter to urbanize beyond its already exhausted quota. Only Chengdu and Chongqing are allowed to trade or purchase agricultural land from other areas to exceed their quotas as a result of their status as experimental areas.[31]

To settle disputes arising from the market circulation of land-contracting and operating rights, a special arbitration committee was created on the basis of Dujiangyan Municipality's Temporary Measures for Arbitrating Disputes Regarding Village Land Contracting Transfer of Village Land Circulation.[32] Administratively under the jurisdiction of the Agricultural Development Bureau, the committee was headed by that office's director and composed of members of the Petitions and Letters Office, Forestry Bureau, National Land Bureau, Court System, and Procurator's Office and other experts with experience in agricultural management.[33]

According to a 2011 report published by a Dujiangyan Municipal Party School research group, there has only been a small margin in the amount of land circulated on the market.[34] In 2011, Dujiangyan contained a total of 278,900 mu (a mu is equal to one fifth of a hectare) of arable land. By December 2010, only 58,700 mu of land was circulated on the market. The annual percentage increased at a snail's pace in 2009 and 2010.[35] Additionally, out of the manifold choices for circulating the land, it is almost exclusively rented at the price of 800–1,200 catties of husked rice (1 catty is equal to 0.5 kilograms).[36] Finally, some lands have become fallow, as a minority of investors "do not genuinely operate the land, but use it to engage in speculation."[37]

In addition to the small amount of land actually being circulated as a commodity on property markets, there are also few interested investors and actual proprietors. Cumulatively there were thirty-seven proprietors by 2008, fifty-two in 2009, and sixty-seven in 2010.[38] The proprietors are roughly divided between specialized cooperative organizations and enterprises; in 2009 out of the fifty-two proprietors, 43.3 percent were specialized cooperatives and 39.2 percent for-profit enterprises. The specialized cooperative organizations are nonprofit/nongovernmental organizations with the role of linking individual household production to larger enterprises and distribution networks. Agriculture is already considered a "weak industry" that requires massive initial capital outlays and promises limited benefits that will accrue only over a long period of time.[39] It is also harder to find investors after an earthquake.

To make matters worse, commercial enterprises that are interested in investing in Dujiangyan's nonagricultural land also faced significant constraints as a result of the legal restrictions on land-use rights and profit distribution. According to the Sichuan Provincial Government's 2011 Document No. 10, "a national tax will be levied on construction of land for new urban areas" and "nongovernmental capital must not participate in the distribution of earnings from construction on new land areas." These two clauses curtailed investment possibilities in the commercial and industrial development of nonagricultural land as well as limited the distribution of profits from prior investments.[40] Consequently, the fulfillment of already promised investments has slowed to avoid further sunk costs. The lack of social investment transfers the burden of funding land reorganization onto the local government—an unsustainable situation over the long term. The Party school report concludes that "without the investment of social capital, Dujiangyan's public finances will be powerless to support it."[41] The theoretical assertion that leading enterprises would initiate a positive cycle of investment and development failed to materialize.[42]

In addition to the structural obstacles discussed above, there is also a lack of political initiative to enact the reforms. According to the Party school report, leading Party cadres are fearful of standing between peasants and their land and, as a result, do not treat the reforms as a priority.[43] The Party cadres responsible for implementing the plan lack adequate knowledge of the law, neglect management responsibilities, "allow problems to drift," and do not closely supervise the transactions of land rights.[44] Careless management has led to the failure to create a sufficient number of intermediary service organizations necessary for linking peasant households with enterprises, assessing land value, offering legal advice, helping to draft contracts, obtaining banking services, and so on. It is worth reflecting on the fact that there is not a natural or organic market that would integrate the needs of peasants with the profit demands of enterprises, let alone do so in a fair and equitable way; where Party involvement was in fact required, it was nowhere to be found because of the high level of governance difficulties and low rate of return. The economic difficulties in the earthquake zone are not the result of state distortion of markets but rather the state's inability to create them.

This lack of regulatory oversight is especially egregious in light of the fact that some of the contracts between peasant households and enterprises were orally agreed on and, as such, have no legal basis for dispute resolution. Written contracts were often drawn up in obscure language that did not clearly specify who signed the contracts, the rights and obligations of each party to the contract, or exact amounts of compensation to be paid to the farmers. In certain cases, this led to the "violation of voluntary will, coerced transfer of land, and encroachment of benefits" that were supposed to help peasants transition to becoming urban residents.[45]

Apart from the Party and state's lack of involvement in the daily operation of land-rights circulation, the plan did not account for, or more precisely, ignored the well-known fact that many farmers are not willing to give up their land-use rights, which they regard as "their very lifeblood" (*ming genzi*).[46] Despite the attractiveness of urban wages, many farmers view the land as their guarantee for food and protection against proletariatization. They may also distrust the intentions of both the Party and outside investors to safeguard their interests.

Not all farmers had land to keep, however, as many were required to transfer their land-use rights to the government as the condition to obtain post-earthquake housing in new concentrated townships. It turns out that these landless peasants may in one aspect be luckier than peasants who retained and rented out their land. As was pointed out to me by the Party secretary of an urban community in Pi County, Dujiangyan's neighbor, and another experimental site, "The people who have it worst are peasants who have not lost their land but rent it out—the rent is very little but because they still have land, they are not eligible for social insurance."[47] This is another way of saying that even when the plan works, it does not work as planned.

Industry

The concentration of industry is slightly more straightforward than the tortuous—and for the People's Republic of China (PRC) unprecedented—registration, marketization, circulation, and management of land-use rights. The post-earthquake industrialization plan followed the national preference and tendency to construct industrial clusters. The goal was to establish dominant industrial clusters for the primary processing of agricultural products and light manufacture. Similar to the metaphor of blood transfusion and generation discussed in chapter 3, the theory was that the clusters would attract outside capital investment as well as factories wanting to relocate from the coastal regions to the interior, in search of cheaper labor, lower operating costs, and preferential conditions. At the same time, the tertiary service industry was supposed to expand to keep pace with the accelerated rate of urbanization. These industrial gains were to provide jobs and income. Contrary to the plan's expectations, Dujiangyan's Puyang Industrial Cluster was beset by incoherence. Instead of rationalized linkages generating market advantages, Puyang suffers from a lack of dominant industry, few large enterprises, inadequate industrial layering, and limited space for industrial development, rendering it unattractive to outside investment. Puyang is further constrained by Chengdu's regional economic planning, which is prioritized in the pecking order of administrative planning over Dujiangyan's local needs. As a result, the post-earthquake revitalization of Dujiangyan's industrial economy suffers from a faint pulse and an inability to absorb labor. To return to the metaphors from chapter 3, the "blood transfused" (*shuxue*) by the earthquake reconstruction has failed to become a "blood-generating cycle" (*zaoxue xunhuan*) in the local economy; instead, Dujiangyan's "ability to produce its own blood is severely deficient" (*zaoxue yanzhong quesun*).[48]

As a result of the weak agricultural base detailed in the previous section, industries that process agricultural products have not fared well.[49] Dujiangyan has not developed any specialty agricultural products that could find a profitable market.[50] A Dujiangyan Party School report bluntly summarizes the problem as follows: "good products are not many; many products are not good."[51]

Dujiangyan's industrial enclaves are also plagued with structural contradictions and inefficiencies. In 2010, the value added from Dujiangyan's total industrial output was 26.37 hundred million RMB ($421.8 million), 16 hundred million ($256.0 million) of which was from the Puyang Industrial Enclave—a dismally low number when compared with the 56.08 hundred million RMB ($891.8 million) of neighboring Pengzhou County. Dujiangyan's industrial performance also pales in comparison with the Chengdu suburbs of Wenjiang and Shuangliu.[52] Given its sizable percentage of overall value added, Puyang

Township's industrial enclave offers a microcosm of Dujiangyan's industrial problems.

One possible reason for Dujiangyan's weak industrialization is its rather diminished importance within Chengdu's regional economy. Chengdu's rule "One area, one main industry" (*yi qu, yi zhu ye*) has required continual adjustments to find a magical industrial formula.[53] The development of the Puyang Industrial Enclave was consequently slowed by its inability to determine a dominant industry. Its lack of a clear and coherent identity as an industrial enclave rendered it difficult to attract other related industries and enterprises that were supposed to in theory form an industrial cluster. As a result, it lacks "industrial conglomeration" (*jituan hangye*), "leading enterprises" (*longtou qiye*), or an influential "name brand" (*pinpai*) that might "influence" (*qidong*) and "assemble" (*jiju*) other industries producing an economic "radiation" (*fushe*) effect.[54] Absent a dominant industry, it follows that the enclave has weak "industrial layering" (*chanye cengci*) and enterprises lack "horizontal" (*hengxiang*) supply chain linkages. In short, the Puyang Industrial Enclave has been unable to achieve industrial advantages of scale.

Instead, many companies are small scale, insufficiently influential, and unable to apply for bank loans and expand their scale of operations. The industrial enclave's credit operation is also severely limited in how much it is authorized to lend. Insufficient capital circulation constrains the ability of enterprises to expand. Somewhat preposterously, a large percentage of companies in the industrial enclave lack legal land use formalities and therefore cannot be claimed as "legal assets" (*hefa zichan*), further undermining linkages between enterprises and the coherency of the enclave.[55] Exacerbating matters, Chengdu Municipality's National Land Bureau has curtailed the amount of land for industrial construction allotted to Puyang. No wonder a report from the Dujiangyan Party School referred to the enclave as having an uncertain future.[56]

The capital shortage of enterprises is passed on to the local state. According to the same report in 2011, the Puyang Industrial Enclave faces a "shortage of capital for follow-up development." There is an estimated capital shortage of 48 hundred million RMB ($767.9 million) originating from state expenditure in construction, infrastructure, and fees related to land appropriation, demolition, and relocation of residents.[57]

In light of the aforementioned problems, Puyang's "ability to absorb the employment needs of labor is weak."[58] Addressing Dujiangyan as a whole, a Party school report concludes that "lack of industrial support makes it difficult to guarantee employment opportunities and means of livelihood for the peasants entering new townships, restricting the development of town-ization."[59] In a similarly harsh indictment of the planning process, the Urban Construction Theory Research journal identifies that "the main shortcoming of the plan to spatially con-centrate villagers is that it failed to satisfactorily consider villager employment needs. . . . The reconstruction plan did not devote much consideration to villa-ger production and lifestyle needs."[60] This lack of employment opportunity and wages has devastating consequences for the now landless peasant-urban resident.

New Urban Citizen Construction

The earthquake offered the local Party and state organs the rare opportunity to rapidly implement the long coveted but politically sensitive relocation of peas-antry. According to official statistics, in rural Dujiangyan the earthquake dam-aged over 123,800 rural households; 43,000 houses required demolition and reconstruction, while 57,000 households needed repair and reinforcement.[61] In urban Dujiangyan, the earthquake damaged over 97,000 households, 40,000 requiring demolition and reconstruction, 57,000 needing repair and reinforce-ment. Given the extensive damage, the Party grasped the opportunity to "break the constraint of the former urban-rural model."[62]

Break the model they did. Post-earthquake housing construction devoured in total 7.7 million square meters.[63] The relocation of rural inhabitants incorporated over 50 percent of Dujiangyan's total rural population into urban communities and incorporation of peripheral townships and former suburbs into the city lim-its, "enormously expanding Dujiangyan's urban radius."[64] Out of Dujiangyan's sixty-nine urban communities, thirty-three were newly constructed after the earthquake, with twenty still under construction as of 2011. Villages administra-tively incorporated into Dujiangyan's city limits were reclassified as communities, village leaders were renamed community directors, and political administration was subtly placed under the category of management in an attempt to nominally transform the state into a service-oriented government. Most of the concen-trated settlements are composed of ten-story buildings (the largest is nineteen stories) with an average of three thousand units (the largest contains 8,100) and are located at the urban periphery constructed on what was prior to the earthquake agricultural land.[65] These communities are mainly monofunctional housing complexes, some of which have "shop fronts" (*pumian*), and the majority of them are gated and operated by residential management companies requiring monthly service fees. New communities are often composites of merged villages requir-ing a new administrative structure; some combine residents who prior to the earthquake lived in urban as well as rural areas, such as the community in which I rented an apartment located on Dujiangyan's urban periphery. Typically, for-merly rural and urban residents are spatially segregated from each other in differ-ent complexes within the same community. Apparently, even the ardent desire to construct new urban citizens reproduces urban-rural hierarchies within its own processes.

Urbanization was also extended in the form of concentrated housing developments into the countryside, creating half-urban, half-village communities (*ban chengshi, ban nongcun shequ*). These concentrated settlements administratively belong to the township they are located in. Consequently, peasants remain in the countryside but live in buildings that resemble urban communities.

This official objective of rationally administered urban space resembled the syndrome of compulsive urban construction that has led to the creation of numerous ghost cities throughout China's urban landscape.[66] According to the *Bluebook of Urban-Rural Integration* (2011), published by the Chinese Academy of Social Sciences, one of the dangers of the national urban-rural integration campaign is the "urbanization of land enormously exceeds the urbanization of people . . . as well as speed of industrialization" resulting in "hollow townships and villages" (*kongxin zhen, kongxin cun*) and a "grave waste of land resources" (*tudi ziyuan de yanzhong langfei*).[67] When I asked a cab driver in Dujiangyan what has changed since the earthquake, he bitterly laughed and responded, "Urban space but nothing else."[68]

Dujiangyan indeed suffers from a glut of empty housing units as well as storefronts, especially in the post-earthquake-built communities on Dujiangyan's periphery. According to the head of a GONGO (government-organized nongovernmental organization) in charge of providing social services for these communities, "many of the new communities were built with an oversupply. For instance, Community A contains thirty thousand housing units and only sixteen thousand of them are filled"[69] already four years after the earthquake occurred. When I visited this community, I noticed that in addition to vacant apartments, the storefronts lining the street were almost entirely empty or abandoned. I interviewed the owner of one of the only restaurants that was open, who explained: "Most people here cannot afford the rent for these storefronts. If someone opens a shop, they have to raise prices to be able to make ends meet. But nobody wants to pay for such raised prices and the store goes under. It is a vicious circle."[70] In an interview with the Party secretary of Community B, he admitted to me that one third of the apartments were empty and that they were in the process of "relocating more villagers" to fill them.[71] Community C was filled with residents, but other complexes within the community were almost entirely empty. More conspicuously, I counted over two hundred empty storefronts wrapping around the perimeter of one complex. These storefronts and the land adjacent to them are sometimes informally occupied by people repairing shoes or selling fruits, meats, and animal skins from the back of a truck. For the most part, though, they were starkly empty. Even worse, in Community D, the Party promised each residential household a storefront; to the residents' dismay and anger, the storefronts were constructed inside the buildings of the gated community, and some were even located on the third floor, undermining any potential economic utility (local officials have refused to allocate any of the storefronts, afraid of the disputes it will raise, so they all remain idle). This led one resident to speculate that "the government is trying to intentionally hurt the people"[72]—for him, there was no other explanation that could possibly explain the irrationality of the planning decision. Apparently, tensions between the local Party branch and residents in Community D over this, as well as other issues (see the following discussion over quality disputes) were exacerbated to the point that the local government allegedly instructed security guards to ban outsiders and especially researchers from entering the community—many residents were surprised I had not been detained and escorted out while I was talking to them.

Local residents speculate that the reason for the tremendous rate of empty apartments is corruption and the vacant apartments will sooner or later, by opaque means, become the assets of local officials. "Local cadres will definitely sell the empty housing as commodity housing. Even if they can't sell it, it still counts as fixed assets on their books. Some have already made over hundreds of thousands of profits from this."[73] Another middle aged-man, sitting in the sun, joked with me that since "reform and opening, our government should enter the Guinness Book of World Records for the most advanced science and technology. They are famous for the size of their irrigated pork"[74] (*guan shui zhu rou*). In Chinese, the characters *guan shui* literally mean to irrigate but have a double connotation of artificially increasing weight (by pumping water into something) or to cook the books through illegal activity. In the words of a cab driver, "After the reconstruction, the Dujiangyan government increased the number of police and frequency of patrols. Do you know why? They are afraid that if residents ever found out how much money was wasted during the earthquake reconstruction, they would set fire to the city and overthrow the government. I am not being reactionary [*fandong*]; I am simply stating the facts."[75] While I do not have evidence to confirm or deny such conjectures, the excessive construction of urban housing according to a plan that in theory was supposed to economize land use and relied on fairly precise population statistics certainly merits questioning. This was clearly not the transformation of a "disorderly, unstructured usage of space into its intensive rationalization."[76]

What is more, many of the new apartments were built on what was previously agricultural land, which as angry villagers called to my attention consists of loose soil that is subject to liquefaction in seismically active regions.[77] In other words, building foundations on loose soil that are not reinforced are more prone to capsize. According to a dozen of villagers I interviewed as a group from Community D, "the government promised us they would use rebar to secure the foundations of the building, but we inspected it, and found out they lied to us."[78] Although it is unclear how the villagers actually inspected and scientifically verified this information, they expressed anxiety over what might happen in case of a future earthquake. The same group of villagers also explained to me that the quality of construction is very poor. According to one villager, "When I was renovating my apartment, I found out that both the paint and concrete were shoddy. Touching it with your hand, the cement in the walls crumbles, and the paint peels right off."[79] While loose soil, peeling paint, and inferior concrete might appear to some as apolitical objects, in Dujiangyan's Community D, such mundane complaints are palpable proof to the villagers of the Party's failure to serve their interests.[80] The intimate and ordinary realm of what people care about, understand, and experience is where Party legitimacy is slowly being eroded in rural China. It also should be kept in mind that Dujiangyan was home to three of the most severe school collapses as a result of the earthquake, resulting in an estimated total of over nine hundred deaths of students and teachers, casting a grim pallor over construction quality disputes.

Problems in daily life are exacerbated by economic stress. According to urban researcher Yan Guo, as a result of Dujiangyan's "radical transformation of economic structure and labour market, a majority of locals lost their essentials for carrying on life in the city. This vulnerable group, usually are ones affected by the Earthquake, has run out of options but been force [sic] to leave home"[81] and migrate for employment opportunities. Sadly, this largely correct account overlooks the fact that many of the newly relocated peasantry lack the necessary skills as well as education levels and are at an age demographic where even the option of migrant labor is largely closed off to them.[82] Yan is correct that most of those who can migrate have already done so, leaving behind residents for whom the rural-to-urban transformation has become a process of treading water with neither shore any longer in sight.[83]

The Dujiangyan Party School conducted a survey of thirty thousand residents who moved into concentrated settlements in 2009. The survey found that 27 percent of this population sample was between forty and fifty years of age, and 21 percent was over the age of fifty-one, which means that more than one-fourth of the "new urban citizens" were too young to retire and likely too old to learn new skills or migrate for work, if they had not done so already. Within the same population sample, 36 percent of residents' highest degree of education was primary school, 42 percent junior high school.[84] Also, 7.8 percent of the sample population received welfare subsidies.

As figures 5 and 6 demonstrate, this high percentage of uneducated middle-aged residents suggests that even if more jobs were available, this group of people probably would not have the qualifications to be hired. Many interview-

Age

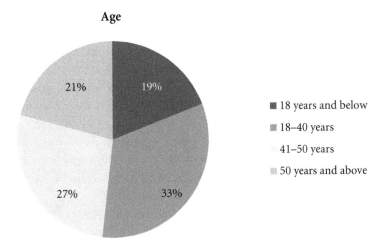

- ■ 18 years and below
- ▨ 18–40 years
- 41–50 years
- ▨ 50 years and above

FIGURE 5.   Sample new urban resident population by age

Education Level

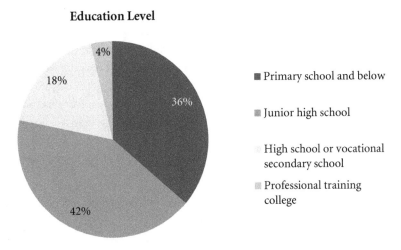

- ■ Primary school and below
- ▨ Junior high school
- High school or vocational secondary school
- ▨ Professional training college

FIGURE 6.   Sample new urban resident population by education level

ees described themselves as unhirable even as migrant laborers. One middle-aged woman exclaimed, "At my age, and with no education, who would hire me? Not even the factories in Guangdong would take someone like me!"[85]

Without land to farm, jobs to work, or places to migrate, most residents are idle.[86] An anthropology professor in Chengdu described idleness as a phenomenology of "having nothing left, a new form of proletariatization that happens when people's original living structures collapse."[87] This new form of proletariatization is composed of stubbornly unmalleable rural bodies, old and exhausted bodies, and crippled bodies (from injuries during the earthquake)—in sum, surplus bodies that cannot be integrated into the circuits of capital taking place elsewhere.[88] In the words of one interviewee, "I wake up and eat breakfast, then walk around until lunch, eat lunch, walk around until dinner, after dinner go to bed and get ready to do the same thing tomorrow."[89] Residents also spend their days playing mahjong and card games or in the winter, sitting around a fire.[90] In dry, clinical, Chinese Communist language, a Dujiangyan Party School research report describes these people as a "surplus population with widespread low quality."[91] This resembles the situation of the left-behind rural population in China's "hollow villages" more than it does a newly urbanized landscape.[92]

The implications of this situation for actual residents are rather bleak. Most of my interviewees complained about not having the space to raise pigs, which to them are a lifeline for food security. As one Dujiangyan villager explained,

> The government's "integrated program" has both advantages and disadvantages. The main advantage of moving to this location is it is more convenient for transportation. The disadvantages are living in these multistory homes. Water, electricity, gas, and food all require money. In the past, I didn't need to pay money in order to burn firewood; we also grew our food, and extracted our own oil. Now we cannot raise pigs and we are far away from our land; to get there is at least half an hour walk. If they let us repair our old houses and build a courtyard-style house where we could raise pigs and chickens, that would be ideal. If I had a choice between this integrated program plan and rebuilding my old home on my own, I would choose the latter.[93]

Many residents are not used to paying for services and goods that were previously free or unnecessary. This is not only a matter of not wanting to or not being accustomed to pay but an inability to pay. A Party school report diagnoses the root of the problem as "living expenses increase, revenue sources supporting life decrease."[94] A common refrain among interviewees was, "Since the reconstruction our quality of life has not improved, only the cost of living has increased" or simply "consumer costs are too high."[95]

When I interviewed residents from Community D, Complex 2, in Dujiangyan, their narratives registered how the disruptions from relocation permeated every aspect of their lives, in both profound and mundane ways. One elderly resident was distraught from losing his ancestral land where he intended to be buried; now he will, in his own words, "die without a proper burial site" (*si wu zang shen zhi di*), lacking money to buy a plot elsewhere.[96] The phrase he used also connotes to suffer a tragic ending as a rootless and spectral being. In fact, the previous homes of residents from Community D, Complex 2, only suffered minimal damage from the earthquake; according to the elderly man, "in the name of the reconstruction plan" their homes were forcibly demolished to make way for the Chengdu-Dujiangyan High-Speed Rail (reducing a one-and-a-half-hour bus trip to under thirty minutes, costing 15 RMB ($2.40) per ticket, even cheaper than the 17 RMB ($2.72) bus ticket). A man in his late fifties complained that the "buildings were too dense" and violated state policy mandating a proportion of "green space" to residential construction surface area.[97]

Many Party cadres and scholars contend that these problems are temporary growing pains that will be resolved in the next generation.[98] The next generation of residents will be accustomed from birth to the amenities of urban life and will have no memory or attachment to life in the countryside, eradicating at least the cultural basis of complaints. Party documents have also started to subtly shift discursive attention and hope to later generations.[99] The present impasse implicitly acknowledges the violence required to transform older generations, poetically described by Tuan Yi-fu:

> To be forcibly evicted from one's home and neighborhood is to be stripped of a sheathing, which in its familiarity protects the human being from the bewilderments of the outside world. As some people are reluctant to part with their shapeless old coat for a new one, so some people—especially older people—are reluctant to abandon their old neighborhood for the new housing development.[100]

Even if the hope placed on future generations comes to fruition, it is based on a logic that relegates the relocated disaster victims to the status of a sacrificial generation.

Some of the younger people I interviewed quite fluently expressed their desires and dreams in the Party discourse of enjoyment, spending, and consumerism. Standing in the doorway of the first floor of her apartment converted into a teahouse, a woman in her thirties informed me that "post-earthquake transformations are huge" and noted specifically an acute rise of "consumer consciousness,"[101] which in Chinese implies developing a reflexive consciousness of oneself as someone who consumes, who is permitted to enjoy and desire consumption—in distinct contrast to Maoist austerity and the cultural tradition of saving money, spending little. A young mother explained that "in the past people were not willing to spend money, and would put all of it in savings. Now, the thinking is, if you should spend money, then spend it!"[102]

The Communist Party's macroeconomic plan to increase domestic demand requires this micro-level transformation of people's daily habits, desires, and practices. The Chinese Communist Party (CCP) is currently leading a massive biopolitical campaign to create new consumer subjectivities.[103] This change in thinking might not, however, be entirely an effect of the Communist Party propaganda machine; some have suggested that new spending impulses are a result of people's traumatic encounter with their own mortality during the earthquake. "You never know when another earthquake will happen, and if you are unlucky that time, what are you going to do with the money you saved after you are dead?"[104] explained a local Chengdu resident. Problem is, even if people do change their subjective desires, there is no guarantee that the economic conditions will be such to support their new desires to buy, decorate, and individualize. The same teahouse proprietor admitted that "right now this community already has six teahouses like this one, so I have to sell tea very cheaply, and make hardly any money."[105] Her hope is that the idleness of community members will be the engine for her business: "so many people have nothing to do here, they need a place where they can relax and be entertained."[106]

Despite indications of an entrepreneurial spirit developing among some of their members, the new urban communities lack economic vitality. This pervasive idleness has ironically pushed the people and the Party closer together, as the people's dependency on the Party has increased, even though its trust and approval of the Party have declined. The government's objective to transform itself into a neutral service-oriented government and withdraw from direct and heavy-handed interference in the functioning of the economy and affairs of daily life has backfired dramatically.[107] Instead, the local state and Party organs are even more enmeshed in the politics of everyday life. According to one local cadre I interviewed, "it was easier to govern in the countryside because everyone was spread out and self-reliant. Now, in these urban communities, if people have any problem, they immediately come to us. Where else can they go? They have no money to resolve problems on their own."[108] A Party secretary from Community F in Pi County disparagingly referred to the state's role in the new urban communities as a "nanny."[109] Over a dozen urban-community cadres I interviewed, in both Dujiangyan and Pi Counties, described governing these communities as a "headache" and "irritating."

When residents have trouble paying their bills or if a pipe leaks in their apartment, without cash or the ability to solve problems on their own, they turn to the Party for help or as the object of their grievances. In their eyes, the Party put them there, so it is the Party's responsibility to solve their problems. According to the Party secretary of Community F of Pi County, "People's dependency is very strong. Any problem and they immediately come to the government asking for help."[110]

This dependency multiplies the encounters and increases the potential surfaces of friction between state and society (or, Party and masses, to use the Party's expression)—it expands the range of objects that can produce political disputes within the territory of everyday life. This also explains why Party officials are obsessively vigilant over small details and mundane disputes, perceiving in them the "sprouts" of social instability.

Not only are new urban residents more dependent on the Party than they were as peasants, but the Party's biopolitical investment in "new urban citizen construction" extends its reach into the realms of ordinary life. According to the Party secretary of Community B in Pi County, "urban-rural integration has been underway here for six years already; people are still spitting melon seeds everywhere, chaotically throwing their trash where they want—all of these are huge problems! Six years already living here and the same problems still persist; the habits have not changed, despite our efforts to educate and train them."[111] Another Party secretary from Community F in Pi County complained about the numerous violations of community rules, such as villagers' growing crops inside their apartments, making fires in the courtyard, and converting their ground floors into mahjong parlors or teahouses, among other public or aesthetic nuisances—phenomena I witnessed on a daily basis in Dujiangyan as well. This Party secretary explained how she was initially very idealistic and eager to help the farmers in their transition, but now, her hair is going white from the stress. "We are understaffed, and we just can't chase after all of them and correct these violations. We have to some extent to tolerate them; otherwise, they will increase tensions between the Party and local residents."[112] I interviewed the Party secretary of Community A in Dujiangyan while he was on his way to hand out "red envelopes" filled with small money gifts to villagers for the upcoming Chinese New Year. When I asked him about these kinds of infractions, he sighed: "We sit down with them, carry out educational campaigns to train them how to live in their new homes, but they do what they want anyway. Management is very difficult."[113]

This suggests that the transition from rural to urban broke down somewhere along the route to modernity and is not spontaneously resuming itself. Even invasive Party tactics cannot seem to push it back on track. Rather than engage in introspective self-criticism that would need to account for the Party's responsibility for the flaws in the urban-rural integration plan and the promises it made, its favored narrative is to blame the recalcitrant character of the peasantry for derailing the process.

During conversations with Party officials and in many restricted access Party documents, continual reference is made to the "traditional peasant mentality" (*xiao nong yishi*) of "waiting, depending, and demanding" (*deng, kao, yao*). The discourse that peasants are "unable to adapt their thinking"[114] conveniently individualizes the problems caused by the reconstruction and redirects blame away from the Party and more intractable structural issues, such as the lack of economic development. "After concentrating the peasantry into housing, their [administrative] identities were transformed into that of urban citizens and their dwelling was modernized, but their thinking, sense, and life-style still require a process."[115] This "antiquated way of thinking" is traced back to "ancestral" patterns of dispersed living that tenaciously "persist in one's old ways,"[116] making the peasantry "resistant" to change. In the Party's eyes, the "low quality [suzhi] of peasants" is responsible for their "lack of indulging in consumerism."[117] People believe that public areas are the state's responsibility and so do nothing to change their "dirty, disorderly, and substandard" behaviors that blemish the aesthetic of utopian urbanism.[118] Strikingly, rural sensibilities, and not the labor market, are also blamed for unemployment. "Initiative to find employment or engage in entrepreneurship is weak. After becoming citizens on paper, some peasants' thinking still has not been transformed in the direction of urban citizens. Their ability to independently start their own ventures or find work for themselves is frail. Their thinking is to depend on the government and subsidies of village committees."[119] This dependence on the government is summed up in a uniquely Chinese phrase, the conceptual significance of which is difficult to capture in English, which literally means "it is hot above, but cold down below" (shangtou re, xiamian leng),[120] implying that villagers will not act without being told what to do. In addition to lacking self-motivation, peasants' difficult economic conditions are often explained as the result of their lack of discipline and dissolute morality. When I asked one Party cadre why so many residents seem to be lacking money, he responded, "We gave them money after the earthquake, but some people went ahead and bought a car they cannot afford to put gas in now, or blew all the money on gambling and now have nothing left. So they come back to the local Party branch complaining and demanding more money."[121]

The Party's position is that idleness is a moral problem rather than a socioeconomic phenomenon. In the new urban communities, cadres typically identify idleness as the main culprit for troublemaking without investigating why people have nothing to do, which would implicate the Party in the picture. A Dujiangyan Party School report nicely captures this sentiment: "some people with nothing to do make trouble out of nothing; small problems can possibly spark contradictions, to the extent of bringing about mass incidents."[122] The government has enlisted NGOs to help fix this problem by organizing community events, leisurely activities, or handicrafts to keep people out of trouble. According to a local Dujiangyan NGO worker, "after becoming urban, most residents don't know what to do and are idle, so we help them do meaningful activities"[123]—an example of how discourse slips amid registers of social management and philanthropy.

Conclusion: Utopian Rationality

With the earthquake as a convenient alibi, the Party seized the opportunity to implement top-down plans for the urbanization of villagers. In the stinging words of Yan Guo, the post-earthquake urban-rural integration plan resulted in a "massive consumption of fertile land for a fantasized urban China."[124]

Utopian urbanism and the fantasies it generates are at the core of China's developmental model. The cold, rationalized jargon of urban-rural integration orbits around the figure of new urban citizens pursuing their own private paradises in a moderately prosperous society (*xiaokang shehui*).[125] This dreamlike status of the figure is protected by a veneer of scientific armor that presents itself as impervious to criticism. The vertiginous stream of statistics the Party publishes on urban-rural integration (or any topic, for that matter) is typically more bewildering than clarifying. Reading statistic upon statistic and campaign slogan after campaign slogan produces a disorienting effect through which reality is negated

FIGURE 7. Dujiangyan planning exhibition wall projection

by its statistical representation. Publishing how many apartments were built, with what infrastructural improvements; how many great strides of development were accomplished; and how many peasants, who have written countless beautiful couplets thanking the Party, were relocated crystallizes the circular, self-referential, and fantasmatic elements of development by theoretical fiat.

Dujiangyan's Planning Exhibition Pavilion is a perfect archive of urban utopia. The basement level of the pavilion contains a miniature model of Dujiangyan, with different sections that light up from pushing the buttons on a control panel. The walls are decorated with blueprints of Dujiangyan's urban construction projects, including government buildings, schools, tourist facilities, and residential complexes. As the figuration of an unrealized future, a road of flowers opens onto a starry sky (see figure 7) and digitized residents are photoshopped into the images—in some cases, missing a face. Fantasy is not the opposite of reality; it is the core around which it is organized.

During the Mao years, the mythical aura of the model worker Lei Feng set the standard for communist subjectivity. In the present, the goal has shifted from the creation of model workers to the creation of model urban consumers. The failure to achieve this dream inscribes itself in unintended consequences. Peasants might lack employment and purchasing power, but they can no longer go back to being peasants.

THE MIRAGE OF DEVELOPMENT

Yingxiu Township

> The Party's governance concept is people-oriented: the entire work
> of post-disaster restoration and reconstruction is organized around
> the people, improving the people's welfare. If we depart from this
> central point, what are we building? How are we building it? Hasn't
> everything lost its original meaning?

—Wenchuan County Party secretary Qing Lidong, 2009

The Communist Party's Hall of Mirrors

One of the main themes of this book is how Communist Party utopianism persists in the production of dreamlike images around which reality is organized. In chapter 1, I explained that the Communist Party's legitimacy depends on a narrow repertoire of discourses through which events are ascribed meaning. In this chapter, I take the argument of discursive path dependence a step further and suggest that the currency of China's political system is the production and circulation of images of success.

In the words of sociologist Sun Liping, China's political system suffers from an endemic "vanity" (xurong) problem. The management of the Party's image biases how information flows through the political system. According to Sun, vanity impairs the cognitive ability to directly confront problems, which is the precondition for their resolution (it is rather useless to solve a poorly posed and misunderstood problem).[1] The Communist Party's epistemological tradition of seeking truth from facts is destroyed when facts precede investigation. Sun's argument is nearly identical to Mao's account of epistemology described in chapter 1. For Sun, the Communist Party decides "what methods to use to resolve problems" on the basis of rigorous and extended investigation that pierces "surface-level appearance" in order to apprehend the substantive as well as genuine causes of the problem at hand. Mao's definition of formalism as a poison that threatens the Communist Party's survival is echoed in Sun's conclusion that China's political future depends on "whether or not it can give up its vanity."

The "disease of formalism" is chronically inflamed by the Party organization's *Nomenklatura* (appointment) system and mechanisms for cadre evaluation and promotion. A Party cadre's career trajectory depends on how higher-level officials perceive and assess his or her performance. Top-down assessment rewards images of success that may or may not accurately represent reality. The opinions of ordinary citizens are rarely incorporated into the promotion decision. As a result of this exclusion, cadres will frequently discount how their actions impact the lives of local residents.

It is telling that the Communist Party's political vocabulary continually borrows from aesthetic terminology. The following example from a restricted access Central Party School report is worth quoting at length:

> Cadres attach importance to conspicuous political achievements and disregard subtler, less visible ones . . . obsessed with the superficial display of projects that give them face. . . . [In some cases] cadres will pursue the display of glory without concern for the masses. . . . Their only fear is that high-level authorities will not pay attention.[2]

The Communist Party's organizational hierarchies, evaluation mechanisms, and appointment system structurally generate formalism. The aestheticization of political criteria is also responsible for the proliferation of large-scale projects that are impractical and wasteful. Yongshun Cai explains, "When politicians are answerable to their superiors, their career goals may drive them to make decisions and allocate resources for the self-serving purpose of image enhancement, with little concern for the economic costs or other negative outcomes of their decisions."[3] Ordinary citizens are then forced to deal with the consequences of the economic costs and negative outcomes of the political achievements of Party officials.

For this reason, tension between the Party and the people originates from the fact that citizens and higher-level officials inhabit different sensible realities. As I discuss in this chapter, what higher-level officials see on a "leadership visit" (*lingdao shicha*) is qualitatively different from how local residents experience reality in their daily lives. Although a provincial-level official on tour of the reconstruction area might be pleased by the beautiful façade of a new house, its interior might be threadbare and inhabitants utterly destitute.

Party officials and earthquake victims evaluated the reconstruction on the basis of different criteria of success. For central- and provincial-level officials, the reconstruction needed to be completed on time and in accord with national-level policy targets. For township- and village-level officials, the validation of success came from the adulation of higher-level officials. For residents, a successful reconstruction project would be one that improved their lives.

Welcome to Yingxiu Township

The bus from Chengdu to the Wenchuan county seat stops halfway along the route outside of Yingxiu Township. To reach Yingxiu from the bus stop, it is necessary to cross a footbridge that traverses the Min River. Standing on the opposite shore for the first time in March 2012, I was struck by the sublime appearance of this township precariously wedged between raging water and mist-shrouded mountains. As I crossed the footbridge and entered Yingxiu, its beauty gave way to an overwhelming sense of forlornness. In the words of one resident, the Party built a "beautiful stage [*xitai*] without any actors [*yanyuan*]."

Since the earthquake, Yingxiu has been rebuilt as a political symbol of Communist Party glory and benevolence. It is another example of a utopian planning, which is not place specific but a composite of dreamlike images. As Yingxiu was the epicenter of the 2008 Sichuan earthquake, its reconstruction was designed in anticipation of higher-level officials on inspection visits, global audiences, and awestruck tourists. According to former Sichuan provincial Party secretary Liu Qibao (currently head of the Central Propaganda Department), Yingxiu's "historic mission" was to become a "world-famous township" and bustling tourist destination.[4]

FIGURE 8.   Yingxiu from across the Min River, 2012

In interviews with more than forty different residents and multiple extended trips to Yingxiu, however, I barely came across anyone who viewed Yingxiu as a successful example of reconstruction. The following joke reveals the deterioration of Communist Party legitimacy in Yingxiu:

> A TV reporter went to Yingxiu to conduct interviews. He asked an elderly man, "Did you hear that Guangdong Province was donating 620 million RMB [$93 million] to build a public cemetery only for Party cadres and government officials? What is your opinion on the matter?" The elderly man paused for a moment to reflect then cheerfully responded, "As long as they will be buried alive."[5]

Many local residents expressed similar indignation. After a two-hour interview, a retired People's Liberation Army (PLA) soldier apologized "for speaking too long" but quickly added that he could "go on for days about how angry" he was with the reconstruction.[6] During the 2013 Spring Festival, a village Party secretary ascended the roof of the local government headquarters with a loudspeaker to broadcast that the township government had not paid him for construction work. From the roof, he hung a banner with the words "The government is black."[7]

Although it is not unusual in a post-disaster context for people to feel abandoned by the state, Yingxiu was not lacking state capacity, presence, and the political will to engineer growth. It was swarming with Party cadres, government officials, famous architects, urban planners, and engineers. The main pattern of discontent was villagers' perception that the Communist Party had used the reconstruction as an opportunity to improve its image and not to improve their lives. As one villager put it, "The government spent so much money on projects the people do not like or need. They entirely neglected to consider how to improve [our] ability to make a living. Instead they only considered how it would appear from the street. Yingxiu looks good, but that is only a feeling; it has no benefit for us."[8] This view was echoed in the account of an anthropologist who also conducted fieldwork in Yingxiu:

> If you try to examine things from the point of view of economic rationality [*jingji de lixing*], you will see so many examples of sheer irrationality, but there is logic; it is a political-poetic [*zhengzhi de shixue*] logic. In Yingxiu Township, the government did not consider whether or not Yingxiu's economy would be sustainable; they wanted to turn it into a symbol and display of the strength of the Party.[9]

The "political-poetic logic" of Yingxiu's reconstruction plan was to create a world-class tourist destination that would host not only tourists but also high-level leaders on inspection visits. As long as Yingxiu attracted favorable attention and publicity, the Communist Party's "miracle" of reconstruction would be validated, regardless of the experiences and opinions of local residents.

The Gift of Reconstruction

After the earthquake, Yingxiu's only economic options were to export migrant labor and develop tourism. The former option has the downside of increasing rural depopulation and does not resolve the need to develop a self-reliant local economy. As a Wenchuan County official rhetorically asked, "If we don't do tourism, what else are we going to do?"[10]

Other options pursued by different disaster localities were not available in Yingxiu. The earthquake ravaged Yingxiu's scarce arable land, thereby ruling out agricultural modernization as a possibility. On top of this, at the time of the earthquake, Yingxiu was already a decade into a process of deindustrialization. Since a county-wide restructuring and privatization campaign that began in 2001, "many firms are in dire financial straits. About half of Wenchuan's industry continues to lose money. Even worse, about 20 percent of industry is polluting and will have to move, close down, or install expensive pollution treatment equipment. . . . Many factories are faced with closure."[11] After the earthquake, almost all of the factories surrounding Yingxiu closed down or relocated in fear of future natural disasters. This fear was not unwarranted. In July 2013, days of torrential rain triggered a landslide that damaged Zhangjiaping Village and other areas of Yingxiu Township. The gas station on the road leading to the village was swept into the river.

The idea of transforming Yingxiu into a tourist destination was also not developed overnight. Prior to the earthquake, county officials had already drafted a plan to construct a regional corridor of tourism. During the Wenchuan County Enlarged Working Conference on July 26, 2007, county Party secretary Wang Bin announced that Yingxiu would become "a quality tourism brand-name."[12] Wang also reminded conference participants that they were still a long way from achieving this goal. "The tourism industry in Wenchuan County has not yet achieved scale; its content is homogenous, product development is lagging, and its market system is incomplete."[13] As of April 30, 2008, it was reported that an estimated 1.6 billion yuan ($235 million USD) was invested in tourism development.[14] Two weeks later, the area was reduced to rubble.

After the earthquake, there was no time to adequately assess Yingxiu's attractiveness as a tourist destination based on its symbolic identity as the epicenter of the earthquake. Instead, a top-down political process dictated the formulation of Yingxiu's reconstruction plan. The basic organizational and chronological details of the planning process went as follows: On February 9, 2009, the Sichuan Provincial

Government convened the Wenchuan County, Yingxiu Township Master Plan Circumstances Report Conference.[15] The purpose of the conference was to convey the spirit of Guangdong Provincial Party Secretary Wang Yang and Sichuan Provincial Party Secretary Liu Qibao's written notes regarding the future of direction of Yingxiu, listen to the Sichuan Province Construction Office's work report on the status of the reconstruction plan, and establish a Yingxiu Township Plan Coordination Small Leadership Group with Deputy Provincial Governor Huang Yanrong serving as the group leader. On April 9, 2009, the Yingxiu Township Post-Disaster Reconstruction International Discussion Forum convened in Chengdu to provide a narrow opportunity for expert consultation. Five days later, the provincial government held a routine meeting conference to deliberate on Yingxiu Township's master reconstruction plan, a process that was then repeated at the prefectural level days later. Finally, on June 3, 2009, Dongguan Municipality— in charge of reconstructing Yingxiu Township under the terms of the provincial partner program—sealed off Yingxiu Township to the outside world and began reconstruction.

The meetings produced a blueprint of utopian futures. According to various plans, Yingxiu was to become an "earthquake tourism brand" (*dizhen lüyou pinpai*), a "warm-hearted small town" with "charming special characteristics," "a gallery of master architects, and a museum of antiseismic architecture."[16]

French architect Paul Andreu (whose masterpieces include the National Theater in Beijing and Charles de Gaulle Airport in France) was commissioned to design the Earthquake Resistant Disaster Reduction International Academic Exchange Center (*kangzhen jianzai guoji xueshu jiaoliu zhongxin*). The architectural firm of Pritzker Prize winner I. M. Pei designed the Youth Activity Center (*qingshaonian huodong zhongxing*). He Jintang (designer of China's Pavilion during the 2010 Shanghai World Expo) was in charge of the Earthquake Memorial Museum (*zhenzhong jinian bowuguan*). These famous architectural buildings are clustered within short walking distance from the Xuankou Middle School Earthquake Relics (*xuankou zhongxue dizhen yizhi*)—Yingxiu's primary tourist attraction. The decision to attract internationally acclaimed architects follows a global trend in which "leaders of a depressed city or an overlooked region want to retool for a new economy of cultural tourism, and believe an architectural symbol that will also serve as a media emblem can help them."[17] In Yingxiu, a cultural zone was constructed via a main shopping avenue littered with vendor stalls connecting the Xuankou relics to the monument and the museum.

In addition to commissioning world-renowned architects for Yingxiu's reconstruction, in 2011 the Wenchuan County Tourism Bureau successfully applied for Yingxiu to become a national AAAA-grade tourist scenic area.[18] In April 2012, it ambitiously decided to pursue AAAAA status, the highest grade possible in China for a tourist destination. This application process was significantly hampered and delayed by the vitriolic Internet controversy it provoked over whether a place in which nearly seven thousand bodies were buried during the earthquake should be commodified as an AAAAA tourist scenic area.[19] A *Xinhua* news report labeled the attempt as having an extremely high "moral risk" and quoted one netizen's description of the idea as "universally shocking and offensive to all of society."[20] The sensitive controversy alarmed Wenchuan County officials. In preparation for an interview with the Wenchuan County Tourism Bureau chief, I was sternly warned by the friend providing the introduction that "under no circumstances" should I "mention the AAAAA application controversy."[21] The interview was canceled at the last minute.

The controversy was not confined to how to properly respect and honor the dead but also brought to light questions about the value and purpose of Yingxiu's new architecture. The convoluted history of the International Academic Exchange Center is a perfect example of a building whose practical uses diverge from its nominal purpose. Initially designed as a center for academic exchanges, the building was privately contracted to a hotel conglomerate, which changed the name to the Yingxiu Hotel (*yingxiu da jiudian*). Photographs of the sign of the hotel's name were posted on the Internet, sparking another controversy in which many netizens expressed their disgust with such attempts to capitalize on the earthquake. The sign was torn down, and the name reverted to the International Academic Exchange Center. But the building nonetheless continued to function as a hotel. A frustrated local resident described the name change as "Different broth, same medicine."[22] Afraid that the name International Academic Exchange Center was driving away potential business, the owners yet again changed the name of the sign, back to the Yingxiu Hotel. An interview with an employee at the hotel revealed, "We rarely have any customers here. The large catering hall is only used when the government hosts official events."[23] Although this story is humorously absurd, in the eyes of local residents it is evidence that they were not intended as the main beneficiaries of the reconstruction process. "Some of these projects are simply a waste of labor and money."[24]

Despite the fact that hundreds of thousands of tourists have visited Yingxiu since the earthquake, local residents have received almost no income from tourism. According to a professor of tourism based at a university in Chengdu, "from the perspective of tourist development, Yingxiu's reconstruction plan was intrinsically flawed" in its conceptualization of space and inclusion of residents.[25] As I demonstrate below, Yingxiu confirms John Donaldson's argument that "the effect of tourism [on poverty alleviation] depends on whether the tourist industry is designed in such a way as to include or exclude the participation of the poor. To understand this, we must analyze not only the volume, but also the distribution and structure of tourism."[26]

One reason for Yingxiu's failure to generate a thriving tourist economy is its distribution of tourist activity, which is condensed around the Xuankou Middle School Earthquake Relics and surrounding architecture. Businesses even a block over, not to mention those located on Yingxiu's periphery, receive almost no foot traffic. Many local residents, however, in anticipation of the officially promised tourism boom, converted their two-story homes into rural guesthouses and opened restaurants and souvenir shops. As of my last trip to Yingxiu in July 2013, several businesses had already closed down, others were barely surviving, and almost none were profitable. A noodle shop owner's admission of selling only "a dozen bowls of noodles every month" reflected a common economic reality for most residents.[27] Guesthouses also hosted only a few lodgers in the entire time they have been open. The fact that dozens of rural guesthouses, restaurants, and souvenir shops exist alongside each other has perniciously created an oversupply for a nonexistent demand. In the words of one resident, "I am without even a little bit of hope" that conditions will improve.[28]

As a result of Yingxiu's anemic economy, many residents decided to migrate to other cities for work.[29] Not all people, however, particularly those in their fifties and sixties, have the ability to migrate. "People who had money already moved out. The rest of us who do not have anything are stuck. What is someone my age [fifty years old] supposed to do? No one will hire me as a migrant worker. I am stuck here without a future."[30]

A second reason for the failure to attract customers is a lack of space to accommodate the needs of tourists. The majority of houses in Yingxiu have two levels with an average surface area of 120 square meters (ranging from 100 to 140 square meters). This dense living space cannot provide adequate or comfortable lodging for tourists. It also restricts the kinds of entrepreneurial activities available to local residents. One resident complained, "Before the earthquake, we used to run a decent business selling women's fashion. But now, in this cramped space, where are we supposed to hang and display the clothing? And how are customers supposed to move around and shop? So, we opened a much less profitable convenience store."[31] Almost 95 percent of my interviewees complained about cramped living quarters.

A third reason is that Yingxiu's regional location works against its ability to attract overnight guests. It is only a one-hour and twenty-minute bus ride from Chengdu, a thirty-minute minivan ride from Dujiangyan, and a twenty-minute minivan ride from Shuimo Township.[32] It is also en route to the stunningly beautiful Jiuzhaigou nature reserve. As a result, most tourists arrive in Yingxiu, spend a few hours in front of the earthquake relics and at the museum (that is really all you need), and then return to Chengdu or proceed to the next destination. Seldom do people spend the night or even stay for dinner. "The largest problem with Yingxiu's tourism industry is that no one stays there. Large tour groups arrive by bus, do a little sightseeing, and leave without staying to eat lunch."[33]

The relative ease with which tourists can leave Yingxiu for other destinations is compounded by the fact that there is no good reason to stay there. Yingxiu lacks anything resembling a nightlife or entertainment facilities. Moreover, Yingxiu's harsh climate and terrain render it unsuitable for tourist development. After heavy rains, the Min River rises dramatically, often triggering serious floods as well as rock and mudslides.[34] Finally, the fact that nearly seven thousand people died during the earthquake, including hundreds schoolchildren, envelops Yingxiu in a somber atmosphere unsuitable for entertainment-driven tourism. Most of the tourists visiting Yingxiu whom I interviewed cited the presence of "ghosts" as a central reason for why they did not want to spend the night. "Too many people died in Yingxiu; there are too many ghosts there. If you stay there for too long, it will bring you bad luck."[35]

The concept of earthquake tourism is also too one-dimensional to be sustainable over the long term. After one visits Yingxiu once, there is no compelling reason to visit there again. As time moves on, the salience of the earthquake in public memory will also fade. A sixty-year-old man who runs a hotel on the bank of the Min River analyzed the situation in the following terms: "Depending on the 'earthquake brand' as our economic lifeline is too dangerous. People's interest in the earthquake will gradually fade. You come once; you won't come a second time. But we have no land and no industry. In eight, ten years, if no tourists come, what then? It will become a problem of having enough food to eat and clothing to keep warm."[36] According to a news report from May 2014, the volume of tourists visiting Yingxiu has steadily decreased, further weakening a tourism industry that was already on the verge of collapse even when it was flourishing.[37]

Perhaps the most damning evidence of Yingxiu's economic woes is the failure of "A Ray of Sunshine Tourism Investment Management Limited Corporation" (yimi yangguang lüyou touzi guanli youxian gongsi). After a 7.0 earthquake devastated the small town of Lijiang, Yunnan Province, in 1996, the tourist development firm A Ray of Sunshine made a fortune by transforming Lijiang into one of China's most popular tourist destinations. The company detected a similar opportunity to turn Yingxiu into a "tourist resort that features earthquake tours and patriotic education" and signed a forty-year contract in early 2011 with the Yingxiu township government.[38] The resort consisted of hotels, teahouses, bars, commercial shops, and a venue for sunbathing.

FIGURE 9.   A Ray of Sunshine abandoned storefronts, Yingxiu, August 2013

Poor planning that resulted from a lack of knowledge regarding local conditions, however, plagued the resort area. According to a local resident, "The development project ran contrary to the laws of nature. How is it even possible to sunbathe in Yingxiu? Yingxiu and Lijiang have different climates. It rains all the time here."[39] The resort area also suffered from a less-than-ideal geographic location. Despite being only a five-minute walk from the Xuankou Middle School Earthquake Relics, it was still too remote to be on the radar of Yingxiu tour groups. After months of losing money, A Ray of Sunshine closed down its Yingxiu operations, withdrawing all employees as well as interior furnishings.

If A Ray of Sunshine could not survive under these conditions, the prospects are rather bleak for local residents whose resources are even more threadbare. Even local officials are nervous. In the words of a village Party secretary, "How can Yingxiu retain tourists? If Yingxiu is unable to develop its tourism industry, villagers will be without income."[40] The extent of economic precariousness can be glimpsed in a series of local responses and criminal behaviors. According to a reliable local source, in the past two years, a handful of destitute local residents have dismantled, stolen, and sold public infrastructures. "People are without work or land so they steal public infrastructure to support themselves. All of the electrical wires in the public park built by Dongguan have been stolen. Some people

FIGURE 10.   Lights stolen from beneath a bridge, Yingxiu, August 2013

have even been dismantling the sewers. Arresting them is no use. When detained, their defense is that they have no other way to support themselves."[41] Several local residents who were unable to afford Yingxiu's new housing have also started to squat in some of Yingxiu's ample supply of empty housing units.[42]

It is no surprise, then, that the topic of tourism and local economic development is now regarded as a politically sensitive issue by the township government. In March 2013, I was prohibited by the township Party secretary from distributing a survey to three hundred persons on the relationship between post-earthquake tourism and household income. The timing of my survey was unfortunate, as angry local residents had been escalating their demands to know exactly how much money was spent on individual projects during the earthquake reconstruction. Despite the central government's requirement of transparency, Yingxiu township officials have refused to release data related to the earthquake reconstruction budget to the public, for fear it could "spark a fire."[43]

Finally, it merits consideration that the "dream palliative" of tourist development is a pervasive phenomenon in the post-earthquake region.[44] During research visits to villages in Mianzhu Municipality, Beichuan County, Qingchuan County, Mao County, and other parts of Wenchuan County, I repeatedly encountered villagers and village Party secretaries who were anxiously hoping to develop tourism as a means of economic salvation. This trend has not gone unnoticed by the international and domestic media. On May 13, 2013, National Public Radio broadcast a report identifying similar issues plaguing Beichuan's new county seat:

> The town center of new Beichuan consists of handsome, sturdy brick and wood buildings, mostly housing tourist shops selling cheap souvenirs. There's one big problem, though: There are few tourists. Having lost their land, residents struggle to get by. "Business is no good here, especially this year," says vendor Zhang Ming, who runs a stall selling cold drinks and homemade tofu. "In this street, almost 70 percent of people are losing money. This year is worse than last year. No one comes here anymore."[45]

Reports suggest that Qinghai Province's Yushu Municipality, which was devastated by an earthquake in 2010, might also suffer from the same post-disaster tourism syndrome:

> The tourists and businesses that residents hoped would materialize after the rebuilding have not appeared. Before the earthquake, the city was a thriving trading hub for the region's Tibetan pastoralists, but government planners have reimagined Yushu as a tourist attraction for Chinese seeking to experience the fetishized mystique of Tibetan culture. The new city is flecked with museums, although none have opened yet.[46]

A worker from a Chengdu-based nongovernmental organization (NGO) accurately captures the perils of depending on tourism for economic life support with his observation that "a [relatively well-known] place like Yingxiu is unable to generate sustainable tourism, [so] how are places like Qingchuan County, five hours away from Chengdu, and without the same national-level attention, supposed to do it?"[47]

Political Tourism

As waves upon waves of central- and provincial-level leaders descended on the earthquake zone on compulsory "leadership inspection visits" (*lingdao shicha*), they would inevitably stop in Yingxiu, the epicenter of the quake. Leadership visits began immediately after the earthquake and continued until the official end of the reconstruction period in 2011. A leader would visit, display compassion for the disaster victims, inspect the progress of reconstruction, and move on to the next stop. Each leadership visit required massive expenditures of resources, which most local residents, and even several village-level cadres, regarded as excessively wasteful. In China's political system, "waste" is a contentious term which suggests the capture and cannibalization of political and economic resources by the Party state's aesthetic machinery.

The theatrical staging of the leadership visit defeats its original purpose as an inspection of local circumstances and an opportunity to gather information and adjust policy direction. Instead, the only information that is transmitted during these visits is a message of success. As Mao put it in 1963 when China was recovering from one of the worst famines in human history, in large part because of the concealment of local conditions, "They show to foreign visitors, comrades from other parts of the country or comrades sent by the central authorities to their area only what is good and not what is bad."[48] For Mao, the ritualization of investigation and fabrication of reporting undermines the Party's ability to formulate policies that adequately address the concrete circumstances and needs of the masses.

The post-earthquake reconstruction did not depart from this formalized pattern of political processes, behavior, and outcomes. In Yi Kang's wonderful description,

> Because the Chinese leadership increasingly realized the viability of a "symbolic management" approach, it attached great importance to it and invested a large amount of resources in it. Following their highups, lower-level officials pursued this approach in a fanatical manner and pushed it to distorted extremes, resulting in affectation and deception. The most telling examples were the "face projects"—the unnecessary reconstruction projects that wasted huge amounts of funding— and the various, pretentious, showy practices [*menmian gongfu*] in administration. For instance, immediately before high-ranking officials, journalists, or foreign guests paid visits to a resettlement site, the administrative staff would mobilize or even force the residents and volunteers to clean and decorate the place. . . . In receiving important guests, a common practice of the local cadres was to block people from raising doubts or complaints publicly.[49]

My own research corroborates Yi Kang's observations, and I further suggest that symbolic management and reputation are not new categories of political management in a globalized era but the path-dependent trajectories of China's political system.

The leadership inspection visit is a liturgical practice during which the Communist Party's glory and benevolence are acclaimed. These visits are occasions for the idealization and cosmetic touching up of Communist Party leaders, traditions, and practices. When one walks into the Yingxiu Earthquake Museum, the first thing one sees are blown-up photographs of leadership visits captioned with descriptions of selfless devotion to the people.

The life of Yingxiu residents was constantly disrupted and influenced by leadership visits. The residents witnessed firsthand the expenditure, violence, and energy that went into the theatrical presentation of their happiness. Many of my interviewees directly associated their experience of leadership visits with their disgust at the wastefulness of the Communist Party.

Before Xi Jinping's official crackdown on governmental excesses, the unwritten rules of Chinese political culture dictated a lavish manner for greeting leaders.[50] The reconstruction budget included aesthetic expenditures on expensive flower arrangements, newly paved roads, banquets, and police entourages. According to a local resident, "Any time a leader visited, township officials would purchase flowers. The moment the leader left, the flowers would be tossed in the garbage. The next day a new leader would arrive, and the cycle would begin all over again."[51] The same interviewee continued, "The night before Prime Minister Wen Jiabao planned to visit the ruins of Xuankou Middle School, I saw construction workers paving an asphalt road in the middle of the night. When I asked a worker, 'Aren't you afraid that paving at night will be uneven?' he responded, 'No, after Prime Minister Wen leaves tomorrow afternoon the road will be torn up.'"[52] The next day, the road was indeed gone.

This cycle of construction and destruction provided a lucrative source of income for local township officials and their extended family members. According to the construction worker mentioned earlier, asphalt was mixed in nearby Pi County by a contractor who was a relative of a Yingxiu township government official. In nearby Shuimo Township, asphalt roads also transiently appeared before and disappeared in the wake of leadership visits. This formed a mutually beneficial relationship in which township officials profited from the allocation of central government funds to finance spectacles consumed by central- and provincial-level leaders. For local residents, these roads were simply evidence of corruption and waste.

A post on the popular Internet service Weibo (similar to Twitter in the United States) vented frustration with similar processes:

> I was taking a nap when I received a call from a friend in Yingxiu's Yuzixi Village. He said to me, because the 5.12 anniversary is almost here, once again central government leaders will come to Yingxiu for an "inspection." The local government wants to do some "image projects" to welcome them. They want to carve the names of former volunteers who helped in the relief effort into a memorial on Compassion Road. My friend nearly exploded with anger when telling me this, disgusted

that the local government cared so much about these "face projects" and "political achievement projects." The only real political achievement is to lead the disaster masses to better lives [*zhenzheng dailing zaihou qunzhong guo shang hao rizi cai shi zhenzheng de zhengji*].[53]

It is worth pointing out that it is not necessarily wasteful to build a wall to honor volunteers who risked their lives in an earthquake relief effort. The ideological and discursive context in which all Communist Party actions are supposed to benefit the people, however, opens up the possibility for this kind of claim.

Leadership visits also required the semblance of participation from the earthquake victims. Leaders want to see completed work projects and satisfied local residents. In the words of a local cadre, this entailed the "careful selection of people who know how to speak and will only express positive opinions."[54] In Yingxiu, this tendency allegedly reached absurd proportions. Before Prime Minister Wen visited hospital tents to console sick patients, township officials transferred the patients to a nearby hospital in Dujiangyan. In their place, village cadres were hooked up to intravenous drips and injected with glucose in order to look like sick patients. Only reporters from the state-run news agencies the People's Daily, Xinhua, and CCTV were granted access to report on the event and enter the tents.[55] According to a local village cadre, "I was upset because Prime Minister Wen only visited the first tent and I was in a tent in the back. I went through all of this and didn't even get a chance to meet him."[56] One local villager described the event as a "collective sickness" (*jiti shengbing*). I also spoke with a young mother who was livid because she was unable to obtain treatment for her son who was actually sick.[57]

Whether or not this event happened is unlikely to be verified, but on a certain level, this is irrelevant. These stories take root in the memory and imagination of local residents and are extremely hard, if not impossible, to dislodge through evidential proof. Even if this particular account is untrue as an empirical fact, I suggest that it is true as a social fact indicative of the fractured relationship between residents and township officials.

People's interests can also be sacrificed in the name of political performance. Prior to the 2011 Spring Festival, the reconstruction of Yingxiu was still incomplete. Although housing structures were finished, the Dongguan Municipal Partnership Reconstruction Team still needed a few more months to address infrastructural issues. Despite the incompleteness of the project, the Yingxiu government decided to relocate villagers to their new homes for Spring Festival. The Wenchuan County government published a celebratory article on its website with the headline "Yingxiu Masses Move into Their New Homes to Celebrate the New Year" including the obligatory photographs of local residents gathering, singing, dancing, and wearing ethnic Qiang costumes.[58] Soon after moving in, the local government was flooded with complaints by angry villagers whose new homes suffered from leaky pipes and other infrastructural issues. To address this problem, the government enlisted a local NGO to conduct household surveys, identify the specific problems, and organize villager repair teams to address them.[59]

In this example, a leaky pipe is not simply a home repair problem. It is a hyperlocalized site in which Communist Party legitimacy is contested. For local officials, moving the residents into houses before Spring Festival displayed Party benevolence. By contrast, local residents measure Party benevolence in terms of working pipes and safe living conditions. The roots of popular contention, and the deteriorating relationship between the Party and society, lie in the clash between different sensible realities and interpretations of benevolence.

The idealized forms of Party legitimacy, however, will always be defended against the complaints of individuals. As Achille Mbembe cautions, "We should not underestimate the violence that can be set into motion to protect the vocabulary . . . [and] safeguard the official forms that underwrite the apparatus of domination."[60] As argued in chapter 1, the Communist Party's demand for earthquake victims to display gratitude for the "gift" of reconstruction was itself a form of political violence. It also ensured that mundane frictions and complaints would be magnified into issues of political significance (an interpretive reflex that has been developed over decades of Maoist political education).

These political sensitivities were heightened during leadership visits because the careers of local township officials were on the line. To protect their political achievements from unscripted voices and unruly bodies, officials often resorted to violent methods. Some Yingxiu residents were forced to remain in their homes, placed under surveillance, threatened with violence, and on occasion beaten up.

In the account of an elderly villager, "When Prime Minister Wen Jiabao visited, the government dispatched the armed police forces not only to protect him, which would be natural, but also to monitor us. They would not let anyone leave their homes without prior authorization. If you tried to go outside for whatever reason, you would be forced back into your home."[61] From the elderly man's account, it can be gathered that police were instructed not only to protect Wen Jiabao's physical security but also to guard his field of vision.

Before the inspection tour of an official from the Provincial Bureau of the Ministry of Finance—referred to by local cadres as the "God of Wealth" in eager anticipation of the rewards to be reaped from a successful visit—a group of "unidentified young men" with an unclear relation to the official public security apparatus patrolled the site of the visit.[62] With terrible timing, a Beijing lawyer on an earthquake disaster tour was in the process of photographing the site when the unidentified security agents ordered him to delete his photographs. When he refused, they gagged his mouth and restrained his hands, and detained him until after the "God of Wealth" departed.[63]

The following blog post describes another violent encounter with the police:

> Recently Wen Jiabao visited Yingxiu and took the road here from Xuankou Township. The government closed the main road, which is totally normal when central-level leaders come on inspection . . . but the other surrounding, smaller roads were also closed. There was a person who tried to cross one of the smaller roads and was almost knocked to the ground by a traffic cop. I rushed over to see if the guy was OK and said to the cop, "Hey! You knocked that guy over." He called me a son of a bitch [*gui erzi*] and said, "I should beat you up and as long as I don't kill you, I won't get in trouble." As soon as I heard this, I nearly exploded with anger and considered getting a metal stick to beat the cop with. I thought to myself, "You are a county traffic police officer; the country trained you [*guojia peiyang ni*] and gave you food to eat, you son of a bitch, and you want to hit common people?"[64]

These examples, and the countless others like them, suggest that the Communist Party's discourse of building a "harmonious society" (*hexie shehui*) and practice of "social stability maintenance" (*weihu shehui wending*) are primarily about maintaining a specific order of appearances and protecting the symbolic forms of Party legitimacy.[65]

High-profile leadership visits often prompted local-level officials to scramble to conceal unflattering evidence. After the emergency relief period ended and reconstruction commenced, rainwater ruined a substantial amount of relief supplies—such as winter tents, blankets, clothing, and rice—that were stored in a warehouse where they went unattended. Before Wen's inspection visit, cadres burnt the evidence of their negligence. As one villager recalled, "We were sitting in our temporary shelter and we saw black plumes of smoke in the distance. When we arrived at the scene, we saw local cadres burning molded relief supplies in preparation for Wen Jiabao's visit. This kind of waste was painful to watch."[66] Some villagers speculated that the relief provisions were not distributed because township officials were hoarding them in order to sell them at a later date.[67] I asked a village Party secretary about the accusation, who responded that "a few hotdogs may have had mold on them."[68]

In some cases, the game of cat and mouse was painfully obvious. Long after Yingxiu was directed to dismantle all tents and move their residents into temporary housing, one temporary encampment remained.[69] Days before Wen arrived on an inspection tour, the entire tent village was hurriedly moved into the mountains, as if a village could simply disappear.[70] Successful dissimulation does not mean that information does not make its way up. On September 5, 2008, Wenchuan County Party secretary Wang Bin warned, "At present, the construction of transitional housing is uneven. . . . In some areas, the problem of formalism is severe; false statements, empty talk, fraudulent reports, falsifying by over- or underreporting still exist. Individual townships and villages have not built temporary housing but reported that the work was already complete."[71]

The similarity of the narratives in this section is striking. Almost each account begins with "Before Prime Minister Wen arrived" and concludes with a range of tactics deployed by township officials in order to choreograph a scene for his gaze. The performance to please higher-level officials inevitably alienates local residents. Yingxiu's villagers do not experience the Party's benevolence when they are locked in their home, attending to leaking pipes, and watching relief goods become cinder.

Conclusion

What does it mean to "serve the people" (*wei renmin fuwu*) in a market economy? The Communist Party has struggled to come up with a compelling and consistent answer to this question in its attempts to reconcile the contradiction between market processes and outcomes that do not follow the same logic as its political commitments.

Note how the following passage from Wenchuan County Party secretary Qing Lidong ambiguously describes the development of Yingxiu's tourism industry as an official promise and moral responsibility to improve people's lives that is simultaneously supposed to follow market logic:

> [Reconstruction] *must be for the people* [*minxin gongcheng*], transparent [*yangguang gongcheng*], and exemplary [*yangban gongcheng*]. . . . It must guide capital flows, develop a rural vacation setting that is relaxing for city dwellers . . . promote the transformation from a village economy toward a tourist economy, and the transformation of a scenic economy into a *people's benefit economy* [*huimin jingji*]; finally, it must facilitate the retention of local labor and *raise the income of local residents* [emphasis added].[72]

For Yingxiu residents, this discourse is far from empty. It provides the normative criteria through which they perceived the reconstruction as a failure of the Communist Party's political and moral obligations.

Yingxiu residents felt betrayed by the wastefulness of the reconstruction. Many of my interviewees described feelings of heartache and rage as they watched the elaborate spectacles of leadership visits. For the earthquake survivors, Yingxiu was not a place to be lived in but a spectacle of Communist Party glory to be admired from afar.

It is not clear, however, how outcomes might have been different. One of the problems with writing about China is that it is difficult to avoid fantasy hypothetical situations. The ghost of the "if only" haunts most conclusions to academic writing. In this chapter, I have found myself repeatedly intimating that if only cadre evaluation mechanisms included the input of ordinary citizens, if only there were channels for popular participation in the reconstruction planning, and if only township officials did not hide reality from higher-level officials, Yingxiu would be better off. To be honest, I am not sure what could be done to substantively improve the lives of Yingxiu residents.

Instead, I would like to point out the danger of falling into the wishful thinking that Communist Party propaganda and repressive state machinery are what is constraining China's future development. Once the hall of mirrors is smashed, we will finally be able to glimpse reality. Is this not also a utopian view?

Imagine a leadership visit where nothing is concealed. Would Yingxiu's future be different?

THE IDEOLOGICAL PURSUIT OF ECOLOGY

Qingchuan County

The curse of politics is precisely that it must translate values into the order of facts.

—Maurice Merleau-Ponty, 1947

Background

Adjacent to Sichuan's capital, Chengdu, Dujiangyan Municipality implemented a massive expansion of the city into the countryside after earthquake. Yingxiu Township developed its post-earthquake tourist economy development plan by leveraging its fame as the epicenter of the 2008 earthquake. As a remote, mountainous, and impoverished county on Sichuan's border with Gansu Province, Qingchuan County lacked these so-called structural advantages of the other cases.

Qingchuan is one of Sichuan's poorest counties. In 2010 the Development Research Center (DRC) of the State Council published a report on Qingchuan's pre- and post-earthquake economic situation. "Qingchuan County is located in a remote mountain area, with inconvenient transportation, and is economically impoverished and backward. Before the earthquake, poverty was already substantially worse [in Qingchuan] than in other national poverty alleviation project areas."[1]

The reasons for Qingchuan's underdevelopment are in part historical. A report from the local paper the *Guangyuan Times* describes Qingchuan's twentieth-century history as a continuous series of "selfless contributions" that permitted Qingchuan "no chance for development."[2] According to the 1985 edition of the Qingchuan County gazetteer, "during the Republican period, [Qingchuan] cultivated opium, was harmed by bandits, and suffered from uninterrupted natural disasters. The people's livelihoods were wretched. In 1936, a long drought resulted in the calamity of cannibalism."[3] Qingchuan's fate did not improve during the first two decades of Chinese Communist Party (CCP) rule. During the height of the Great Leap Forward in 1959 and 1960, Qingchuan's population growth rate decreased precipitously, by −10.98 percent and −42.76 percent, respectively, with an estimated total of 11,807 deaths out of a total population of 133,498 for the entire four-year campaign period (1958–62). The massive death toll went beyond people. "In the month of May 1958, with great fanfare all of the sparrows and mice were exterminated during the 'four harms' campaign, using guns and medicinal poison to surround and annihilate, piling up the corpses of birds and mice."[4]

Qingchuan also participated in Mao's "Third Front" campaign (1964–71) to relocate strategic industrial and military bases to China's mountainous interior to secure them in case of foreign attack in an increasingly volatile geopolitical climate.[5] "During Third Front Construction, Qingchuan 'donated' without compensation over seven hundred mu of land. In the 1990s, however, the military construction factories successively moved away, depleting the county's financial revenue by one fifth."[6] Qingchuan's industrial development never recovered.

Qingchuan continued to suffer during the reform and opening period (1978 to the present). In 1984, the construction of the Baodian reservoir severed Qingchuan's primary outbound highway, which was only reopened to regular traffic in 1998. Six townships adjacent to the reservoir were prohibited from new construction for fourteen years; over thirty thousand mu of fertile land and forests were submerged under water; nearby enterprises migrated, while private enterprises "died"; Qingchuan's GDP slid by one third during the process. The economic effects of the reservoir construction still linger today. According to a State Council DRC report, currently 10,971 people out of the 15,673 total relocated population are categorized as below the poverty line.[7] Some villagers still rely on boats as their main means of transport to market towns.

The May 12, 2008 Sichuan earthquake showed Qingchuan County no mercy. Four earthquake rupture fronts are dispersed throughout Qingchuan, rendering it extremely seismically active.[8] Many county officials I interviewed declared that Qingchuan was the only county to suffer comprehensive damage to its entire surface area during the 2008 earthquake. Out of Qingchuan's total population of approximately 250,000 people, an official estimate of 4,697 people died and over 15,000 people were injured. In Donghekou Village alone, 184 households composed of 780 people were buried under one hundred meters of a collapsed mountain.[9] The village is now a national memorial.

Almost all of Qingchuan's residents suffered varying degrees of damage to their homes, and nearly the entirety of Qingchuan's public infrastructure, including schools, hospitals, and roadways, were damaged if not destroyed. After

FIGURE 11. Donghekou Village memorial site

the earthquake, 1,507 landslides and a countless number of aftershocks challenged relief efforts and delayed reconstruction.[10]

Qingchuan's fragile ecology, which had constrained its development in the past, deteriorated tremendously as a result of the earthquake. Most of Qingchuan's 3,271-square-kilometer surface area is mountainous land with high slopes unsuitable for agriculture and suffers from soil erosion. The earthquake damaged 42,529 hectares of arable land, among which 1,234 hectares were "extinguished."[11]

In the face of such massive devastation, Qingchuan's only developmental path was to "restore its ecology" and capitalize on its natural resources.[12] The county's post-earthquake economic development plan drew from prior strategies of increasing the scale and modernizing the technology of agricultural production;[13] developing specialty agricultural products at the township and village levels with market potential;[14] integrating Qingchuan into regional, provincial, and national markets through the expansion of transportation and distribution infrastructures;[15] and converting uncultivated and excess agricultural land into forests as part of a national campaign to increase forest coverage.[16] Similar to that in Dujiangyan and Yingxiu, post-quake economic development revolved around the intensification and acceleration of plans that were already underway prior to the earthquake.

What is unique about the Qingchuan case is the emergence of the ideology and discourse of "ecological civilization" (*shengtai wenming*). Several years before the earthquake, Qingchuan officials and local media promoted the county as an ecological society and an experimental pioneer in rethinking development in ecological terms.[17] Qingchuan's ecological consciousness and dialectical strategy of protecting the environment and advancing the economy were said to differentiate Qingchuan from other agricultural counties. This new discourse transformed Qingchuan's developmental constraints into political advantages.

Serendipitously for Qingchuan, the concept of ecological civilization gained national prominence when it was mentioned in the Seventeenth Party Congress Report in October 2007 and continues to increase in importance under Xi Jinping.[18] During the Eighteenth Party Congress, it was elevated into one of the "Five-in-One Constructions" (*wuwei yiti*), next to economic construction, political construction, cultural construction, and social construction. These are the five pillars for China's ultimate goal of becoming a "moderately prosperous society" (*xiaokang shehui*). Needless to say, Qingchuan government officials I interviewed were extremely proud of their advanced thinking and conceptual precedent setting. The discursive consolidation of ecological civilization at the national level guaranteed the term's centrality in all of Qingchuan's post-earthquake planning documents. Qingchuan's previous experiments and struggles in agricultural production were recast in the glowing ideological light of "ecological civilization."

Ecological Civilization: Definitions and Contradictions

Ecological civilization is best understood as a regulative ideal under which a set of exploratory practices, developmental models, and pedagogies are clustered.[19] Interpretive latitude is built into the concept that allows it to be refined in order to address local conditions and adapt to the specific needs of different economic sectors and administrative bureaus.[20]

The concept originated as part of a Party discussion on the "global ecological crisis" triggered by the ongoing mode of industrial development and insatiable capitalist growth.[21] Professor Zhao Jianjun from the Central Party School (where government and Party leaders are trained and advised) formulates the construction of ecological civilization as an urgent imperative for the survival of humanity.[22] He concludes, "The earth no longer has the capability to support industrial civilization's development in this way."[23] Another restricted access Central Party School publication argues that without a structural shift in the global mode of economic development, "humanity will bring disaster to itself."[24] Ecological civilization is the Party's vision for a new horizon emerging from the twilight of industrial civilization.[25]

Ideology is articulated in policy through political objectives and cadre performance measures. Instead of the mantra of development at all costs, measured in GDP growth, the Party is experimenting with new definitions and measures of development in its attempt to chart a course of sustainable development, green economy, and people orientation in order to remediate the devastating environmental and human costs of uneven capitalist development.[26]

Ecological civilization, however, is rife with contradiction. To borrow one of Mao's concepts, the primary contradiction is between the profit structure of global capitalism and the barrier of environmental protection. In the words of one Party report, "without a doubt, economic development and the protection of the environment are from start to finish contradictory."[27] The closure of polluting industries, the cost of retrofitting and salvaging other industries, the forgoing of profits to be gained from the extraction of natural resources, and the loss of jobs entailed by all of the above (and the list can go on) contradict the dynamic relationship between late global capitalism and China's economic development.

In an underdeveloped county such as Qingchuan, these contradictions are exacerbated. Qingchuan's 12th Five-Year Plan (2011–15) clearly spells out its predicament in these terms. "We must abandon the mode of large-scale growth. For underdeveloped counties, this undoubtedly increases difficulties for development."[28] Despite the fact that Qingchuan's total economic output is 0.09 percent of the provincial economy, it cannot rely on large-scale industrialization to close the developmental gap. Consequently, the demands for industrial upgrade, environmental protection, and optimization of land resources further constrain Qingchuan's margin for development. The report laments that Qingchuan's "environment and restricted development zones severely curtail its growth, resulting in an extremely prominent contradiction between limited environmental capacity and demands for accelerated development."[29] In this candid admission, the dialectical opposites resist unification in a magical formula—they are revealed as genuine tensions between environmental protection and economic growth. The plan also discretely admits Qingchuan's inability to overcome the structural relations in which it is embedded:

> As the processes of industrialization and urbanization are driven forward at a rapid speed, China's national economy has entered into a new stage of high-speed growth. Across the country, competition increases developmental speed and intense contestation over market access and essential factors of production. Qingchuan's economic strength is weak; distribution costs are high; level of industrialization is low; and competitive

ability is relatively inferior. This phase of large-scale economic growth has not fundamentally changed. . . . We face increasingly higher pressure participating in market competition.[30]

Qingchuan is unable to extricate itself from the contradictions between national economic dynamics, increased regional competition, and its own low level of economic infrastructure. Without massive structural reforms of the national economy (not to mention global economy), Qingchuan will remain pinched between the demands for rapid growth and environmental protection.

These contradictions are not limited to Qingchuan or post-disaster settings. According to an internal central-level analysis of Dengjiang County in Yunnan Province, the experiment to turn the county into a model of ecological civilization has been placed at risk by the threat of being financially unsustainable. After shutting down the surrounding mines that previously supported the local economy, "the county government faces a contradiction between income and expenditure of its fiscal balance sheet. . . . Future development funds are insufficient as a result of the contradictions between development and protection. . . . Ordinary residents are lacking principal sources of income."[31]

According to Communist Party epistemology, one of the solutions to large-scale political economic contradictions is transforming people's subjective beliefs and attitudes. The ideological mechanisms promoting ecological civilization borrow heavily from the Maoist tradition of "political thought work" (*sixiang gongzuo*), defined as the inculcation of officially sanctioned values in the behaviors, attitudes, and opinions of the mass public through the mobilization of the political apparatus. Thought work's rationale is the Maoist principle that "correct thinking" is the groundwork for developmental success, whereas "backward thinking" is responsible for economic stagnation. Any major political-economic transformation or shift requires a corresponding change in language and how people think.

Ecological civilization is also a new iteration of the Party's ongoing Maoist biopolitical campaigns to improve the population's overall quality (*suzhi*) through the cultivation of environmentally friendly behaviors and attitudes.[32] The goal of ecological civilization thought work is to educate people in how to think and ethically relate differently to their natural surroundings. Protecting the environment requires "a transformation of concepts," "behaviors," and "attitudes" as the foundation for a new "value-system" and "ecological consciousness" at the individual level.[33] The public is encouraged to no longer conceptualize the environment as a "conquerable object" (*zhengfu de duixiang*) but as the indispensable basis of human life. As stressed throughout the book, the Party's political epistemology entails a multiscalar approach that dialectically grasps the relationship between Beijing's macroeconomic bird's eye view and the thoughts and habits of a Qingchuan peasant.

A member of Qingchuan County's Guanghui Village Political Thought Supervision Group provides an illustrative account of thought work in the context of environmental protection: "People in the mountains rely on chopping trees and selling them as firewood in order to buy oil and salt. It is now forbidden to cut down trees. 'What are we supposed to do?' they ask. 'What do you mean create a forest? If we have to wait for the trees to grow up, we will already be in the ground.'"[34] He explains that the purpose of thought work is to answer such concerns and provide policy education so that the conservation of trees will appear more valuable than the profit to be gained from cutting and selling timber.

According to the Party's political understanding, without mass work, ecological civilization will fall victim to formalism. In the words of the Party secretary of Qingchuan's Hongguang Township, "Ecological civilization means constructing a foundation, training villagers, developing the ways they think about production—and proceeding step-by-step. This kind of mass work is the basis of great leap development. Without the foundation of the masses, it has no meaning; it is just a pile of formalism."[35] In fact, various Party documents suggest that environmental protection is especially susceptible to perils of formalism. According to a *People's Daily* op-ed published in 2013, "You request greening the environment, you get a desolate mountain painted with green lacquer and a bunch of dried up trees with new branches stuck in them. You request the reduction of emissions and energy-saving, you get a temporary stoppage of electricity harming local residents to go a few days without electricity."[36] Another example of environmental protection campaigns with questionable results but visual prominence is Xi'an's mist cannon that is alleged to reduce car exhaust, dust, and PM 2.5 levels (fine particulate matter which causes air pollution). A tweet on May 10, 2014 from *New York Times* reporter Chris Buckley sarcastically captions the photograph of the mist cannon as "a visual definition of futility."[37] It does not matter if this truck is only minimally reducing environmental pollutants; it matters that it presents the state in action.

In chapter 3, I explored how state planning is necessary to create and sustain the trappings of market activity in peripheral areas; in chapter 4, I explained Dujiangyan's plan for urban-rural integration as an example of utopian urbanism that works in theory but not in practice; and in chapter 5 I examined how Yingxiu Township's tourism plan is an example of the aestheticization of development in lieu of economic sustainability. In the remainder of this chapter, I demonstrate how these tendencies converged and interacted in Qingchuan's plan to become a "model example of an ecological county."[38]

Qingchuan's 12th Five-Year Plan

Qingchuan County's National Economic and Social Development 12th Five-Year Plan Essential Points articulates the guiding principles for the county's developmental ambitions; describes how they conform to national, provincial, and regional objectives; and provides detailed instructions for development at the zone and township levels for the 2011–15 planning cycle. Officially concluded in 2011, the post-earthquake reconstruction is the foundation for the 12th Five-Year Plan's next step of "revitalized development" (*zhenxing fazhan*).[39]

The preface describes the action plan as a "magnificent blueprint for a new great leap" of socioeconomic development. The first chapter summarizes and assesses the "miraculous" achievements of the 11th Five-Year Plan (2007–11) that de facto merged with the reconstruction plan for the post-2008 Sichuan earthquake. It performs the embedding work of linking Qingchuan's local situation to global economic dynamics, national macroeconomic adjustments, and specific campaigns and directives handed down from the center.[40] These linkages are important because they legitimize Qingchuan's developmental strategy according to national objectives and position it as a likely recipient for central-level aid. This section identifies Qingchuan's market potential in its abundance of natural resources as part of the goal of constructing a new ecological civilization.[41]

The second chapter enumerates the "Guiding Ideas and Development Goals." It subdivides Deng's mantra "Development is still the overriding principle"[42] (*fazhan cai shi ying daoli*) into six interlocking subtypes of development. There is "rapid development" (the growth component), "coordinated development" (the regional component), "innovative development" (the technological component), "low carbon development" (the ecological component), and "harmonious development" (the social component). The new prism of development is refracted through these categories. The second chapter, third section, enumerates the intended percentages of increase for each economic sector during the five-year planning cycle.

The third chapter outlines the "optimization of spatial arrangements."[43] This chapter is unique because it assigns functional capacities to individual zones and townships. It geographically divides the county into ecological protection zones and conservation districts, industrial clusters, and residential areas. The spatial arrangement of productive capacities is organized according to a specialized plan of "one axis, two wings."[44] The industrial hub of Zhuyuan located in the county's southern region forms a central axis with the county seat Qiaozhuang in the northern region. This geographical division of labor was not accidental but was engineered as part of the reconstruction plan. The eastern and western wings were also assigned different developmental objectives based on their natural resources and productive capabilities.

The second section spatially arranges agricultural production into a model of "five zones, five parks."[45] Each zone is categorized according to indigenous resources and market advantages. The zones overlap in certain places, meaning that some townships are engaged in two or more types of production. Zone 1 is for tea production; zone 2 is for mushroom production; zone 3 is for walnut, Chinese olive oil, and wood oilseed production; zone 4 is for raw forest materials; zone 5 is for animal husbandry; and oddly, a sixth zone is added at the bottom of the paragraph for aquatic products such as artificial ponds for the cultivation of the Chinese giant salamander (*Andrias davidianus*; *wawa yu*). Each zone is meticulously subdivided into lines and areas that link individual townships together into production subunits. These linkages operate according to the strategies of "one village, one product" and "specialized township, specialized village, specialized large family" (*zhuanye xiang, zhuanye cun, zhuanye dahu*).[46]

The chapter's third section administratively maps industry into three large concentrated economic areas. These are the Zhuyuan Economic Development Zone, the Chuan-Zhe Cooperative Industrial Park, and the Agricultural By-Product Processing Area. The fourth section optimizes the spatial arrangement of the service industry, namely, tourism. This section is graded along a descending scale into zones, areas, slices, and points.

This administrative cartography of economic development reveals the continuation of a "command mentality," at least at the county level. The problems discussed in the chapters on Dujiangyan, Yingxiu, and now Qingchuan share the same underlying problem that technocratic planning does not guarantee market success. The examples of economically viable Special Economic Zones (SEZ) and industrial parks are in the aggregate relatively small compared to the number of remote and poor counties like Qingchuan attempting to engineer integrated markets single-handedly by policy fiat. It would be inappropriate to label state intervention a form of market distortion because the market is precisely what it is attempting to construct. On the other hand, what other options can the county government realistically pursue?

The fourth chapter, "Enthusiastically Develop Ecological Agriculture," spells out a clear rubric for agricultural development down to the village level. Given that 80 percent of Qingchuan's population is agricultural, modernization of Qingchuan's agricultural industry is the key to its economic development. This chapter is framed by another set of nested guiding principles, which are standardization, specialization, scientific and technological innovation, and marketization.[47] For agriculture to be profitable it needs to achieve a larger production scale and expand market networks, infrastructure, and distribution. These are standard developmental tropes in circulation for the past two decades.

Among the reasons why these transformations undergo indefinite durations is that local residents are reluctant to participate in them. According to an interview with a high-level government official from Zhejiang Province's Provincial Assistance Team,

> [the] methods [of Qingchuan villagers] were old-fashioned and their thinking was passive. They would hand pick the mushrooms and wait for people to come and buy them or they would use them at home. The goal now is increasing the scale of production. At first villagers did not believe these new production methods. They were worried that industrialization of production methods would not be able to sell more products. They worried there would be no market and were not willing to invest even a little of their own money.[48]

Exemplified in the preceding passage is the Communist Party tradition of linking epistemology and development. In this context, thought work addresses how villagers think about production, scale, and profit. "Backward thinking" slows down the modernization of agriculture and the insinuated wealth to be generated from it. This passage also reveals the awkward position of villagers whose understandable skepticism of their own market potential and reluctance to part with their life savings are viewed as an obstacle by local Party and state agents. As a result, local cadres make promises of development based on a raft of assumptions and guarantees that they ultimately cannot provide. To address villagers' subjective anxieties, the Zhejiang Provincial Assistance Team in tandem with Qingchuan County returned to a familiar strategy in the CCP's developmental playbook. "We encouraged large households to undertake these kinds of production experiments first. Then we used the profits they obtained as a 'leading model example' to 'provide impetus' to smaller households to follow their example. We also invited local Qingchuan farmers to Zhejiang to 'study' our methods of large tent planting, as well as dispatched cadres from the Zhejiang Agricultural Bureau to provide on-site training in Qingchuan."[49] The method of example setting is a mainstay of Maoist governance techniques that continues in the present repurposed to fit a different developmental agenda. Consequently, Qingchuan's 12th Five-Year Plan is replete with familiar references to models, example setting, and linkages between large and small households.

Another peculiar reason for the slowness of the process is the relatively scant amount invested in agriculture during the reconstruction period:

The Qingchuan County post-earthquake reconstruction plan contained a total investment of 169 hundred million RMB [2.62 billion]. The estimated total investment for village construction was 28 hundred million RMB [$434.1 million], only 16.57 percent of the total investment. Moreover, this amount was mainly concentrated in village reconstruction and infrastructural facilities. Investment in farmland infrastructural construction was relatively small. There was a prominent contradiction of insufficient investment in agricultural production.[50]

Many of my interviewees were convinced that the reconstruction process was saturated with corruption. According to a man in his fifties, "the central government and Zhejiang Provincial government gave Qingchuan tons of money for the reconstruction, but each hand it passes through, money gets skimmed from the top; when it gets to its destination—the people—not much is left."[51]

Most Qingchuan villagers exhausted their savings and took out loans to pay for the portion of the reconstruction of their homes not covered by state subsidies.[52] As a consequence, they had no money left to invest in their own means of production; many residents plunged below the poverty line.[53] In 2009, the DRC of the State Council conducted a randomly sampled survey of 150 agricultural households in Qingchuan and found that 63.5 percent of peasant households surveyed experienced a decline in standard of living relative to pre-earthquake levels and 30 percent lacked any primary source of income. The survey revealed that on average Qingchuan peasants took out 25,300 RMB ($4,047.61) in loans to finance the reconstruction of their homes (an interview with the deputy mayor pegs the average at 30,000 RMB [$4,799.53] in his township), and 49.7 percent of survey respondents worried that the loans would be difficult to repay.[54] According to an interview in May 2013 with the head of the Qingchuan County Poverty Alleviation and Immigration Bureau, Qingchuan has over 53,700 residents living below the poverty line, roughly 26.96 percent of the total population.[55] Despite such questionable county-level resource allocation and priorities, hard budget constraints, financial shortfalls, and exacerbated poverty, the 12th Five-Year Plan continues to extol Qingchuan's virtue as an "ecological agriculture pilot scheme county."[56]

The fourth chapter of the plan sets production targets for each of the five primary zones of agricultural production. For example, by 2015 tea production was supposed to increase its base of operations by adding 17,000 mu of land, including an "organic" tea production park of 5,000 mu, contributing to a total 150,000 mu of land designated for tea production. Tea output is set at 3,400 tons.[57] Even though agricultural communes were dismantled and the command economy discarded, counties in rural areas continue to set production targets for market transactions.

The remaining fifty pages of Qingchuan's 12th Five-Year Plan continue with meticulous plans for a variety of governmental affairs. These topics include but are not limited to the "ecologization" of industry (in Chinese, the suffix *hua* converts an abstract noun into a process of becoming loosely equivalent to the English suffix—ization; in plain English, "the ecologization of industry" means greening industrial production), investments in tourism infrastructure, comprehensive urban-rural integration, transportation networks, irrigation facilities, flood-prevention engineering, energy resources, informatization, poverty alleviation, environmental protection, educational and medical facilities, spiritual civilization construction, social management, and disaster prevention. This short list reveals relatively no space outside of the capture, in varying degrees, of the planning apparatus.

The Communist Party's planning apparatus and interventionism struggle with the structural conundrum: how to create market activity and allocate economic opportunity in places that are not deemed profitable from a market perspective and in the case of Qingchuan, how to pursue development that will not further damage the environment? The ideology and discourse of ecological civilization is an attempted synthesis of these contradictions. For Qingchuan's residents, however, these contradictions, pressures, and tensions are present in their everyday lives, discourses, and material realities.

Local Perspectives

Qingchuan's Hongguang Township contains several villages (two of which I visited) whose local economy revolves around raising rabbits and shearing and selling the fur.[58] According to the township Party secretary,

> Villagers raised rabbits before the earthquake but did not earn any money. It was more of a hobby. It lacked scale and did not produce any economic benefit. Today, their enthusiasm is slowly increasing, which is a good thing. We have scientific methods of feeding and defending against disease. In the past, peddlers would come to purchase the fur and take it to the market. This is now a standardized process to improve the price of sales. Next, we plan on expanding the scale and number of households involved. We call this leading by model example. We introduce to villagers new kinds of breeds as well as policy guidelines. If their heart is afraid of investing, the government provides preferential policies to overcome their worries. Policy support means the government provides subsidies and the villagers provide some of their own money too.[59]

Analysis of the Party secretary's description reveals two important patterns of how local officials conceptualize post-earthquake development. One pattern is that the Party secretary repeatedly distinguishes the scientific scale, standardization, and economic benefit from the disorganization and nonprofitable practices of the past. The other pattern is that he emphasizes villagers' subjective attitudes and thoughts, their fears as well as enthusiasm, as the motor of economic development.

I accompanied an official from the Hongguang township government to visit Village W and inspect their rabbit-raising farms. As soon as we arrived, angry villagers surrounded our car and prevented us from inspecting the rabbit cages or photographing the village. After the yelling in local dialect between my government escort and the villagers subsided, my escort pulled me aside and explained that the County Animal Husbandry and Food Bureau promised the village's nineteen rabbit-raising households "development capital" of 3,000 RMB ($479.95) per household. After finding out only five households received the subsidy, villagers were furious over the inequity of what they assumed were back-channel patronage networks. The official actually complained the entire car ride back to the township government office that he was helpless because this issue is beyond his jurisdiction and was frustrated that local villagers failed to make this distinction. There was an acute contradiction between this official's sense of his own diminished place in the political pecking order and the villagers' exaggerated impression of his powers as a Party agent who would have the ability to get things done.[60] The villagers were not concerned, however, with the particular job responsibilities of this particular official. After the argument settled down, I spoke with an older villager who explained, "If we don't make a scene, we won't get the money."[61] The township government official admitted candidly, "The villagers know that this rabbit farm is one of Qingchuan's only economic 'bright spots.' Higher-level officials and media are often brought here to see the example of Qingchuan's post-earthquake success. Blocking access hurts the government."[62] For the villagers, it was also a matter of egalitarian distribution. In the words of the township official, "It would have been better not to give any subsidies rather than only five."[63]

In addition to an expectation of fairness, villagers also expected the Party to protect them against market failure. Party discourse contradictorily encourages these expectations through its socialist promises to guarantee economic development at the same time that it rebukes villagers for a mentality of "waiting, depending, and demanding."[64]

As China attempts to digitize governance and complaint handling, the Mayor's Mailbox (*shizhang xinxiang*) can be an interesting data source. Local residents are encouraged to publicly post queries and complaints that the Mayor's Mailbox Office relays to appropriate members of the government to handle and respond to publicly. Based on the handful of selections I read from within the past year, responses typically are posted within two weeks after appropriate time is spent on investigation. In one letter, a villager from Yaodu township profusely thanks the county government for its benevolent policies to help villagers "become rich." He then tactfully embeds his village's mushroom production operation into the official state discourse of enriching the peasantry ("our village's development of mushroom cultivation has allowed peasants to see the hope of becoming rich").[65] The next sentence cannily frames his letter as a "succinct work report" of the village's production situation to the Party secretary. In 2011 the government "took the lead" in cultivating mushrooms (the words "to take the lead" implicitly ascribe responsibility to the state to ensure the plan succeeds) and organized several households, along with the Guangyuan Municipality State Investment Company, to invest a total of 500,000 RMB ($79,992.32) in mushroom production. The author explains, "Because of a shortage of technology and experience two thirds of the production were ruined. We were not discouraged and made use of the remaining one third to redeem some of our loss." In an appeal to national policy objectives of revitalizing the countryside, the letter continues: "this has allowed us to create many jobs and allowed villagers to remain in their native place without having to migrate to other cities," thus discursively aligning itself with Party objectives. Finally, the letter summarizes its main point that "last year we did not make any profits. We saw the hope of becoming rich but did not become rich" as a transition to its ultimate request for subsidization. "This year we want to continue planting and expand production, with 'one household bringing along many households' and provide our village with employment opportunities. Because of a capital shortage, our equipment is out-of-date. . . . We hope that the government can give us support and allow us to become more confident. We are definitely able to set off a single spark to ignite the entire countryside and lead villagers to prosperous days." This letter is a good example of how villagers expect the Party to protect them against market risk, and compensate them in case of failure. In addition to interweaving state policy and Party discourse into the letter, the author integrates Mao's famous call to revolution, "A single spark can start a prairie fire" (*xingxingzhihuo, keyi ranyuan*), into the mantra associated with Deng Xiaoping that "wealth is glorious."[66] A dialectical masterpiece!

The county sent Yaodu Township's Party and Government Committee to investigate, which determined that joint ventures in neighboring villages did not face similar production difficulties (the logic of market competition). As a compromise, the township government offered subsidies for each bag of mushrooms produced and free provision of steel frameworks for canopies to protect the mushrooms from the heat (the logic of Party benevolence). The response ends with a gesture of encouragement for leading the "development of special-characteristic [agricultural] industries." While the reader is most likely not terribly interested in the fate of mushroom production in an obscure village in a remote county, this exchange reveals the terms through which the Party and society speak to each other.

The county's plan for economic development promises prosperity it cannot guarantee. In most cases, the reality is that government-led programs for special crop production are tenuous processes with mixed results. Besides out-migration for work, villagers typically experiment with combinations of crop cultivation in order to support their livelihoods. The following excerpt from an interview with a Party secretary from a village adjacent to Qingchuan's county seat exemplifies the makeshift production strategies adopted by peasants as a means to ensure their precarious survival:

> Before the earthquake we had no source of income. We mainly grew grain, raised pigs, and sometimes burnt firewood to turn it into charcoal. In 2007, we tried raising sheep, but most of them died as a result of disease. We also had no grass to feed them during the winter. For those that survived, the prices we got for them were low. We've also tried to grow fruit, but the water and soil quality is too acidic. Also, we have no flat land here—we are surrounded on both sides by mountains. About thirty years ago, we tried to cultivate Chinese medicine, but all of these are not ways of thinking that will produce wealth. In 2004, we tried to grow tea leaves [goes into a long explanation of tea cultivation methods] but the manual labor required is not worth the money it fetches on the market. Anyone who is young has migrated elsewhere to find work.[67]

He was interviewed in 2009, and his assessment of the post-earthquake future is not reassuring. "Right now, we have no plans. If we do not come up with something soon, the reconstruction subsidies offered to us will be taken away." The unspoken point here is that people manage to survive; they only do not manage to do so profitably.

Another villager's post-earthquake account describes an existence maintained on the periphery of the market economy:

> What would we do if we left the village? We have nothing. If we moved, we would also have to find a way of earning money and the state again would not take responsibility for this. The first six months after the earthquake we lived on a livelihood subsistence of 300 RMB [$48.07] per month. After that, the government only provided a 200 RMB [$32.05] per month subsistence to the elderly and children. They also gave us rice and oil. . . . Each year we raise five pigs and sell four on the market for 5,000 RMB [$801.26]. We also sell some of the potatoes we grow. Young people from the village all migrate for work. We have no savings, but in this way

we manage to get by. Right now our anxiety is that you need to pay money to see the doctor, and money to send children to school. Each year we only receive an 800 RMB [$128.20] subsidy from planting trees on the mountain.[68]

This account is representative of interviews I conducted with other Qingchuan County villagers, as well as villagers in other earthquake zones. Villagers find themselves pinched between increasing expenses (school, medicine) and scant resources, including meager state welfare, with which to make ends meet.

When farmers shift to nonagricultural modes of labor, their prospects for earning money are also rather bleak.[69] The following narrative discloses a sadly familiar scene of cruel optimism and faith in the Party's benevolence.[70]

We borrowed money from family and friends in 1999 in order to buy land and build a house. In 2008, we sold our old car and borrowed more money in order to buy a truck for transporting merchandise. That way, we hoped to repay the loans in a few years. When the earthquake happened, our house was damaged beyond repair; my husband and other family members died; our belongings were stolen; and, the truck was crushed. . . . A friend lent me 6,000 RMB [$961.52] to open a convenience store. But people with money moved out and the people who stayed behind don't have any money. I do not even sell 1000 RMB [$160.25] of goods a month. There are also more than ten convenience stores on the town's two streets. . . . The government had a policy of assisting disaster victims by providing over ninety public welfare jobs. Each person could earn 450 RMB [$72.11] a month by performing tasks such as sweeping streets. Mine is the only family in town who lost relatives during the earthquake but I was denied a post. This was so unfair! I went to the County Labor Bureau and Petition Letter Office. . . . I forced the person at the Labor Bureau, who was unwilling at first, to let me look at the name list of people who were given these jobs. When I looked at the list, I saw the family name of even the head of the local hospital. I told them, "If you do not investigate this situation, I will immediately give my child to the County Party Secretary so it will be his problem!"[71]

After she left the Labor Bureau, the Petition Letter Office refused to accept her claim according to the stipulation that they were not allowed to accept petitions related to the earthquake. The Petition Letter Office helped her call the township Party secretary, who explained to her that she was not offered a public welfare job because she ran her own business and already possessed an income source. She demanded an investigation of her financial situation by pleading, "I am in debt;

I do not earn money from the store. I am a single woman who has to support two elderly people and two children."[72] In other parts of the transcript, she admits her shame over asking for help, which she justifies as a measure of desperation. The transcript also deals with a demolition compensation dispute carried over from before the earthquake, accusations of patronage networks, embezzlement of relief supplies, and an accumulating sense of bitterness.

This particular case is symptomatic of contemporary conditions in China's countryside. It complexly weaves together all of the major themes of rural township politics: private loans to acquire the capital to engage in nonagricultural work, aspirations for upward mobility, the inability to survive financially without support from Party benevolence and state policy, recriminations over the fairness and opacity of policy implementation, power hierarchies and the relative futility of petitioning, and, ultimately, the erosion of Party legitimacy.

Accounts like these offer an inverted reflection of macroeconomic policies and trajectories. The individual narratives presented in detail above are linked together by the common theme of the inability to survive in a market economy and resultant expectation, dependence, and resentment toward the Party and the state. These are also global themes of peasants existing precariously at the margins of the global capitalist economy, in a painful limbo between partial inclusion and exclusion. In China, they are given the added twist of a socialist legacy that authorizes claims to be made on the Communist Party to provide for the basic means of existence.

When local residents perceive official development projects as wastes of money, labor, and resources on gratuitous face projects, their economic insecurity assumes the form of a political grievance. The controversy over Qingchuan's plan to green the county seat Qiaozhuang is an example of how the Communist Party's legitimating principle to serve the people is turned against local state formalism.

An Excess of Parks and Struggle over Space

After the earthquake struck on May 12, 2008, it took more than one year to formulate a reconstruction blueprint for the County Seat, which is anomalous in light of the central-level pressure to complete the reconstruction in under two years. The primary reason for the delay was the scientific evaluation that the old area rested on three active earthquake fault lines and was prone to landslides. This resulted in protracted and opaque bureaucratic negotiations concerning whether to move the county seat farther south to the city of Zhuyuan or remain in Qiaozhuang.[73]

Under such uncertain circumstances, the Ningbo Urban Planning Research Center from Zhejiang Province in charge of designing the blueprint for the new area refused to include in its plans the old area constructed prior to the earthquake. As time passed, it was tentatively decided to adapt the county seat's original 2003 Detailed Comprehensive Plan. This was an unpalatable option, however, as the plan was out of date and did not conform to modern safety standards.

In June 2009, then Sichuan Province Party secretary Liu Qibao issued the following directive: "Create a comprehensive plan for the construction of Qiaozhuang and Zhuyuan; create a comprehensive plan for the construction of Qiaozhuang's new and old areas."[74] This meant that Zhuyuan was to become the industrial center of Qingchuan and Qiaozhuang was to remain the administrative, cultural, tourist, and residential center. It also meant that the old area needed to be immediately incorporated into the overall plan for the county seat. As a result, the Provincial-Level Housing and Urban-Rural Construction Planning Office swiftly formulated a revised plan.

Shortly after, in the name of public safety and disaster prevention, the county government issued a directive to demolish the buildings constructed on the fault lines and relocate the local residents into the newly constructed residential settlements located at the periphery of the county seat. According to Sichuan Provincial Housing and Urban-Rural Construction Office head planner Qiu Jian,

> The revised plan of Qingchuan's new county seat has eight defining features. It is people oriented; safety is its priority; houses along the three earthquake fault zones and three landslide avoidance points must be entirely demolished; increase green space and develop an ecological park city; excavate the essential properties of urban space and manifest the special characteristics of culture; increase cultural elements and raise the city's aesthetic appreciation; respect nature, respect reality; attach importance to improvement and upgrade and strive to build a safe, livable, ecological, cultural, and modern landscape county seat.[75]

This passage breathlessly knots together discourses of safety, ecology, demolition, and aesthetics. The violence of compulsory demolition is neatly erased by incorporation into the other semiotic elements.

The three fault lines were transformed into three "green zones."[76] In place of the houses, trees were planted and over a dozen public parks were created. It is important to notice how ecological and aesthetic discourses converge in a tautological loop. Whatever is green is beautiful and whatever is beautiful is green. According to the provincial planner in charge of the project, "Narrow streets do not have any room for urban parks. Right now, when I look at the blueprint, I feel comfortable. After construction is complete, it will definitely look even more comfortable! Every day many people come to see the plan and think it is great. After they see it become reality, they will say it is very beautiful."[77] The aesthetic sensibilities of the speaker and imagined sensibilities of future residents and tourists form the underlying definition of ecology. It does not matter if the new parks genuinely benefit the environment, and it matters less how the parks impact the lives of local residents. What matters is that they produce a pleasing sensation. According to Qingchuan County Party secretary Xiang Cide, "the county must be beautified" (*meihua xiancheng*) for its application to become a nationally ranked AAAA status tourist destination.[78] The similarities with Yingxiu are unmistakable.

Forestry bureau chief Li Mingjie (now under investigation for corruption) firmly advocated the plan to green the county seat.[79] The logic he offered in support of it is a wonderful example of ideological alchemy:

> Our bureau and the construction bureau are working inseparably close to accelerate the pace of the greening of the county seat. We optimized procedures . . . that saved us twenty days for each greening project. By Chinese New Year, the county seat will include twelve leisure parks. Turning the three fault zones into three green zones was an ingenious way of transforming harm into benefit [*hua hai wei li*] and peril into safety [*zhuan wei wei an*]. There will be forty square meters of green space per capita—rare in both the nation and province. After completion of construction, Qingchuan will rival Europe's eco-cities and towns![80]

The local residents I interviewed rejected this logic as formalism. A primary source of state-society tension in Qiaozhuang is the perceived waste, cost, and uselessness of the parks: "The parks are face projects."[81] "No one likes the parks; 95 percent of ordinary people oppose the construction of parks."[82] "The government wasted a fortune to build parks and engage in 'face projects' and we cannot afford to rebuild our homes. We are still living in a temporary shelter. How is this fair?"[83] "The parks are empty because no one uses them."[84] Local residents also denounced the construction of a memorial "wall of gratitude" in the center of the city as one more "face project."[85]

Only one month after Sichuan provincial Party secretary Liu's visit in July 2009, the demolitions commenced. According to official statistics, 927,900 total square meters were demolished (80 percent of the total surface area of the county seat).[86] What these numbers indicate, which was confirmed to me by a source within the county government, is that the demolished surface area was not limited to the demarcated old area alone.

Given the magnitude and sensitivity of the project, a Demolition Supervision Work Group composed of 220 cadres from the functional bureaus from Guangyuan City (administratively responsible for Qingchuan) and Qingchuan County were responsible for "propaganda, policy explanation work, assistance for the resolution of contradictions, concentrating strength to accelerate the demolition and relocation process, and distribution of tents to households."[87] In addition to the work group, a Qingchuan county seat Planning and Construction Leadership Small Group was also created. The demolition process was described in the media as a military campaign.[88]

Contradictions start to emerge, however, within the official narrative. According to an article in the *Guangyuan Times*, by November 2010 the demolition and relocation were 94 percent complete, carried out "according to the law and in a harmonious fashion."[89] However, on February 12, 2012, the Qingchuan government's official Web page reported a summary of the proceedings of a "county seat fault zone demolition work conference" led by the Qingchuan National People's Congress deputy director concerning the massive difficulties slowing down the implementation.[90] The purpose of the meeting was to increase the resolve, discipline, and management of cadres undertaking the demolition process. Qingchuan County Party secretary Xiang was quoted during the meeting: "As long as our thinking does not slide, our methods will always be able to handle our difficulties."[91] The conference stipulated three primary goals: (1) accelerate demolition pace, (2) resolve contradictions, and (3) conscientiously and with great fanfare engage in a model example of policy dissemination and propaganda. This posting was later removed from the Qingchuan County government website.

When I interviewed the personal secretary of the county magistrate in May 2013, he informed me that "all of the buildings were already demolished." When I asked him if there were any protests or resistance, he denied any discontent on the grounds that "all of the residents accepted the objective 'science' behind the decision."[92]

During an interview later that week with the deputy magistrate of a nearby township who resides in the county seat, he confided that there were still several hundred "nail houses" (*dingzihu*)—a term for people who continue to remain in their homes resisting demolition. He explained that the delay resulted from the need to use "different resolution methods for different houses. For the houses with connections, their compensation rates are discreetly determined on an individual basis. The people without connections are screwed. But that's the way things are." He poetically continued, "Where there is sunshine, there are also shadows."[93] A local resident I interviewed described one of those other methods as the employment of local crime networks to help with the demolition process and "resolve problems the government is unable to resolve."[94] I also heard reports of similar intimidation tactics in Mianzhu City.[95] These findings support the argument of Hurst, Liu, Liu, and Tao that local state reliance on mafia is prevalent in China's underdeveloped regions.[96]

The next day I interviewed the proprietors of a few nail houses. They were dissatisfied because in their view the compensation offered by the government was too low and relocation destination too peripheral. All of the residents I interviewed stated that local county officials never once solicited their opinions on the reconstruction plan for the county seat. A motorcycle repair shop owner explained that the proposed relocation would adversely impact his business. "I don't care too much about where I live—the important issue is my store front. If we are moved to the periphery, how will we do business? Even here, the population is small and business is bad; don't even mention what it would be like on the outskirts of the city."[97] A neighbor added, "The government negotiates with each house directly on an individual basis. If you don't have any 'connections,' you don't have any power." Asked if her family organizes collectively with other nail houses, she responded, "It is impossible because of the individualized process of the negotiations."[98] A few houses down, an elderly gentleman summarized the post-earthquake political economy as a cycle of "demolish, repair, demolish, repair, demolish, repair . . ." His wife sighed: "All of these parks and all of this demolition have absolutely nothing to do with improving people's lives."[99]

One local resident filed a request with the county court to repeal the administrative ruling of the demolition because compensation was too low. The court denied his request on the grounds that many demolitions and relocations were already completed, thus granting an individual appeal would disturb the work schedule of the reconstruction and potentially harm the public interest. To resolve the case, the court's president and deputy vice president personally met with the claimant to explain the law and importance of the reconstruction process. Functional bureaus responsible for the demolition also contributed to the negotiations until the claimant "revoked some of his irrational requests" and finally dropped the lawsuit.[100] This example conforms to broader tendencies in China to settle disputes in personalized mediation outside of the courtroom. It also highlights the official compulsion to manage discourse and repair damage to the Party's image. After admitting the "irrationality" of his request, the plaintiff allegedly converted his views and "fully supported the reconstruction as well as expressed his gratitude to the county court for their contribution to the reconstruction work."[101]

Perhaps as a result of the ongoing nail house encampments, perhaps as a product of intentional oversupply and inflated market prices or a combination thereof, Qingchuan's new area also contains vast swathes of empty apartments. The surface area of Qingchuan's county seat "expanded two, three times larger than it was before the earthquake. . . . New roads are over twelve meters wide. . . . The county seat is larger and even more beautiful."[102] The reporter of this story, however, subtly interjects a cynical tone. "Mayor Ma Hua of Guangyuan Municipality proudly introduced Qingchuan's county seat as 'a great leap of twenty years.' . . . This reporter saw numerous brand new residential apartments that were as empty as anything."[103] My latest research trip in July 2013 confirmed this description of numerous empty apartments. Again, the similarities with Dujiangyan and Yingxiu are unmistakable.

The contestations over ecological land use are not limited to urban space but have also penetrated the capillaries of rural space. During the post-earthquake reconstruction period, in a village adjacent to Qingchuan's county seat, the local Party secretary recounts county regulations to achieve a specific "natural" aesthetic. In addition to their reconstruction subsidy of 16,000 to 22,000 RMB ($2,559.75 to $3,519.66) depending on household size, local residents were also provided with a 4,000 RMB ($639.93) "style remodeling subsidy" to purchase cast stones to adorn the façade of their homes.[104] The literal translation of cast stones in Chinese is *wenhua shi*, "cultural stones." This translation shifts the connotation of the stone. According to Baidu, China's version of Wikipedia, cultural stones "maintain a natural, original style . . . keeping with people's reverence of nature and the concept of returning to nature. As a result, people collectively refer this kind of stone as a 'cultural stone.' Using this kind of stone decoration creates a bright wall full of implicit cultural charm and natural atmosphere."[105] The aesthetics of the cultural stone is an ersatz embodiment of ecological civilization.

In a village belonging to Qingchuan's Hongguang Township, village officials ordered residents to plant grass around their homes in order to beautify the village and meet the policy targets of increasing green space. Local villagers deemed the request uneconomical. As a result, they defied political pressure and planted an assortment of vegetables instead. Eventually, local authorities conceded to the voluntary selection of vegetables. In other earthquake areas, however, villagers lost similar landscaping struggles. In a village in Pengzhou (near Chengdu), villagers already planted vegetables but were forced to tear them up and plant grass in preparation for the visit of a higher-level official. A local village cadre explained the decision in aesthetic terms: "Villagers are indifferent to hygiene. Vegetable fields are planted chaotically without any attention to tidiness. This has an extreme impact on what is pleasing to the eyes."[106] These accounts reveal the aesthetic priorities of local officials who would rather present a tidy landscape of manicured grass than allow villagers to plant sideline crops from which they could earn money or that they could use for subsistence. They are also further evidence that the Party's relationship with society is negotiated in mundane spaces. Persisting "unruly" village habits in new urban space in Dujiangyan, complaints over leaking pipes in Yingxiu, and disputes over vegetable fields in Qingchuan and Pengzhou are examples of a Party-state apparatus that has never stopped planning the details of rural life.

Planning is a desire for control and not necessarily the exercise of it. Even though the post-earthquake reconstruction provided Qingchuan with a serious infrastructural facelift, it did not improve the basic economic situation and livelihoods of the peasantry. In the words of one of my interviewees, "Although the post-earthquake reconstruction advanced the quality of basic infrastructure, transportation, and other aspects by twenty years, the livelihood of ordinary people has not changed. We still have no money and the vast majority of us still need to migrate for work."[107]

Conclusion

After the 2008 Sichuan earthquake, because of its lack of development and fragile ecosystem, Qingchuan County became an experimental laboratory for promoting the Party leadership's newly proposed mode of development based on "ecological civilization." To pursue this vision, county-level Party and state officials merged the post-earthquake reconstruction and 11th Five-Year Plans into a comprehensive strategy for the meticulous reorganization of rural production down to the village level, including even the kinds of grass to be planted. The plans for long-term changes in the mode of production were to be supported by thought work at the individual level in order to promote ecological awareness and a new set of values. The attempts to make Qingchuan green resulted in disputes between cadres and local residents over the utilization of space and allocation of resources.

If we revisit one of the examples from this chapter, which is more valuable, the commodity of timber or conservation of a protected forest? The choice between them is not so much of a choice but a gap between opposing discursive frames, value systems, and political economies. Rational choice models argue from the conviction that commensurability (in which money is the common measure of two or more objects) is the paramount source of value. This is an ideological position based on a specific political economic mode of production, which models human behavior and motivations on the basis of consumer choice. Conversely, the argument that the preservation of forests is intrinsically worthwhile, regardless of financial cost, depends on an entirely different system of values and economic production no longer organized around profit maximization. These positions cannot be reduced to banal differences of opinion, as they belong to the ideological, discursive, political, and economic formations in which individuals learn to speak, esteem, and act.

The frames that form the basis for our innermost thoughts do not belong entirely to us. The decentering of the liberal subject was conveniently hidden through the condemnation of twentieth-century Communist totalitarianism. Representations of the Soviet Union and Maoist China brain-washing their citizens made it possible, for a time, to ignore the ways in which the lives of citizens in liberal democracies are also the products of thought work of a more subtle variety.[108] The alternative between Communist indoctrination and liberal freedom of expression is already constructed from the premises of liberalism.

It is helpful to consider thought work as the process of translating values into facts—politics as a world-making activity and mode of constituent power. According to this definition, political systems determine the different agents and mechanisms through which thought work is conducted. In China, the state and Party apparatus continues to set the parameters for expression in a visible and often heavy-handed manner, whereas in liberal democracies, those parameters are drawn through disparate assemblages of power. Thought work exposes the socially mediated and contingent quality of the frames that allow thinking to take place.

What stands out about China is that the Communist Party unabashedly accepts that ideology, discourse, and propaganda are vital functions of the state. At the risk of sounding heretical, I suggest that there is nothing intrinsically wrong with this position. In a positive light, the CCP has developed a reflexive awareness and insight into the relationship between politics, language, and power that is missing from liberal accounts of the political. The link between politics, epistemology, and language is inscribed within the Chinese word for ideology (*yishixingtai*), which means consciousness (*yishi*) of patterns and forms (*xingtai*). Communist Party discourse also appropriated the word for Buddhist enlightenment (*juewu*) to describe political awareness (*zhengzhi juewu*) as the activity of rousing from sleep in order to apprehend the truth of reality. The epistemological and political project of thought work is to shape how people perceive and act in the world to accord with a set of core values and vision of the future.

While ecological civilization might have potential to constitute a new horizon for China's future, its transformative power is limited by China's capitalist mode of production and integration into the global economy. Experiments in peripheral counties like Qingchuan have little chance of flourishing without changes to regional, national, and international political economic systems.[109] In China's present circumstances, the ideology and discourse of ecological civilization is not powerful enough on its own to resolve the contradictions between profit-driven capitalist production, social prosperity and stability, and environmental protection. For the Communist Party to liberate China from the shackles of these contradictions, it will need to perform a miracle.

CONCLUSION

In a letter addressed to Voltaire about the significance of the 1755 Lisbon earthquake and tsunami that was created by it that ravaged the city, Jean-Jacques Rousseau questioned whether the disaster was indeed natural. "It was hardly nature," he wrote, "who assembled [in Lisbon] twenty-thousand houses of six or seven stories. If the residents of this large city had been more evenly dispersed and less densely housed, the losses would have been fewer or none at all."[1] In drawing attention to how human inattentiveness to the ways of nature had amplified the disaster, Rousseau's observation in effect highlights the limitations of cognition when confronted by the full force and power of nature.

Anxieties over how to read and understand nature have been at the heart of Chinese cosmology, history, and statecraft for millennia. The "careful noting of natural calamities has been a continuous feature of Chinese record keeping as far back as the Shang oracle-bone records."[2] In the *Book of Change*, the ancient oracular text organized around sixty-four symbolic diagrams, the hexagram *zhen* signifies both quakes in the earth (*dizhen*) and heavenly thunder.[3] The interplay between nature and the human realm underpinned the cosmological tradition of Chinese power. Not only might natural disasters cause political chaos; they were also portents of administrative disarray and moral turpitude. A natural disaster was seen as a reflection of failed leadership. In today's China, natural disasters are officially regarded not as inauspicious omens but as opportunities for the Communist Party to perform, renew, and record its essential role as savior of the Chinese people. Indeed, managing disaster, manipulating the language that describes and resolves problems revealed by disasters, and rebuilding in an effort to constantly create "miracles in the human realm" (*renjian qiji*) are a core Party mission, along with national sovereignty, economic construction, and the revitalization of the Chinese nation.

In Defense of Interpretive Methods

This book studies how Communist Party ideology and discourse determined the official decisions and responses to the 2008 Sichuan earthquake. My work emphasizes the need to take China seriously, which entails study of China's politics and society through a grounded literacy in the political concepts, discourses, and vocabularies of the Communist Party itself. To dismiss China's official discourse as empty propaganda makes China and Chinese realities harder to understand, not easier. The Party expends vast resources on developing, maintaining, and advancing its discursive imaginary. The secretive Party structure and its internal and exogenous security apparatuses ensure that the state's national priorities are never publicly challenged. The Party accordingly seeks to control the semantic environment of China, that is, to ensure that the meanings assigned to the words making up an argument, idea, or thought and the way words are spoken and written do not deviate too much from its own discourse.

A critical engagement with the Sinophone world requires not merely fluency in Chinese but some familiarity with the conceptual and linguistic world of the Chinese Communist Party. This does not mean that the big-picture questions and debates in political science are incommensurable with the problems that a more finely textured area studies approach would address. Some might regard the study of specifically Chinese political issues to be of limited interest and relevance to broader considerations of comparative politics and political theory. I suggest that the opposite is true. By navigating Chinese culture, language, and its palimpsests of meaning to consider what matters as politics in a non-European and non-American context, we are more likely to open a vista on what Geremie Barmé has poetically described as our *"shared humanity."*[4] The point of comparative investigation is not to replace one conceptual system with another; rather, it is to engage in a process of conceptual defamiliarization and discovery through continuous acts of cultural translation.

In my work, I attempt a "particular kind of tacking back and forth between theoretical insights and empirical evidence so that theoretical work illuminates the empirical world and the empirical world also raises questions about our longstanding theoretical presuppositions and findings."[5] This approach is meant to illuminate the hidden assumptions in how we view and understand empirical reality, and it sheds light on how we ground abstract concepts in concrete practices and circumstances.

Interpretive methods, as distinct from the more common recourse to analytical methods in political research, do not mean forgoing analyses of Party history, institutional arrangements, organizational behaviors, and material realities. In fact, they are meant to clarify how the Chinese Communist Party sees and governs itself, responds to crises, manages the economy, and interacts with society. My methodological approach is based on the assumption that the discursive realm and the real world are not discrete variables that can be studied in isolation from each other.

By calling on those who would engage with contemporary China and its political behaviors to read and reflect on the Communist Party's ideological work and discursive formulations, I am not defending the relativity of values or giving an apology for Chinese political arrangements.[6] Interpretations of state and public discourse can offer valuable insight into how power works. Acknowledging the power of language is not only different from defending the language of power.[7] It helps us notice how the effects of power are exercised in and as language.

The Communist Party and the People

As is so often repeated by the Party's leaders, "while the waters can bear the boat, they can also sink it" (*shui neng zai zhou, yi neng fu zhou*). The Party's source of legitimacy is the heartfelt affirmation and acclamation of the Chinese people. "Those who gain the hearts of the people gain all under heaven; those who lose the hearts of the people lose the world" (*de renxinzhe de tianxia, shi renxinzhe shi tianxia*). These ideas are the framework of the Party's discursive imaginary. The Communist Party acts and speaks of itself not only as being the ultimate choice of the Chinese people in 1949 but as being the sole representative and agent of the weal and welfare of the Chinese people today. Since the Communist Party claims this role solely for itself, it also makes itself responsible for all that is good and bad in the society. For this reason, Party leaders are acutely sensitive to what they call the "seeds" (*miaotou*) and "germinations" (*mengya*) of disquiet among the people.

Based on the frequent reports of social unrest in China, it would seem as if China is continuously in a state of emergency. It should be emphasized, however, that the police murders of young black men, the mundane event of daily mass shootings, ballooning student loan debt, and home foreclosures in the United States do not provoke the same diagnosis of systemic dysfunction. The meaning of discontent is not immediately obvious without an understanding of the broader discursive contexts through which it is articulated. As Lauren Berlant puts it, "negative political feelings provide important openings for measuring injustice but their presence or absence isn't really evidence of anything."[8]

In China, whenever there is a major earthquake, a train disaster, or an industrial explosion, the Communist Party is immediately held responsible in the public mind.[9] In particular, the local Party committees bear responsibility for everything that happens in society. To preserve its moral authority and legitimacy in the aftermath of a crisis, Party central attempts to placate public outrage and maintain social order by punishing "corrupt" and "negligent" local officials, strictly managing how events are represented in the media, and silencing key voices that tell a different story through what are often Draconian measures. The perception that all expressions of discontent are of a political nature is a product of the Communist Party's worldview.

In the United States, people may question local government competence, but they will not question the very notion of the American polity and blame its core political system for their circumstances. This contrast between China and the United States is exemplified by a conversation I had with a professor from Beijing who was in New York during Hurricane Sandy in 2012. Referring to blackouts and the several days it took to repair the electricity grid in certain parts of New York, she said, "If that happened in Beijing, the people would be demanding the heads of the Party officials responsible!" In my understanding, she was not arguing that the Chinese government is more efficient when it comes to disaster responsiveness and emergency management but rather that in China, such failures would be ascribed a political meaning. People affected by the hurricane in New York and New Jersey (where I am from) were frustrated by the inefficient response and delay in repairing the grid, but with the exception of a few protests, they did not articulate their frustration as a political grievance. Most of the media reports focused on technical issues about improving New York City's disaster resilience and updating its electricity grid.[10]

Compare the relatively understated public response to Hurricane Sandy to the outpouring of popular fury after Yuyao City, Zhejiang Province, was flooded by record-breaking amounts of precipitation caused by Typhoon Fitow in October 2013. Residents gathered outside of the local government and Party headquarters to protest against what they perceived to be an inadequate official relief effort. They demanded that both the mayor and the Party secretary resign. One group tore down the Party slogan "Serve the People" at the entrance of the government building.[11] The protesters felt that the Party had not only failed in basic government service but also failed to live up to their stated ideals. Mao's speech "Serve the People" remains emblematic for people because it indicates the relationship between the Party and what it calls the "masses."[12] It features on the entrance of every government office and more often than not means "Keep out!"

Shaken Authoritarianism

Communist Party rule in China depends on a number of factors: its historical standing in the creation of an independent and sovereign state for the Chinese nation, economic management and increased prosperity for the society as a whole, protection of the status and integrity of the nation-state itself, and its claim to represent what it formulates as the true interests and long-term benefit of the vast majority of Chinese. The Communist Party's mechanisms for maintaining and renewing that legitimacy are various: high standards of political performance, social stability maintained by a complex skein of social ethics and behaviors intermingled with a constant policing by the Party and its security apparatus, and above all, the way the Party enables people to think and speak about what it does. This is what I call China's discursive environment. The discursive sectors I describe in this book range from the public (that is, the spectrum of language that gives form to political ideas and that also informs political articulations) to the private (in which the individual, family, or community express ideas and emotions, in the context of both the politically allowable and the personally significant).

In this book, I have argued that the Communist Party is *discursively path dependent*, repeatedly performing a repertoire of legitimating narratives that it can neither abandon nor fulfill. To protect its legitimating narratives, the Communist Party cannot openly acknowledge any gap between its own interests and those of the people.[13] Each time a crisis activates this fault line, it shakes the foundation of the Party's authority. Most events result in small tremors that can hardly be felt outside their immediate vicinity. Others are national catastrophes that, like the Sichuan earthquake, caused discursive tremors far away in Beijing. As we have seen, the Communist Party has developed extensive methods for responding to crises and concealing rifts between itself and the people.

The official account of the 2008 Sichuan earthquake declared that it was a "natural disaster" (*tianzai*), not a "manmade catastrophe" (*renhuo*). That is to say, the damage and loss of life that occurred were unavoidable. The Party was not culpable; in fact, it was the agent of salvation.

This narrative was challenged by the deaths of over five thousand schoolchildren that occurred when "tofu-dregs" (*doufuzha*) schoolhouses collapsed during the earthquake. This scandal exposed the corruption, fraud, and incompetence of the local government and pointed beyond itself to a broader dynamic of Party-state rule in which profit accumulation and rapid development had taken priority over the protection, value, and sanctity of human lives.

The revelation of collapsed schools, however, did not bring down the Sichuan authorities or result in an overhaul of Party governance. The public security apparatus arrested, monitored, and silenced protesting parents, activists, and lawyers who demanded an explanation to be given honestly and in public of why the schools collapsed and resulted in the deaths of their children. Instead, the Party expended a considerable amount of material and ideological resources on educating the public on how to tell the difference between a natural and a manmade disaster. In addition, local authorities demanded that people think positively and channel their attention and energy into support for the upcoming Beijing Olympics in August that year. Apart from the continuing expressions of parental grief in the earthquake zone and several documentary films and art installations produced outside China, the collapsed schools and their dead have disappeared from public memory.[14]

The unprecedented and "tremendous surge of volunteers, civic associations, enterprises and media from across the country"[15] momentarily unsettled the Communist Party's representation of itself as the best and only guarantee of the prosperity and safety of the Chinese people. Although the Party initially praised the humanitarianism and dedication of the volunteers, it also reasserted control over the context and meaning of their actions. The spontaneous self-organization and compassion demonstrated by ordinary citizens were recoded and transformed into a Party-led activity of nation-building.

Perhaps a bit too eagerly, many observers saw in post–2008 earthquake events a watershed moment for the emergence of civil society and nongovernmental organizations (NGOs) in China. In light of the Party's understanding of how power works, it was only a matter of time before this opening was also firmly shut. Authorities steadily curbed the influence of NGOs in the earthquake zone, disbanded those that completed their mission and were no longer needed, cracked down on organizations alleged to have murky religious and foreign affiliations, and pulled the rest into line with official priorities.

The Chinese Communist Party not only represses dissenting voices. It also has to live up to its promise to perform miracles. In the earthquake zone the Party thus sought to foreground its capabilities for reconstruction while also using coercive methods to maintain and rebuild the authority of its unelected rule. As I explained in chapter 2, the Communist Party defends its legitimacy in ways that are distinctively different from those of political organizations in countries with universal suffrage and fixed-term elections.

In China, political legitimacy is negotiated through the daily encounters between cadres and people. The Party's claim to serve the people in all of its actions has to be embodied by individual cadres, performed in daily interactions and demonstrated through elaborate symbolic arrangements. For this reason, I believe that each cadre bears the weight of maintaining, embodying, and upholding the Communist Party's symbolic apparatus. The discourse of Party spirit (*dangxing*) marks the cadre (*ganbu*) off as being different from a Weberian bureaucrat and professional politician in other political systems. The evocation of Party spirit, in times of crisis, sets a standard for cadres to behave in a selfless manner.

In the earthquake zone, Party spirit was to be demonstrated in the cadre's ability and willingness to "eat bitterness" (*chiku*) and suffer alongside the survivors, which was meant to reaffirm the "intimate" (*qinmi*) relationship between the Party and the people. As might be expected, Party propaganda organs churned out volumes of generic accounts of injured Party cadres rushing from their hospital beds to return to the reconstruction effort at tremendous risk to their personal health and safety. Cadres were literally "dying to get back to work." Although it is easy to dismiss these accounts as being patently absurd and comically mechanical, they provide valuable insight into the normative pressures on cadres to act, behave, and talk in certain ways. For cadres, pressures to comply with the Party's political goals and discursive requirements "can be uncomfortable, even excruciating."[16] As the pressures of achieving high reconstruction targets intensified, local cadres who were also earthquake survivors began to display symptoms of physical, emotional, and mental distress. A few cadres even committed suicide, eliciting attention, concern, and consternation from Beijing about cadre well-being in the earthquake zone.

Post-earthquake reconstruction was also an opportunity for the Party to transfer wealth from China's affluent coastal regions to poor counties in the earthquake zone. The reconstruction was conceptualized and described as a process of "blood transfusion" (*shu xue*) that would eventually transform into a local source of "blood generation" (*zao xue*).[17]

Authorities poured massive resources into a reconstruction effort it believed would demonstrate the Party's care for the people and the moral authority of its rule. The new homes, roads, schools, and hospitals were proof of the Communist Party's benevolence, power, and glory. In return for its generosity, the Party expected the recipients to feel as well as display a deep sense of gratitude. The ultimate acclamation of Party legitimacy would be for the earthquake survivors to acknowledge in words and deeds the contentment they were expected to find in their new lives.

The Communist Party's promises also worked against it as people lost faith in its ability, and in some cases intention, to provide for their well-being. What the Party built was not always what the people wanted, and in some cases made their lives worse off than they were before the earthquake. Even though most people's complaints revolved around normal conflicts of interest, in the discursive context of China's political system they exposed the gap between Party promises and reality. In response, the Party launched a "gratitude education" (*gan'en jiaoyu*) campaign to transform unappreciative and unruly peasants into compliant and well-mannered urban citizens.

"Shaken authoritarianism" means that the Communist Party's grip on power is fragile as a result of its attempt to control and manipulate every outcome to conform to its legitimating narratives. The nature of the one-party system keeps the Party leadership and the cadres below them perpetually anxious about unforeseen events and unexpected problems. In the eyes of many international observers, each new crisis is expected to expose the "tofu-dregs" foundations of China's political system. Yet despite predictions of collapse, the Communist Party has to date demonstrated an admirable resilience in its ability to absorb the exogenous, and internal, shocks that shake its authority. Crises are moments of vulnerability not only for the political system but also for the people who are continuously reminded by the discursive environments they inhabit that their lives depend on the Communist Party and it alone.

Notes

INTRODUCTION

1. James Daniell, "Sichuan 2008: A Disaster on an Immense Scale," last updated May 9, 2013, available at www.bbc.com/news/science-environment-22398684.

2. Ma Yuan and Nan Yang, "Guanyu yufang zaihou dongyuan pingtai qi fasheng shehui xinren weiji de sikao yu duice" [Precautionary reflections and countermeasures regarding post-disaster mobilization platforms and social trust crisis], *Lingdao Canyue* [Leadership reference] 17, no. 459 (June 15, 2008): 15–19. Restricted circulation publication.

3. Yang Jisheng, *Tombstone: The Untold Story of Mao's Great Famine*, trans. Stacy Mosher and Guo Jian (New York: Farrar, Straus and Giroux, 2012); Frank Dikötter, *Mao's Great Famine: The History of China's Most Devastating Catastrophe, 1958–1962* (New York: Walker, 2011); Ralph Thaxton, *Catastrophe and Contention in Rural China: Mao's Great Leap Forward Famine and the Origins of Righteous Resistance in Da Fo Village* (Cambridge: Cambridge University Press, 2008).

4. Zhang Shuyan, "Liu Shaoqi yao 'tuifan' Mao Zedong: Jiantao 'dayuejin' jing qiangdiao 'renhuo'" [Liu Shaoqi wants to "overthrow" Mao Zedong: Examination of the "Great Leap Forward" emphasizes "human catastrophe"], *Renmin wang* [People's Daily Online], December 12, 2011, available at http://history.people.com.cn/GB/205396/1668 2372.html.

5. Chen Donglin, "'San nian ziran zaihai' yu 'dayuejin'—'Tianzai,' 'Renhuo' guanxi de jiliang lishi kaocha" ["Three years of natural disaster and the Great Leap Forward—The relationship between "natural disaster" and "human catastrophe" as a measurement and test of history], *Zhongguo nongye lishi yu wenhua* [Chinese agricultural history and culture], available at http://agri-history.ihns.ac.cn/scholars/others/cdl.htm.

6. Zhonghua renmin gongheguo tufa shijian yingdui fa [Emergency Response Law of the People's Republic of China] 2007, available in both Chinese and English at www .lawinfochina.com/display.aspx?lib=law&id=6358.

7. As Patricia Thornton argues, "the labeling and articulation of particular social problems or issues as crises can prove a valuable tool in the hands of a central executive, particularly one seeking to overcome bureaucratic immobilism or local intransigence." Patricia Thornton, "Crisis and Governance: SARS and the Resilience of the Chinese Body Politics," *China Journal* 61 (January 2009): 26.

8. "Return to Repression," *Washington Post*, June 23, 2008 available at www.washington post.com/wp-dyn/content/article/2008/06/22/AR2008062201586.html.

9. Even the earthquake might not be as natural as it appears, as there have been scientific allegations that the construction of China's Three Gorges Dam and Zipingpu Dam may have altered tectonic activity and increased the likelihood of an earthquake along the Longmenshan fault line. Party reports swiftly condemned these "assertions" (*shicheng*) as "rumors" (*yaoyan*), which accordingly were censored. See Zhongguo shekeyuan xinwen yu chuanbo yanjiusuo [The Chinese Academy of Social Sciences News and Broadcast Research Institute], "Jiji zuo hao kangzhen jiuzai yuqing yindao gongzuo" [Actively engage in anti-earthquake disaster relief public sentiment guidance work], *Lingdao Canyue* [Leadership reference] 15, no. 456 (May 25, 2008). Restricted circulation publication; also Sharon

LaFraniere, "Possible Link between Dam and China Quake," *New York Times*, February 5, 2009, available at www.nytimes.com/2009/02/06/world/asia/06quake.html?pagewanted =all&_r=0.

10. Mianyangshi renmin zhengfu [Mianyang Municipal People's Government], "Mianyangshi zaihou nongfang chongjian he kunnan qunzhong mianlin shenghuo jiuzhu deng qingkuang baogao" [Mianyang municipal government work report regarding post-disaster reconstruction of rural housing and assistance to masses facing livelihood difficulties] (October 28, 2008).

11. Christian Sorace, "China's Vision for Developing Sichuan's Post-Earthquake Countryside: Turning Unruly Peasants into Grateful Urban Citizens," *China Quarterly* 218 (June 2014): 404–27.

12. Tania Branigan, "China Jails Investigator into Sichuan Earthquake Schools," *The Guardian*, February 9, 2010 available at http://www.theguardian.com/world/2010/feb/09/china-eathquake-schools-activist-jailed; for a summary of Tan's research into the collapsed schools, see Tan Zuoren, "Longmenshan: Qing wei Beichuan haizimen" [Longmen Mountains: Please testify for Beichuan's children], in possession of author.

13. Christian Sorace, "China's Last Communist: Ai Weiwei," *Critical Inquiry* 40, no. 2 (February 2014): 396–419; Christian Sorace, "In Rehab with Weiwei," *The China Story*, October 14, 2015, available at http://www.thechinastory.org/2015/10/in-rehab-with -weiwei/.

14. U.S. Consulate in Chengdu, "Wife of Sichuan Dissident Huang Qi Discusses His Case," *WikiLeaks* Confidential Cable, January 6, 2010, available at https://search.wikileaks .org/plusd/cables/10CHENGDU6_a.html.

15. Ibid.

16. Christian Sorace, "The Communist Party's Miracle? The Alchemy of Turning Post-Disaster Reconstruction into Great Leap Development," *Comparative Politics* 47, no. 4 (July 2015): 458–77.

17. I obtained this document from an archive in the Sichuan Provincial Communist Party School. Because of the sensitivity of the document, the author's name and work unit were omitted. It appears to be the report of a temporary work group specially created to stabilize the social unrest. "Guanyu Dujiangyanshi xuexiao shewen wenti youguan qingkuang de huibu" [Situation report concerning problems involving collapsed schools in Dujiangyan Municipality].

18. U.S. Consulate in Chengdu, "Human Rights Activist Huang Qi: Attorney Provides More Details on Court Case; How Communist Party Arranges Convictions"; *WikiLeaks* Confidential Cable, January 15, 2010, available at https://search.wikileaks.org/plusd /cables/10CHENGDU12_a.html.

19. Mao Zedong, "Speech at the Ninth Plenum of the Eighth CPC Central Committee" (September 24, 1962), translation public, available at www.marxists.org/reference /archive/mao/selected-works/volume-8/mswv8_63.htm.

20. Kevin O'Brien, "Studying Chinese Politics in an Age of Specialization," *Journal of Contemporary China* 20, no. 71 (2011): 536. For a different perspective, see Marie-Ève Reny, "What Happened to the Study of China in Comparative Politics?" *Journal of Contemporary East Asian Studies* 11, no. 1 (2011): 105–35.

21. Michael Schoenhals, *Doing Things with Words in Chinese Politics: Five Studies* (Berkeley: Institute of East Asian Studies, University of California, 1992), 3.

22. Vivien A. Schmidt, "Discursive Institutionalism: The Explanatory Power of Ideas and Discourse," *Annual Review of Political Science* 11 (2008): 304–5.

23. Haifeng Huang's argument that propaganda is mainly used "to signal the government's strength in maintaining social control and political order" downplays the Party's obsessive control over the wording and content of propaganda. The fact that propaganda

may be badly written does not make it arbitrary. Huang Haifeng, "Propaganda as Signaling," *Comparative Politics* (July 2015): 419–20.

24. Simon Leys, "The Art of Interpreting Nonexistent Inscriptions Written in Invisible Ink on a Blank Page," *New York Review of Books*, October 11, 1990, available at www.nybooks.com/articles/1990/10/11/the-art-of-interpreting-nonexistent-inscriptions-w/.

25. Frank N. Pieke, *The Good Communist: Elite Training and State Building in Today's China* (Cambridge: Cambridge University Press, 2009), 4.

26. Anne-Marie Brady, *Marketing Dictatorship: Propaganda and Thought Work in Contemporary China* (Lanham, MD: Rowman and Littlefield, 2009), 183.

27. Timothy Cheek, "The Names of Rectification: Notes on the Conceptual Domains of CCP Ideology in the Yan'an Rectification Movement," Indiana University East Asian Studies Center working paper series (January 1996).

28. Confucius, *The Analects*, ed. Michael Nylan, trans. Simon Leys (New York: W. W. Norton, 2014), chap. 13, sec. 3, 37.

29. See Børge Bakken, *The Exemplary Society: Human Improvement, Social Control, and the Dangers of Modernity* (Oxford: Oxford University Press, 2000).

30. Xu Quanxing, "Mao zedong lun kongzi 'zheng ming'" [Mao Zedong's view on Confucius's doctrine of the "rectification of names"], *Mao Zedong shuzi tushuguan* [Mao Zedong digital library], available at www.mzdlib.com/libszzy/maozedongxingjiushujuku/5188.html.

31. Vladimir Lenin, "What Is to Be Done?" in *The Lenin Anthology*, ed. Robert C. Tucker (New York: W. W. Norton, 1975), 19.

32. Xu, "Mao zedong lun kongzi."

33. Mao Zedong, "Oppose Stereotyped Party Writing," (1942) trans. public, available at www.marxists.org/reference/archive/mao/selected-works/volume-3/mswv3_07.htm.

34. Louis Althusser made a similar point in the late 1960s: "In scientific and philosophical reasoning, the words (concepts, categories) are 'instruments' of knowledge. But in political, ideological and philosophical struggle, the words are also weapons, explosives or tranquillizers and poisons. Occasionally, the whole class struggle may be summed up in the struggle for one word against another word. Certain words struggle amongst themselves as enemies. Other words are the site of an ambiguity: the stake in a decisive but undecided battle." Louis Althusser, "Philosophy as a Revolutionary Weapon" in *Lenin and Philosophy and Other Essays*, trans. Ben Brewster (New York: Monthly Review Press, 2001), 21.

35. David E. Apter and Tony Saich, *Revolutionary Discourse in Mao's Republic* (Cambridge, MA: Harvard University Press, 1994), chap. 8: 263–93.

36. Louis Althusser, *Machiavelli and Us*, trans. Gregory Elliott (London: Verso, 1999).

37. I have in mind here the classic and remarkably relevant text for understanding the Communist Party even today: Franz Schurmann, *Ideology and Organization in Communist China* (Berkeley: University of California Press, 1968).

38. Yu Liu, "Maoist Discourse and the Mobilization of Emotions in Revolutionary China," *Modern China* 36 (2011): 334.

39. Ann Anagnost, *National Past-Times: Narrative, Representation, and Power in Modern China* (Durham, NC: Duke University Press, 1997), 27.

40. Thaxton, *Catastrophe and Contention*, 294.

41. Ban Wang, "In the Beginning Is the Word: Popular Democracy and Mao's Little Red Book," in *Mao's Little Red Book: A Global History*, ed. Alexander C. Cook (Cambridge: Cambridge University Press), 266.

42. On the "royal touch," see Marc Bloch, *The Royal Touch: Sacred Monarchy and Scrofula in England and France* (Kingston, ON: McGill-Queen's University Press, 1973). The sacredness of the written word in China is not an invention of the Mao cult. During

the Qing Dynasty (1644–1912), for example, officials were required to give "sacred lectures" (*xuanjiang*) and recitations of the Sacred Maxims of the Emperor. The state's "textual control also extended to prescribing standard forms for all script" and regulation over what kind of parchment to use. Reverence for Mao's writing taps into a long history and tradition of regarding official edicts and the paper on which they are written as sacred documents. See Endymion Wilkinson, *Chinese History: A New Manual*, 4th ed. (Cambridge, MA: Harvard University Asia Center, 2015).

43. "A Circular Concerning the Withdrawal from Circulation of Quotations from Chairman Mao" (February 12, 1979) in Geremie R. Barmé, *Shades of Mao: The Posthumous Cult of the Great Leader* (London: Routledge, 1996), 7.

44. The main difference is that now the Party is attempting to engineer new, civilized urban citizen consumers rather than an army of austere and selfless communists. Luigi Tomba, *The Government Next Door: Neighborhood Politics in Urban China* (Ithaca, NY: Cornell University Press, 2014).

45. He was formerly a professor in the powerful Central Party School of the Communist Party of China, where he allegedly ghostwrote several of Xi Jinping's speeches; Li Shulei, "Zaizao yuyan" [Restoring language], *Zhanlüe yu guanli* [Strategy and management] (2001), available at www.21ccom.net/articles/lsjd/jwxd/article_20140218100761.html.

46. On the contrary, as Luigi Tomba argues, "governing has always implied, for the Chinese Communist Party, the aspiration to create citizens in harmony with the existing developmental project of the nation and willing to support it." Tomba, *Government Next Door*, 88.

47. Louis Althusser, *On Ideology*, trans. Ben Brewster (London: Verso, 2008), 43.

48. Ibid., 42.

49. I would argue that the political authority of the Chinese Communist Party is also maintained through sacred doxologies and liturgies, not to mention the inquisition of heretics, who are forced to confess and apologize for their political sins.

50. Althusser, *On Ideology*, 44–51.

51. Judith Butler, *The Psychic Life of Power: Theories in Subjection* (Stanford, CA: Stanford University Press, 1997), 108.

52. Ibid., 107.

53. Tomba, *Government Next Door*, 14.

54. Banu Bargu, "Althusser's Materialist Theater: Ideology and Its Aporias," *differences* 26, no. 3 (2015): 97.

55. Étienne Balibar, "Althusser's Dramaturgy and the Critique of Ideology," *differences* 26, no. 3 (2015): 11.

56. I am referring specifically here to O'Brien and Li's account of "rightful resistance," in which peasants "use the vocabulary of the regime to advance claims" and "act as if they take the values and programs of political and economic elites to heart, while demonstrating that some authorities do not." The insinuation of the "as if" is that peasants inwardly do not take the ideology and discourse of the elites to heart, and are untouched in their thoughts and desires by the vocabulary of the regime. Kevin O'Brien and Lianjiang Li, *Rightful Resistance in Rural China* (Cambridge: Cambridge University Press, 2006), 5.

57. In this article, Mitchell criticizes the work of James Scott, which is a theoretical reference point for O'Brien and Li. Timothy Mitchell, "Everyday Metaphors of Power," *Theory and Society* 19, no. 5 (October 1990): 545.

58. The eternity of ideology does not mean that change is impossible but that transformation of social reality proceeds at scales and temporalities beyond the scope of individual comprehension and intention—what Althusser refers to in his later work as the unpredictable and contingent structure of history as a kind of "aleatory materialism" open to

chance encounters. See Louis Althusser, *Philosophy of the Encounter: Later Writings, 1978–1987*, trans. G. M. Goshgarian (London: Verso, 2006).

59. Geremie R. Barmé, "1989, 1999, 2009: Totalitarian Nostalgia," *China Heritage Quarterly* 18 (June 2009), available at http://www.chinaheritagequarterly.org/features.php ?searchterm=018_1989nostalgia.inc&issue=018.

60. *The Gate of Heavenly Peace*, movie directed by Richard Gordon and Carma Hinton; transcript is available at www.tsquare.tv/film/transcript.html; also see Geremie R. Barmé, "Confession, Redemption, and Death: Liu Xiaobo and the Protest Movement of 1989," in *The Broken Mirror: China After Tiananmen*, ed. George Hicks (London: Longmans: 1990): 52–99.

61. In the aftermath of the Tianjin chemical explosion in 2015 that killed over 160 people, which even the Party could not deny was a manmade catastrophe, Tianjin authorities unveiled plans to transform the disaster site into a "pleasant ecological park"—another example of the ways in which the authorities use the built environment to conceal catastrophe as well as aestheticize its own legitimacy and power. Fergus Ryan, "Tianjin Blasts: Plans to Turn Site into 'Eco Park' Mocked on Chinese Social Media," *The Guardian*, September 6, 2015, available at http://www.theguardian.com/world/2015/sep/06/tianjin -blasts-plans-to-turn-site-into-eco-park-mocked-on-chinese-social-media.

62. In February 2016, activist Huang Qi (mentioned earlier) was detained in Mianyang on his way to "speak to some of the people protesting the government's seize of Yang's [another activist] land under the pretext of post-quake reconstruction." See Xin Lin and Huang Qi, "Interview: 'The Authorities Fear We Will Expose the Scandal of Post-Quake Reconstruction,'" *Radio Free Asia*, March 4, 2016, available at http://www.rfa.org/english /news/china/china-huang-03042016153923.html.

63. The term "emotionally unbalanced" was frequently employed in official social stability discourse to describe the parents of deceased students who continued to protest and cause public disturbances.

64. My research sites include Chengdu Municipality, Dujiangyan Municipality, Mianyang Municipality, Wenchuan County Seat, Yingxiu Township, A'Er Village, Caopo Township, Jinbo Village, Qingchuan County Seat, Hongguan Township, Mianzhu Municipality, Hanwang Township, Qingping Township, Beichuan County, Shuixiu Village, Mao County Seat, Taiping Township, Lianghekou Village, Niushikou Village, Li County, An County, Xiaoba Township, Pi County, and finally Qinghai Province, Yushu (where an earthquake occurred on April 14, 2010) and Ya'an Prefectural-Level City and several surrounding villages (where an earthquake occurred on April 20, 2013—I was in Chengdu at the time and could feel the entire building shake; I also volunteered to do relief work in Ya'an for one week).

65. See Sorace, "China's Vision."

66. Su Dongbo, "Zhan zai guojia yu shehui chongjian de gaodushang yong gaige kaifang siwei zhidao zaihou chongjian" [A bird's-eye perspective on state and society reconstruction: Using reform and opening thinking to guide post-disaster reconstruction], *Gaige neican jueceban* [Reform decision-making] 19 (2008): 23–27.

67. Timothy Mitchell, "The Work of Economics: How a Discipline Makes the World," *European Journal of Sociology* 46, no. 2 (August 2005): 317.

68. For a discussion of the national scope of this phenomenon, see Lynette H. Ong, "State-Led Urbanization in China: Skyscrapers, Land Revenue and 'Concentrated Villages,'" *China Quarterly* 217 (March 2014): 162–79.

69. "Yingxiu zhaokai chongjian yantaohui" [Yingxiu convenes reconstruction discussion session], Wenchuan County government website, May 25, 2009, available at http:// www.wenchuan.gov.cn/p/st_news_items_i_x634089993846730000/.

1. THE COMMUNIST PARTY'S MIRACLE

1. Jessica Teets, "Post-Earthquake Relief and Reconstruction Efforts: The Emergence of Civil Society in China?" *China Quarterly* 198 (2009): 332. Also see Shawn Shieh and Deng Guosheng, "An Emerging Civil Society: The Impact of the 2008 Sichuan Earthquake on Grass-Roots Associations in China," *China Journal* 65 (2011): 181–94; Xu Bin,"Consensus Crisis and Civil Society: The Sichuan Earthquake Response and State-Society Relations," *China Journal* 71 (January 2014): 91–108; Yang Guobin, "A Civil Society Emerges from the Earthquake Rubble," *Yale Global Online* (June 5, 2008), available at http://yaleglobal.yale.edu/print/4739.

2. Patricia Thornton argues that "the reform-era state is neither suffering from a hidden crisis of governance nor is it curiously adept at responding to critical challenges by redesigning its core institutions: rather, crisis itself may have emerged as a mode of governance in its own right during the post-revolutionary era." Patricia Thornton, "Crisis and Governance: SARS and the Resilience of the Chinese Body Politics," *China Journal* 61 (2009): 25. As Gloria Davies points out however, the discourse of crisis and phenomenon of "anxiety consciousness" (*youhuan yishi*) are not Communist Party inventions but belong to traditional definitions of what it means to be an intellectual in China. Gloria Davies, *Worrying about China: The Language of Chinese Critical Inquiry* (Cambridge, MA: Harvard University Press, 2007).

3. Bin Xu, "Consensus Crisis," 101; also see Bin Xu, "Grandpa Wen: Scene and Political Performance," *Sociological Theory* 30, no. 2 (2012): 114–29.

4. Charlene Makley, "Spectacular Compassion: 'Natural' Disasters and National Mourning in China's Tibet," *Critical Asian Studies* 46, no. 3 (September 2014): 374.

5. Yi Kang, *Disaster Management in China in a Changing Era* (New York: Springer, 2015): 6–8.

6. Wu Jingshi, "Sichuan dizhen hou chongjian zhanlüe de jianyi" [Post-Sichuan earthquake reconstruction strategy and suggestions], *Gaige neican jueceban* [Reform decision-making] 19 (2008): 27–29.

7. Vivien Schmidt challenges traditional accounts of historical institutionalism on the grounds that "the institutions they defined have had a tendency to be overly 'sticky,' and the agents (where they exist) have been largely fixed in terms of preferences or fixated in terms of norms. The turn to ideas and discourse by scholars . . . represents their effort to unstick institutions and to unfix preferences and norms." What Schmidt overlooks is how the "stickiness" and inertia of discourses can be more resistant to change than institutions. Vivien A. Schmidt, "Discursive Institutionalism: The Explanatory Power of Ideas and Discourse," *Annual Review of Political Science*, 11 (2008): 313.

8. Sebastian Heilmann and Elizabeth J. Perry, eds., *Mao's Invisible Hand: The Political Foundations of Adaptive Governance in China* (Cambridge, MA: Harvard University Press, 2011).

9. Ren Zhongping, "Wenchuan teda dizhen san zhounian zhi" [On the third anniversary of the Wenchuan earthquake]. *Renmin ribao* [People's Daily], May 11, 2011, available at http://news.sina.com.cn/c/2011-05-11/113422444531.shtml.

10. The pseudonym Ren Zhongping came into existence in 1993 under the auspices of writing commentaries for the *People's Daily* advocating the importance of Deng Xiaoping's reform and opening policies. "When big incidents occur, the CCP publishes articles by Ren Zhongping to boost public morale, and so many high-level officials pay close attention to articles appearing under his name." Tsai Wen-Hsuan and Kao Peng-Hsiang, "Secret Codes of Political Propaganda: The Unknown System of Writing Teams," *China Quarterly* 214 (2013): 400.

11. Zhang Guolong, "Wen Jiabao: Zhengqu liangnian shijian wancheng huifu chongjian" [Wen Jiabao: Strive to complete reconstruction in two years], June 23, 2008, available at http://stock.hexun.com/2008-06-23/106889791.html.

12. Ren Zhongping, "Wenchuan."

13. Gu Songqing, *Fazhanxing chongjian zaihou jueqi de Sichuan moshi* [Development model reconstruction: The emergence of the post-disaster Sichuan method] (Chengdu, Sichuan renmin chubanshe, 2011), 37.

14. As Ren Zhongping points out with a degree of schadenfreude, several people were still homeless or living in temporary trailers in New Orleans six years after Katrina. Ren Zhongping, "Wenchuan."

15. See Tsai Wen-Hsuan and Nicola Dean, "The CCP's Learning System: Thought Unification and Regime Adaptation," *China Journal* 69 (January 2013): 87–107.

16. Ren Zhongping, "Wenchuan."

17. Ibid.

18. Ibid.

19. Karl Marx, "The Eighteenth Brumaire of Napoleon Bonaparte," in *The Marx-Engels Reader*, 2nd ed., ed. Robert C. Tucker (New York: W. W. Norton, 1978), 595.

20. Mao Zedong, "The Foolish Old Man Who Removed the Mountains" (June 11, 1945), in *Mao Selected Works*, vol. 3, trans. public, available at www.marxists.org/reference/archive/mao/selected-works/volume-3/mswv3_26.htm.

21. Mara Hvistendahl, "China's Three Gorges Dam: An Environmental Catastrophe?" *Scientific American*, March 25, 2008, available at http://www.scientificamerican.com/article/chinas-three-gorges-dam-disaster/; Christina Larson, "World's Largest River Diversion Project Now Pipes Water to Beijing," *Bloomberg News*, December 16, 2014, available at www.bloomberg.com/news/articles/2014-12-15/world-s-largest-river-diversion-project-now-pipes-water-to-beijing; Ian Johnson, "As Beijing Becomes a Supercity, the Rapid Growth Brings Pains," *New York Times*, July 19, 2015, available at www.nytimes.com/2015/07/20/world/asia/in-china-a-supercity-rises-around-beijing.html?_r=1; Jonathan Kaiman, "China to Flatten 700 Mountains for New Metropolis in the Desert," *The Guardian*, December 7, 2012, available at http://www.theguardian.com/world/2012/dec/06/china-flatten-mountain-lanzhou-new-area.

22. It would be interesting to read and apply Deleuze and Guattari's distinction between "molar" large-scale changes and "molecular" small-scale shifts in the Chinese context. See Gilles Deleuze and Felix Guattari, *A Thousand Plateaus*, trans. Brian Massumi (Minneapolis: University of Minnesota Press, 2003).

23. George Urban, ed., *The Miracles of Chairman Mao: A Compendium of Devotional Literature, 1966–1970* (London: Tom Stacey, 1971).

24. Ibid., 120.

25. Ibid., 121.

26. Interestingly, in this passage, Weber defines politics as the transformation of the possible through striving for the impossible. "Politics is a strong and slow boring of hard boards. It requires passion as well as perspective. Certainly all historical experience confirms—that man would not have achieved the possible unless time and again he had reached out for the impossible. But to do that, a man must be a leader, and more than a leader, he must be a hero as well, in a very sober sense of the word. And even those who are neither leaders nor heroes must arm themselves with that resolve of heart which can brave even the failing of all hopes. This is necessary right now, otherwise we shall fail to attain that which it is possible to achieve today. Only he who is certain not to destroy himself in the process should hear the call of politics; he must endure even though he finds the world too stupid or too petty for that which he would offer. In the face of that he must

have the resolve to say 'and yet,'—for only then does he hear the 'call' of politics." Max Weber, "Politik als Beruf" (lecture delivered before the Freistudentischen Bund of the University of Munich); both the German and English versions of the passage can be found together online at *Harper's Magazine* available at https://harpers.org/blog/2008/06/weber-on-the-political-vocation/.

27. David E. Apter and Tony Saich, *Revolutionary Discourse in Mao's Republic* (Cambridge, MA: Harvard University Press, 1994), 85.

28. Ibid., 97.

29. Yongnian Zheng, "Calamities and China's Re-emergence," University of Nottingham *China Policy Institute Blog*, June 3, 2008, available at https://www.nottingham.ac.uk/cpi/china-analysis~/china-policy-institute-blog/2008-entries/03-06-2008.aspx.

30. Xi Jinping, *Xi Jinping guanyu shixian zhonghua minzu weida fuxing de zhongguo meng lunshu zhaibian* [Xi Jinping on the realization of the great rejuvenation of the Chinese dream discourse], Zhonggong zhongyang wenxian yanjiu shi bian [Central Committee of the Communist Party Document Research Office], December 2013.

31. Zhongguo shekeyuan xinwen yu chuanbo yanjiusuo [Chinese Academy of Social Sciences News and Broadcast Research Institute], "Jiji zuo hao kangzhen jiuzai yuqing yindao gongzuo" [Actively engage in anti-earthquake disaster relief public sentiment guidance work], *Lingdao Canyue* [Leadership reference] 15, no. 456 (May 25, 2008): 12.

32. Ibid.

33. Makley, "Spectacular Compassion," 373.

34. Ren Zhongping, "Chuanyue zainan yingjie guangrong" [Overcoming calamity, welcoming glory], *Renmin ribao* [People's Daily], August 20, 2008, available at http://cpc.people.com.cn/GB/64093/64099/7692888.html.

35. "Spiritual Atom Bomb Aids Harvest," Peking Radio, January 2, 1969, quoted in Urban, *Miracles of Chairman Mao*, also found online at www.morningsun.org/red/deafmute/spiritual_atom_bomb.html.

36. After the chemical warehouse explosion in the Binhai New Area Port outside of Tianjin killed over a hundred people on August 12, 2015, David Bandurski described the media climate as follows: "The primary objective of China's leadership can be summed up in a single phrase that will most probably make its way (or already has) into propaganda directives: 'Do not do reports of a reflective nature' (*bu zuo fansixing baodao*). 'Reflecting back,' or *fansi*, refers to any reporting of a probing or profound nature." David Bandurski, "The Politics of Senseless Tragedy," *medium*, August 17, 2015, available at https://medium.com/@cmphku/the-politics-of-senseless-tragedy-12cc9230fa4#.f06pmy94l.

37. Interview with professor at X University, Chengdu, February 2012.

38. Mao Zedong, "On the Correct Handling of Contradictions among the People," February 27, 1958, trans. public, available at www.marxists.org/reference/archive/mao/selected-works/volume-5/mswv5_58.htm. When the immune system becomes too powerful, it begins to harm the system it was designed to protect. In its extreme form, it becomes an autoimmune disorder, which attacks the very body politic it is meant to protect. See Roberto Esposito, *Immunitas: The Protection and Negation of Life*, trans. Zakiya Hanafi (Cambridge: Polity Press, 2011).

39. *After the Tangshan Earthquake: How the Chinese People Overcame a Major Natural Disaster* (Peking: Foreign Languages Press, 1976): 3–4.

40. Kathryn Jean Edgerton-Tarpley, "From 'Nourish the People' to 'Sacrifice for the Nation': Changing Responses to Disaster in Late Imperial and Modern China," *Journal of Asian Studies* 73, no. 2 (May 2014): 452.

41. Gu, *Fazhanxing chongjian*, 10.

42. Guowuyuan fazhan yanjiu zhongxin [Development Research Center of the State Council], "Wenchuan dizhen zaihou chongjian de ruogan zhongyao wenti" [Several impor-

tant problems concerning the post-Wenchuan earthquake reconstruction] 90, no. 3202 (June 20, 2008), 5. Restricted access publication.

43. Gu, *Fazhanxing chongjian*, 37.

44. Dujiangyanshi dangxiao [Dujiangyan Communist Party School], *Huifu, fazhan, chuangxin: 2009 nian zaihou chongjian youxiu yanjiu wenji xuanbian* [Reconstruction, development, innovation: Selected works of excellent research reports regarding the 2009 post-disaster reconstruction situation], 17.

45. Qiu Baoxing, "Zaihou chengxiang chongjianguihua de wenti, fang'an he zhanlüe" [Problems in post-disaster urban-rural reconstruction planning: Guidelines and strategies], Zaihou chongjian guihua duikouzhiyuan gongzuo huiyishang de jianghua [Speech delivered at a conference on post-disaster reconstruction planning and the provincial partner-assistance program] (July 3, 2008), available at http://www.512ngo.org.cn/news _detail.asp?id=1167.

46. Chen Guaming, *Wenchuan dizhenhou huifu chongjian zhuyao fali wenti* [Research on main legal issues in post-Wenchuan earthquake rehabilitation and reconstruction] (Beijing, Falü chubanshe, 2010), 62.

47. Wan Penglong and Ma Jian, eds., *Cong beizhuang xiang haomai: Kangji Wenchuan teda dizhen zaihai de Sichuan shijian* [From tragedy to heroism: The Sichuan practice of resistance against the great Wenchuan earthquake] (Chengdu, Sichuan renmin chubanshe, 2011), 21.

48. Ma Yuan and Nan Yang, "Guanyu yufang zaihou dongyuan pingtai qi fasheng shehui xinren weiji de sikao yu duice" [Precautionary reflections and countermeasures regarding post-disaster mobilization platforms and social trust crisis], *Lingdao Canyue* [Leadership reference] 17, no. 459 (June 15, 2008): 15–19.

49. WeChat post, relayed to author on May 28, 2014.

50. Gu, *Fazhanxing chongjian*, 91.

51. Wang Fenyu, He Guangxi, Ma Ying, Deng Dasheng, and Zhao Yandong, "Wenchuan dizhen zaiqu jumin de shenghuo zhuangkuang yu zhengce xuqiu" [Wenchuan earthquake disaster-area residents living circumstance and policy needs] (January 13, 2009), available at http://www.china.com.cn/aboutchina/zhuanti/09zgshxs/content_17099440_5 .htm. This is similar to Dorothy Solinger's finding that recipients of the Minimum Livelihood Quarantee [*dibao*] still have faith in the benevolence of the Party. Dorothy J. Solinger, "A Question of Confidence: State Legitimacy and the New Urban Poor," in *Chinese Politics: State, Society, and the Market*, edited by Peter Hays Greis and Stanley Rosen, 243–57. New York: Routledge, 2010.

52. Dujiangyanshi dangxiao, *Huifu, fazhan, chuangxin*, 91.

53. Mao Zedong, "Oppose Book Worship" (1930), trans. public, available at www .marxists.org/reference/archive/mao/selected-works/volume-6/mswv6_11.htm.

54. Ibid.

55. Ibid.

56. Mao Zedong, "The Role of the Chinese Communist Party in the National War" (October 1938), trans. public, available at www.marxists.org/reference/archive/mao/selected -works/volume-2/mswv2_10.htm.

57. Mao Zedong, "Reform Our Study" (May 1941), trans. public, available at https:// www.marxists.org/reference/archive/mao/selected-works/volume-3/mswv3_02.htm.

58. Mao Zedong, "Oppose Stereotyped Party Writing" (1942), trans. public, available at https://www.marxists.org/reference/archive/mao/selected-works/volume-3/mswv3_07 .htm.

59. Vivienne Shue, "Legitimacy Crisis in China?" in *State and Society in 21st Century China: Crisis, Contention, and Legitimation*, ed. Peter Hays Gries and Stanley Rosen (New York: Routledge, 2004), 24–49.

60. Mao Zedong, "Some Questions Concerning Method of Leadership" (June 1943), trans. public, available at www.marxists.org/reference/archive/mao/selected-works/volume -3/mswv3_13.htm.

61. Mao Zedong, "On the Chungking Negotiations" (1945), trans. public, available at www.marxists.org/reference/archive/mao/selected-works/volume-4/mswv4_06.htm; "Xi Jinping Vows 'Power within Cage of Regulations," *Xinhua News Agency*, January 23, 2013, available at http://www.china.org.cn/china/2013-01/23/content_27767102_2.htm.

62. Mao Zedong, "Methods of Work Party Committees" (March 13, 1949), trans. public, available at www.marxists.org/reference/archive/mao/selected-works/volume-4 /mswv4_59.htm.

63. "Offprint of Mao's Work Published after Xi's Comments," *Xinhua News Agency*, February 26, 2016, available at http://news.xinhuanet.com/english/2016-02/26/c_135134761 .htm.

64. Mao Zedong, "On Practice: On the Relation between Knowledge and Practice, between Knowing and Doing" (1937), trans. public, available at www.marxists.org /reference/archive/mao/selected-works/volume-1/mswv1_16.htm.

65. I am in full agreement with Lin Chun's argument that "whenever the People's Republic failed the people, it turned out not to be because it defied the Western models of government and their colonial extension, but because it departed from its own visionary inspiration and promises of democracy." Lin Chun, *The Transformation of Chinese Socialism* (Durham, NC: Duke University Press, 2006), 136.

66. Wang Hui, *China's Twentieth Century: Revolution, Retreat, and the Road to Equality* (London: Verso, 2016), 172.

67. See He Baogang and Mark E. Warren, "Authoritarian Deliberation: The Deliberative Turn in Chinese Political Development," *Perspectives on Politics* 9, no. 2 (2011): 269–89; Suzanne Ogden, book review in *Perspectives on Politics* 7, no. 3 (2009): 697–99; Steve Hess, "Deliberative Institutions as Mechanisms for Managing Social Unrest: The Case of the 2008 Chongqing Taxi Strike," *China: An International Journal* 7, no. 2 (2009): 336–52; Mark Leonard, *What Does China Think?* (New York: Perseus Books, 2008): 51–81; Jessica Teets, "Let Many Civil Societies Bloom: The Rise of Consultative Authoritarianism in China," *China Quarterly* 213 (March 2013): 19–38; and Steve Tsang, "Consultative Leninism: China's New Political Framework," *Journal of Contemporary China* 18, no. 62 (2009): 865–80.

68. See Ogden, book review.

69. Wang Hui, *China's Twentieth Century*, 153–78.

70. Guowuyuan [State Council], Wenchuan dizhen zaihou huifu chongjian tiaoli [Regulations on post-Wenchuan earthquake restoration and reconstruction] (Order No. 526), June 2008 available at http://www.gov.cn/zwgk/2008-06/09/content_1010710 .htm.

71. Zhu Jiangang and Hu Ming, "Duoyuan gongzhi: Dui zaihou shequ chongjian zhong canyushi fazhan lilun de fanying" [Pluralized public governance: Theoretical reflections on participatory development in post-disaster reconstruction], *Open Times* 10 (2011).

72. Wang Zhuo, "Canyushi fangfa dui zaihou xiangcun chongjiang de zuoyong he yingxiang" [The function and impact of participation in post-disaster township reconstruction], from an internal archive in the Sichuan Communist Party School.

73. Interview, Chengdu, March 2013.

74. Interview, Guangzhou, December 2012.

75. Mao, "Oppose Stereotyped Party Writing."

76. Wang Guangxin, "Xingshizhuyi shi zheteng de biaoxian" [Formalism is an expression of waste], *Jiefangjun bao* [PLA Daily], May 1, 2012, available at http://theory.people .com.cn/GB/49150/100788/16797347.html.

77. The following discussion of formalism draws from a variety of official sources on Party theory; see Diao Xingze, "Xingshizhuyi de pingpan biaozhun" [Criteria for appraising formalism], *Lilun renmin wang* [People's Daily Online, Theory section], December 4, 2013, available at http://theory.people.com.cn/n/2013/1204/c40537-23743924.html; "Xingshizhuyi: Yi zhong cuowei de zhengzhiguan" [Formalism: A type of erroneous judgment of political achievement], *Henan ribao* [Henan Daily], October 10, 2013), available at http://theory.people.com.cn/n/2013/1023/c49150-23296160.html; Shi Wenlong, "Zhidu xingshizhuyi: Zhidu jianshe de di yi wanzheng" [Institutional formalism: The first stubborn illness of institutional building], *Zhongguo qingnian bao* [China Youth Daily], February 26, 2014, available at http://cpc.people.com.cn/pinglun/n/2014/0226/c78779-24469002.html; and Li Shirong, "Fangzhi fenquan quanxian chengwei lingyi zhong xingshizhuyi" [Prevent the separation and limitation of authority from becoming another kind of formalism], *Guangdong ribao* [Guangdong Daily], January 27, 2014, available at http://opinion.people.com.cn/BIG5/n/2014/0127/c1003-24238892.html.

78. Mao Zedong, "On Contradiction" (August 1937), trans. public, available at https://www.marxists.org/reference/archive/mao/selected-works/volume-1/mswv1_17.htm.

79. Yongshun Cai, "Irresponsible State: Local Cadres and Image-Building in China," *Journal of Communist Studies and Transition Politics* 20, no. 4 (2004): 20–41.

80. Ibid., 22.

81. Chen Guaming, *Wenchuan dizhenhou huifu chongjian zhuyao falü wenti*, 62.

82. Interview with villager, Mianzhu, March 2012.

83. Interview at Y University, Chengdu, March 2012.

84. Mao, "Oppose Book Worship."

85. Françoise Thom, *Newspeak: The Language of Soviet Communism*, trans. Ken Connelly (London: Claridge, 1989).

86. Ibid., 27.

87. Ibid., 42.

88. Ibid., 102.

89. Ibid., 44.

90. I disagree with Thom's argument that there is something special about Communist Party discourse that "paralyzes reason." Her theoretical touchstone, George Orwell, also had a rather dim view of the use of language in democracies. In "Politics and the English Language," Orwell skewers the "ready-made phrases" and "meaningless words" that pass for political discourse and debate in liberal democracies, which has only intensified in the age of communicative capitalism's sound bites and Internet memes. "When one watches some tired hack on the platform mechanically repeating the familiar phrases . . . one often has a curious feeling that one is not watching a live human being but some kind of dummy. . . . The appropriate noises are coming out of his larynx, but his brain is not involved, as it would be if he were choosing his words for himself." Orwell describes political discourse as an unconscious habit of speech "as one is when one utters the responses in church." One could even categorize today's neoliberal management speak as a *langue du bois*. Thom's exclusive focus on Communist Party discourse is an unfortunate by-product of the historical period and ideological perspective of antitotalitarianism from which it was written. George Orwell, "Politics and the English Language" (1946), available at http://www.orwell.ru/library/essays/politics/english/e_polit/.

91. Alexei Yurchak, *Everything Was Forever, Until It Was No More: The Last Soviet Generation* (Princeton, NJ: Princeton University Press, 2005).

92. Ibid., 13–14 and 35.

93. Ibid., 29.

94. Jacques Derrida quoted in John D. Caputo and Michael J. Scanlon, eds., *God, the Gift, and Postmodernism* (Bloomington: Indiana University Press, 1999), 59.

95. Han Feizi, *Basic Writings*, trans. Burton Watson (New York: Columbia University Press, 2003), 87. In an anthology of heroic deeds compiled after the 1976 Tangshan earthquake, I found an especially graphic version of Han Fei's parable. It is the story of a PLA medical assistant who discovered a wounded peasant "unable to urinate because of a ruptured ureter [*sic*]" and "did not hesitate to crouch down beside the victim, insert a catheter and apply suction with his mouth." *After the Tangshan Earthquake*, 55.

96. Eric L. Santner, *The Weight of All Flesh: On the Subject-Matter of Political Economy* (Oxford: Oxford University Press, 2015), 54.

97. Sina Najafi, David Serlin, and Lauren Berlant, "The Broken Circuit: An Interview with Lauren Berlant," *Cabinet Magazine*, no. 31 (Fall 2008), available at www.cabinetmagazine.org/issues/31/najafi_serlin.php.

98. Gu, *Fazhanxing chongjian*, 11.

99. Wangcang xian qi yi zhong xue [Wangcang County Qiyi middle school], "Nongcun chuzhong gan'en jiaoyu de shijian yu yanjiu: Shiyan fang'an" [Village junior high school gratitude education practice and research: Experimental plan] (2010).

100. Shifang jian di long ju zhongxin xiaoxue [Shifang jian di long ju zhongxin elementary school] "Mingji dang'en, fenfa ziqiang jiaoyu huodong jihua yu shishi fangan" [Plan and implementation guidelines to engrave in memory the Party's kindness and strive for self-improvement education activities] (2009).

101. Zhonggong chengdu wuhou xincheng jianshe gongzuo weiyuanhui [Communist Party of Chengdu Wuhou new city construction working committee], "Guanyu kaizhan zaihou huifu chongjian gan'en wenming jiaoyu you jiang zheng wen huodong de tongzhi" [Notification regarding the launch of post-disaster restoration and reconstruction gratitude civilization education literary award campaign] (February 16, 2011).

102. Interview with Dujiangyan Party School professor, Dujiangyan, December 2012.

103. Qing Lidong, "Hongyang gan'en wenhua, jianxing gan'en zeren" [To promote gratitude culture and implement gratitude responsibility] (speech given at the Wenchuan County Chinese People's Consultative Conference, January 24, 2010).

104. Emily T. Yeh, *Taming Tibet: Landscape Transformation and the Gift of Chinese Development* (Ithaca, NY: Cornell University Press, 2013), 5.

105. Ibid., 6.

106. Ibid.

107. Jie Yang, *Unknotting the Heart: Unemployment and Therapeutic Governance in China* (Ithaca, NY: Cornell University Press, 2015), 51.

108. Yan Lianke, *Lenin's Kisses*, trans. Carlos Rojas (New York: Grove Press, 2013).

109. See Yan Lianke, "Finding Light in China's Darkness: Yan Lianke on Writing in China," *New York Times*, October 23, 2014, available at http://www.nytimes.com/2014/10/23/opinion/Yan-Lianke-finding-light-in-chinas-darkness.html?_r=0; and Yan Lianke, "On China's State-Sponsored Amnesia," *New York Times*, April 2, 2013, available at http://www.nytimes.com/2013/04/02/opinion/on-chinas-state-sponsored-amnesia.html?_r=0; Yan Lianke, "Understand the Enemy," video interview on *The Louisiana Channel*, October 28, 2015, available at https://www.youtube.com/watch?v=cwPa3utBWYsm.

110. Yan, *Lenin's Kisses*, 3.

111. Ibid., 56.

112. Ibid., 77.

113. Ibid., 77.

114. Ibid., 94.

115. Ibid., 97.

116. Ibid., 99.

117. Ibid., 100.

2. PARTY SPIRIT MADE FLESH

1. Lisa Wedeen, "Concepts and Commitments in the Study of Democracy," in *Problems and Methods in the Study of Politics*, ed. Ian Shapiro, Rogers M. Smith, and Tarek E. Masoud (Cambridge: Cambridge University Press, 2004), 278.

2. Dan Slater, "Democratic Careening," *World Politics* 65, no. 4 (October 2013): 731.

3. Xi Jinping, "Lingdao ganbu yao renrenzhenzhen xuexi, laolaoshishi zuoren, ganganjingjing ganshi" [Leading cadres must earnestly study, honestly behave with integrity, and clean work], *Zhongzhong zhongyang dangxiao baogao xuan* [Central Party School selected reports] no. 8 (2008), 5. Restricted access publication.

4. Max Weber, quoted in Lewis Coser, *Masters of Sociological Thought*, 2nd ed. (New York: Harcourt, 1997), 230–31.

5. Ban Wang, *The Sublime Figure of History: Aesthetics and Politics in Twentieth Century China* (Stanford, CA: Stanford University Press, 1997), 2.

6. Joseph V. Stalin, "On the Death of Lenin" (January 30, 1924), trans. public at https://www.marxists.org/reference/archive/stalin/works/1924/01/30.htm.

7. It is important to note that the definition of Party spirit has a complex and contested history that can only be mentioned in passing here. During the Mao era, Party spirit manifested the "class character" (*jiejixing*) of the Communist Party. After Mao's death and the abandonment of class struggle as the Party's guiding platform, theorist and propagandist Hu Qiaomu presciently warned in 1982, "If we leave class struggle and discuss the character of the people [*renminxing*], we will have lost our direction." Without the ideology of class struggle as its animating principle and goal, Hu worried that Party spirit would be emptied of its ideological content, vitality, and charisma. Hu Qiaomu, "Guanyu xinwen gongzuo de dangxing he 'renminxing' wenti" [Regarding the problem of party spirit and popular character in news work], in *Hu Qiaomu ji di er juan* [The collected works of Hu Qiaomu, vol. 2] (Beijing, Renmin chubanshe, 1993), 527.

8. The Party Oath can be found in Chinese at http://cpc.people.com.cn/GB/64156 /65682/4440819.html.

9. A complete English version text of the Constitution of the Chinese Communist Party is available at http://english.cpc.people.com.cn/206972/206981/8188090.html (updated as of March 29, 2013).

10. "Zhongguo gongchandang lianjie zilü zhunze" [Chinese Communist Party standards on integrity and self-restraint], available in Chinese at http://politics.people.com .cn/n/2015/1022/c1001-27726471.html with commentary provided by legal scholar Flora Sapio available on her blog *Forgotten Archipelagos* at http://florasapio.blogspot.com.au /2015/10/chinese-communist-party-standards-on.html.

11. Flora Sapio, "Sources of CCP Law, CCP Regulations on Disciplinary Punishments," October 10, 2015, available at http://florasapio.blogspot.com.au/2015/10/chapter -2-sources-of-ccp-law-ccp.html.

12. Liu Shaoqi, *How to Be a Good Communist* (1939), trans. public at https://www .marxists.org/reference/archive/liu-shaoqi/1939/how-to-be/ch06.htm.

13. In Chinese philosophy, there is a deep-rooted conviction in human malleability and the importance of education in shaping one's moral character. In the terse words of Xunzi, "People's nature is bad. Their goodness is a matter of deliberate effort." Xunzi compares human nature to "crooked wood" that must be straightened through the "transforming influence of teachers and models." The CCP adopted a similar worldview that continues to shape the Party's propaganda efforts and governance strategies. Xunzi, *The Complete Text*, trans. Eric L. Hutton (Princeton, NJ: Princeton University Press, 2014), 248. For an overview of "exemplarity" in Chinese statecraft, see Børge Bakken, *The Exemplary Society: Human Improvement, Social Control, and the Dangers of Modernity* (Oxford: Oxford University Press, 2000).

14. Frank N. Pieke, *The Good Communist: Elite Training and State Building in Today's China* (Cambridge: Cambridge University Press, 2009).

15. Augustine, *The City of God against the Pagans*, ed. R. W. Dyson (Cambridge: Cambridge University Press, 1998), 961. For a selective list of political theological readings of the Communist Party, see David E. Apter and Tony Saich, *Revolutionary Discourse in Mao's Republic* (Cambridge, MA: Harvard University Press, 1994); Wang Ban, "In the Beginning Is the Word: Popular Democracy and Mao's Little Red Book," in *Mao's Little Red Book: A Global History*, ed. Alexander C. Cook (Cambridge: Cambridge University Press), 266–77; Michael Dutton, "Mango Mao: Infections of the Sacred," *Public Culture* 16, no. 2 (2004): 161–87; Christian Sorace, "Saint Mao," *Telos* 151 (Summer 2010): 173–91.

16. My understanding of the flesh as a modern political category and production site of legitimacy is inspired by the work of Eric L. Santner, *The Royal Remains: The People's Two Bodies and the Endgames of Sovereignty* (Chicago: University of Chicago Press, 2011); and Santner, *The Weight of All Flesh: On the Subject-Matter of Political Economy* (Oxford: Oxford University Press, 2015).

17. I am drawing from Franz Schurmann's classic argument that the CCP governs its own members through the dual mechanisms of ideological and organizational control. Franz Schurmann, *Ideology and Organization in Communist China* (Berkeley: University of California Press, 1968).

18. Ken Jowitt, *New World Disorder: The Leninist Extinction* (Berkeley: University of California Press, 1993).

19. The term "acclamation of glory" is borrowed from Giorgio Agamben, *The Kingdom and the Glory: For a Theological Genealogy of Economy and Government*, trans. Lorenzo Chiesa (with Matteo Mandarini) (Stanford, CA: Stanford University Press, 2011). For a discussion of "glory" as a pillar of Party legitimacy, see Vivienne Shue, "Legitimacy Crisis in China?" in *State and Society in 21st Century China: Crisis, Contention, and Legitimation*, ed. Peter Hays Gries and Stanley Rosen (New York: Routledge, 2004), 24–49.

20. There are also other benefits to crisis governance. "Deftly employed, the rhetoric of crisis helps to legitimate extraordinary interventions by social and political elites, subvert the standard bureaucratic procedures that characterize normal politics and create political space for extraordinary mobilizations of resources to overcome challenges." Patricia Thornton, "Crisis and Governance: SARS and the Resilience of the Chinese Body Politics," *China Journal* 61 (2009): 26.

21. Anne-Marie Brady, *Marketing Dictatorship: Propaganda and Thought Work in Contemporary China* (Lanham, MD: Rowman and Littlefield, 2009), 188.

22. In the commentary on his translation of *The Analects*, Simon Leys compares this line to Shakespeare's *Richard II*: "The tongues of dying men / Enforce attention, like deep harmony." Confucius, *The Analects*, ed. Michael Nylan, trans. Simon Leys (New York: W. W. Norton, 2014), 35.

23. Haiyan Lee, "The Charisma of Power and the Military Sublime in Tiananmen Square," *Journal of Asian Studies* 70, no. 2 (May 2011): 409.

24. Ibid., 406.

25. Ibid., 399.

26. Bakken, *Exemplary Society*, 194.

27. Anita Chan, *Children of Mao: Personality Development and Political Activism in the Red Guard Generation* (London: Macmillan, 1985); Wu Si, *Qian guize: Zhongguo lishi zhong de zhenshi youxi* [The hidden rules: Real games of Chinese history] (Shanghai: Fudan daxue chubanshe, 2009); Jiwei Ci, *Moral China in the Age of Reform* (Cambridge: Cambridge University Press, 2014); Xiaoying Wang, "The Post-Communist Personality: The Spectre of China's Capitalist Market Reforms," *China Journal* 47 (January 2002): 1–17.

28. Clifford Geertz, "Centers, Kings, and Charisma: Reflections on the Symbolics of Power," in *Rites of Power: Symbolism, Ritual, and Politics since the Middle Ages*, ed. Sean Wilentz (Philadelphia: University of Pennsylvania Press, 1985): 13–38.

29. Charles A. Laughlin, *Chinese Reportage: The Aesthetics of Historical Experience* (Durham, NC: Duke University Press, 2002), 259.

30. Ibid.

31. Geremie R. Barmé, *In the Red: On Contemporary Chinese Culture* (New York: Columbia University Press, 2000): 107–8.

32. The *ci* was also a poetic form favored by Mao Zedong. Indeed, Mao's song lyrics were even set to music and sung during the Cultural Revolution. Xi's poem recently made headlines during Xi's state visit to the United Kingdom in October 2015 when the Chinese embassy arranged for a British student to recite Xi's poem as a tribute of respect. "Xi Jinping: China Has Taught UK Schools Discipline—and Has Learned about Play," *The Guardian*, October 22, 2015, at http://www.theguardian.com/world/2015/oct/22/xi-jinping-china-taught-uk-schools-discipline-learned-about-play.

33. Ibid.; the Chinese original can be found on Baidu at http://baike.baidu.com/view/12514523.htm.

34. "Xi Jinping chongfang lankao: Jiao yulu jingshen shi yonghengde" [Xi Jinping returns to Lankao: The Jiao Yulu spirit is eternal], *Xinhua*, March 17, 2014, available at http://news.xinhuanet.com/politics/2014-03/17/c_119810080.htm.

35. Zheng Degang, "Kangzhen jiuzai bairi: 67 ming ganbu yin linzhen tuisuo deng xingwei bei chufen" [100 days of earthquake resistance and disaster relief: 67 cadres disciplined for getting cold feet], *Renmin ribao* (August 19, 2008).

36. *Wenchuanxian ganbu duiwu zhuangkuang gongzuo huibao* [Wenchuan County cadre ranks situation work report]. I acquired this document from an internal archive within the Sichuan Party School, and its identifying author and document serial number have been removed. It is likely that it originated from the Party's Organization Department.

37. Ibid.

38. Wenchuanxian jiwei jianchaju [Wenchuan County Discipline Inspection Commission Supervisory Office], "Zuo dang de zhongcheng weishi, dang qunzhong de tiexin ren, Wenchuanxian jiwei jianchaju yong xingdong quanshi jijian ganbu de biaozhun" [To serve as a loyal guardian of the party and person intimate with the masses: Using actions to perform the standards of a disciplinary inspection cadre], document undated, from Sichuan Party School archive.

39. Yu Zaigu and Li Yang, "Wei bao chongjian wuzi Pengzhoushi cun zhuren Huang shunquan shoushang jiezhi" [Protecting reconstruction materials Pengzhou Municipality village head Huang Shunquan sustained injuries that required amputation], *Chengdu wanbao* (October 27, 2008), available at http://sichuan.scol.com.cn/sczh/20081027/2008102770332.htm.

40. Xie Yue, "The Political Logic of *Weiwen* in Contemporary China," *Issues & Studies* 48, no. 2 (2012): 1–41.

41. Zhonggong qingchuan xianwei qunzhong gongzuo ju [Qingchuan County Party Mass Work Bureau], "Guanyu bao song '5.12' dadizhen wo xian xinfang ganbu suo zuo gongzuo de bao gao" [Work report regarding county letters and visits cadres work following the great 5.12. earthquake] (June 5, 2008). Restricted access party document.

42. Xie Huachi, "CPC Members Told to Think of the People," *Xinhua English*, September 25, 2013, available at http://news.xinhuanet.com/english/china/2013-09/25/c_132750401.htm.

43. Wang Bin, "Zai shi jie xianwei di 32 ci changwei (kuoda) huiyishang de jianghua" [Speech given at the 32nd meeting of the tenth county standing committee enlarged conference] (September 5, 2008).

44. Qing Lidong, "Pa poshang kan zhua zhongdian, xushi tupo yu kuayue" [Climbing up a slope on the threshold of grasping the important points, store up power to break through and step across], Zai jiakuai tuijin shi da zhongdian gongzuo dongyuan huishang de jianghua [Speech given at the conference for the accelerated promotion of ten large important points of work mobilization], no. 5/96 (2010).

45. *Wenchuanxian ganbu duiwu zhuangkuang gongzuo huibao.*

46. Interview, Wenchuan County Seat, March 2013.

47. Interview with Dujiangyan Municipal Communist Party School teacher, Dujiangyan, January 2013.

48. Wang Bin, "Zai zhonggong wenchuan xianwei shi jie qi ci quanti (kuoda) huiyi shang de jianghua" [Speech given at the seventh meeting of the Entire Tenth County Standing Committee Enlarged Conference] (September 5, 2008).

49. Interview with township official, Qingchuan, May 2013.

50. "Feixu shang da xie Qingchuan—Qingchuanxian kexue tuijin zaihou huifu chongjian jishi" [Writing Qingchuan on the ruins—Qingchuan County scientifically advancing post-disaster restoration and reconstruction record of events], *Sichuan ribao* [Sichuan Daily], May 5, 2010, available at http://sichuandaily.scol.com.cn/2010/05/05/2010050 563722402441.htm.

51. Dujiangyanshi dangxiao [Dujiangyan Communist Party School], *Huifu, fazhan, chuangxin: 2009 nian zaihou chongjian youxiu yanjiu wenji xuanbian* [Reconstruction, development, innovation: Selected works of excellent research reports regarding the 2009 post-disaster reconstruction situation], restricted circulation publication: 5–8; Arthur Kleinman, "Neurasthenia and Depression: A Study of Somatization and Culture in China," *Culture, Medicine, Psychiatry* 6, no. 2 (1982): 117–90.

52. Chen Qiu and Yan Qianmin, "Zaihou wenchuan jiceng ganbu xinli jiankang zhuangkuang diaocha ji tiaoshi duice yanjiu" [Post-disaster Wenchuan grassroots cadres psychological health situation investigation and proposed remedies], *Xinan minzu daxue xuebao* [Southwestern University for Nationalities Journal] 2 (2011): 85–89.

53. Interview with township-level cadre, Qingchuan, May 2013.

54. Interview with village-level Party secretary, Mao County, June 2012.

55. Chen and Yan, "Zaihou wenchuan jiceng ganbu," 88.

56. Ibid.

57. Interview with village Party secretary, Yingxiu, June 2012.

58. A Jian, *Zai nanzhong: Shendu fangtan beichuan xiangzhen shuji* [In the midst of difficulty: In-depth interviews with Beichuan Township party secretaries] (Beijing: Renmin wenxue chubanshe, 2009), 285.

59. Ibid., 277.

60. Ibid., 279.

61. Ibid., 281.

62. *Beichuan ganbu zhenhou shangwang fankuibao* [Post-earthquake information report on the injury and death situation of Beichuan cadres], Confidential Party organization document.

63. Interview with NGO leader in charge of social work, Guangzhou, December 2012.

64. Chen Tao, "Social Workers as Conflict Mediator: Lessons from the Wenchuan Earthquake," *China Journal of Social Work* 3 (2009): 181.

65. "5.12 da dizhen hou 5 ge yue beichuan nongban zhuren zisha" [Five months after the 5.12 great earthquake Beichuan agricultural office director commits suicide], *Huaxi dushi bao* (October 8, 2008), available at http://sichuan.scol.com.cn/dwzw/20081008 /200810853617.htm.

66. Ibid.

67. "Dizhen zhounian ji, dangxin zisha fengchao laixi" [On the first anniversary of the earthquake, on the lookout for a wave of suicides] (May 14, 2009), available at http://www.rdzx.net/xlzx/ShowArt.asp?id=114.

68. Ibid.

69. Feng Xiang, "Haizi, tiantangli meiyou dizhen" [Child, there are no earthquakes in heaven], *Sina Weibo Blog* (May 21, 2008), available at http://blog.sina.com.cn/s/blog _4fcbc32a01009a4u.html.

70. For an analysis of post-earthquake national mourning, see Xu Bin, "For Whom the Bell Tolls: State-Society Relations and the Sichuan Earthquake Mourning in China," *Theory and Society* 42, no. 5 (2013): 509–42; also see my discussion of Ai Weiwei's counter-politics of mourning and grief, in Christian Sorace, "China's Last Communist: Ai Weiwei," *Critical Inquiry* 40, no. 2 (February 2014): 394–410.

71. Interview with township-level cadre, Qingchuan, May 2013.

72. On depression and its relationship to politics in modern China, see Sing Lee, "Depression: Coming of Age in China," in *Deep China: The Moral life of the Person*, ed. Arthur Kleinman et al. (Berkeley: University of California Press, 2011): 177–212.

73. Wang Bin, Speech given at the Seventh Meeting of the Entire Tenth County Standing Committee Enlarged Conference, September 5, 2008.

74. Zhonggong beichuan Qiangzu zizhi xian wei bangongshi [Beichuan Qiangzu Ethnicity Autonomous County Party Committee Office], "Beichuan ganbu ying zhen hou shou ge shuangxiu guanfang huiying dong yufei zisha" [Beichuan cadres welcome post-earthquake first double-relaxation: The official response to Dong Yufei's suicide], *Guangzhou ribao* (October 12, 2008), available at http://sichuan.scol.com.cn/dwzw /20081012/2008101293651.htm.

75. *Wenchuanxian ganbu duiwu zhuangkuang gongzuo huibao.*

76. Interview with Wenchuan County leading cadre, Wenchuan County Seat, March 2013.

77. Wu Chutong, "Yi Dong yufei zisha wei jian: Zaiqu ganbu 'xinling chongjian'" [The example of Dong Yufei's suicide: Disaster-area cadres "mental health reconstruction"], *Tianfu zaobao* (October 22, 2008), available at http://sichuan.scol.com.cn/dwzw /20081022/2008102252714.htm.

78. Tao Ling, "Sichuan shouci jizhong dui zaiqu jiceng ganbu kaizhan xinli fudao" [Sichuan's first time carrying out psychological counseling focused on grassroots cadres], *Huaxi dushibao* (October 22, 2008), available at http://sichuan.scol.com.cn/dwzw /20081022/2008102270004.htm.

79. For a fascinating perspective on "therapeutic governance" applied to laid-off workers from China's state-owned enterprises, see Jie Yang, *Unknotting the Heart: Unemployment and Therapeutic Governance in China* (Ithaca, NY: Cornell University Press, 2013).

80. Zhonggong Wenchuanxian wei zuzhibu [Wenchuan County Party Organization Department], "Guanyu 'shi yi wu' gongzuo zongjie 2011 nian gongzuo anpai de baogao" [Summary of the "11th Five-Year Plan" and 2011 work plan report], December 2, 2010.

81. Sun Liping, "Zouxiang jiji de shehui guanli" [Trend toward proactive social management], *Shehuixue yanjiu* [Sociological studies] 4 (2011): 22–32.

82. Ibid.

83. Benjamin Schwartz, "The Reign of Virtue: Some Broad Perspectives on Leader and Party in the Cultural Revolution," in *Party Leadership and Revolutionary Power in China*, ed. John Wilson Lewis (Cambridge: Cambridge University Press, 1970): 149–69.

84. Max Weber, *Politik als Beruf* [Politics as vocation] lecture; Joel Andreas, *Rise of the Red Engineers: The Cultural Revolution and the Origins of China's New Class* (Stanford, CA: Stanford University Press, 2009), 223; Jean Oi, "The Role of the Local State in China's Transitional Economy," *China Quarterly* 144 (1995), 1137; Dali L. Yang, *Remaking the Chi-*

nese Leviathan: Market Transitions and the Politics of Governance in China (Stanford, CA: Stanford University Press, 2004).

85. Liu, How to Be a Good Communist. In hindsight, this passage is heartbreaking.

86. Liu, How to Be a Good Communist.

87. Huang Xianghuai, "Xin Jinping lun jiankang zhengzhi shengtai" [Xin Jinping's theory on healthy political ecology], Zhongguo gongchandang xinwen wang [Chinese Communist Party news website], June 3, 2015, available at http://theory.people.com.cn/n /2015/0603/c168825-27099150.html.

3. BLOOD TRANSFUSION, GENERATION, AND ANEMIA

1. Vivienne Shue, "Epilogue: Mao's China—Putting Politics in Perspective," in Maoism at the Grassroots: Everyday Life in China's Era of High Socialism, ed. Jeremy Brown and Matthew D. Johnson (Cambridge, MA: Harvard University Press, 2015), 378.

2. Jason Zweig, "Memo to China: Your Market Moves Are Doomed to Fail," Wall Street Journal, July 10, 2015, available at http://blogs.wsj.com/moneybeat/2015/07/10 /memo-to-china-your-market-moves-are-doomed-to-fail/; S.R. "China's Stockmarket Crash: A Red Flag," The Economist, July 7, 2015, available at http://www.economist.com /blogs/freeexchange/2015/07/chinas-stockmarket-crash.

3. Lingling Wei, "China Presses Economists to Brighten Their Outlooks," Wall Street Journal, May 3, 2016, available at http://www.wsj.com/articles/china-presses-economists -to-brighten-their-outlooks-1462292316; Tom Phillips, "Chinese Reporter Makes On-Air 'Confession' after Market Chaos," The Guardian, available at http://www.theguardian .com/world/2015/aug/31/chinese-financial-journalist-wang-xiaolu-makes-alleged -on-air-confesssion-after-market-chaos confession; Banyan editorial, "A Confession to Make," The Economist, January 30, 2016, available at http://www.economist.com/news /china/21689620-what-current-vogue-televised-confessions-and-apologies-says-about -xi-jinpings-china.

4. "Ideology: The Return of Correct Thinking," The Economist, April 23, 2016, available at http://www.economist.com/news/china/21697266-keep-party-and-public-line-xi-jinping -using-marxist-classics-return-correct; Didi Kirsten Tatlow, "China Seeks to Promote the 'Right' Western Philosophy: Marxism," New York Times, September 23, 2015, available at http://sinosphere.blogs.nytimes.com/2015/09/23/peking-university-china-marx/.

5. This conceptual framework and historical narrative have given rise to a cottage industry of Xi/Mao comparisons; see Chris Buckley, "China's President Returns to Mao's (and His) Roots in Yan'an," New York Times, February 13, 2015, available at http:// sinosphere.blogs.nytimes.com/2015/02/13/chinese-president-returns-to-maos-and-his -roots-in-yanan/?_r=0; "Does Xi Represent a Return to the Mao Era?" roundtable discussion, The China File, June 16, 2015, available at http://www.chinafile.com/reporting -opinion/features/does-xi-jinping-represent-return-mao-era; Edward Wong, "Chinese Security Laws Elevate the Party and Stifle Dissent. Mao Would Approve," New York Times, May 30, 2015, available at http://www.nytimes.com/2015/05/30/world/asia/chinese -national-security-law-aims-to-defend-party-grip-on-power.html; Willy Lam, "A Modern Cult of Personality? Xi Jinping Aspires to be the Equal of Mao and Deng," China Brief 15, no. 5, March 6, 2015; the list could go on for pages and pages.

6. Zhao Dingxin, "The Mandate of Heaven and Performance Legitimation in Historical and Contemporary China," American Behavioral Scientist 53, no. 3 (2009): 418.

7. Ibid., 422.

8. Ibid.

9. Ibid.

10. Ibid., 425.

11. Andrew J. Nathan, "Authoritarian Resilience," *Journal of Democracy* 14, no. 1 (January 2003): 6–17.

12. Slavoj Žižek, *Living in the End Times* (London: Verso, 2011).

13. Deng Xiaoping, "Uphold the Four Cardinal Principles" (March 30, 1979). English version available at http://en.people.cn/dengxp/vol2/text/b1290.html.

14. "Xi Says China Must Adapt to 'New Normal' of Slower Growth," *Bloomberg News*, May 11, 2014, available at http://www.bloomberg.com/news/articles/2014-05-11/xi-says-china-must-adapt-to-new-normal-of-slower-growth; Hu Angang, "Embracing China's New Normal: Why the Economy Is Still on Track," *Foreign Affairs* (May–June 2015), available at https://www.foreignaffairs.com/articles/china/2015-04-20/embracing-chinas-new-normal.

15. Glancing at the following headlines, it is no wonder that the Communist Party believes it is locked in an ideological struggle with the West! David Shambaugh, "The Coming Chinese Crackup," *Wall Street Journal*, March 6, 2015, available at http://www.wsj.com/articles/the-coming-chinese-crack-up-1425659198; Minxin Pei, "Will the Chinese Communist Party Survive the Crisis? How Beijing's Shrinking Economy May Threaten One-Party Rule," *Foreign Affairs*, May 12, 2009, available at https://www.foreignaffairs.com/articles/asia/2009-03-12/will-chinese-communist-party-survive-crisis; Jamil Anderlini, "How Long Can the Communist Party Survive in China?" *Financial Times*, September 20, 2013, available at http://www.ft.com/cms/s/2/533a6374-1fdc-11e3-8861-00144feab7de.html#slide0; Michael Auslin, "The Twilight of China's Communist Party," *Wall Street Journal*, January 29, 2015, available at http://www.wsj.com/articles/michael-auslin-the-twilight-of-chinas-communist-party-1422551788; "When Will China's Government Collapse?" roundtable at Foreign Policy (March 13, 2015), available at http://foreignpolicy.com/2015/03/13/china_communist_party_collapse_downfall/.

16. Based on her ethnographic fieldwork in an impoverished factory town on the outskirts of Harbin, Mun Young Cho argues that the "management of urban poverty is not merely a technical project of alleviating individual need but a contested arena for the nation-state and its subjects." Mun Young Cho, *The Specter of "the People": Urban Poverty in Northeast China* (Ithaca, NY: Cornell University Press, 2013), 4.

17. Hannah F. Pitkin, *The Concept of Representation* (Berkeley, CA: University of California Press, 1972), 1.

18. Mao, "On Contradiction" (August 1937), trans. public, available at https://www.marxists.org/reference/archive/mao/selected-works/volume-1/mswv1_17.htm.

19. Ibid.

20. Mao Zedong, "On the Ten Major Relationships" (April 25, 1956) trans. public, available at https://www.marxists.org/reference/archive/mao/selected-works/volume-5/mswv5_51.htm.

21. Barry Naughton, *Growing Out of the Plan: Chinese Economic Reform 1978–1993* (Cambridge: Cambridge University Press, 1995), 5.

22. Dali L. Yang, *Remaking the Chinese Leviathan: Market Transitions and the Politics of Governance in China* (Stanford, CA: Stanford University Press, 2004), 21.

23. The Party's nearly ubiquitous usage of the terms "construction" (*jianshe*) and "transformation" (*zhuanbian*) in its planning documents suggest that in its own esteem the process is nowhere near complete.

24. "This privileging of the urban and disparaging of the rural led to what has been called the 'spectralization' of agriculture and the countryside, as villages became ghostly reminders of the past, a wasteland inhabited only by the 'left-behind,' particularly children and the elderly." Emily T. Yeh, Kevin J. O'Brien, and Jingzhong Ye, "Rural Politics in Contemporary

China," *Journal of Peasant Studies* 40, no. 6 (2013): 917. Also see Yan Hairong, "Spectralization of the Rural: Reinterpreting the Labor Mobility of Rural Young Women in Post-Mao China," *American Ethnologist* 30, no. 4: 1–19.

25. Sebastian Heilmann and Oliver Melton, "The Reinvention of Development Planning in China, 1993–2012," *Modern China* 39, no. 6 (August 2013): 581.

26. Ibid., 582.

27. Hu Angang, "The Distinctive Transition of China's Five-Year Plans," *Modern China* 39, no. 6 (August 2013): 629–30.

28. Heilmann and Melton, "Reinvention of Development Planning," 585.

29. The ongoing process of constructing markets in the countryside is a national priority. Zhengce fagui chu [Policy and Legislation Office], "Buduan tuijin nongcun jingji shichanghua jianshe he fazhan—jianshe shehuizhuyi xin nongcun fazhan jizhi tanjiu" [Continuously advance village economic marketization construction and development—construct socialism new village development mechanism investigation], *Quyu jingji cankao* [Regional economic reference] 16, no. 65 (July 10, 2008): 45–50. Restricted access publication.

30. In a recent news article, the People's Bank of China was described as in possession of a "toolkit [that] now includes more surgical armaments." Enda Curran, "In China, Focus of Monetary Easing Turns to Surgical Strikes," *Bloomberg*, April 29, 2015, available at http://www.bloomberg.com/news/articles/2015-04-29/in-china-focus-of-monetary -easing-turns-to-surgical-strikes.

31. Liu Tie, *Duikouzhiyuan de yunxing jizhi jiqi fazhihua: Jiyu Wenchuan dizhen zaihou huifu chongjian de shizheng fenxi* [On the operation and legalization of partner assistance: An empirical study based on the post-disaster reconstruction of the Wenchuan earthquake] (Beijing, Falü chubanshe, 2010), 84.

32. Ibid., 38.

33. Chen Guaming, *Wenchuan dizhenhou huifu chongjian zhuyao falü wenti* [Research on main legal issues in post-Wenchuan earthquake rehabilitation and reconstruction], Falü chubanshe (2010), 53.

34. Jessica Teets, "Post-Earthquake Relief and Reconstruction Efforts: The Emergence of Civil Society in China?" *China Quarterly* 198 (2009): 330–47; Bin Xu, "Consensus Crisis and Civil Society: The Sichuan Earthquake Response and State-Society Relations," *China Journal* 71 (January 2014): 91–108; Charlene Makley, "Spectacular Compassion: 'Natural' Disasters and National Mourning in China's Tibet," *Critical Asian Studies* 46, no. 3 (September 2014): 371–404; Kathryn Jean Edgerton-Tarpley, "From 'Nourish the People' to 'Sacrifice for the Nation': Changing Responses to Disaster in Late Imperial and Modern China," *Journal of Asian Studies* 73, no. 2 (May 2014): 447–69; Christian Sorace, "China's Vision for Developing Sichuan's Post-Earthquake Countryside: Turning Unruly Peasants into Grateful Urban Citizens," *China Quarterly* 218 (June 2014): 404–27.

35. Ren Zhongping, "Wenchuan teda dizhen san zhounian zhi" [On the third anniversary of the Wenchuan earthquake], *Renmin ribao* [People's Daily], May 11, 2011, available at http://news.sina.com.cn/c/2011-05-11/113422444531.shtml; Gu Songqing, *Fazhanxing chongjian zaihou jueqi de Sichuan moshi* [Development model reconstruction: The emergence of the post-disaster Sichuan method], Sichuan renmin chubanshe (2011), 324.

36. Ibid., 303.

37. Liu, *Duikouzhiyuan*, 110–11.

38. Hou Shuiping, *Wenchuan dadizhen zaihou huifu chongjian xiangguan zhongda wenti yanjiu* [Wenchuan post-earthquake recovery- and reconstruction-related important research problems] (Sichuan: Sichuan renmin chubanshe, 2010), 400.

39. Ibid., 500.

40. Kenneth Bradsher, "Chinese Officials Cancel Plant Project amid Protests," *New York Times,* July 5, 2012, available at http://www.nytimes.com/2012/07/05/world/asia /chinese-officials-cancel-plant-project-amid-protests.html?_r=0.

41. Alia, "Traces on Weibo: How a NIMBY Protest Turned Violent in a Small Sichuan City," *Offbeat China,* July 2, 2012, available at http://offbeatchina.com/traces-on-weibo -how-a-nimby-protest-turned-violent-in-a-small-sichuan-city.

42. Liu, *Duikouzhiyuan,* 28.

43. Christian Sorace and William Hurst, "China's Phantom Urbanisation and the Pathology of Ghost Cities," *Journal of Contemporary Asia* 46, no. 2 (2016): 304–22.

44. Kenneth Lieberthal and Michel Oksenberg, *Policy Making in China: Leaders, Structures, and Processes* (Princeton, NJ: Princeton University Press, 1988); Andrew Mertha, "Fragmented Authoritarianism 2.0: Political Pluralization in the Chinese Policy Process," *China Quarterly* 200 (December 2009): 995–1012; Andrew Mertha, *Brothers in Arms: Chinese Aid to the Khmer Rouge* (Ithaca, NY: Cornell University Press, 2014). For an elaboration of the fragmented authoritarianism paradigm in the aftermath of the Sichuan earthquake, see: Christian Sorace " 'When One Place Is in Trouble, Help Comes from All Sides': Fragmented Authoritarianism in Post-Disaster Reconstruction," in *Chinese Politics as Fragmented Authoritarianism: Earthquakes, Energy, and Environment,* ed. Kjeld Erik Brødsgaard (London: Routledge, 2016): 135–55.

45. Chen, *Falü wenti,* 61.

46. Ibid., 62; Interviews with party cadres involved in partner assistance, Guangzhou 2012 and Zhejiang January 2013.

47. Zhao Hongzhu, "Zhejiang shengwei shuji, shengrenda changweihui zhuren zhao hongzhu, jianghua yaodian" [Essential points of speech by Zhejiang provincial party secretary, director of standing committee of Provincial People's Congress, Zhao Hongzhu], (Zhejiang Province, June 9, 2008).

48. Hou, *Wenchuan da dizhen,* 404.

49. Interview with cadre, Zhejiang, January 2013.

50. Liu, *Duikouzhiyuan,* 72.

51. Interview with cadre, Qingchuan, May 2013.

52. Sorace, "China's Vision," 414.

53. Interview with party cadre, Zhejiang, January 2013.

54. Ibid.

55. Ibid.

56. Interview with cadre, Qingchuan, May 2013.

57. Ibid.

58. Zhejiang sheng zhiyuan qingchuanxian zaihou huifu chongjian gongzuo bangongshi, Zhejiangsheng zhiyuan Qingchuanxian zaihou huifu chongjian zhihuibu, Qingchuanxian renmin zhengfu [Zhejiang Province assistance to Qingchuan County post-disaster restoration and reconstruction work office; Zhejiang Province assistance to Qingchuan County post-disaster restoration and reconstruction command center; Qingchuan County people's government], *Zhejiangsheng zhiyuan Qingchuanxian zaihou huifu chongjian guihua shishi pinggu baogao huiji* [Zhejiang Province assistance to Qingchuan County post-disaster restoration and reconstruction planning and implementation assessment report compilation] (December 2010). Referred to as *Zhejiang Report.*

59. Hou, *Wenchuan da dizhen,* 404.

60. Wang Hongxin and He Lijun, "Wenchuan dizhen zaiqu nongcun huifu chongjian, fupin kaifa yu kechixu fazhan: Jiyu yu tiaozhan" [Restoration and recovery of post-Wenchuan earthquake villages: Poverty alleviation development and sustainable development: Opportunities and challenges] in *Wenchuan dizhen zaihou pinkun cun chongjian*

jincheng yu tiaozhan [The reconstruction of post-Wenchuan earthquake poverty villages: Process and challenges], ed. Huang Chengwei and Chen Hanwen (Beijing, Shehui kexue wenxian chubanshe, 2010), 256.

61. Zhu Ling, "Ba jianshao pinkun de mubiao naru zaiqu chongjian jihua" [Incorporate the goal of poverty reduction into disaster-area reconstruction planning], *Guanli Xinxi* [Management information] (2008): 12–13. Restricted access publication.

62. Chen, *Falü wenti*, 127.

63. Hou, *Wenchuan da dizhen*, 403.

64. Zhao Gang, "Yingdui zaimin de liyi he gongyi suqiu xuyao zhuyi de jige wenti" [Several problems to pay attention to when handling disaster victims' benefits and righteous demands], *Lingdao canyue* [Leadership reference] (2008): 13–15. Restricted access publication.

65. Yongshun Cai, "Irresponsible State: Local Cadres and Image-Building in China," *Journal of Communist Studies and Transition Politics* 20, no. 4 (2004): 31.

66. Zhao, "Yingdui zaimin de liyi," 13.

67. This is a compelling reason for the indispensability of ethnographic research on its own and as a necessary supplement to quantitative analysis.

68. Chen, *Falü wenti*, 60.

69. Yushuzhouwei dangxiao ketizu [Qinghai Province, Yushu Prefecture Chinese Communist Party School Task Group], "Shiming yu chuangxin: Yushu zaihou chongjian moshi yanjiu" [Mission and innovation: Research on Yushu's post-disaster reconstruction methods], *Lilun dongtai* [Theoretical trends] 19, no. 8 (December 20, 2015): 5–39.

70. Lao Chunshen, "Zhongyang shou xuan bai ming youxiu ganbu duikou zhiyuan Qinghai shenyi he zai?" [The profound meaning of the center's selection of over 100 excellent cadres for the partner assistance to Qinghai], *Zhongguo gongchandang xinwenwang* [Chinese Communist Party News Network] (August 4, 2010), available at http://cpc.people .com.cn/GB/64093/64103/12345443.html.

71. Yushu Party School, "Shiming yu chuangxin," 30.

72. Interview with cab driver from Sichuan working temporarily in Yushu, Yushu, 2012.

73. Guowuyuan fazhan yanjiu zhongxin [Development Research Center of the State Council], "Chuangxin yuanzang fangshi zaofu xizang renmin," [Innovative Tibetan assistance methods: Benefit for the Tibetan people], (October 15, 2009), *Diaocha yanjiu baogao* [Investigation research report] 129: 1–11.

74. Luo Shuzhen, "Jinyibu zuohao fayuan xitong duikou yuanjiang gongzuo, qieshi weihu bianjiang shehui wending he chang zhi jui ai" [Progressively improve the work of court system partner assistance to Xinjiang, conscientiously maintain border-area social stability and long-term peace], *Renmin fayuan bao* [People's Court report] (December 18, 2014).

75. Anne Norton, *95 Theses on Politics, Culture, & Method* (New Haven, CT: Yale University Press, 2004), 9.

76. Ibid., 8.

4. THE UTOPIA OF URBAN PLANNING

1. David Bray, "Urban Planning Goes Rural: Conceptualising the 'New Village,'" *China Perspectives* 3 (2013): 53–63.

2. The concept of "utopian urbanism" was suggested to me by Luigi Tomba.

3. Guowuyuan fazhan yanjiu zhongxin [Development Research Center of the State Council], "Wo guo chengshibing de tizhi chengyin fenxi" [An analysis of the systemic causes of China's urban pathologies] 67 (2012): 1–13.

4. Ye Xingqing, "China's Urban-Rural Integration Policies," trans. Flemming Christiansen, *Journal of Current Chinese Affairs* 4 (2009): 117–43.

5. Ninth Plenum of Eleventh Chengdu Municipal Party Congress, cited in Wang Fang, "Qianxi xiao chengzhen fazhan jianshe 'jie' yu 'jie'" [Preliminary analysis of urban development construction "combining" and "loosening"], in ed. Dujiangyanshi dangxiao [Dujiangyan Municipal Communist Party School] *Xin sixiang, xin silu, xin chengguo: Dujiangyanshi di shisiqi qingnian ganbu peixunban diaoyan wenji huibian* [New thoughts, new thinking, new results: Dujiangyan Municipality fourteenth young cadre training class research collection of works] (2012), 75, restricted access publication.

6. Daniel Abramson and Yu Qi, "Urban–Rural Integration in the Earthquake Zone: Sichuan's Post-Disaster Reconstruction and the Expansion of the Chengdu Metropole," *Pacific Affairs* 84, no. 3 (2011): 507.

7. Yan Guo, "Emergence of an Integral Post-Disaster Urbanism: On the Crisis of Urban Resilience and Absence of Socio-Spatial Justice Resulted from the Post-Disaster Planning in Sichuan, China," paper presented at Asian Planning Schools Association Eleventh International Conference (2011).

8. Li Bin, "Dujiangyan dazao chongjian yangban he shifan shiyan qu" [Dujiangyan: The creation of a reconstruction template and model example test area], *Chengdu Wanbao* [Chengdu evening news] (October 21, 2009), available at http://news.sina.com.cn/o/2009 -10-21/053116472002s.shtml.

9. Abramson and Yu, "Urban-Rural Integration," 497.

10. Christian Sorace and William Hurst, "China's Phantom Urbanisation and the Pathology of Ghost Cities," *Journal of Contemporary Asia* 46, no. 2 (2016): 305.

11. Luigi Tomba, *The Government Next Door: Neighborhood Politics in Urban China* (Ithaca, NY: Cornell University Press, 2014); Carolyn Cartier, "Governmentality and the Urban Economy: Consumption, Excess, and the 'Civilized City' in China," in *New Mentalities of Government in China*, ed. David Bray and Elaine Jeffreys (London: Routledge, 2016): 56–73.

12. Dujiangyanshi dangxiao [Dujiangyan Party School], *Huifu, fazhan, chuangxin: 2009 nian zaihou chongjian youxiu yanjiu wenji xuanbian* [Reconstruction, development, innovation: Selected works of excellent research reports regarding the 2009 post-disaster reconstruction situation], restricted circulation publication, 19 and 17.

13. Dujiangyanshi tongchou chengxiang gongzuoju wenjian [Dujiangyan Municipality Overall Planning Urban-Rural Work Department], "Guanyu shenhua tongchou chengxiang zonghe peitao gaige tuijin chengxiangyitihua de yijian" [Opinions regarding deepening comprehensive integration reform promoting urban-rural integration], Document No. 55 (2009), 2 (hereafter referred to as "Document No. 55").

14. Wang Jiquan, "Zou tese fazhan zhi lu, fuwu Chengdu dadushi—Dujiangyan tuijin dushi xiandai nongye fazhande zuofa yu qishi" [Walking the road of specialized development, serving the Chengdu Metropolis—Dujiangyan promotes metropolitan modern agricultural methods and enlightenment], *Sichuan jingji xinxi wang* [Sichuan Economic Information Network], July 16, 2012, available at http://www.sc.cei.gov.cn/dir1009/130736 .htm; Ma Zhigang, "Ziben xiaxiang dayoukewei" [Capital goes to the countryside with great prospects for the future], *Jingji Ribao* [Economic daily], January 30, 2014, available at http://theory.people.com.cn/n/2014/0130/c40531-24268536.html.

15. Dujiangyan Party School, *Huifu, fazhan, chuangxin*, 38.

16. Wang Fang, "Qianxi xiao chengzhen fazhan jianshe 'jie' yu 'jie'" [Preliminary analysis of urban development construction "combining" and "loosening"], in ed. Dujiangyanshi dangxiao [Dujiangyan Municipal Communist Party School] *Xin sixiang, xin silu, xin chengguo: Dujiangyanshi di shisiqi qingnian ganbu peixunban diaoyan wenji huibian*

[New thoughts, new thinking, new results: Dujiangyan Municipality fourteenth young cadre training class research collection of works] (2012), restricted access publication, 75–77.

17. Gu Songqing, *Fazhanxing chongjian zaihou jueqi de Sichuan moshi* [Development model reconstruction: The emergence of the post-disaster Sichuan method], Sichuan renmin chubanshe (2011), 10, 37. The fact that the Sichuan earthquake occurred in 2008 at the beginning of the global financial crisis (and in many restricted access Party journals, the reconstruction and financial crisis are analytically linked and studied together) forms the broader macroeconomic context shaping the particulars of the reconstruction plan. Guowuyuan fazhan yanjiu zhongxin [Development Research Center of the State Council], "Wenchuan dizhen zaihai dui woguo jingji zengzhang de yingxiang pinggu" [Assessment of the Wenchuan earthquake's Impact on national economic growth] 8, no. 3201 (June 20, 2008): 1–24.

18. Abramson and Yu, "Urban-Rural Integration," 510.

19. *Chengxiangyitihua: Chengdu de kexue fazhan zhi lu* [Urban-rural integration as the road to Chengdu's scientific development] (Chengdu shidai chubanshe, 2007), 5. For national-level discussions of village property reform, see Zhong Huaining, "Nongcun chanquan gaige yao yi guoqi gaige wei jing" [Village property-right reform must use state-enterprise reform as mirror], *Gaige Neican* (Reform internal reference) 19 (2008): 4–5. For a negative account, see Yan Hairong, "The Myth of Private Ownership," *China Left Review* 1 (2008).

20. During the writing of this book, Li Chuncheng was expelled from the Party and placed under criminal investigation accused of "bribe taking, 'feudal' superstition, and personal depravity." See Michael Forsythe and Chris Buckley, "China's Ruling Party Expels and Investigates Official," *New York Times*, April 29, 2014, available at http://www.nytimes.com/2014/04/30/world/asia/chinas-communist-party-expels-senior-official.html?_r=0; *Dujiangyan: Minyi de chongjian* [Dujiangyan: Reconstruction according to the will of the people], CCTV Documentary (May 2011), available at http://news.cntv.cn/china/20110521/105513.shtml.

21. Interview with Dujiangyan Party School professor, Dujiangyan, January 2013.

22. Document No. 55, p. 5.

23. Ibid., 6.

24. Liu Junlin quoted in *Dujiangyan: Minyi de chongjian*.

25. It is worth pointing out that this document was published in February 2008, three months prior to the earthquake, to emphasize the continuity in pre- and post-earthquake planning. Dujiangyanshi nongcun chanquan zhidu gaige gongzuo lingdao xiaozu bangongshi wenjian [Dujiangyan Municipality Village Property Rights System Reform Leadership Working Small Group], *Dujiangyanshi jititudi suoyouquan quequan banzheng caozuo banfa, shixing* [Dujiangyan Municipality collective land property rights: Work methods for confirmation of rights and conferral of proof, pilot], Document No. 1 (February 2008).

26. Dujiangyan Party School, *Huifu, fazhan, chuangxin*, 37.

27. Dujiangyanshi nongcun chanquan zhidu gaige gongzuo lingdao xiaozu bangongshi wenjian [Dujiangyan Municipality Village Property Rights System Reform Leadership Working Small Group], *Guanyu jianli nongcun chanquan zhidu gaige maodun jiufen yufang, tiaochu, huajie gongzuo jizhi de yijian* [Opinions regarding the establishment of a precaution, investigation and resolution work system for the contradictions and disputes of the reform of the village property rights system reform], Document No. 7 (2008).

28. Document No. 55, p. 5; Dujiangyanshi dangxiao [Dujiangyan Communist Party School], *Gongchandang, haowubian: Houchongjian shidai dangyuan ganbu dangxing jiaoyu*

wenji xuanbian [The party's heroism and shared responsibility: Selected works on post–reconstruction era party member and cadre education], 50. Restricted access publication.

29. Ibid.

30. Wang Fang, "Qianxi xiao chengzhen fazhan," 75.

31. Interview with Dujiangyan Party School professor, Dujiangyan, January 2013.

32. Dujiangyanshi nongcun chanquan zhidu gaige gongzuo lingdao xiaozu bangongshi wenjian [Dujiangyan Municipality Village Property-Rights System Reform Leadership Working Small Group], Dujiangyan Municipality's Temporary Measures for Arbitrating Disputes Regarding Village Land Contracting Transfer of Village Land Circulation, Document No. 6 (2008).

33. Ibid., 3.

34. Dujiangyan Party School, *Gongchandang, haowubian*, 59.

35. Ibid., 59.

36. Ibid., 60.

37. Ibid., 61.

38. Ibid., 59.

39. Ibid., 61.

40. Ibid., 70.

41. Ibid.

42. Qian Forrest Zhang and John A. Donaldson, "The Rise of Agrarian Capitalism with Chinese Characteristics: Agricultural Modernization, Agribusiness and Collective Land Rights," *China Journal* 60 (July 2008): 25–47.

43. Dujiangyan Party School, *Gongchandang, haowubian*, 59.

44. Ibid., 60.

45. Ibid., 62.

46. Ibid., 61.

47. Interview with Community F party secretary, Pi County, February 2013.

48. Dujiangyan Party School, *Gongchandang, haowubian*, 127.

49. Ibid., 94.

50. Ibid.

51. Ibid.

52. Ibid., 121.

53. Ibid.

54. Ibid., 122.

55. Ibid., 123.

56. Deng Rong, "Nongcun juzhu xingtai gaibian yu shengchan fangshi, guanli moshi de chonggou: Guanyu Dujiangyanshi nongmin jizhong juzhu hou xiangguan wenti de diaocha yu sikao" [Transformations in the circumstances of village living and modes of production, reconstructing modes of management: Investigation and reflection concerning problems in the concentration of peasant housing in Dujiangyan], in *Dujiangyanshi di shi san qi qingnian ganbu peixunban diaoyan wenji huibian* [Collected essays from Dujiangyan youth cadre training class], ed. Dujiangyan shiwei dangxiao [Dujiangyan Party School] (July 2011), 37. Restricted access publication.

57. Dujiangyan Party School, *Gongchandang, haowubian*, 122.

58. Ibid., 97.

59. Deng Rong, "Nongcun juzhu xingtai gaibian," 37.

60. Li Bo, "Dujiangyan linpanshi nongcun jujidian" [Dujiangyan "LinPan-style" rural aggregation], *Chengshi jianshi lilun yanjiu* [Urban construction theory research] (2012). According to Elizabeth Perry, there is precedence for this behavior during New Socialist Village Construction Campaigns in which: "Local governments are criticized for reverting to old Mao-era habits in trying to force peasant compliance without due consideration for

local conditions and preferences." Elizabeth J. Perry, "From Mass Campaigns to Managed Campaigns: 'Constructing a New Socialist Countryside,'" in *Mao's Invisible Hand: The Political Foundations of Adaptive Governance in China*, ed. Sebastian Heilmann and Elizabeth J. Perry (Cambridge, MA: Harvard University Press, 2011): 41–42.

61. Dujiangyan Party School, *Huifu, fazhan, chuangxin*, 15.

62. Ibid., 16.

63. Ibid., 29–30.

64. Ibid.

65. Yan Guo, "Emergence of an Integral Post-Disaster Urbanism."

66. Sorace and Hurst, "China's Phantom Urbanisation."

67. *Zhongguo chengxiantyitihua fazhan baogao* [*Bluebook of Urban-Rural Integration*], Ru xin and Fu chonglan, eds. (Beijing, Shehuikexue wenxian chubanshe, 2011), 48.

68. Interview with local cab driver, Dujiangyan, April 2013.

69. Interview with GONGO leader, Dujiangyan, February 2013.

70. Interview with restaurant owner, Dujiangyan, January 2013.

71. Interview with Community B party secretary, Dujiangyan, February 2013.

72. Interview with Community D local resident 2, Dujiangyan, March 2013.

73. Interview with Community D local resident 3, Dujiangyan, March 2013.

74. Interview with Community D resident 4, Dujiangyan, March 2013.

75. Interview with cab driver 2, Dujiangyan, May 2013.

76. Dujiangyan Party School, *Huifu, fazhan, chuangxin*, 29.

77. Interview with Community D resident 7, Dujiangyan, March 2013.

78. Ibid.

79. Ibid.

80. Julie Chu, "When Infrastructures Attack: The Workings of Disrepair in China," *American Ethnologist* 41, no. 2 (2014): 351–67.

81. Yan Guo, "Emergence of an Integral Post-Disaster Urbanism."

82. Dorothy J. Solinger, "The Chinese Work Unit and Transient Labor in the Transition from Socialism," *Modern China* 21, no. 2 (April 1995): 155–83; Tamara Jacka, *Rural Women in Urban China: Gender Migration, and Social Change* (Armonk, NY: M. E. Sharpe, 2005); Rachel Murphy and Ran Tao, "No Wage and No Land: New Forms of Unemployment in Rural China," in *Unemployment in China: Economy, Human Resources and Labour Market*, ed. G. Lee and M. Warner (London: Routledge, 2006): 128–49; and William Hurst, *The Chinese Worker after Socialism* (Cambridge: Cambridge University Press, 2009).

83. Ye Jinzhong, Wang Chunyu, Wu Huifang, He Congzhi, and Liu Juan, "Internal Migration and Left-Behind Populations in China," *Journal of Peasant Studies* 40, no. 6 (2013): 1119–46.

84. Dujiangyan Party School, *Huifu, fazhan, chuangxin*, 31; for a discussion of the similarly low educational credentials of laid off state-sector workers, see Hurst, *Chinese Worker after Socialism*.

85. Interview with local resident 21, Dujiangyan, April 2013.

86. For comparative examples of boredom and waiting as political economic symptoms, see Bruce O'Neill, "Cast Aside: Boredom, Downward Mobility, and Homelessness in Post-Communist Bucharest," *Cultural Anthropology* 29, no. 1 (February 2014): 8–31; Craig Jeffrey, *Timepass: Youth, Class, and the Politics of Waiting in India* (Stanford, CA: Stanford University Press, 2010).

87. Interview with professor from N University, Chengdu, May 2013.

88. For comparative and theoretical accounts of precarious existence at the periphery of global capital, see Anne Allison, *Precarious Japan* (Durham, NC: Duke University Press, 2013); Tania Murray Li, "To Make Live or Let Die? Rural Dispossession and the

Protection of Surplus Populations," *Antipode* 41 (2009): 66–93; Elizabeth A. Povinelli, *Economies of Abandonment: Social Belonging and Endurance in Late Liberalism* (Durham, NC: Duke University Press 2011).

89. Interview with local resident 15, Dujiangyan, May 2013.

90. Huddling by a fire is a traditional pastime in rural Sichuan; these fires, however, are illegal in urban communities because of the hazards they pose.

91. Dujiangyan Party School, *Huifu, fazhan, chuangxin*, 43.

92. Ye et al., "Internal Migration," 1129–30.

93. *Wenchuan dadizhen yizhounian zaiqu qunzhong fangtanlü* [Wenchuan earthquake first anniversary disaster masses interview transcripts] (2009), restricted circulation publication, 96.

94. Dujiangyan Party School, *Huifu, fazhan, chuangxin*, 32.

95. Multiple interviewees, Dujiangyan (common throughout the earthquake zone). These complaints are also national phenomena. See Lynette H. Ong, "State-Led Urbanization in China: Skyscrapers, Land Revenue and 'Concentrated Villages,'" *China Quarterly* 217 (March 2014): 162–79.

96. Interview with Community D resident 8, Dujiangyan, March 2013.

97. Interview with Community D resident 19, Dujiangyan, March 2013.

98. Interview with Dujiangyan Party School professor, Dujiangyan, January 2012; Interview with professor from S University, Chengdu, November 2012.

99. Dujiangyan Party School, *Huifu, fazhan, chuangxin*, 34.

100. Tuan Yi-Fu, *Topophilia: A Study of Environmental Perception, Attitudes and Values* (New York: Columbia University Press, 1990), 99.

101. Interview with teahouse owner, Dujiangyan, December 2012.

102. Interview with local resident 27, Dujiangyan, June 2013.

103. Tomba, *Government Next Door.*

104. Interview with Chengdu resident, Chengdu, October 2012.

105. Interview with teahouse owner, Dujiangyan, December 2012.

106. Ibid.

107. Dujiangyan Party School, *Huifu, fazhan, chuangxin*, 19.

108. Interview with grassroots cadre, Dujiangyan, January 2013.

109. Interviews with grassroots cadre and Party secretary Pi County, February 2013. I have included data from Pi County here not only because it borders Dujiangyan but also because it did not suffer severe damage from the earthquake. As a result, Pi County's "urban-rural integration" developed according to normal conditions, whereas Dujiangyan's was accelerated under the auspices of post-earthquake reconstruction. Despite these different conditions, Pi County and Dujiangyan's urban-rural integration problems are nearly identical.

110. Interview with Party Secretary Pi County, February 2013.

111. Interview with party secretary, Community B, Pi County, February 2013.

112. Interview with party secretary, Community F, Pi County. Adding to the stress levels, new urban communities are understaffed with often twelve cadres for a community of ten thousand people and overwhelmed with administrative obligations delegated by higher-level officials in the township, not to mention demands from below. The Party secretary cited the phrase "the higher-levels have a thousand threads, but below, there is only one needle" (*shang mian qian tiao xian, xia mian yi gen zhen*).

113. Interview with Party secretary, Community A, Dujiangyan, January 2013.

114. Dujiangyan Party School, *Huifu, fazhan, chuangxin*, 32; Deng Rong, "Nongcun juzhu xingtai gaibian," 37–38.

115. Dujiangyan Party School, *Xin sixiang, xin silu, xin chengguo*, 38–39.

116. Interview with Party secretary, Community B, Pi County, February 2013; Deng Rong, "Nongcun juzhu xingtai gaibian," 37.

117. Ibid., 38.

118. Ibid.

119. Ibid., 37.

120. Ibid., 38.

121. Interview with local cadre, Dujiangyan, January 2013.

122. Dujiangyan Party School, *Huifu, fazhan, chuangxin*, 16.

123. Interview with NGO worker, Dujiangyan, January 2013.

124. Yan Guo, "Emergence of an Integral Post-Disaster Urbanism."

125. Zhang Li, *In Search of Paradise: Middle-Class Living in a Chinese Metropolis* (Ithaca, NY: Cornell University Press 2010).

5. THE MIRAGE OF DEVELOPMENT

1. Sun Liping, *Chongjian shehui: Zhuanxing shehui de zhixu zaizao* [Reconstructing society: To rebuild social order in transformational China] (Beijing: Shehui kexue wenxian chubanshe [Social Sciences Academic Press], 2009): 235–36.

2. Zhongyang dangxiao shengbuji ganbu jinxiuban [Central Committee of the Communist Party School, Provincial Level Cadre Advanced Studies Group], "Ba zhengji kaoping jizhi chuangxin zuowei jingji fazhan fangshi zhuanbian de guanjian zhuashou" [Innovations in the mechanisms for evaluating political achievement as a critical starting point for transforming the mode of economic development], *Baogaoxuan* [Chinese Communist Party school selected reports] 6 (2010): 28–29.

3. Yongshun Cai, "Irresponsible State: Local Cadres and Image-Building in China," *Journal of Communist Studies and Transition Politics* 20, no. 4 (2004): 22.

4. Tang Shuquan, "Sichuan shengwei shuji chengyao yingxiu dazao cheng 'shijie mingzhen'" [Sichuan provincial party secretary calls for Yingxiu to become a "world famous township"], *Zhongguo xinwenwang* [China News], May 8, 2010, available at http://politics.people.com.cn/GB/14562/11547445.html.

5. This joke was sent to me via the popular social network platform WeChat on May 13, 2013, one day after the fifth anniversary of the earthquake by a local Yingxiu resident.

6. Interview with retired PLA cadre, Yingxiu, March 2012. During the course of the interview, he professed nostalgia for the harsh rectification campaigns of the Mao era that disciplined the wayward behavior of local Party cadres.

7. Interview with local resident 1, Yingxiu, June 2013.

8. Interview with local resident 31, Yingxiu Township, June 2012.

9. Interview with professor from N University, Chengdu, May 2012.

10. Interview with Wenchuan County government official, February 2013.

11. Christopher McNally, "Sichuan: Driving Capitalist Development Westward," *China Quarterly* 178 (2004): 442–43.

12. Wang Bin, "Zai Zhonggong Wenchuanxian shi jie er ci quanwei (kuada) huishang de jianghua" [Speech given at the second meeting of the tenth Wenchuan County Communist Party Committee enlarged conference] (July 26, 2007).

13. Ibid.

14. Wang Bin, "Zai quanxian yijidu jingji xingshi fensi huiyishang de jianghua" [Speech given at the Wenchuan County First Quarter Economic Circumstances Analysis Conference] (April 30, 2008).

15. *Dongguanshi yuanjian yingxiu gongzuo dashiji jingxuan* [Dongguan Municipality reconstruction assistance work hand-selected record of major events] (2010).

16. "Yingxiu zhaokai chongjian yantaohui" [Yingxiu convenes reconstruction discussion session], Wenchuan County government website, May 25, 2009, available at http://www.wenchuan.gov.cn/p/st_news_items_i_x634089993846730000/; "Wenchuanxian Yingxiuzhen tese meili guihua" [Wenchuan County Yingxiu Township special characteristic charm plan], Aba Prefecture government website, December 2010, available at http://www.abazhou.gov.cn/ztjs/sbgc/cgzssbgc/tsmlxzsbgc2/wcsbgc3/201012/t20101227_309 299.html; Luo Zhenyu, "Dashi yunji, liangdian fencheng, gongjian zhenzhong Yingxiu—Yingxiuzhen jianshe 'xiandai kangzhen jianzhu bowuguan'" [A convergence of great masters, a brilliantly varied highlight, working together to construct the earthquake epicenter Yingxiu—The construction of Yingxiu Township's "modern anti-seismic architecture museum"]. From archive of Sichuan Provincial Party School.

17. Hal Foster, "After the White Cube," *London Review of Books* 37, no. 6 (March 2015): 25–26.

18. Wenchuan lüyouju [Wenchuan County Tourism Bureau], "Guanyu baosong 'Shiyiwu' gongzuo zongjie ji 2011 nian gongzuo anpai de baogao" [Report concerning the summary of 11th Fifth-Year Plan work and work plans for 2011], Document No. 141 (2010).

19. "Wenchuan 5A jingqu bei zhiyi: xiaofei zainan shangkou mo yan shi daode bangjia haishi shang qian baide" [Skepticism over Wenchuan's 5A scenic era: the consumption of disaster, wiping salt in a wound, is it the abduction of morality or evil business conduct?], *Shidai zhoubao* [Time Weekly], March 8, 2012, available at www.time-weekly.com/story/2012-03-08/122611.html.

20. Wang Xiaofang, "Sichuan lüyouju: Wei jiedao Wenchuan Yingxiu dizhen yizhi 5A jingqu shenbao cailiao" [Tourism Bureau has not yet received application information for Wenchuan County Yingxiu Township's earthquake ruins to become a 5A scenic attraction], *Xinhua*, February 23, 2012, available at http://news.xinhuanet.com/local/2012-02/23/c_122742857.htm.

21. Interview with tourism professor, L University, Chengdu, June 2012.

22. Interview with local resident 36, Yingxiu, June 2013.

23. Interview with hotel employee, Yingxiu, July 2012.

24. Interview with villager 55, Yingxiu, July 2012.

25. Interview with tourism professor, L University, Chengdu, April 2012.

26. John A. Donaldson, "Tourism, Development and Poverty Reduction in Guizhou and Yunnan," *China Quarterly* 190 (2007): 335.

27. Interview with noodle shop owner, Yingxiu, March 2012.

28. Many villagers expressed a sense of economic precariousness and lack of hope for ways to improve their situation. Interview with local resident 34, Yingxiu, July 2013.

29. Interview with several local residents, Yingxiu, July 2012.

30. Interview with local resident 61, Yingxiu, July 2012.

31. Interview with local husband and wife, Yingxiu, July 2012.

32. In April 2011, Shuimo Township was awarded the "Global Best Implementation of Post-Disaster Reconstruction" award at the United Nations Sixth Global Forum on Human Settlement; see http://news.xinhuanet.com/english2010/china/2011-04/26/c_13845512.htm. According to many local Shuimo residents, the situation there is scarcely better than the one in Yingxiu. Many businesses have already closed down for lack of business. Interviews with local residents, Shuimo Township, February 2013.

33. Interview with tourism professor, L University, Chengdu, April 2012.

34. See discussion in this chapter of July 2013 floods.

35. Interview with tourist from Shanghai in Yingxiu, February 2013.

36. Interview with small hotel owner, Yingxiu, July 2012.

37. "Sichuan Yingxiu: Dizhen lüyou houxu fazhan fali" [Yingxiu, Sichuan: The continued development of earthquake tourism lacking in strength], *Fenghuang shipin*, May 13,

2014, available at http://v.ifeng.com/news/society/2014005/01e9bf18-0d11-40e2-8ee9
-1f428ce78b03.shtml.

38. Li Li, "County Rebuilds after Quake," *China Daily*, February 1, 2011.

39. Interview with local resident 31, Yingxiu Township, July 2013.

40. Sun Xin, "Huidao dizhen zhongxin cunwei shuji de Yingxiu zhi huo" [Returning to the earthquake epicenter, Yingxiu's party secretary is puzzled], *Zhongguo qiyejia* [Chinese entrepreneur] (May 2011), available at http://finance.jrj.com.cn/biz/2011/05/12111 59949990.shtml.

41. Interview with local reporter, Yingxiu, July 2013.

42. Ibid.

43. Interview with local resident 31, Yingxiu, July 2013.

44. Interview with professor from B University, Hong Kong, May 2012.

45. Louisa Lim, "Five Years after a Quake, Chinese Cite Shoddy Reconstruction," *National Public Radio*, May 14, 2013, available at http://www.npr.org/blogs/parallels/2013 /05/14/183635289/Five-Years-After-A-Quake-Chinese-Cite-Shoddy-Reconstruction.

46. Andrew Jacobs, "4 Years after Quake, Some See a Resurrected Chinese City, Others Dashed Dreams," *New York Times*, May 21, 2014, available at http://www.nytimes .com/2014/05/22/world/asia/4-years-after-quake-some-see-a-resurrected-chinese-city -others-dashed-dreams.html?_r=0.

47. Interview with local Chengdu NGO worker, January 2013.

48. Mao Zedong, "Strive to Learn From Each Other and Don't Stick to the Beaten Track and Be Complacent," (December 1963), available at http://www.marxists.org/reference /archive/mao/selected-works/volume-9/mswv9_10.htm.

49. Yi Kang, *Disaster Management in China in a Changing Era* (New York: Springer, 2015), 58–59.

50. Chairman Xi Jinping's nationwide crackdown on undesirable work styles, such as lavish banqueting, official car use, and other special privileges, launched in 2013 is an attempt to manage this contradiction. See Dexter Roberts, "Xi Jinping Is No Fun," *Businessweek* (October 3, 2013), available at http://www.businessweek.com/articles/2013-10-03/china -president-xi-jinping-revives-self-criticism-sessions-in-maoism-lite.

51. Interview with local reporter, Yingxiu, June 2013.

52. Ibid. The reporter was explicitly warned by township officials not to develop too close of a relationship with me.

53. Weibo post. Downloaded file in author's possession.

54. Interview with Pi County official, February 2013.

55. Interview with local reporter, Yingxiu, June 2013.

56. Interview with villager 51, Yingxiu, April 2013.

57. Interview with villager 47, Yingxiu, July 2012.

58. "Yingxiu qunzhong qian xin ju guo xinnian" [Yingxiu masses move into their new homes to celebrate the new year"] Wenchuan County government, January 31, 2011, available at http://www.wenchuan.gov.cn/p/st_news_items_i_x634321492011450000/.

59. Interview with leader of grassroots NGO, Wenchuan County, February 2013.

60. Achille Mbembe, *On the Postcolony* (Berkeley: University of California Press, 2011), 111.

61. Interview with retired PLA cadre, March 2012.

62. William Hurst, Mingxing Liu, Yongdong Liu, and Ran Tao, "Reassessing Collective Petitioning in Rural China: Civic Engagement, Extra-State Violence, and Regional Variation," *Comparative Politics* 46, no. 4 (July 2014): 459–82.

63. "Wenchuan Yingxiuzhen qingyang ying 'caishen' lushi ailu bei kaowuzui" [Wenchuan County Yingxiu Township clearing the space to welcome the "God of Wealth": Lawyer

blocking road is manacled and gagged], October 18, 2010, available at http://www.360doc
.com/content/10/1018/10/84177_61936983.shtml.

64. *Wenchuan dadizhen yizhounian zaiqu qunzhong fangtanlü* [Wenchuan earthquake first anniversary disaster masses interview transcripts] (2009), restricted circulation publication.

65. Prior to the earthquake, Wenchuan County struggled with how to rectify overly
aggressive police behavior. At a 2006 conference dedicated to the education and rectification of the behavior of police cadres, Wenchuan Party secretary Wang raised the following concerns (which employ nearly identical terms used in Xi Jinping's current
speeches, indicating that these tropes have been in circulation long before Xi's tenure as
party secretary). "A police cadre's sole objective is to wholeheartedly serve the people. . . .
But there is a minority of police cadres who lack affection, understanding, and communication with the masses. When receiving the masses, they are impatient, unenthusiastic, and
aloof. Their door is hard to enter [*men nan jin*], facial expression is ugly to look at [*lian
nan kan*], and language is coarse [*hua nan ting*]. . . . Some cadres' law enforcement style is
simply rough and cruel with little respect for the persons involved, and totally ignorant of
the suffering of the people. . . . These problems injure our relationship with the masses. . . .
As soon as you put on a police uniform, and wear the national emblem, you have already
delivered yourself over to the nation; your each and every moment represents the national
interest and image of the nation" (*guojia de xingxiang*). Wang Bin, "Zai quanxian zhengfa
duiwu jingshi jiaoyu ji jizhong jiaoyu zhengdun dongyuan dahuishang de jianghua"
[Speech given at the Wenchuan County Politics and Law Troops and Concentrated Education Rectification Mobilization Large Conference] (December 16, 2006).

66. Interview with villager 47, Yingxiu, June 2012.

67. Interview with villagers 33, 39, 47, and 59, Yingxiu, March 2012.

68. Interview with Yingxiu X village party secretary, June 2012.

69. The fact that the township government never publicly disclosed why this village
was not given temporary housing unsurprisingly resulted in a proliferation of rumors
among the villagers. According to one account, a conglomerate owned by Deng Xiaoping's
eldest daughter previously purchased the land assigned to the village for the construction
of temporary housing. Local government officials did not want to "ruin" the property
by constructing temporary housing. Interview with villager 55, Yingxiu Township,
June 2013.

70. Interview with professor from B University who conducted social work in Yingxiu
Township, Hong Kong, May 2012.

71. Wang, Speech at Wenchuan Tenth Standing Committee Meeting, September
2008.

72. Qing Lidong, "Pa poshang kan zhua zhongdian, xushi tupo yu kuayue" [Climbing
up a slope on the threshold of grasping the important points, store up power to break
through and step across], Zai jiakuai tuijin shi da zhongdian gongzuo dongyuan huishang
de jianghua [Speech given at the conference for the accelerated promotion of ten large
important points concerning work mobilization] no. 5/96 (2010).

6. THE IDEOLOGICAL PURSUIT OF ECOLOGY

1. Guowuyuan fazhan yanjiu zhongxin [Development Research Center of the State
Council], "Sichuan sheng dizhen zaiqu hou chongjian shiqi: Jidai jiejue de wenti ji jianyi—
yi qingchuanxian wei li" [Sichuan Province earthquake post-disaster reconstruction period: Problems in urgent need of resolution and suggestions—the example of Qingchuan
County] 164, no. 3695 (September 10, 2010). Restricted access publication. Hereafter cited
as DRC Qingchuan.

2. "Kaifang zhuang ge han shanyue—qingchuan xian kuoda dui nei kaifang jishi" [The magnificent song of opening up shakes the lofty mountains—Qingchuan County enlarging internal openness to the outside], *Guangyuan shibao* [Guangyuan Times], September 15, 1999.

3. *Qingchuan xianzhi* [Qingchuan County annals], 1985 edition: 8 and 157.

4. Ibid.

5. Barry Naughton, "The Third Front: Defence Industrialization in the Chinese Interior," *China Quarterly* 115 (September 1988): 351–86.

6. "Kaifang zhuang ge."

7. DRC Qingchuan, 6.

8. According to the U.S. Geological Survey earthquake glossary, "the rupture front [or point] is the instantaneous boundary between the slipping and locked parts of a fault during an earthquake." See http://earthquake.usgs.gov/learn/glossary/?term=rupture%20 front.

9. *Wenchuan dadizhen yizhounian zaiqu qunzhong fangtanlü* [Wenchuan earthquake first anniversary disaster masses interview transcripts] (2009), restricted circulation publication.

10. DRC Qingchuan, 2.

11. Ibid., 6.

12. Ibid.

13. In Qingchuan, the post-earthquake Provincial Partner Assistance Program originated in a prototype experiment in 2001 when Zhejiang Province dispatched cadres from its Science and Technology Bureau to help Qingchuan upgrade its agricultural production methods and cultivate *grifola frondosa*, a polypore mushroom commonly known as "Sheep's Head" in English. As a result of this long-standing relationship, Zhejiang Province was paired to assist Qingchuan's reconstruction. "Hui shu hua 'hua' kai Qingchuan" [The blooming of *Grifola Frondosa* in Qingchuan], *Sichuan ribao* [Sichuan Daily], March 28, 2002.

14. An important goal of post-earthquake economic development in Qingchuan was for each village to produce a specific agricultural product associated with its name. This strategy, referred to as "one village, one product," dates back to at least 1995 when the *People's Daily* published an article on Qingchuan's cultivation methods. "Qingchuan linye xiaoyi lian nian dizeng" [Qingchuan's forestry increasing efficiency over time], *Rennmin ribao*, August 25, 1995.

15. Qingchuan's strategy of linking large-scale enterprises with individual peasant households in order to facilitate market linkage has a long history and is a national model for agricultural development. These linkages were central to the reconstruction strategy. "Qingchuan zhuanbian jingji zengzhang fangshi tuijin kechixu fazhan jishi" [Qingchuan promoting sustainable development and transforming economic growth model—record of events], *Guangyuan ribao*, March 15, 2006.

16. Reforestation was a popular policy in Qingchuan since the late 1990s. "Qingchuan xian shishi shengtai jianshe shiji" [Qingchuan County implementing ecological construction—record of events], *Guangyuan ribao*, September 27, 2005. Also, for a regional-level discussion, see Christine Jane Trac, Amanda H. Schmidt, Stevan Harrell, and Thomas M. Hinckley, "Is the Returning Farmland to Forest Program a Success? Three Case Studies from Sichuan," *Environmental Practice* 15, no. 3 (September 2013): 350–66; Alicia S. T. Robbins and Stevan Harrell, "Paradoxes and Challenges for China's Forests in the Reform Era," *China Quarterly* 218 (June 2014): 381–403.

17. "Qingchuan xian shishi shengtai jianshe."

18. Zhao Jianjun, "Jianshe shengtai wenming de ruogan sikao" [A few thoughts on building ecological civilization], *Lilun dongtai* [Theoretical trends] 1794 (October 20,

2008): 20–28. Restricted access publication; Qiu Baoxing, "Shengtai wenming shidai xiangcun jianshe de jiben duice" [The age of ecological civilization, fundamental measures for township and village construction] *Baogao xuan* [Selected reports] no. 4 (2008): 1–22. Restricted access publication.

19. Ketizu [Task Group], "Tansuo jingji he shengtai wenming xietiao fazhan de xin daolu" [Exploration of the new road of economic and ecological civilization coordinated development], *Lilun Dongtai* [Theoretical trends] 1817 (June 10, 2009): 34–40. Restricted access publication.

20. Sebastian Heilmann, "Policy Making through Experimentation: The Formation of a Distinctive Policy Process," in *Mao's Invisible Hand: The Political Foundations of Adaptive Governance in China*, ed. Sebastian Heilmann and Elizabeth J. Perry (Cambridge, MA: Harvard University Press, 2011), 62–101.

21. For an analysis of capitalism and ecological catastrophe, see Slavoj Žižek, *Living in the End Times* (London: Verso, 2011).

22. Frank N. Pieke, *The Good Communist: Elite Training and State Building in Today's China* (Cambridge: Cambridge University Press, 2009).

23. Zhao, "Jianshe shengtai wenming," 25.

24. Zhou Shengxian, "Nuli tuijin shengtai wenming jianshe: Jiji tansuo zhongguo huanjing baohu xin daolu" [Strive to promote ecological civilization construction: Actively explore a new road for China's environmental protection], *Baogao xuan* [Selected reports] 8, no. 320 (May 18, 2010): 6. Restricted access publication.

25. Ibid., 15.

26. Zhao, "Jianshe shengtai," 20; Zhou, "Nuli tuijin shengtai wenming," 8.

27. Zhonggong zhongyang dangxiao baokan she ketizu [Central Committee of the Communist Party of China Party School Press Research Group], "Jiakuai shengtai baohu diqu shengtai buchang jizhi de jianli" [Accelerate environmental protection areas and the construction of ecological compensation mechanisms], *Lilun Dongtai* [Theoretical trends] 1867 (October 30, 2010): 29–34. Restricted access publication.

28. *Qingchuan xian guomin jingji he shehui fazhan "shi er wu" guihua gangyao* [Qingchuan County national economy and social development 12th Five-Year Plan outline], hereafter Qingchuan 12th Five-Year Plan.

29. Ibid.

30. Ibid.

31. Task Group, "Tansuo jingji he shengtai wenming," 37.

32. Ann Anagnost, "The Corporeal Politics of Quality (Suzhi)," *Public Culture* 16, no. 2 (2004):189–208.

33. Cai Xia, "Jiefang sixiang xuyao shenme" [What is needed for the liberation of thinking?]. *Lilun Dongtai* [Theoretical Trends] 1171 (February 29, 2008): 10–17. Restricted access publication; Zhao, "Jianshe shengtai," 20–28; Zhou, "Nuli tuijin shengtai wenming," 6.

34. Ibid.

35. Interview with Qingchuan County, Hongguang Township, Party secretary, May 2013.

36. "Fandui xingshizhuyi, zhong zai wushi" [Oppose formalism and deal with concrete issues again], *Renmin ribao pinglun bu* [People's Daily Commentary Section] June 20, 2013 available at http://opinion.people.com.cn/n/2013/0620/c1003-21902561.html.

37. May 10, 2014, Twitter.

38. Qingchuan xianwei [Qingchuan County Party Committee], "Chuangjian shengtai wenming shifan xian de jueding" [Decision to establish ecological civilization model county], Document No. 357 (November 11, 2011); "Qingchuan 'Shengtai wenming shifan xian' jianshe zhashi tuijin" [Qingchuan "ecological civilization model county" construction

advances firmly] *Meili Zhongguo* [Charismatic China] (January 26, 2014), available at http://ml.china.com.cn/html/mingxian/csfc/20140126/308375.html.

39. Qingchuan 12th Five-Year Plan.

40. These include the Open Up the West and Build a New Socialist Countryside Campaigns.

41. Qingchuan 12th Five-Year Plan.

42. Ibid.

43. Ibid.

44. Ibid.

45. Ibid.

46. DRC Qingchuan, 4.

47. Qingchuan 12th Five-Year Plan.

48. Interview, Zhejiang Province, January 2013.

49. Ibid.

50. DRC Qingchuan, 6.

51. Interview with local resident, Qingchuan, June 2013.

52. DRC Qingchuan, 7.

53. DRC Qingchuan, 5.

54. On the basis of my interviews in other earthquake counties, even into late 2013, loan repayment continued to be a major anxiety and difficulty for local residents. One visibly anxious village Party secretary from Mao County told me that "although the houses look good from the outside, villagers are unable repay their loans. They put it off for as long as they can, and in the meantime, the inside of their houses remain empty." Interview with Party secretary from X Village, Mao County, July 2012.

55. The Qingchuan government is also engaged in a series of "poverty alleviation" projects that mainly consist in assigning leading cadres, including the ten members of the Qingchuan County Party standing committee, responsibility for improving the economic situation of poor, individual households. These cadres form a "poverty alleviation leadership small group." These "one-on-one" pairings enable cadres to individually provide "investment capital" and "technology training" to impoverished households. The county also set up a "poverty alleviation hotline" for people to call in case of economic and production emergencies. Interview with Qingchuan County Poverty Alleviation and Migration Bureau bureau chief, Qingchuan, May 2013.

56. Qingchuan 12th Five-Year Plan.

57. Ibid.

58. In 2000, Qingchuan villagers started a "rabbit-raising fur-growing association." "Qingchuan nongmin yi shang cu nong" [Qingchuan villagers doing business to promote agriculture], *Sichuan nongcun ribao* [Sichuan Village Daily], (February 2, 2003).

59. Interview with Qingchuan County, Hongguang Township party secretary, May 2013.

60. This is a common trope in scholarship on local governance in China (especially rural China).

61. Interview with villager, Qingchuan, May 2013.

62. Interview with township official, Qingchuan, May 2013.

63. Ibid.

64. See discussion in chapter 3.

65. Guangyuanshi shizhang xinxiang [Guangyuan City Mayor's Mailbox] "Dailing nongcun zhifu" [Leading the village to become rich] (February 15, 2012), available at http://gymail.gy169.net/article.asp?id=57581.

66. Mao Zedong, "A Single Spark Can Start a Prairie Fire" (January 5, 1930). Translation public, available at https://www.marxists.org/reference/archive/mao/selected-works

/volume-1/mswv1_6.htm; the Chinese phrase *zhifu guangrong*, meaning "wealth is glorious"—often misquoted as "to get rich is glorious"—is commonly attributed to Deng Xiaoping, although there is no proof that he uttered the phrase. Evelyn Iritani, "Great Idea but Don't Quote Him," *Los Angeles Times*, September 9, 2004 available at http://articles .latimes.com/2004/sep/09/business/fi-deng9.

67. *Wenchuan dadizhen fangtanlü.*

68. Ibid.

69. The transformation of labor from agricultural to nonagricultural (*zhuanyi laodong*) is a policy objective that is included in cadre evaluation indices.

70. Lauren Berlant, *Cruel Optimism* (Durham, NC: Duke University Press, 2011).

71. *Wenchuan dadizhen fangtanlü.*

72. Ibid.

73. Ibid.

74. Xu Kai, "Qingchuan quanli jiakuai xin xiancheng chongjian jianwen" [Qingchuan all-out acceleration of reconstruction of new county seat information], *Fenghuang* (November 24, 2010), available at http://news.ifeng.com/gundong/detail_2010_11/24 /3214194_0.shtml.

75. Ibid.

76. Ibid.

77. Ibid.

78. "Anzhao 4A ji jingqu shengji Qingchuan xiancheng" [According to 4A grade scenic area improve the Qingchuan's county seat], *Guangyuan xinwen* [Guangyuan News], May 15, 2012, available at http://www.gysta.gov.cn/gyjmgzt/lybz/system/2012/05/15 /000154483.html.

79. In March 2014 it was announced that forestry bureau chief Li was under investigation for charges of disciplinary violations, corruption, and the acceptance of bribes. No further details were released. "Sichuan Guangyuan dui fubai ling rongren: Qunian chachu 15 ming xianji ganbu" [Sichuan's Guangyuan shows zero tolerance for corruption: Last year 15 county-level cadres investigated] *Zhongguo xinwen wang* [China News Net], March 11, 2014, available at http://www.nd.chinanews.com/News/xwdc/20140311 /1682855.html.

80. Xu Kai, "Qingchuan quanli jiakuai xin xiancheng chongjian."

81. Interview with local resident, Qingchuan, May 2013.

82. Ibid.

83. Ibid.

84. Ibid.

85. Interviews with local residents, Qingchuan, May 2013.

86. Xu Kai, "Qingchuan quanli jiakuai xin xiancheng chongjian"; interview with Qingchuan X Township deputy mayor, May 2013.

87. Xu Kai, "Qingchuan quanli jiakuai xin xiancheng chongjian."

88. Ibid.

89. Ibid.

90. Qingchuanxian waixuan ban [Qingchuan County External Propaganda Office], "Wo xian kai xiancheng duanlie dai chaichu chaiqian gongzuo huiyi" [County-Seat Fault-Zone Demolition Work Conference] reported on February 15, 2012. Web page has been subsequently removed.

91. Ibid.

92. Interview with secretary of county mayor, Qingchuan, May 2013.

93. Interview with Qingchuan Township X deputy mayor, Qingchuan, May 2013.

94. Ibid.

95. Interview with NGO worker, Mianzhu, March 2012.

96. William Hurst, Mingxing Liu, Yongdong Liu, and Ran Tao, "Reassessing Collective Petitioning in Rural China: Civic Engagement, Extra-State Violence, and Regional Variation," *Comparative Politics* 46, no. 4 (July 2014): 459–82.

97. Interview with local nail house resident, Qingchuan, May 2013.

98. Ibid.

99. Interview with husband and wife, Qingchuan, May 2013.

100. "Fayuan li quan dingzihu zhu tui Qingchuan zaihou chongjian" [Court strenuously urges nail houses to assist in pushing forward Qingchuan's post-disaster reconstruction], *Meili Zhongguo* [Charismatic China], October 24, 2013, available at http://ml.china.com.cn/guangyuan/zfbd/20131024/257195.html.

101. Kwai Hang Ng and Xin He, "Internal Contradictions of Judicial Mediation in China," *Law & Social Inquiry* 39, no. 2 (Spring 2014): 285–312.

102. Wu Yue, "Wenchuan zaiqu chongjian gao mianzi gongcheng: Zhengfu dalou 'zui chaobiao'" [Wenchuan earthquake zone reconstruction engages in face projects: Government buildings that exceed the acceptable limit] *Sohu*, May 11, 2012, available at http://news.sohu.com/20120511/n342984097.shtml.

103. Ibid.

104. *Wenchuan dadizhen fangtanlü.*

105. See http://baike.baidu.com/view/146488.htm.

106. Interview with local cadre, Pengzhou, March 2012.

107. Interview with local resident, Qingchuan County, June 2013.

108. Jason Stanley, *How Propaganda Works* (Princeton, NJ: Princeton University Press, 2015).

109. Wang Hui, *China's Twentieth Century: Revolution, Retreat, and the Road to Equality* (London: Verso, 2016), 298.

CONCLUSION

1. Letter from Rousseau to Voltaire, August 18, 1758, in J. A. Leigh, ed., *Correspondence complète de Jean Jacques Rousseau*, vol. 4, trans. R. Spang (Geneva, 1967): 37–50.

2. Endymion Wilkinson, *Chinese History: A New Manual, Fourth Edition* (Cambridge, MA: Harvard University Asia Center, 2015), 198.

3. *I Ching* (Yijing) [The Book of Change], trans. with an intro. and commentary by John Minford (New York: Penguin, 2015), 716–17.

4. Geremie R. Barmé, "New Sinology," first published in the *Chinese Studies Association of Australia Newsletter* no. 31 (2005), available online at http://ciw.anu.edu.au/new_sinology/.

5. Lisa Wedeen, memo for the National Science Foundation Workshop, unpublished manuscript (2005).

6. My argument to take seriously Communist Party discourse calls for a practice of critical reading and should not be conflated with the Communist Party's claim to have monopoly over the "discursive rights" (*huayuquan*) to tell the China story. See Dai Mucai, "Cong sixiang he jiazhiguan shang dazao 'zhongguo huayuquan'" [Creating "China's discursive authority/right on the basis of its thought and value system], *Hongqi wengao* (March 23, 2015), available at http://theory.people.com.cn/n/2015/0323/c143844-26737090.html.

7. "Discourses are not once and for all subservient to power or raised up against it. . . . We must make allowances for the complex and unstable process whereby a discourse can be both an instrument and an effect of power, but also a hindrance, a stumbling point of resistance and a starting point for an opposing strategy. Discourse transmits and produces power; it reinforces it, but also undermines and exposes it, renders it fragile and makes it possible to thwart." Michel Foucault, *The History of Sexuality: An Introduction*, trans. Robert Hurley (London: Penguin Books, 1990), 100–101.

8. Lauren Berlant, Sina Najafi, and David Serlin, "The Broken Circuit: An Interview with Lauren Berlant," *Cabinet Magazine* 31 (Fall 2008), available at www.cabinetmagazine .org/issues/31/najafi_serlin.php.

9. In 2015 alone, the Chinese state had to respond to and manage the following "emergencies" (*tufa shijian*): on January 1, the New Year's Eve stampede in Shanghai during which thirty-six people were trampled to death; springtime flooding in the south of China that resulted in over one hundred fatalities; on June 1 in Hubei Province, 440 people drowned when the Oriental Star Ferry cruise ship capsized; the Binhai New Area chemical warehouse explosion in Tianjian on August 12 that resulted in over 170 casualties, massive property destruction, and an enormous crater at the blast site; coal-mine fires in Heilongjiang Province on November 20 and December 16 during which forty-one people died; and, on December 20, the deadly landslide in Shenzhen caused by the collapse of a mountain of illegally dumped construction waste. See Russell Goldman, "A Year of Disasters in China," *New York Times*, December 21, 2015, available at http://www.nytimes.com /interactive/2015/12/21/world/asia/china-diaster-landslide-ship-coal-mine-explosion .html.

10. David Sheppard and Scott Disavino, "Superstorm Sandy Cuts Power to 8.1 Million Houses," *Reuters*, October 30, 2012, available at http://www.reuters.com/article/us-storm -sandy-powercuts-idUSBRE89T10G20121030.

11. Sui-Lee Wee, "China Sends Riot Police to Block New Protests by Flood Victims," *Reuters*, October 16, 2013, available at http://www.reuters.com/article/us-china-protest -idUSBRE99F0BN20131016?utm.

12. Mao Zedong, "Serve the People," translation public (September 8, 1944), available at https://www.marxists.org/reference/archive/mao/selected-works/volume-3/mswv3_19 .htm.

13. This gap was exposed in the Internet scandal that erupted in 2009 in Zhengzhou, the capital of Henan Province, as a result of a local reporter's investigation into a dispute over land demolition. After the departmental vice director of urban planning Lu Jun examined the petition materials prepared by a local resident, he addressed the reporter: "Do you speak for the Party or the people? (*ti dang shuohua, haishi ti laobaixing shuohua*)?" The admission of a gap between the interests of the Party and those of the people was scandalous not because it revealed anything new about state-led dispossession of rural land but because it publicly acknowledged the inadmissible. See Anne Henochowicz, "Do You Speak for the Party or the People?" *China Digital Times*, March 17, 2016, available at http:// chinadigitaltimes.net/2016/03/speak-party-people.

14. Christian Sorace, "Ai Weiwei: China's Last Communist," *Critical Inquiry* 40, no. 2 (February 2014): 412–15.

15. Shawn Shieh and Deng Guosheng, "An Emerging Civil Society: The Impact of the 2008 Sichuan Earthquake on Grass-Roots Associations in China," *China Journal*, vol. 65 (2011): 181.

16. Andrew Mertha, "Stressing Out": Cadre Calibration and Affective Proximity to the CCP in Reform-Era China," *China Quarterly*, forthcoming.

17. The failure of these industrial "transplants" and capital "transfusions" to promote sustainable development resulted in an "anemic" (*pin xue*) economy in the earthquake zone.

Glossary of Terms and Phrases

anemia	贫血	pínxùe
benevolence	仁爱	rén'ài
bid farewell to sorrow and face the future	告别创痛，面向未来	gàobié chuāngtòng, miànxiàng wèilái
blood generation	造血	zàoxùe
blood transfusion	输血	shūxùe
cadre	干部	gànbù
calamity prompts renewal and awakens the nation	多难兴邦	duōnàn xīngbāng
capital to the countryside	资本下乡	zīběn xiàxiāng
capitalization of village resources	农村资源变资本	nóngcūn zīyuán biàn zīběn
catch sparrows blindfolded (to act blindly)	闭塞眼睛捉麻雀	bìsè yǎnjīng zhuō máquè
confer a favor and seek reciprocity	施恩望报	shī'ēn wàngbào
construction	建设	jiànshè
crisis	危机	wēijī
criticism	批评	pīpíng
cultivation	修养	xiūyǎng
democratic centralism	民主集中制	mínzhǔjízhōngzhì
demonstrate or prove through argument	论证	lùnzhèng
dragonfly touching water lightly (superficial contact)	蜻蜓点水	qíngtīng diǎnshuǐ
earthquake	地震	dìzhèn
[an] earthquake doesn't care, the Party does	地震无情，党有情	dìzhèn wúqíng, dǎng yǒuqíng
ecological civilization	生态文明	shēngtài wénmíng
emergency	突发事件	tūfā shìjiàn
expansion of domestic demand	扩大内需	kuòdà nèixū

face project	面子工程	miànzi gōngchéng
faith	信仰	xìnyǎng
formalism	形式主义	xíngshìzhǔyì
fruitless flower (flashy exterior but hollow inside)	华而不实	huá'ér bùshí
glory	光荣	guāngróng
gratitude education	感恩教育	gǎn'ēn jiàoyù
great leap development	跨越式发展	kuàyuèshì fāzhǎn
great rejuvenation of the Chinese nation	中华民族伟大复兴	zhōnghuámínzú wěidà fùxīng
harmonious society	和谐社会	héxié shèhuì
human nature	人性	rénxìng
ideology	意识形态	yìshíxíngtài
idle	闲	xián
inciting the subversion of state power	煽动颠覆国家政权	shāndòng diānfù guójiā zhèngquán
industrial relocation	产业转移	chǎnyè zhuǎnyí
intimate	亲密	qīnmì
irrigated pork (statistical inflation)	灌水猪肉	guànshuǐ zhūròu
leadership inspection visit	领导视察	lǐngdǎo shìchá
look at flowers from horseback (superficial understanding)	走马观花	zǒumǎ guānhuā
mandate of heaven	天命	tiānmìng
manmade catastrophe	人祸	rénhuò
marginalized and vulnerable group	弱势群体	ruòshì qúntǐ
mass line	群众路线	qúnzhòng lùxiàn
methods in line with local circumstances	因地制宜	yīndì zhìyí
miracle	奇迹	qíjì
moderately prosperous society	小康社会	xiǎokāng shèhuì
mountains of paperwork and a sea of mountains	文山会海	wénshān huìhǎi
nail house	钉子户	dīngzihù
natural disaster	天灾	tiānzāi
new normal	新常态	xīn chángtài
new urban citizen construction	新市民建设	xīn shìmín jiànshè

no difficulties can defeat the heroism of the Chinese people	任何困难都难不倒英雄的中国人民中国人民	rènhé kùnnan dōu nánbùdǎo yīngxióng de zhōngguó rénmín
partner assistance program	对口支援	duìkǒu zhīyuán
party image	党的形象	dǎngde xíngxiàng
party spirit	党性	dǎngxìng
post-disaster settlement	集中安置点	jízhōng ānzhìdiǎn
recall the bitterness of the old society and savor the sweetness of the present	忆苦思甜	yìkǔ sītían
rectification of names	正名	zhèngmíng
reflection	反思	fǎnsī
same boat under wind and rain	风雨同舟	fēngyǔ tóngzhōu
saving oneself through production (self-help)	生产自救	shēngchǎn zìjiù
seek truth from facts	实事求是	shíshì qiúshì
self-reliance	自力更生	zìlì gēngshēng
serve the people	为人民服务	wèi rénmín fúwù
shed blood and sweat but not tears; shed skin, shed flesh, but do not fall behind	流血流汗不流泪，掉皮掉肉不掉队	liúxuè liúhàn bù liúlèi, diàopí diàoròu bù diàoduì
a single word may rejuvenate a country; a single word may bring disaster to a country	一言兴邦，一言丧邦	yīyán xīngbāng, yīyán sāng bāng
social stability maintenance	维护社会稳定	wéihù shèhuì wěndìng
speaking bitterness	诉苦	sùkǔ
sustainable development	可持续发展	kěchíxù fāzhǎn
those who gain the hearts of the people gain all under heaven; those who lose the hearts of the people lose the world	得人心者得天下，失人心者失天下	dé rénxīnzhě de tiānxià, shī rénxīnzhě shī tiānxià
thought work	思想工作	sīxiǎng gōngzuò
three concentrations	三个集中	sānge jízhōng
tofu-dregs schoolhouses	豆腐渣校舍	dòufuzhā xiàoshè
transition	转变	zhuǎnbiàn
treat the disease to save the patient	治病救人	zhìbìng jiùrén

urban pathologies	城市病	chéngshìbìng
urban-rural integration	城乡一体化	chéngxiāngyītǐhuà
waiting, depending, and demanding	等，靠，要	děng, kào, yào
when drinking water, remember the well-digger; we rely on the Communist Party for happiness	吃水不忘挖井人，幸福全靠共产党	chīshuǐ bù wàng wā jǐng rén, xìngfú quán kào gòngchǎndǎng
while the waters can bear the boat, they can also sink it	水能载舟，亦能覆舟	shuǐ néng zài zhōu, yì néng fù zhōu
without the Party organization, I would not be alive	没有党组织，就没有我的生命	méiyǒu dǎng zǔzhī, jiù méiyǒu wǒde shēngmìng
work style	工作作风	gōngzuò zuòfēng
vanity	虚荣	xūróng

Bibliography

A Jian. *Zai nanzhong: Shendu fangtan beichuan xiangzhen shuji* [In the midst of difficulty: In-depth interviews with Beichuan Township party secretaries]. Beijing: Renmin wenxue chubanshe, 2009.

Abramson, Daniel, and Yu Qi. "Urban–Rural Integration in the Earthquake Zone: Sichuan's Post-Disaster Reconstruction and the Expansion of the Chengdu Metropole." *Pacific Affairs* 84, no. 3 (2011): 495–523.

After the Tangshan Earthquake: How the Chinese People Overcame a Major Natural Disaster. Peking: Foreign Languages Press, 1976.

Agamben, Giorgio. *The Kingdom and the Glory: For a Theological Genealogy of Economy and Government.* Translated by Lorenzo Chiesa (with Matteo Mandarini). Stanford, CA: Stanford University Press, 2011.

Alia. "Traces on Weibo: How a NIMBY protest turned violent in a small Sichuan city?" *Offbeat China,* July 2, 2012, available at http://offbeatchina.com/traces-on-weibo-how-a-nimby-protest-turned-violent-in-a-small-sichuan-city.

Allison, Anne. *Precarious Japan.* Durham, NC: Duke University Press, 2013.

Althusser, Louis. *Machiavelli and Us.* Translated by Gregory Elliott. London: Verso, 1999.

——. *On Ideology.* Translated by Ben Brewster. London: Verso, 2008.

——. "Philosophy as a Revolutionary Weapon." In *Lenin and Philosophy and Other Essays,* translated by Ben Brewster, 1–10. New York: Monthly Review Press, 2001.

——. *Philosophy of the Encounter: Later Writings, 1978–1987.* Translated by G. M. Goshgarian. London: Verso, 2006.

Anagnost, Ann. "The Corporeal Politics of Quality (Suzhi)." *Public Culture* 16, no. 2 (2004): 189–208.

——. *National Past-Times: Narrative, Representation, and Power in Modern China.* Durham, NC: Duke University Press, 1997.

Anderlini, Jamil. "How Long Can the Communist Party Survive in China?" *Financial Times,* September 20, 2013, available at http://www.ft.com/cms/s/2/533a6374-1fdc-11e3-8861-00144feab7de.html#slide0.

Andreas, Joel. *Rise of the Red Engineers: The Cultural Revolution and the Origins of China's New Class.* Stanford, CA: Stanford University Press, 2009.

"Anzhao 4A ji jingqu shengji Qingchuan xiancheng" [According to 4A grade scenic area improve the Qingchuan's county seat]. *Guangyuan xinwen* [Guangyuan News]. May 15, 2012, available at http://www.gysta.gov.cn/gyjmgzt/lybz/system/2012/05/15/000154483.html.

Apter, David E., and Tony Saich. *Revolutionary Discourse in Mao's Republic.* Cambridge, MA: Harvard University Press, 1994.

Augustine. *The City of God against the Pagans.* Edited by R. W. Dyson. Cambridge: Cambridge University Press, 1998.

Auslin, Michael. "The Twilight of China's Communist Party." *Wall Street Journal,* January 29, 2015, available at http://www.wsj.com/articles/michael-auslin-the-twilight-of-chinas-communist-party-142255178.

Bakken, Børge. *The Exemplary Society: Human Improvement, Social Control, and the Dangers of Modernity.* Oxford: Oxford University Press, 2000.

Balibar, Étienne. "Althusser's Dramaturgy and the Critique of Ideology." *differences* 26, no. 3 (2015): 1–22.

Bandurski, David. "The Politics of Senseless Tragedy." *medium*, August 17, 2015, available at https://medium.com/@cmphku/the-politics-of-senseless-tragedy-12cc9230fa4# .f06pmy94l.

Banyan editorial. "A Confession to Make." *The Economist*, January 30, 2016, available at http://www.economist.com/news/china/21689620-what-current-vogue-televised -confessions-and-apologies-says-about-xi-jinpings-china.

Bargu, Banu. "Althusser's Materialist Theater: Ideology and Its Aporias." *differences* 26, no. 3 (2015): 81–106.

Barmé, Geremie R. "Confession, Redemption, and Death: Liu Xiaobo and the Protest Movement of 1989." In *The Broken Mirror: China After Tiananmen*. Edited by George Hicks, 52–99. London, Longmans, 1990.

——. *In the Red: On Contemporary Chinese Culture*. New York: Columbia University Press, 2000.

——. "New Sinology." First published in the *Chinese Studies Association of Australia Newsletter*, no. 31 (2005), available at http://ciw.anu.edu.au/new_sinology/.

——. "1989, 1999, 2009: Totalitarian Nostalgia." *China Heritage Quarterly* 18 (June 2009).

——. *Shades of Mao: The Posthumous Cult of the Great Leader*. London: Routledge, 1996.

Beichuan ganbu zhenhou shangwang fankuibao [Post-Earthquake information report on the injury and death situation of Beichuan cadres]. Confidential party document.

Berlant, Lauren. *Cruel Optimism*. Durham, NC: Duke University Press, 2011.

Bloch, Marc. The Royal Touch: Sacred Monarchy and Scrofula in England and France. Kingston, ON: McGill-Queen's University Press, 1973.

Bradsher, Kenneth. "Chinese Officials Cancel Plant Project amid Protests." *New York Times*, July 5, 2012, available at http://www.nytimes.com/2012/07/05/world/asia/chinese -officials-cancel-plant-project-amid-protests.html?_r=0.

Brady, Anne-Marie. *Marketing Dictatorship: Propaganda and Thought Work in Contemporary China*. Lanham, MD: Rowman and Littlefield, 2009.

Branigan, Tania. "China Jails Investigator into Sichuan Earthquake Schools." *The Guardian*, February 9, 2010, available at http://www.theguardian.com/world/2010/feb/09 /china-eathquake-schools-activist-jailed.

Bray, David. "Urban Planning Goes Rural: Conceptualising the 'New Village.'" *China Perspectives* (2013): 53–63.

Buckley, Chris. "China's President Returns to Mao's (and His) Roots in Yan'an." *New York Times*, February 13, 2015, available at http://sinosphere.blogs.nytimes.com/2015/02 /13/chinese-president-returns-to-maos-and-his-roots-in-yanan/?_r=0.

Butler, Judith. *The Psychic Life of Power: Theories in Subjection*. Stanford, CA: Stanford University Press, 1997.

Cai Xia. "Jiefang sixiang xuyao shenme" [What is needed for the liberation of thinking?]. *Lilun Dongtai* [Theoretical Trends] Vol. 1171 (February 29, 2008): 10–17. Restricted access publication.

Cai Yongshun. "Irresponsible State: Local Cadres and Image-Building in China." *Journal of Communist Studies and Transition Politics* 20, no. 4 (2004): 20–41.

Caputo, John D., and Michael J. Scanlon, eds. *God, the Gift, and Postmodernism*. Bloomington: Indiana University Press, 1999.

Cartier, Carolyn. "Governmentality and the Urban Economy: Consumption, Excess, and the 'Civilized City' in China." In *New Mentalities of Government in China*, edited by David Bray and Elaine Jeffreys, 56–73. London: Routledge, 2016.

Chan, Anita. *Children of Mao: Personality Development and Political Activism in the Red Guard Generation*. London: Macmillan, 1985.

Cheek, Timothy. "The Names of Rectification: Notes on the Conceptual Domains of CCP Ideology in the Yan'an Rectification Movement." Indiana University East Asian Studies Center working paper series (January 1996).

Chen Donglin. "'San nian ziran zaihai' yu 'dayuejin'—'Tianzai,' 'Renhuo' guanxi de jiliang lishi kaocha" [Three years of natural disaster and the Great Leap Forward—The relationship between "natural disaster" and "human catastrophe" as a measurement and test of history]. *Zhongguo nongye lishi yu wenhua* [Chinese agricultural history and culture], available at http://agri-history.ihns.ac.cn/scholars/others/cdl.htm.

Chen Guaming. *Wenchuan dizhenhou huifu chongjian zhuyao falü wenti* [Research on main legal issues in post–Wenchuan earthquake rehabilitation and reconstruction]. Beijing: Falü chubanshe, 2010.

Chen Qiu, and Yan Qianmin. "Zaihou wenchuan jiceng ganbu xinli jiankang zhuangkuang diaocha ji tiaoshi duice yanjiu" [Post-Disaster Wenchuan grassroots cadres psychological health situation investigation and proposed remedies]. *Xinan minzu daxue xuebao* [Southwestern University for Nationalities Journal] 2 (2011): 85–89.

Chen Tao. "Social Workers as Conflict Mediator: Lessons from the Wenchuan Earthquake." *China Journal of Social Work* 3 (2009): 179–87.

Chengxiangyitihua: Chengdu de kexue fazhan zhi lu [Urban-rural integration as the road to Chengdu's scientific development]. Chengdu: Chengdu shidai chubanshe, 2007.

"China's Stockmarket Crash: A Red Flag." *The Economist*, July 7, 2015, available at http://www.economist.com/blogs/freeexchange/2015/07/chinas-stockmarket-crash.

Cho, Mun Young. *The Specter of "the People": Urban Poverty in Northeast China*. Ithaca, NY: Cornell University Press, 2013.

Chu, Julie. "When Infrastructures Attack: The Workings of Disrepair in China." *American Ethnologist* 41, no. 2 (2014): 351–67.

Ci, Jiwei. *Moral China in the Age of Reform*. Cambridge: Cambridge University Press, 2014.

Confucius. *The Analects*. Edited by Michael Nylan, translated by Simon Leys. New York: W. W. Norton, 2014.

Coser, Lewis. *Masters of Sociological Thought*, 2nd ed. 230–31. New York: Harcourt, 1997.

Curran, Enda. "In China, Focus of Monetary Easing Turns to Surgical Strikes." *Bloomberg*, April 29, 2015, available at http://www.bloomberg.com/news/articles/2015-04-29/in-china-focus-of-monetary-easing-turns-to-surgical-strikes.

Dai Mucai. "Cong sixiang he jiazhiguan shang dazao 'zhongguo huayuquan'" [Creating 'China's discursive authority/right' on the basis of its thought and value system]. *Hongqi wengao*, March 23, 2015, available at http://theory.people.com.cn/n/2015/0323/c143844-26737090.html.

Daniell, James. "Sichuan 2008: A Disaster on an Immense Scale." *BBC*, last updated May 9, 2013, available at www.bbc.com/news/science-environment-22398684.

Davies, Gloria. *Worrying about China: The Language of Chinese Critical Inquiry*. Cambridge, MA: Harvard University Press, 2007.

Deleuze, Gilles, and Felix Guattari. *A Thousand Plateaus*, translated by Brian Massumi. Minneapolis: University of Minnesota Press, 2003.

Deng Rong. "Nongcun juzhu xingtai gaibian yu shengchan fangshi, guanli moshi de chonggou: Guanyu Dujiangyanshi nongmin jizhong juzhu hou xiangguan wenti de diaocha yu sikao" [Transformations in the circumstances of village living and modes of production, reconstructing modes of management: Investigation and reflection concerning problems in the concentration of peasant housing in Dujiangyan]. In *Dujiangyanshi di shi san qi qingnian ganbu peixunban diaoyan wenji* huibian [Collected essays from Dujiangyan youth cadre training class], edited by Dujiangyan shiwei dangxiao [Dujiangyan Party School]. (July 2011). Restricted circulation publication.

Deng Xiaoping. "Uphold the Four Cardinal Principles." (March 30, 1979), available at http://en.people.cn/dengxp/vol2/text/b1290.html.

Diao Xingze. "Xingshizhuyi de pingpan biaozhun" [Criteria for Appraising Formalism]. *Lilun renmin wang* [People's Daily Online, Theory section], December 4, 2013, available at http://theory.people.com.cn/n/2013/1204/c40537-23743924.html.

Dikötter, Frank. *Mao's Great Famine: The History of China's Most Devastating Catastrophe, 1958–1962.* New York: Walker, 2011.

"Dizhen zhounian ji, dangxin zisha fengchao laixi" [On the first anniversary of the earthquake, on the lookout for a wave of suicides]. May 14, 2009, available at http://www.rdzx.net/xlzx/ShowArt.asp?id=114.

"Does Xi Represent a Return to the Mao Era?" *The China File* roundtable discussion. June 16, 2015, available at http://www.chinafile.com/reporting-opinion/features/does-xi-jinping-represent-return-mao-era.

Donaldson, John A. "Tourism, Development and Poverty Reduction in Guizhou and Yunnan." *China Quarterly* 190 (2007): 333–51.

Dongguanshi yuanjian yingxiu gongzuo dashiji jingxuan [Dongguan Municipality reconstruction assistance work hand-selected record of major events] (2010).

Dujiangyan: Minyi de chongjian [Dujiangyan: Reconstruction according to the will of the people]. CCTV documentary (May 2011), available at http://news.cntv.cn/china/20110521/105513.shtml.

Dujiangyanshi dangxiao [Dujiangyan Communist Party School]. *Gongchandang, haowubian: Houchongjian shidai dangyuan ganbu dangxing jiaoyu wenji xuanbian* [The party's heroism and shared responsibility: Selected works on post–reconstruction era Party member and cadre education]. Restricted access publication.

———. *Huifu, fazhan, chuangxin: 2009 nian zaihou chongjian youxiu yanjiu wenji xuanbian* [Reconstruction, development, innovation: Selected works of excellent research reports regarding the 2009 post-disaster reconstruction situation]. Restricted circulation publication.

Dujiangyanshi nongcun chanquan zhidu gaige gongzuo lingdao xiaozu bangongshi wenjian [Dujiangyan Municipality Village Property Rights System Reform Leadership Working Small Group]. *Dujiangyanshi jititudi suoyouquan quequan banzheng caozuo banfa, shixing* [Dujiangyan Municipality collective land property rights: Work methods for confirmation of rights and conferral of proof, pilot]. Document No. 1 (February 2008).

———. Dujiangyan Municipality's Temporary Measures for Arbitrating Disputes Regarding Village Land Contracting Transfer of Village Land Circulation. Document No. 6 (2008).

———. *Guanyu jianli nongcun chanquan zhidu gaige maodun jiufen yufang, tiaochu, huajie gongzuo jizhi de yijian* [Opinions regarding the establishment of a precaution, investigation and resolution work system for the contradictions and disputes of the reform of the village property rights system reform]. Document No. 7 (2008).

Dujiangyanshi tongchou chengxiang gongzuoju wenjian [Dujiangyan Municipality Overall Planning Urban-Rural Work Department]. "Guanyu shenhua tongchou chengxiang zonghe peitao gaige tuijin chengxiangyitihua de yijian" [Opinions regarding deepening comprehensive integration reform promoting urban-rural integration]. Document No. 55 (2009).

Dutton, Michael. "Mango Mao: Infections of the Sacred." *Public Culture* 16, no. 2 (2004): 161–87.

Edgerton-Tarpley, Kathryn Jean. "From 'Nourish the People' to 'Sacrifice for the Nation': Changing Responses to Disaster in Late Imperial and Modern China." *Journal of Asian Studies* 73, no. 2 (May 2014): 447–69.

Esposito, Roberto. *Immunitas: The Protection and Negation of Life.* Translated by Zakiya Hanafi. Cambridge: Polity Press, 2011.

"Fandui xingshizhuyi, zhong zai wushi" [Oppose formalism and deal with concrete issues again]. *Renmin ribao pinglun bu* [People's Daily Commentary Section], June 20, 2013, available at http://opinion.people.com.cn/n/2013/0620/c1003-21902561.html.

"Fayuan li quan dingzihu zhu tui Qingchuan zaihou chongjian" [Court strenuously urges nail houses to assist in pushing forward Qingchuan's post-disaster reconstruction]. *Meili Zhongguo* [Charismatic China], October 24, 2013, available at http://ml.china .com.cn/guangyuan/zfbd/20131024/257195.html.

Feng Xiang. "Haizi, tiantangli meiyou dizhen" [Child, there are no earthquakes in heaven]. Sina Weibo Blog (May 21, 2008), available at http://blog.sina.com.cn/s/blog _4fcbc32a01009a4u.html.

Forsythe, Michael, and Chris Buckley. "China's Ruling Party Expels and Investigates Official." *New York Times*, April 29, 2014, available at http://www.nytimes.com/2014 /04/30/world/asia/chinas-communist-party-expels-senior-official.html?_r=0.

Foster, Hal. "After the White Cube." *London Review of Books* 37, no. 6 (March 2015): 25–26.

Foucault, Michel. *The History of Sexuality: An Introduction.* Translated by Robert Hurley. London: Penguin Books, 1990.

The Gate of Heavenly Peace. Movie directed by Richard Gordon and Carma Hinton. Transcript available at www.tsquare.tv/film/transcript.html.

Geertz, Clifford. "Centers, Kings, and Charisma: Reflections on the Symbolics of Power." In *Rites of Power: Symbolism, Ritual, and Politics since the Middle Ages*, edited by Sean Wilentz, 13–38. Philadelphia: University of Pennsylvania Press, 1985.

Glaeser, Andreas. *Political Epistemics: The Secret Police, the Opposition, and the End of East German Socialism.* Chicago: University of Chicago Press, 2011.

Goldman, Russell. "A Year of Disasters in China." *New York Times*, December 21, 2015, available at http://www.nytimes.com/interactive/2015/12/21/world/asia/china -diaster-landslide-ship-coal-mine-explosion.html.

Guangyuanshi shizhang xinxiang [Guangyuan City Mayor's Mailbox]. "Dailing nongcun zhifu" [Leading the village to become rich], February 15, 2012, available at http:// gymail.gy169.net/article.asp?id=57581.

"Guanyu Dujiangyanshi xuexiao shewen wenti youguan qingkuang de huibu" [Situation report concerning problems involving collapsed schools in Dujiangyan Municipality]. From confidential Party archive.

Gu Songqing. *Fazhanxing chongjian zaihou jueqi de Sichuan moshi* [Development model reconstruction: The emergence of the post-disaster Sichuan method]. Chengdu: Sichuan renmin chubanshe, 2011.

Guowuyuan [State Council]. Wenchuan dizhen zaihou huifu chongjian tiaoli [Regulations on post-Wenchuan earthquake restoration and reconstruction]. (Order No. 526), June 2008 available at http://www.gov.cn/zwgk/2008-06/09/content_1010710.htm.

Guowuyuan fazhan yanjiu zhongxin [Development Research Center of the State Council]. "Chuangxin yuanzang fangshi zaofu xizang renmin" [Innovative Tibetan assistance methods: Benefit for the Tibetan people]. *Diaocha yanjiu baogao* [Investigation Research Report] 129 (October 15, 2009): 1–11.

——. "Sichuan sheng dizhen zaiqu hou chongjian shiqi: Jidai jiejue de wenti ji jianyi—yi qingchuanxian wei li" [Sichuan Province earthquake post-disaster reconstruction period: Problems in urgent need of resolution and suggestions—the example of Qingchuan County] 164, no. 3695 (September 10, 2010).

——. "Wenchuan dizhen zaihai dui woguo jingji zengzhang de yingxiang pinggu" [Assessment of the Wenchuan earthquake's impact on China's economic growth] 8, no. 3201 (June 20, 2008): 1–24.

———. "Wenchuan dizhen zaihou chongjian de ruogan zhongyao wenti" [Several important problems concerning the post-Wenchuan earthquake reconstruction] 90, no. 3202 (June 20, 2008).

———. "Wo guo chengshibing de tizhi chengyin fenxi" [An analysis of the systemic causes of China's urban pathologies] 67 (2012): 1–13.

Han Feizi. *Basic Writings.* Translated by Burton Watson. New York: Columbia University Press, 2003.

He Baogang and Mark E. Warren. "Authoritarian Deliberation: The Deliberative Turn in Chinese Political Development." *Perspectives on Politics* 9, no. 2 (2011): 269–89.

Heilmann, Sebastian. "Policy-Making through Experimentation: The Formation of a Distinctive Policy Process." In *Mao's Invisible Hand: The Political Foundations of Adaptive Governance in China,* edited by Sebastian Heilmann and Elizabeth J. Perry, 62–101. Cambridge, MA: Harvard University Press, 2011.

Heilmann, Sebastian, and Oliver Melton. "The Reinvention of Development Planning in China, 1993–2012." *Modern China* 39, no. 6 (August 2013): 580–628.

Heilmann, Sebastian, and Elizabeth J. Perry, eds., "Embracing Uncertainty." In *Mao's Invisible Hand: The Political Foundations of Adaptive Governance in China* Cambridge, MA: Harvard University Press, 2011: 1–29.

———, eds., *Mao's Invisible Hand: The Political Foundations of Adaptive Governance in China* (Cambridge, MA: Harvard University Press, 2011).

Henochowicz, Anne. "Do You Speak for the Party or the People?" *China Digital Times,* March 17, 2016, available at http://chinadigitaltimes.net/2016/03/speak-party -people.

Hess, Steven. "Deliberative Institutions as Mechanisms for Managing Social Unrest: The Case of the 2008 Chongqing Taxi Strike." *China: An International Journal* 7, no. 2 (2009): 336–52.

Hou Shuiping. *Wenchuan dadizhen zaihou huifu chongjian xiangguan zhongda wenti yanjiu* [Wenchuan post-earthquake recovery- and reconstruction-related important research problems]. Sichuan: Sichuan renmin chubanshe, 2010.

Hu Angang. "The Distinctive Transition of China's Five-Year Plans." *Modern China* 39, no. 6 (August 2013): 629–39.

———. "Embracing China's New Normal: Why the Economy Is Still on Track." *Foreign Affairs* (May–June 2015), available at https://www.foreignaffairs.com/articles/china /2015-04-20/embracing-chinas-new-normal.

Hu Qiaomu. "Guanyu xinwen gongzuo de dangxing he 'renminxing' wenti" [Regarding the problem of Party spirit and popular character in news work]. In *Hu Qiaomu ji di er juan* [The collected works of Hu Qiaomu], Vol. 2. Renmin chubanshe, 1993.

Huang Haifeng. "Propaganda as Signaling." *Comparative Politics* 47, no. 4 (July 2015): 419–44.

Huang Xianghuai. "Xin Jinping lun jiankang zhengzhi shengtai" [Xin Jinping's theory on healthy political ecology]. *Zhongguo gongchandang xinwen wang* [Chinese Communist Party news website], June 3, 2015, available at http://theory.people.com.cn/n /2015/0603/c168825-27099150.html.

"Hui shu hua 'hua' kai Qingchuan" [The blooming of *Grifola Frondosa* in Qingchuan]. *Sichuan ribao* [Sichuan Daily], March 28, 2002.

Hurst, William. *The Chinese Worker after Socialism.* Cambridge: Cambridge University Press, 2009.

———. "Mass Frames and Worker Protest." In *Popular Protest in China,* edited by Kevin J. O'Brien, 71–87. Cambridge, MA: Harvard University Press, 2008.

Hurst, William, Mingxing Liu, Yongdong Liu, and Ran Tao. "Reassessing Collective Petitioning in Rural China: Civic Engagement, Extra-State Violence, and Regional Variation." *Comparative Politics* 46, no. 4 (July 2014): 459–82.

Hvistendahl, Mara. "China's Three Gorges Dam: An Environmental Catastrophe?" *Scientific American*, March 25, 2008, available at http://www.scientificamerican.com/article/chinas-three-gorges-dam-disaster/.

I Ching (Yijing) [The Book of Change]. Translated with an introduction and commentary by John Minford. New York: Penguin, 2015.

"Ideology: The Return of Correct Thinking." *The Economist*, April 23, 2016, available at http://www.economist.com/news/china/21697266-keep-party-and-public-line-xi-jinping-using-marxist-classics-return-correct.

Iritani, Evelyn. "Great Idea but Don't Quote Him." *Los Angeles Times*, September 9, 2004, available at http://articles.latimes.com/2004/sep/09/business/fi-deng9.

Jacka, Tamara. *Rural Women in Urban China: Gender Migration, and Social Change.* Armonk, NY: M. E. Sharpe, 2005.

Jacobs, Andrew. "4 Years after Quake, Some See a Resurrected Chinese City, Others Dashed Dreams." *New York Times*, May 21, 2014, available at http://www.nytimes.com/2014/05/22/world/asia/4-years-after-quake-some-see-a-resurrected-chinese-city-others-dashed-dreams.html?_r=0.

Jeffrey, Craig. *Timepass: Youth, Class, and the Politics of Waiting in India.* Stanford, CA: Stanford University Press, 2010.

Johnson, Ian. "As Beijing Becomes a Supercity, the Rapid Growth Brings Pains." *New York Times*, July 19, 2015, available at www.nytimes.com/2015/07/20/world/asia/in-china-a-supercity-rises-around-beijing.html?_r=1.

Jowitt, Ken. *New World Disorder: The Leninist Extinction.* Berkeley: University of California Press, 1993.

"Kaifang zhuang ge han shanyue—qingchuan xian kuoda dui nei kaifang jishi" [The magnificent song of opening up shakes the lofty mountains—Qingchuan County enlarging internal openness to the outside]. *Guangyuan shibao* [Guangyuan Times], September 15, 1999.

Kaiman, Jonathan. "China to Flatten 700 Mountains for New Metropolis in the Desert." *The Guardian*, December 7, 2012, available at http://www.theguardian.com/world/2012/dec/06/china-flatten-mountain-lanzhou-new-area.

Kang Yi. *Disaster Management in China in a Changing Era.* New York: Springer, 2015.

Ketizu [Task Group]. "Tansuo jingji he shengtai wenming xietiao fazhan de xin daolu" [Exploration of the new road of economic and ecological civilization coordinated development]. *Lilun Dongtai* [Theoretical trends]. Vol. 1817 (June 10, 2009): 34–40. Restricted access publication.

Kleinman, Arthur. "Neurasthenia and Depression: A Study of Somatization and Culture in China." *Culture, Medicine, Psychiatry* 6, no. 2 (1982): 117–90.

LaFraniere, Sharon. "Possible Link between Dam and China Quake." *New York Times*, February 5, 2009, available at www.nytimes.com/2009/02/06/world/asia/06quake.html?pagewanted=all&_r=0.

Lam, Willy. "A Modern Cult of Personality? Xi Jinping Aspires to be the Equal of Mao and Deng." *China Brief* 15, no. 5, March 6, 2015.

Larson, Christina. "World's Largest River Diversion Project Now Pipes Water to Beijing." *Bloomberg News*, December 16, 2014, available at www.bloomberg.com/news/articles/2014-12-15/world-s-largest-river-diversion-project-now-pipes-water-to-beijing.

Laughlin, Charles A. *Chinese Reportage: The Aesthetics of Historical Experience.* Durham, NC: Duke University Press, 2002.

Lee, Haiyan. "The Charisma of Power and the Military Sublime in Tiananmen Square." *Journal of Asian Studies* 70, no. 2 (May 2011): 397–424.

Lee, Sing. "Depression: Coming of Age in China." In *Deep China: The Moral Life of the Person*, edited by Arthur Kleinman et al., 177–212. Berkeley: University of California Press, 2011.

Lenin, Vladimir. "What Is to Be Done?" In *The Lenin Anthology*, edited by Robert C. Tucker, 12–114. New York: W. W. Norton, 1975.

Leonard, Mark. *What Does China Think?* New York: Perseus Books, 2008.

Leys, Simon. "The Art of Interpreting Nonexistent Inscriptions Written in Invisible Ink on a Blank Page." *New York Review of Books*, October 11, 1990, available at www.nybooks.com/articles/1990/10/11/the-art-of-interpreting-nonexistent -inscriptions-w/.

———. *The Hall of Uselessness: Collected Essays*. New York: New York Review of Books Classics, 2013.

Li Bin. "Dujiangyan dazao chongjian yangban he shifan shiyan qu" [Dujiangyan: The creation of a reconstruction template and model example test area]. *Chengdu Wanbao* [Chengdu evening news], October 21, 2009, available at http://news.sina.com.cn/o /2009-10-21/053116472002s.shtml.

Li Bo. "Dujiangyan linpanshi nongcun jujidian" [Dujiangyan "LinPan-style" rural aggregation]. *Chengshi jianshi lilun yanjiu* [Urban construction theory research] 4 (2012).

Li Li. "County Rebuilds after Quake." *China Daily*, February 1, 2011, available at http:// www.chinadaily.com.cn/china/2011-02/01/content_11950279.htm.

Li Shirong. "Fangzhi fenquan quanxian chengwei lingyi zhong xingshizhuyi" [Prevent the separation and limitation of authority from becoming another kind of formalism]. *Guangdong ribao* [Guangdong Daily], January 27, 2014, available at http://opinion .people.com.cn/BIG5/n/2014/0127/c1003-24238892.html.

Li Shulei. "Zaizao yuyan" [Restoring language]. *Zhanlüe yu guanli* [Strategy and management] (2001), available at www.21ccom.net/articles/lsjd/jwxd/article_20140218100761 .html.

Li, Tania Murray. "To Make Live or Let Die? Rural Dispossession and the Protection of Surplus Populations." *Antipode* 41 (2009): 66–93.

Lieberthal, Kenneth, and Michel Oksenberg. *Policy Making in China: Leaders, Structures, and Processes*. Princeton, NJ: Princeton University Press, 1988.

Lim, Louisa. "Five Years after a Quake, Chinese Cite Shoddy Reconstruction." *National Public Radio*, May 14, 2013, available at http://www.npr.org/sections/parallels/2013/05/14 /183635289/Five-Years-After-A-Quake-Chinese-Cite-Shoddy-Reconstruction.

Lin Chun. *The Transformation of Chinese Socialism*. Durham, NC: Duke University Press, 2006.

Liu Shaoqi. *How to Be a Good Communist* (1939). Translation public, available at https:// www.marxists.org/reference/archive/liu-shaoqi/1939/how-to-be/ch06.htm.

———. *On the Party* (1945). Translation public, available at https://www.marxists.org /reference/archive/liu-shaoqi/1945/on-party/index.htm.

Liu Tie. *Duikouzhiyuan de yunxing jizhi jiqi fazhihua: Jiyu Wenchuan dizhen zaihou huifu chongjian de shizheng fenxi* [On the operation and legalization of partner assistance: An empirical study based on the post-disaster reconstruction of the Wenchuan earthquake]. Beijing: Falü chubanshe, 2010.

Liu Yu. "Maoist Discourse and the Mobilization of Emotions in Revolutionary China." *Modern China* 36 (2011): 329–62.

Luo Shuzhen. "Jinyibu zuohao fayuan xitong duikou yuanjiang gongzuo, qieshi weihu bianjiang shehui wending he changzhijiuai" [Progressively improve the work of court system partner assistance to Xinjiang, conscientiously maintain border area social stability and long-term peace]. *Renmin fayuan bao* [People's Court report] (December 18, 2014).

Luo Zhenyu. "Dashi yunji, liangdian fencheng, gongjian zhenzhong Yingxiu—Yingxiuzhen jianshe 'xiandai kangzhen jianzhu bowuguan'" [A convergence of great masters, a brilliantly varied highlight, working together to construct the earthquake epicenter Yingxiu—The construction of Yingxiu Township's "modern anti-seismic architecture museum"]. From archive of Sichuan Provincial Party School.

Ma Yuan and Nan Yang. "Guanyu yufang zaihou dongyuan pingtai qi fasheng shehui xinren weiji de sikao yu duice" [Precautionary reflections and countermeasures regarding post-disaster mobilization platforms and social trust crisis]. *Lingdao Canyue* [Leadership reference] 17, no. 459 (June 15, 2008): 15–19. Restricted circulation publication.

Ma Zhigang. "Ziben xiaxiang dayoukewei" [Capital goes to the countryside with great prospects for the future]. *Jingji Ribao* [Economic daily], January 30, 2014, available at http://theory.people.com.cn/n/2014/0130/c40531-24268536.html.

Makley, Charlene. "Spectacular Compassion: 'Natural' Disasters and National Mourning in China's Tibet." *Critical Asian Studies* 46, no. 3 (September 2014): 371–404.

Mao Zedong. "A Single Spark Can Start a Prairie Fire" (January 5, 1930). Translation public, available at https://www.marxists.org/reference/archive/mao/selected-works/volume-1/mswv1_6.htm.

——. "The Foolish Old Man Who Removed the Mountains" (June 11, 1945). Translation public, available at www.marxists.org/reference/archive/mao/selected-works/volume-3/mswv3_26.htm.

——. "Methods of Work Party Committees" (March 13, 1949). Translation public, available at www.marxists.org/reference/archive/mao/selected-works/volume-4/mswv4_59.htm.

——. "On the Chungking Negotiations" (October 17, 1945). Translation public, available at www.marxists.org/reference/archive/mao/selected-works/volume-4/mswv4_06.htm.

——. "On Contradiction" (August 1937). Translation public, available at https://www.marxists.org/reference/archive/mao/selected-works/volume-1/mswv1_17.htm.

——. "On the Correct Handling of Contradictions among the People" (February 27, 1958). Translation public, available at www.marxists.org/reference/archive/mao/selected-works/volume-5/mswv5_58.htm.

——. "On Guerilla Warfare," (1937). Translation public, available at: https://www.marxists.org/reference/archive/mao/works/1937/guerrilla-warfare/.

——. "On Practice: On the Relation between Knowledge and Practice, between Knowing and Doing" (July 1937). Translation public, available at www.marxists.org/reference/archive/mao/selected-works/volume-1/mswv1_16.htm.

——. "On Protracted War" (May 1938). Translation public, available at https://www.marxists.org/reference/archive/mao/selected-works/volume-2/mswv2_09.htm.

——. "On the Ten Major Relationships" (April 25, 1956). Translation public, available at https://www.marxists.org/reference/archive/mao/selected-works/volume-5/mswv5_51.htm.

——. "Oppose Book Worship" (May 1930). Translation public, available at www.marxists.org/reference/archive/mao/selected-works/volume-6/mswv6_11.htm.

——. "Oppose Stereotyped Party Writing" (February 8, 1942). Translation public, available at https://www.marxists.org/reference/archive/mao/selected-works/volume-3/mswv3_07.htm.

——. "Rectify the Party's Style of Work" (February 1, 1942). Translation public, available at https://www.marxists.org/reference/archive/mao/selected-works/volume-3/mswv3_06.htm.

——. "Reform Our Study" (May 1941). Translation public, available at https://www.marxists.org/reference/archive/mao/selected-works/volume-3/mswv3_02.htm.

——. "The Role of the Chinese Communist Party in the National War" (October 1938). Translation public, available at www.marxists.org/reference/archive/mao/selected-works/volume-2/mswv2_10.htm.

——. "Serve the People" (September 8, 1944). Translation public, available at https://www.marxists.org/reference/archive/mao/selected-works/volume-3/mswv3_19.htm.

——. "Some Questions Concerning Method of Leadership" (June 1943). Translation public, available at www.marxists.org/reference/archive/mao/selected-works/volume-3/mswv3_13.htm.

——. "Speech at the Ninth Plenum of the Eighth CPC Central Committee" (September 24, 1962). Translation public, available at www.marxists.org/reference/archive/mao/selected-works/volume-8/mswv8_63.htm.

——. "Strive to Learn from Each Other and Don't Stick to the Beaten Track and Be Complacent" (December 1963). Translation public, available at http://www.marxists.org/reference/archive/mao/selected-works/volume-9/mswv9_10.htm.

——. "Talk on Questions of Philosophy" (August 18, 1964). Translation public, available at https://www.marxists.org/reference/archive/mao/selected-works/volume-9/mswv9_27.htm.

——. "Twenty Manifestations of Bureaucracy" (February 1970). Translation public, available at https://www.marxists.org/reference/archive/mao/selected-works/volume-9/mswv9_85.htm.

Marx, Karl. "The Eighteenth Brumaire of Napoleon Bonaparte." In *The Marx-Engels Reader*, 2nd ed., edited by Robert C. Tucker. New York: W. W. Norton, 1978.

Mbembe, Achille. "The Banality of Power and the Aesthetics of Vulgarity in the Postcolony." *Public Culture* 4, no. 2 (Spring 1993): 1–30.

——. *On the Postcolony*. Berkeley: University of California Press, 2011.

McNally, Christopher. "Sichuan: Driving Capitalist Development Westward." *China Quarterly* 178 (2004): 426–47.

Merleau-Ponty, Maurice. *Humanism and Terror: An Essay on the Communist Problem*. Translated by John O'Neill. Boston: Beacon, 1969.

Mertha, Andrew. *Brothers in Arms: Chinese Aid to the Khmer Rouge*. Ithaca, NY: Cornell University Press, 2014.

——. *China's Water Warriors: Citizen Action and Policy Change*. Ithaca, NY: Cornell University Press, 2008.

——. "Fragmented Authoritarianism 2.0: Political Pluralization in the Chinese Policy Process." *China Quarterly* 200 (December 2009): 995–1012.

——. "Stressing Out": Cadre Calibration and Affective Proximity to the CCP in Reform-Era China." *China Quarterly*, forthcoming.

Mianyang shi renmin zhengfu [Mianyang Municipal People's Government]. "Mianyang shi zaihou nongfang chongjian he kunnan qunzhong mianlin shenghuo jiuzhu deng qingkuang baogao" [Mianyang muncipal government work report regarding post-disaster reconstruction of rural housing and assistance to masses facing livelihood difficulties] (October 28, 2008).

Mitchell, Timothy. "Everyday Metaphors of Power." *Theory and Society* 19, no. 5 (October 1990): 545–77.

——. "The Work of Economics: How a Discipline Makes the World." *European Journal of Sociology* 46, no. 2 (August 2005): 297–320.

Murphy, Rachel, and Ran Tao. "No Wage and No Land: New Forms of Unemployment in Rural China." In *Unemployment in China: Economy, Human Resources and Labour Markets*, edited by Grace O. M. Lee and Malcolm Warner, 128–49. London: Routledge, 2006.

Najafi, Sina, David Serlin, and Lauren Berlant. "The Broken Circuit: An Interview with Lauren Berlant. *Cabinet Magazine*, no. 31 (Fall 2008), available at www.cabinetmagazine .org/issues/31/najafi_serlin.php.

Nathan, Andrew J. "Authoritarian Resilience." *Journal of Democracy* 14, no. 1 (January 2003): 6–17.

Naughton, Barry. *Growing Out of the Plan: Chinese Economic Reform 1978–1993*. Cambridge: Cambridge University Press, 1995.

———. "The Third Front: Defence Industrialization in the Chinese Interior." *China Quarterly* 115 (September 1988): 351–86.

Ng, Kwai Hang, and Xin He. "Internal Contradictions of Judicial Mediation in China." *Law & Social Inquiry* 39, no. 2 (Spring 2014): 285–312.

Norton, Anne. *95 Theses on Politics, Culture, & Method*. New Haven, CT: Yale University Press, 2004.

O'Brien, Kevin. "Studying Chinese Politics in an Age of Specialization." *Journal of Contemporary China* 20, no. 71 (2011): 535–41.

O'Brien, Kevin, and Lianjiang Li. *Rightful Resistance in Rural China*. Cambridge: Cambridge University Press, 2006.

"Offprint of Mao's Work Published after Xi's Comments." *Xinhua News Agency*, February 26, 2016, available at http://news.xinhuanet.com/english/2016-02/26/c_135134761 .htm.

Ogden, Suzanne. Book Review in *Perspectives on Politics* 7, no. 3 (2009): 697–99.

Oi, Jean. "The Role of the Local State in China's Transitional Economy." *China Quarterly* 144 (1995): 1132–49.

O'Neill, Bruce. "Cast Aside: Boredom, Downward Mobility, and Homelessness in Post-Communist Bucharest." *Cultural Anthropology* 29, no. 1 (February 2014): 8–31.

Ong, Lynette H. "State-Led Urbanization in China: Skyscrapers, Land Revenue and 'Concentrated Villages.'" *China Quarterly* 217 (March 2014): 162–79.

Orwell, George. "Politics and the English Language" (1946), available at http://www.orwell .ru/library/essays/politics/english/e_polit/.

Pei Minxin. "Will the Chinese Communist Party Survive the Crisis? How Beijing's Shrinking Economy May Threaten One-Party Rule." *Foreign Affairs*, May 12, 2009, available at https://www.foreignaffairs.com/articles/asia/2009-03-12/will-chinese-communist -party-survive-crisis.

Peng Dapeng. "Cunmin zizhi yijing meiyou yiyi le ma?" [Is villager autonomy already meaningless?"]. *San nong Zhongguo* [China village research network] (2011) at http://www.snzg.cn/article/2011/0519/article_23894.html.

Perry, Elizabeth J. "From Mass Campaigns to Managed Campaigns: 'Constructing a New Socialist Countryside.'" In *Mao's Invisible Hand: The Political Foundations of Adaptive Governance in China*, edited by Sebastian Heilmann and Elizabeth J. Perry, 30–61. Cambridge, MA: Harvard University Press, 2011.

Phillips, Tom. "Chinese Reporter Makes On-Air 'Confession' after Market Chaos." *The Guardian*, August 31, 2015, available at http://www.theguardian.com/world/2015 /aug/31/chinese-financial-journalist-wang-xiaolu-makes-alleged-on-air -confesssion-after-market-chaos confession.

Pieke, Frank N. *The Good Communist: Elite Training and State Building in Today's China*. Cambridge: Cambridge University Press, 2009.

Pitkin, Hannah F. *The Concept of Representation*. Berkeley: University of California Press, 1972.

Povinelli, Elizabeth A. *Economies of Abandonment: Social Belonging and Endurance in Late Liberalism*. Durham, NC: Duke University Press, 2011.

"Qingchuan linye xiaoyi lian nian dizeng" [Qingchuan's forestry increasing efficiency over time]. *Rennmin ribao*, August 25, 1995.

"Qingchuan nongmin yi shang cu nong" [Qingchuan villagers doing business to promote agriculture]. *Sichuan nongcun ribao* [Sichuan Village Daily], (February 2, 2003).

"Qingchuan 'Shengtai wenming shifan xian' jianshe zhashi tuijin" [Qingchuan "ecological civilization model county" construction advances firmly]. *Meili Zhongguo* [Charismatic China] (January 26, 2014), available at http://ml.china.com.cn/html/mingxian/csfc/20140126/308375.html.

Qingchuan xian guomin jingji he shehui fazhan "shi er wu" guihua gangyao [Qingchuan County national economy and social development 12th Five-Year Plan outline] (2011).

"Qingchuan xian shishi shengtai jianshe shiji" [Qingchuan County implementing ecological construction—record of events]. *Guangyuan ribao*, September 27, 2005.

Qingchuan xian waixuan ban [Qingchuan County External Propaganda Office]. "Wo xian kai xiancheng duanlie dai chaichu chaiqian gongzuo huiyi" [County-Seat Fault-Zone Demolition Work Conference] reported on February 15, 2012. Webpage has been subsequently removed.

Qingchuan xianwei [Qingchuan County Party Committee]. "Chuangjian shengtai wenming shifan xian de jueding" [Decision to establish ecological civilization model county]. Document no. 357 (November 11, 2011).

Qingchuan xianzhi [Qingchuan County annals]. 1985 edition.

"Qingchuan zhuanbian jingji zengzhang fangshi tuijin kechixu fazhan jishi" [Qingchuan promoting sustainable development and transforming economic growth model—record of events]. *Guangyuan ribao*, March 15, 2006.

Qing Lidong. "Hongyang gan'en wenhua, jianxing gan'en zeren" [To promote gratitude culture and implement gratitude responsibility]. Speech given at the Wenchuan County Chinese People's Consultative Conference (January 24, 2010).

———. "Jiefang sixiang, kuaizhongqiuhao, nuli shixian sannian huifu chongjian renwu liangnian jiben wancheng mubiao" [Liberate thinking, pursue the good with speed, industriously implement and complete the goal of three-year reconstruction within two years]. *Zai Zhonggong Wenchuanxianwei shi jie jiu ci quantihuiyishang de jianghua* [Speech given at the Wenchuan County Communist Party General Congress, 10th plenary session]. No. 28/85 (October 2009).

———. "Pa poshang kan zhua zhongdian, xushi tupo yu kuayue" [Climbing up a slope on the threshold of grasping the important points, store up power to break through and step across]. Zai jiakuai tuijin shi da zhongdian gongzuo dongyuan huishang de jianghua [Speech given at the conference for the accelerated promotion of ten large important points concerning work mobilization]. No. 5/96 (2010).

Qiu Baoxing. "Shengtai wenming shidai xiangcun jianshe de jiben duice" [The age of ecological civilization, fundamental measures for township and village construction]. *Baogao xuan* [Selected reports]. No. 4 (2008): 1–22. Restricted access publication.

———. "Zaihou chengxiang chongjianguihua de wenti, fang'an' he zhanlüe." [Problems in post-disaster urban-rural reconstruction planning: Guidelines and strategies]. Zaihou chongjian guihua duikouzhiyuan gongzuo huiyishang de jianghua [Speech delivered at a conference on post-disaster reconstruction planning and the provincial partner-assistance program] (July 3, 2008), available at http://www.512ngo.org.cn/news_detail.asp?id=1167.

Ren Zhongping. "Chuanyue zainan yingjie guangrong" [Overcoming calamity, welcoming glory]. *Renmin ribao* [People's Daily], August 20, 2008, available at http://cpc.people.com.cn/GB/64093/64099/7692888.html.

——. "Wenchuan teda dizhen san zhounian zhi" [On the third anniversary of the Wenchuan earthquake]. *Renmin ribao* [People's Daily], May 11, 2011, available at http://news.sina.com.cn/c/2011-05-11/113422444531.shtml.

Reny, Marie-Ève. "What Happened to the Study of China in Comparative Politics?" *Journal of Contemporary East Asian Studies* 11, no. 1 (2011): 105–35.

"Return to Repression." *Washington Post*, June 23, 2008 available at www.washingtonpost.com/wp-dyn/content/article/2008/06/22/AR2008062201586.html.

Robbins, Alicia S. T., and Stevan Harrell. "Paradoxes and Challenges for China's Forests in the Reform Era." *China Quarterly* 218 (June 2014): 381–403.

Roberts, Dexter. "Xi Jinping Is No Fun." *Businessweek*, October 3, 2013, available at http://www.businessweek.com/articles/2013-10-03/china-president-xi-jinping-revives-self-criticism-sessions-in-maoism-lite.

Rousseau, Jean Jacques. Letter to Voltaire, August 18, 1758. In *Correspondence complète de Jean Jacques Rousseau*, edited by J. A. Leigh, translated by R. Spang. Vol. 4, 37–50. Geneva, 1967.

Ryan, Fergus. "Tianjin Blasts: Plans to Turn Site into 'Eco Park' Mocked on Chinese Social Media." *The Guardian*, September 6, 2015, available at http://www.theguardian.com/world/2015/sep/06/tianjin-blasts-plans-to-turn-site-into-eco-park-mocked-on-chinese-social-media.

Santner, Eric L. *The Royal Remains: The People's Two Bodies and the Endgames of Sovereignty*. Chicago: University of Chicago Press, 2011.

——. *The Weight of All Flesh: On the Subject-Matter of Political Economy*. Oxford: Oxford University Press, 2015.

Sapio, Flora. "Sources of CCP Law, CCP Regulations on Disciplinary Punishments." October 10, 2015, available at http://florasapio.blogspot.com.au/2015/10/chapter-2-sources-of-ccp-law-ccp.html.

Schmidt, Vivien A. "Discursive Institutionalism: The Explanatory Power of Ideas and Discourse," *Annual Review of Political Science* 11 (2008): 303–26.

Schoenhals, Michael. *Doing Things with Words in Chinese Politics: Five Studies*. Berkeley: Institute of East Asian Studies, University of California, 1992.

Schurmann, Franz. *Ideology and Organization in Communist China*. Berkeley: University of California Press, 1968.

Schwartz, Benjamin. "The Reign of Virtue: Some Broad Perspectives on Leader and Party in the Cultural Revolution." In *Party Leadership and Revolutionary Power in China*, edited by John Wilson Lewis, 149–69. Cambridge: Cambridge University Press, 1970.

Shambaugh, David. "The Coming Chinese Crackup." *Wall Street Journal*, March 6, 2015, available at http://www.wsj.com/articles/the-coming-chinese-crack-up-1425659198.

Sheppard, David, and Scott Disavino. "Superstorm Sandy Cuts Power to 8.1 Million Houses." *Reuters*, October 30, 2012, available at http://www.reuters.com/article/us-storm-sandy-powercuts-idUSBRE89T10G20121030.

Shieh, Shawn, and Deng Guosheng. "An Emerging Civil Society: The Impact of the 2008 Sichuan Earthquake on Grass-Roots Associations in China." *China Journal* no. 65 (2011): 181–94.

Shifang jian di long ju zhongxin xiaoxue [Shifang jian di long ju zhongxin elementary school]. "Mingji dang'en, fenfa ziqiang jiaoyu huodong jihua yu shishi fangan" [Plan and implementation guidelines to engrave in memory the party's kindness and strive for self-improvement education activities] (2009).

Shi Wenlong. "Zhidu xingshizhuyi: Zhidu jianshe de di yi wanzheng" [Institutional formalism: The first stubborn illness of institutional building]. *Zhongguo qingnian bao* [China Youth Daily], February 26, 2014, available at http://cpc.people.com.cn /pinglun/n/2014/0226/c78779-24469002.html.

Shue, Vivienne. "Epilogue: Mao's China—Putting Politics in Perspective." In *Maoism at the Grassroots: Everyday Life in China's Era of High Socialism*, edited by Jeremy Brown and Matthew D. Johnson, 365–80. Cambridge, MA: Harvard University Press, 2015.

——. "Legitimacy Crisis in China?" In *State and Society in 21st Century China: Crisis, Contention, and Legitimation*, edited by Peter Hays Gries and Stanley Rosen, 24–49. New York: Routledge, 2004.

"Sichuan Guangyuan dui fubai ling rongren: Qunian chachu 15 ming xianji ganbu" [Sichuan's Guangyuan shows zero tolerance for corruption: Last year 15 county-level cadres investigated]. *Zhongguo xinwen wang* [China News Net], March 11, 2014, available at http://www.nd.chinanews.com/News/xwdc/20140311/1682855.html.

"Sichuan Yingxiu: Dizhen lüyou houxu fazhan fali" [Yingxiu, Sichuan: The continued development of earthquake tourism lacking in strength]. *Fenghuang shipin* [Fenghuang video], May 13, 2014, available at http://v.ifeng.com/news/society /2014005/01e9bf18-0d11-40e2-8ee9-1f428ce78b03.shtml.

Slater, Dan. "Democratic Careening." *World Politics* 65, no. 4 (October 2013): 729–63.

Solinger, Dorothy J. "The Chinese Work Unit and Transient Labor in the Transition from Socialism." *Modern China* 21, no. 2 (April 1995): 155–83.

——. "A Question of Confidence: State Legitimacy and the New Urban Poor." In *Chinese Politics: State, Society and the Market*, edited by Peter Hays Gries and Stanley Rosen, 243–57. New York: Routledge, 2010.

Sorace, Christian. "China's Last Communist: Ai Weiwei." *Critical Inquiry* 40, no. 2 (February 2014): 396–419.

——. "China's Vision for Developing Sichuan's Post-Earthquake Countryside: Turning Unruly Peasants into Grateful Urban Citizens." *China Quarterly* 218 (June 2014): 404–27.

——. "The Communist Party's Miracle? The Alchemy of Turning Post-Disaster Reconstruction into Great Leap Development." *Comparative Politics* 47, no. 4 (July 2015): 458–77.

——. "In Rehab with Weiwei." *The China Story*, October 14, 2015, available at http://www .thechinastory.org/2015/10/in-rehab-with-weiwei/.

——. "Saint Mao." *Telos* 151 (Summer 2010): 173–91.

——. " 'When One Place Is in Trouble, Help Comes from All Sides': Fragmented Authoritarianism in Post-Disaster Reconstruction." In *Chinese Politics as Fragmented Authoritarianism: Earthquakes, Energy, and Environment*, edited by Kjeld Erik Brødsgaard, 135–55. London: Routledge, 2016.

Sorace, Christian, and William Hurst. "China's Phantom Urbanisation and the Pathology of Ghost Cities." *Journal of Contemporary Asia* 46, no. 2 (2016): 304–22.

Stalin, Joseph V. "On the Death of Lenin" (January 30, 1924). Translation public, available at https://www.marxists.org/reference/archive/stalin/works/1924/01/30.htm.

Stanley, Jason. *How Propaganda Works*. Princeton, NJ: Princeton University Press, 2015.

The State Planning Group of Post-Wenchuan Earthquake Restoration and Reconstruction; National Development and Reform Committee (NDRC); The People's Government of Sichuan Ministry of Housing and Urban-Rural Development (MOHURD). *Wenchuan dizhen zaihou huifu chongjian zongti guihua* [The overall plan for the post-Wenchuan earthquake restoration and reconstruction], 2008.

Su Dongbo. "Zhan zai guojia yu shehui chongjian de gaodushang yong gaige kaifang siwei zhidao zaihou chongjian" [A bird's-eye perspective on state and society reconstruction: Using reform and opening thinking to guide post-disaster reconstruction]. *Gaige neican jueceban* [Reform decision making] 19 (2008): 23–27.

Sun Liping. *Chongjian shehui: Zhuanxing shehui de zhixu zaizao* [Reconstructing society: To rebuild social order in transformational China]. Beijing: Shehui kexue wenxian chubanshe [Social Sciences Academic Press], 2009.

——. "Zouxiang jiji de shehui guanli" [Trend toward proactive social management]. *Shehuixue yanjiu* [Sociological studies] 4 (2011): 22–32.

Sun Xin. "Huidao dizhen zhongxin cunwei shuiji de Yingxiu zhi huo" [Returning to the earthquake epicenter, Yingxiu's party secretary is puzzled]. *Zhongguo qiyejia* [Chinese entrepreneur], May 2011, available at http://finance.jrj.com.cn/biz/2011/05 /1211159949990.shtml.

Tan Zuoren. "Longmenshan: Qing wei Beichuan haizimen" [Longmen Mountains: Please testify for Beichuan's children]. In possession of author.

Tang Shuquan. "Sichuan shengwei shuji chengyao yingxiu dazao cheng 'shijie mingzhen'" [Sichuan provincial party secretary calls for Yingxiu to become a "world famous township"]. *Zhongguo xinwenwang* [China News], May 8, 2010, available at http:// politics.people.com.cn/GB/14562/11547445.html.

Tao Ling. "Sichuan shouci jizhong dui zaiqu jiceng ganbu kaizhan xinli fudao" [Sichuan's first time carrying out psychological counseling focused on grassroots cadres]. *Huaxi dushibao* (October 22, 2008), available at http://sichuan.scol.com.cn/dwzw/20081022 /2008102270004.htm.

Tatlow, Didi Kirsten. "China Seeks to Promote the 'Right' Western Philosophy: Marxism." *New York Times*, September 23, 2015, available at http://sinosphere.blogs.nytimes .com/2015/09/23/peking-university-china-marx/.

Teets, Jessica. "Let Many Civil Societies Bloom: The Rise of Consultative Authoritarianism in China." *China Quarterly* 213 (March 2013): 19–38.

——. "Post-Earthquake Relief and Reconstruction Efforts: The Emergence of Civil Society in China?" *China Quarterly* 198 (2009): 330–47.

Thaxton, Ralph. *Catastrophe and Contention in Rural China: Mao's Great Leap Forward Famine and the Origins of Righteous Resistance in Da Fo Village*. Cambridge: Cambridge University Press, 2008.

Thom, Françoise. *Newspeak: The Language of Soviet Communism*. Translated by Ken Connelly. London: Claridge, 1989.

Thornton, Patricia. "Crisis and Governance: SARS and the Resilience of the Chinese Body Politics." *China Journal* 61 (January 2009): 23–48.

Tomba, Luigi. *The Government Next Door: Neighborhood Politics in Urban China*. Ithaca, NY: Cornell University Press, 2014.

Trac, Christine Jane, Amanda H. Schmidt, Stevan Harrell, and Thomas M. Hinckley. "Is the Returning Farmland to Forest Program a Success? Three Case Studies from Sichuan." *Environmental Practice* 15, no. 3 (September 2013): 350–66.

Tsai Wen-Hsuan and Kao Peng-Hsiang. "Secret Codes of Political Propaganda: The Unknown System of Writing Teams." *China Quarterly* 214 (2013): 394–410.

Tsai Wen-Hsuan and Nicola Dean. "The CCP's Learning System: Thought Unification and Regime Adaptation." *China Journal* 69 (January 2013): 87–107.

Tsang, Steve. "Consultative Leninism: China's New Political Framework." *Journal of Contemporary China* 18, no. 62 (2009): 865–80.

Tuan Yi-Fu. *Topophilia: A Study of Environmental Perception, Attitudes and Values*. New York: Columbia University Press, 1990.

Urban, George, ed. *The Miracles of Chairman Mao: A Compendium of Devotional Literature 1966–1970*. London: Tom Stacey, 1971.

U.S. Consulate in Chengdu. "Human Rights Activist Huang Qi: Attorney Provides More Details on Court Case; How Communist Party Arranges Convictions." *WikiLeaks*

Confidential Cable, January 15, 2010, available at https://search.wikileaks.org/plusd
/cables/10CHENGDU12_a.html.

———. "Wife of Sichuan Dissident Huang Qi Discusses His Case." *WikiLeaks* Confidential
Cable, January 6, 2010, available at https://search.wikileaks.org/plusd/cables
/10CHENGDU6_a.html.

Wan Penglong and Ma Jian, eds. *Cong beizhuang xiang haomai: Kangji Wenchuan teda
dizhen zaihai de Sichuan shijian* [From tragedy to heroism: The Sichuan practice of
resistance against the great Wenchuan earthquake]. Chengdu: Sichuan renmin
chubanshe, 2011.

Wang Ban. "In the Beginning Is the Word: Popular Democracy and Mao's Little Red Book."
In *Mao's Little Red Book: A Global History*, edited by Alexander C. Cook, 266–77.
Cambridge: Cambridge University Press.

———. *The Sublime Figure of History: Aesthetics and Politics in Twentieth Century China*.
Stanford, CA: Stanford University Press, 1997.

Wang Bin. "Zai quanxian yijidu jingji xingshi fensi huiyishang de jianghua" [Speech given
at the Wenchuan County First Quarter Economic Circumstances Analysis Confer-
ence] (April 30, 2008).

———. "Zai quanxian zhengfa duiwu jingshi jiaoyu ji jizhong jiaoyu zhengdun dongyuan
dahuishang de jianghua" [Speech given at the Wenchuan County Politics and Law
Troops and Concentrated Education Rectification Mobilization Large Conference]
(December 16, 2006).

———. "Zai shi jie xianwei di 32 ci changwei (kuoda) huiyishang de jianghua" [Speech given
at the 32nd meeting of the tenth county standing committee enlarged conference]
(September 5, 2008).

———. "Zai xinren kejiganbu peixunban jieye dianlishang de jianghua" [Speech given at
the graduation ceremony for newly trained technical cadres] (September 20,
2007).

———. "Zai zhonggong wenchuan xian shi jie er ci quanwei (kuada) huishang de jianghua"
[Speech given at the Second Meeting of the Tenth Wenchuan County Communist
Party Committee Enlarged Conference] (July 26, 2007).

———. "Zai zhonggong wenchuan xianwei shi jie qi ci quanti (kuada) huiyishang de jianghua
" [Speech given at the Seventh Meeting of the Entire Tenth County Standing Committee Enlarged Conference] (September 5, 2008).

Wangcang xian qi yi zhong xue [Wangcang County Qiyi Middle School]. "Nongcun
chuzhong gan'en jiaoyu de shijian yu yanjiu: Shiyan fang'an" [Village junior high
school gratitude education practice and research: Experimental plan] (2010).

Wang Fang. "Qianxi xiao chengzhen fazhan jianshe 'jie' yu 'jie'" [Preliminary analysis of
urban development construction "combining" and "loosening"]. In Dujiangyanshi
Dangxiao [Dujiangyan Municipal Communist Party School] ed., *Xin sixiang, xin
silu, xin chengguo: Dujiangyanshi di shisiqi qingnian ganbu peixunban diaoyan
wenji huibian* [New thoughts, new thinking, new results: Dujiangyan Municipality
fourteenth young cadre training class research collection of works] (2012). Restricted
access publication.

Wang Fenyu, He Guangxi, Ma Ying, Deng Dasheng, and Zhao Yandong. "Wenchuan dizhen
zaiqu jumin de shenghuo zhuangkuang yu zhengce xuqiu" [Wenchuan earthquake
disaster-area residents living circumstances and policy needs]. *China.com*, January 13, 2009, available at http://www.china.com.cn/aboutchina/zhuanti/09zgshxs
/content_17099440_5.htm.

Wang Guangxin. "Xingshizhuyi shi zheteng de biaoxian" [Formalism is an expression of
waste]. *Jiefangjun bao* [PLA Daily], May 1, 2012, available at http://theory.people
.com.cn/GB/49150/100788/16797347.html.

Wang Hongxin and He Lijun. "Wenchuan dizhen zaiqu nongcun huifu chongjian, fupin kaifa yu kechixu fazhan: Jiyu yu tiaozhan" [Restoration and recovery of post-Wenchuan earthquake villages: Poverty alleviation development and sustainable development: Opportunities and challenges]. In *Wenchuan dizhen zaihou pinkun cun chongjian jincheng yu tiaozhan* [The reconstruction of post-Wenchuan earthquake poverty villages: Process and challenges], edited by Huang Chengwei and Chen Hanwen. Beijing: Shehui kexue wenxian chubanshe, 2010.

Wang Hui. *China's Twentieth Century: Revolution, Retreat, and the Road to Equality.* London: Verso, 2016.

Wang Jiquan. "Zou tese fazhan zhi lu, fuwu Chengdu dadushi—Dujiangyan tuijin dushi xiandai nongye fazhande zuofa yu qishi" [Walking the road of specialized development, serving the Chengdu Metropolis—Dujiangyan promotes metropolitan modern agricultural methods and enlightenment]. *Sichuan jingji xinxi wang* [Sichuan Economic Information Network] (July 16, 2012), available at http://www.sc.cei.gov.cn/dir1009/130736.htm.

Wang Xiaofang. "Sichuan lüyouju: Wei jiedao Wenchuan Yingxiu dizhen yizhi 5A jingqu shenbao cailiao" [Sichuan Tourism Bureau has not yet received application information for Wenchuan County Yingxiu Township's earthquake ruins to become a 5A scenic attraction]. *Xinhua*, February 23, 2012, available at http://news.xinhuanet.com/local/2012-02/23/c_122742857.htm.

Wang Xiaoyi. "Duiyu jinxing Wenchuan dizhen zaiqu shehui wangluo huifu chongjian yu pinggu wenti de jianyi" [Regarding implementing social network restoration and reconstruction in the post-Wenchuan earthquake disaster areas: Evaluation of problems and suggestions]. *Zhongguo shehuixue wang* [China Sociology Web], (July 25, 2008).

Wang, Xiaoying. "The Post-Communist Personality: The Spectre of China's Capitalist Market Reforms." *China Journal* 47 (January 2002): 1–17.

Wang Zhuo. "Canyushi fangfa dui zaihou xiangcun chongjiang de zuoyong he yingxiang" [The function and impact of participation in post-disaster township reconstruction], from an internal archive in the Sichuan Communist Party School, (October 16, 2008).

Weber, Max. *Politik als Beruf* [Politics as vocation], lecture delivered before the Freistudentischen Bund of the University of Munich]. Both the German and English versions of the passage can be found together online at *Harper's Magazine*: https://harpers.org/blog/2008/06/weber-on-the-political-vocation/.

Wedeen, Lisa. *Ambiguities of Domination: Politics, Rhetoric, and Symbols in Contemporary Syria.* Chicago: University of Chicago Press, 1999.

———. "Concepts and Commitments in the Study of Democracy." In *Problems and Methods in the Study of Politics*, edited by Ian Shapiro, Rogers M. Smith, and Tarek E. Masoud, 274–306. Cambridge: Cambridge University Press, 2004.

———. Memo for the National Science Foundation Workshop, unpublished manuscript (2005).

Wee, Sui-Lee. "China Sends Riot Police to Block New Protests by Flood Victims." *Reuters*, October 16, 2013, available at http://www.reuters.com/article/us-china-protest-idUSBRE99F0BN20131016?utm.

Wei, Lingling. "China Presses Economists to Brighten Their Outlooks." *Wall Street Journal*, May 3, 2016, available at http://www.wsj.com/articles/china-presses-economists-to-brighten-their-outlooks-1462292316.

Wenchuan dadizhen yizhounian zaiqu qunzhong fangtanlü [Wenchuan earthquake first anniversary disaster masses interview transcripts] (2009). Restricted circulation publication.

Wenchuanxian ganbu duiwu zhuangkuang gongzuo huibao [Wenchuan County cadre ranks situation work report].

Wenchuanxian jiwei jianchaju [Wenchuan County Discipline Inspection Commission Supervisory Office]. "Zuo dang de zhongcheng weishi, dang qunzhong de tiexin ren, Wenchuanxian jiwei jianchaju yong xingdong quanshi jijian ganbu de biaozhun" [To serve as a loyal guardian of the party and person intimate with the masses: Using actions to perform the standards of a disciplinary inspection cadre]. Document undated, from Sichuan Party School archive.

Wenchuanxian lüyouju [Wenchuan County Tourism Bureau]. "Guanyu baosong 'Shiyiwu' gongzuo zongjie ji 2011 nian gongzuo anpai de baogao" [Report concerning the summary of 11th Fifth-Year Plan work and work plans for 2011]. Document no. 141 (2010).

"Wenchuan Yingxiuzhen qingyang ying 'caishen' lushi ailu bei kaowuzui" [Wenchuan County Yingxiu Township clearing the space to welcome the "God of Wealth": Lawyer blocking road is manacled and gagged]. October 18, 2010, available at http://www.360doc.com/content/10/1018/10/84177_61936983.shtml.

"Wenchuanxian Yingxiuzhen tese meili guihua" [Wenchuan County Yingxiu Township special characteristic charm plan]. *Aba Prefecture government website*, December 2010, available at http://www.abazhou.gov.cn/ztjs/sbgc/cgzssbgc/tsmlxzsbgc2/wcsbgc3/201012/t20101227_309299.html.

"Wenchuan 5A jingqu bei zhiyi: xiaofei zainan shangkou mo yan shi daode bangjia haishi shang qian baide" [Skepticism over Wenchuan's 5A scenic era: the consumption of disaster, wiping salt in a wound, is it the abduction of morality or evil business conduct?]. *Shidai zhoubao* [Time Weekly], March 8, 2012, available at www.time-weekly.com/story/2012-03-08/122611.html.

"When Will China's Government Collapse?" *Foreign Policy* roundtable, March 13, 2015, available at http://foreignpolicy.com/2015/03/13/china_communist_party_collapse_downfall/.

Wilkinson, Endymion. *Chinese History: A New Manual*. 4th ed. Cambridge, MA: Harvard University Asia Center, 2015.

Wong, Edward. "Chinese Security Laws Elevate the Party and Stifle Dissent. Mao Would Approve." *New York Times*, May 30, 2015, available at http://www.nytimes.com/2015/05/30/world/asia/chinese-national-security-law-aims-to-defend-party-grip-on-power.html.

Wu Chutong. "Yi Dong yufei zisha wei jian: Zaiqu ganbu 'xinling chongjian'" [The example of Dong Yufei's suicide: Disaster-area cadres "mental health reconstruction"]. *Tianfu zaobao* (October 22, 2008), available at http://sichuan.scol.com.cn/dwzw/20081022/2008102252714.htm.

Wu Jingshi. "Sichuan dizhen hou chongjian zhanlüe de jianyi" [Post–Sichuan earthquake reconstruction strategy and suggestions]. *Gaige neican jueceban* [Reform decision making] 19 (2008): 27–29.

Wu Si. *Qian guize: Zhongguo lishi zhong de zhenshi youxi* [The hidden rules: Real games of Chinese history]. Shanghai: Fudan daxue chubanshe, 2009.

Wu Yue. "Wenchuan zaiqu chongjian gao mianzi gongcheng: Zhengfu dalou 'zui chaobiao'" [Wenchuan earthquake zone reconstruction engages in face projects: Government buildings that exceed the acceptable limit]. *Sohu*, May 11, 2012, available at http://news.sohu.com/20120511/n342984097.shtml.

"Xi Jinping: China Has Taught UK Schools Discipline—and Has Learned about Play." *The Guardian*, October 22, 2015, at http://www.theguardian.com/world/2015/oct/22/xi-jinping-china-taught-uk-schools-discipline-learned-about-play.

——. "Lingdao ganbu yao renrenzhenzhen xuexi, laolaoshishi zuoren, ganganjingjing ganshi" [Leading cadres must earnestly study, honestly behave with integrity, and clean work]. *Zhongzhong zhongyang dangxiao baogao xuan* [Central Party School selected reports] no. 8 (2008). Restricted access publication.

"Xi Jinping chongfang lankao: Jiao yulu jingshen shi yonghengde" [Xi Jinping returns to Lankao: The Jiao Yulu spirit is eternal]. *Xinhua News Agency*, March 17, 2014, available at http://news.xinhuanet.com/politics/2014-03/17/c_119810080.htm.

Xi Jinping guanyu shixian zhonghua minzu weida fuxing de zhongguo meng lunshu zhaibian [Xi Jinping on the realization of the great rejuvenation of the Chinese dream discourse]. Zhonggong zhongyang wenxian yanjiu shi bian [Central Committee of the Communist Party Document Research Office] (December 2013).

"Xi Jinping Vows 'Power within Cage of Regulations." *Xinhua News Agency*, January 23, 2013, available at http://www.china.org.cn/china/2013-01/23/content_27767102_2 .htm.

"Xi Says China Must Adapt to 'New Normal' of Slower Growth." *Bloomberg News*, May 11, 2014, available at http://www.bloomberg.com/news/articles/2014-05-11/xi-says -china-must-adapt-to-new-normal-of-slower-growth.

Xie Huachi. "CPC Members Told to Think of the People." *Xinhua English*, September 25, 2013, available at http://news.xinhuanet.com/english/china/2013-09/25/c _132750401.htm.

Xie Yue. "The Political Logic of *Weiwen* in Contemporary China." *Issues & Studies* 48, no. 2 (2012): 1–41.

Xin Lin, and Huang Qi. "Interview: 'The Authorities Fear We Will Expose the Scandal of Post-Quake Reconstruction.'" *Radio Free Asia*, March 4, 2016, available at http:// www.rfa.org/english/news/china/china-huang-03042016153923.html.

"Xingshizhuyi: Yi zhong cuowei de zhengzhiguan" [Formalism: A type of erroneous judgment of political achievement]. *Henan ribao* [Henan Daily], October 10, 2013), available at http://theory.people.com.cn/n/2013/1023/c49150-23296160.html.

Xiong Jingming. "Yi shengming de mingyi huiwang lishi—dizhen hou du beichuan xianzhi" [In the name of life, a historical reflection: Reading the Beichuan County annals in the aftermath of the earthquake]. *Political China* (2010), available at http:// www.aisixiang.com/data/31544.html.

Xu Bin. "Consensus Crisis and Civil Society: The Sichuan Earthquake Response and State-Society Relations." *China Journal* 71 (January 2014): 91–108.

——. "For Whom the Bell Tolls: State-Society Relations and the Sichuan Earthquake Mourning in China." *Theory and Society* 42, no. 5 (2013): 509–42.

——. "Grandpa Wen: Scene and Political Performance." *Sociological Theory* 30, no. 2 (2012): 114–29.

Xu Kai. "Qingchuan quanli jiakuai xin xiancheng chongjian jianwen" [Qingchuan all-out acceleration of reconstruction of new county seat information]. *Fenghuang* (November 24, 2010), available at http://news.ifeng.com/gundong/detail_2010_11/24 /3214194_0.shtml.

Xu Quanxing. "Mao zedong lun kongzi 'zheng ming'" [Mao Zedong's view on Confucius's doctrine of the "rectification of names"]. *Mao Zedong shuzi tushuguan* [Mao Zedong digital library] available at www.mzdlib.com/libszzy/maozedongxingjiushujuku /5188.html.

Xunzi. *The Complete Text*. Translated by Eric L. Hutton. Princeton, NJ: Princeton University Press, 2014.

Yan Guo. "Emergence of an Integral Post-Disaster Urbanism: On Crisis of Urban Resilience and Absence of Socio-Spatial Justice Resulted from the post-disaster Planning in Sichuan, China." Paper presented at Asian Planning Schools Association Eleventh International Conference (2011).

Yan Hairong. "The Myth of Private Ownership." *China Left Review* 1 (2008).

——. "Spectralization of the Rural: Reinterpreting the Labor Mobility of Rural Young Women in Post-Mao China." *American Ethnologist* 30, no. 4: 1–19.

Yan Lianke. "On China's State-Sponsored Amnesia." *New York Times*, April 2, 2013, available at http://www.nytimes.com/2013/04/02/opinion/on-chinas-state-sponsored -amnesia.html?_r=0.

——. "Finding Light in China's Darkness: Yan Lianke on Writing in China." *New York Times*, October 23, 2014, available at http://www.nytimes.com/2014/10/23/opinion /Yan-Lianke-finding-light-in-chinas-darkness.html?_r=0.

——. *Lenin's Kisses*. Translated by Carlos Rojas. New York: Grove Press, 2013.

——. "Understand the Enemy," video interview on *The Louisiana Channel*, October 28, 2015, available at https://www.youtube.com/watch?v=cwPa3utBWYsm.

Yang, Dali L. *Remaking the Chinese Leviathan: Market Transitions and the Politics of Governance in China*. Stanford, CA: Stanford University Press, 2004.

Yang Guobin. "A Civil Society Emerges from the Earthquake Rubble." *Yale Global Online* (June 5, 2008), available at http://yaleglobal.yale.edu/print/4739.

Yang Jie. *Unknotting the Heart: Unemployment and Therapeutic Governance in China*. Ithaca, NY: Cornell University Press, 2013.

Yang Jisheng. *Tombstone: The Untold Story of Mao's Great Famine*. Translated by Stacy Mosher and Guo Jian. New York: Farrar, Straus and Giroux, 2012.

Ye Jinzhong, Wang Chunyu, Wu Huifang, He Congzhi, and Liu Juan. "Internal Migration and Left-Behind Populations in China." *Journal of Peasant Studies* 40, no. 6 (2013): 1119–46.

Ye Xingqing. "China's Urban-Rural Integration Policies." Translated by Flemming Christiansen. *Journal of Current Chinese Affairs* 4 (2009): 117–43.

Yeh, Emily T. *Taming Tibet: Landscape Transformation and the Gift of Chinese Development*. Ithaca, NY: Cornell University Press, 2013.

Yeh, Emily T., Kevin J. O'Brien, and Jingzhong Ye. "Rural Politics in Contemporary China." *Journal of Peasant Studies* 40, no. 6 (2013): 915–28.

"Yingxiu qunzhong qian xin ju guo xinnian" [Yingxiu masses move into their new homes to celebrate the new year]. *Wenchuan County government website*, January 31, 2011, available at http://www.wenchuan.gov.cn/p/st_news_items_i_x63432149201145 0000/.

"Yingxiu zhaokai chongjian yantaohui" [Yingxiu convenes reconstruction discussion session]. *Wenchuan County government website*, May 25, 2009, available at http://www .wenchuan.gov.cn/p/st_news_items_i_x634089993846730000/.

Yurchak, Alexei. *Everything Was Forever, Until It Was No More: The Last Soviet Generation*. Princeton, NJ: Princeton University Press, 2005.

Yushuzhouwei dangxiao ketizu [Qinghai Province, Yushu Prefecture Chinese Communist Party School Task Group]. "Shiming yu chuangxin: Yushu zaihou chongjian moshi yanjiu" [Mission and innovation: Research on Yushu's post-disaster reconstruction methods]. *Lilun dongtai* [Theoretical trends] 19, no. 8 (December 20, 2015): 5–39.

Yu Zaigu, and Li Yang. "Wei bao chongjian wuzi Pengzhou shi cun zhuren Huang shunquan shoushang jiezhi" [Protecting reconstruction materials Pengzhou Municipality village head Huang Shunquan sustained injuries that required amputation]. *Chengdu wanbao* (October 27, 2008), available at http://sichuan.scol.com.cn/sczh /20081027/2008102770332.htm.

Zhang Guolong. "Wen Jiabao: Zhengqu liangnian shijian wancheng huifu chongjian" [Wen Jiabao: Strive to complete reconstruction in two years]. *Hexun.com*, June 23, 2008, available at http://stock.hexun.com/2008-06-23/106889791.html.

Zhang Li. *In Search of Paradise: Middle-Class Living in a Chinese Metropolis*. Ithaca, NY: Cornell University Press, 2010.

Zhang, Qian Forrest, and John A. Donaldson. "The Rise of Agrarian Capitalism with Chinese Characteristics: Agricultural Modernization, Agribusiness and Collective Land Rights." *China Journal* 60 (July 2008): 25–47.

Zhang Shuyan. "Liu Shaoqi yao 'tuifan' Mao Zedong: Jiantao 'dayuejin' jing qiangdiao 'renhuo'" [Liu Shaoqi wants to "overthrow" Mao Zedong: Examination of the "Great Leap Forward" emphasizes "human catastrophe"]. *Renmin wang* [People's Daily Online], December 12, 2011, available at http://history.people.com.cn/GB /205396/16682372.html.

Zhao Dingxin. "The Mandate of Heaven and Performance Legitimation in Historical and Contemporary China." *American Behavioral Scientist* 53, no. 3 (2009): 416–33.

Zhao Gang. "Yingdui zaimin de liyi he gongyi suqiu xuyao zhuyi de jige wenti" [Several problems to pay attention to when handling disaster victims' benefits and righteous demands]. *Lingdao canyue* [Leadership reference] (2008): 13–15. Restricted access publication.

Zhao Hongzhu. "Zhejiang shengwei shuji, shengrenda changweihui zhuren zhao hongzhu, jianghua yaodian" [Essential points of speech by Zhejiang provincial Party secretary, director of standing committee of Provincial People's Congress, Zhao Hongzhu]. (June 9, 2008).

Zhao Jianjun. "Jianshe shengtai wenming de ruogan sikao" [A few thoughts on building ecological civilization]. *Lilun dongtai* [Theoretical trends] 1794 (October 20, 2008): 20–28. Restricted access publication.

Zhejiang sheng zhiyuan Qingchuanxian zaihou huifu chongjian gongzuo bangongshi, Zejiangsheng zhiyuan Qingchuanxian zaihou fuifu chongjian zhihuibu, Qingchuanxian renmin zhengfu [Zhejiang Province assistance to Qingchuan County post-disaster restoration and reconstruction work office; Zhejiang Province assistance to Qingchuan County post-disaster restoration and reconstruction command center; Qingchuan County people's government]. *Zhejiangsheng zhiyuan Qingchuanxian zaihou huifu chongjian guihua shishi pinggu baogao huiji* [Zhejiang Province assistance to Qingchuan County post-disaster restoration and reconstruction planning and implementation assessment report compilation] (December 2010).

Zhengce fagui chu [Policy and Legislation Office]. "Buduan tuijin nongcun jingji shichanghua jianshe he fazhan—jianshe shehuizhuyi xin nongcun fazhan jizhi tanjiu" [Continuously advance village economic marketization construction and development—construct socialism new village development mechanism investigation]. *Quyu jingji cankao* [Regional economic reference] 16, no. 65 (July 10, 2008): 45–50. Restricted access publication.

Zheng Degang. "Kangzhen jiuzai bairi: 67 ming ganbu yin linzhen tuisuo deng xingwei bei chufen" [100 days of earthquake resistance and disaster relief: 67 cadres disciplined for getting cold feet]. *Renmin ribao* (August 19, 2008).

Zheng Yongnian. "Calamities and China's Re-emergence." University of Nottingham *China Policy Institute Blog*, June 3, 2008, available at https://www.nottingham.ac.uk/cpi /china-analysis~/china-policy-institute-blog/2008-entries/03-06-2008.aspx.

Zhonggong beichuan qiangzu zizhi xian wei bangongshi [Beichuan Qiangzu Ethnicity Autonomous County Party Committee Office]. "Beichuan ganbu ying zhen hou shou ge shuangxiu guanfang huiying dong yufei zisha" [Beichuan cadres welcome post-earthquake first double-relaxation: The official response to Dong Yufei's suicide]. *Guangzhou ribao* (October 12, 2008), available at http://sichuan.scol.com.cn /dwzw/20081012/2008101293651.htm.

Zhonggong chengdu wuhou xincheng jianshe gongzuo weiyuanhui [Communist Party of Chengdu Wuhou New City Construction Working Committee]. "Guanyu kaizhan zaihou huifu chongjian gan'en wenming jiaoyu you jiang zheng wen huodong de tongzhi" [Notification regarding the launch of post-disaster restoration and reconstruction gratitude civilization education literary award campaign] (February 16, 2011).

Zhonggong qingchuan xianwei qunzhong gongzuo ju [Qingchuan County Party Mass Work Bureau]. "Guanyu bao song '5.12' dadizhen wo xian xinfang ganbu suo zuo gongzuo de bao gao" [Work report regarding county letters and visits cadres work following the great 5.12. earthquake] (June 5, 2008). Restricted access party document.

Zhonggong qinghai sheng yushu zhou wei dangxiao ketizu [Qinghai Yushu Prefectural Committee Party School Task Group report]. "Shiming yu chuangxin: Yushu zaihou chongjian moshi yanjiu" [Mission and innovation: Yushu's post-disaster reconstruction model research]. *Lilun dongtai* [Theoretical trends] 1908 (December 20, 2011): 25–39. Restricted access publication.

Zhonggong wenchuanxian wei zuzhibu [Wenchuan County Party Organization Department]. "Guanyu 'shi yi wu' gongzuo zongjie 2011 nian gongzuo anpai de baogao" [Summary of the "11th Five-Year Plan" and 2011 work plan report]. December 2, 2010.

Zhonggong zhongyang dangxiao baokan she keti zu [Central Committee of the Communist Party of China Party School Press Research Group]. "Jiakuai shengtai baohu diqu shengtai buchang jizhi de jianli" [Accelerate environmental protection areas and the construction of ecological compensation mechanisms]. *Lilun Dongtai* [Theoretical trends] 1867 (October 30, 2010): 29–34. Restricted access publication.

Zhongguo chengxiantyitihua fazhan baogao [Annual report on China's urban-rural integration]. Edited by Ru xin and Fu chonglan. Beijing: Shehuikexue wenxian chubanshe, 2011.

"Zhongguo gongchandang lianjie zilü zhunze" [Chinese Communist Party standards on integrity and self-restraint]. Available in Chinese at http://politics.people.com.cn/n /2015/1022/c1001-27726471.html.

Zhongguo shekeyuan [Chinese Academy of Social Sciences Social Studies Agricultural Development Group]. "Sichuan dizhen zaiqu nongcun huifu fazhan de xingshi fenxi" [Analysis of Sichuan earthquake disaster zones villager reconstruction development circumstances]. *Guanli xinxi* [Management information] 11, no. 250 (2008). Restricted circulation publication.

Zhongguo shekeyuan [Chinese Academy of Social Sciences Social Studies Post-Disaster Social Reconstruction Group]. "Zaihou yongjiuxing zhufang anzhi yao qinfang sanlei qingxiang" [Post-disaster permanent housing settlement must diligently avoid three types of trends]. *Guanli xinxi* [Management information] 11, no. 250 (2008). Restricted circulation publication.

Zhongguo shekeyuan xinwen yu chuanbo yanjiusuo [Chinese Academy of Social Sciences News and Broadcast Research Institute]. "Jiji zuo hao kangzhen jiuzai yuqing yindao gongzuo" [Actively engage in antiearthquake disaster relief public sentiment guidance work]. *Lingdao Canyue* [Leadership reference] 15, no. 456 (May 25, 2008). Restricted circulation publication.

Zhong Huaining. "Nongcun chanquan gaige yao yi guoqi gaige wei jing" [Village property-right reform must use state-enterprise reform as a mirror]. *Gaige Neican* [Reform Internal Reference] 19 (2008): 4–5.

Zhonghua renmin gongheguo tufa shijian yingdui fa [Emergency Response Law of the People's Republic of China] 2007. Available in both Chinese and English at www .lawinfochina.com/display.aspx?lib=law&id=6358.

Zhongyang dangxiao shengbuji ganbu jinxiuban [Central Committee of the Communist Party School, Provincial Level Cadre Advanced Studies Group]. "Ba zhengji kaoping jizhi chuangxin zuowei jingji fazhan fangshi zhuanbian de guanjian zhuashou" [Innovations in the mechanisms for evaluating political achievement as a critical starting point for transforming the mode of economic development]. *Baogaoxuan* [Chinese Communist Party School selected reports] 6 (2010). Restricted access publication.

Zhou Shengxian. "Nuli tuijin shengtai wenming jianshe: Jiji tansuo zhongguo huanjing baohu xin daolu" [Strive to promote ecological civilization construction: Actively explore a new road for China's environmental protection]. *Baogao xuan* [Selected reports] 8, no. 320 (May 18, 2010). Restricted access publication.

Zhu Jiangang and Hu Ming. "Duoyuan gongzhi: Dui zaihou shequ chongjian zhong canyushi fazhan lilun de fanying" [Pluralized public governance: Theoretical reflections on participatory development in post-disaster reconstruction]. *Open Times* 10 (2011).

Zhu Ling. "Ba jianshao pinkun de mubiao naru zaiqu chongjian jihua" [Incorporate the goal of poverty reduction into disaster-area reconstruction planning]. *Guanli Xinxi* [Management information] (2008): 12–13. Restricted access publication.

Žižek, Slavoj. *Living in the End Times*. London: Verso, 2011.

Zweig, Jason. "Memo to China: Your Market Moves Are Doomed to Fail." *Wall Street Journal*, July 10, 2015, available at http://blogs.wsj.com/moneybeat/2015/07/10/memo -to-china-your-market-moves-are-doomed-to-fail/.

"5.12 da dizhen hou 5 ge yue beichuan nongban zhuren zisha" [Five months after the 5.12 great earthquake Beichuan agricultural office director commits suicide]. *Huaxi dushi bao* [West China City Daily] October 8, 2008, available at http://sichuan.scol.com .cn/dwzw/20081008/200810853617.htm.

Index

Page numbers in italics refer to figures and tables.

AAAA status tourist areas, 110–11, 142
Abazhou Prefecture, 54
Abramson, Daniel, 82
aesthetics, 16, 44, 73, 76, 101–2, 106, 117–18, 130, 141–42, 145–46, 161n61
affect, 22–23, 36–37
aftershocks, 1, 49–50, 54, 126
agricultural land, 16, 83–91, 95, 109, 126, 134
agricultural products, 91; production targets, 134; Qingchuan County, 126, 132–34, 137–39, 188nn13–15
Ai Weiwei, 5, 173n70
Althusser, Louis, 1, 8, 10–12, 159n34, 160n58
Anagnost, Ann, 9
Analects (Confucius), 7, 170n22
Andreu, Paul, 110
anemic economy, 15, 65, 74, 112, 193n17
anxiety, 22, 36, 50, 56–57, 96, 133, 155, 162n2
approval ratings. *See* public opinion
Apter, David, 22
Augustine, 43

"backward thinking," 129, 133
Baidu Baike, 20, 145
Bakken, Børge, 44
Balibar, Étienne, 11
Bandurski, David, 164n36
Baodian reservoir, 125
Bargu, Banu, 11
Barmé, Geremie, 12, 45, 149
Beichuan County, 12, 51–52, 54, 115
Beijing, 5, 10, 20, 37, *67, 68,* 70, 77, 78, 110, 129, 151–54
Beijing Olympics (2008), 22, 153
belief, 9–11, 61–62, 129
benevolence: Communist Party, 34, 107, 117, 120, 122, 137, 139, 154; Qing Dynasty, 24
Berlant, Lauren, 34, 151
biopolitics, 100–101, 129
blood generation, 15, 59, 65, 69, 91, 154. *See also* economic development
blood transfusion, 15, 59, 65, 66, 69–76, 91, 154. *See also* partner assistance program

Bluebook of Urban-Rural Integration (2011), 94
Book of Change, 148
border areas, 78
bottom-up participation, 30, 56. *See also* participation
Bradsher, Kenneth, 70
Brady, Anne-Marie, 7
Buckley, Chris, 130
bureaucrats, professional, 15, 40–41, 57, 154. *See also* cadres
businesses: closure of, 109, 112, 114, 128, 185n32; contracts, 90; empty storefronts, 94–95; relocation of coastal enterprises, 69; scale of operations, 92. *See also* agricultural products; industrialization; partner assistance programs

cadres: demolition supervision, 143; evaluation, 54, 106, 123, 184n6, 191n69; land reform implementation, 90; models, 44–48; negotiating Party legitimacy, 40–42, 50, 57–58, 153–54; psychological conditions, 48–58; self-care, 53–56; self-sacrifice, 41, 43, 46–50, 154; spheres of governance, 63; suicides, 42, 50, 52–53, 55–57, 154; understaffed, 183n112; work style, 27–28, 40–41, 54–55. *See also* corruption; Party spirit
Cai Yongshun, 32, 106
capital, 92, 136, 137
capitalism, 61, 64, 147; command capitalism, 70–71, 80; global, 128
CCP. *See* Chinese Communist Party
CCTV, 119
celebrity disaster zones, 75–76
censorship, 2, 13, 23
Central Party School, 40, 48, 58, 106, 127, 160n45
Cheek, Timothy, 7
Chen Boda, 8
Chengdu: academic community, 13; National Land Bureau, 92; proximity to Yingxiu,

Chengdu (*continued*)
    112–13; regional economy, 91–92;
    urban-rural integration, 82–84,
    87–88
Chengdu-Dujiangyan High-Speed Rail, 99
Chen Guaming, 25
Chen Qiu, 50
Chiang Kai-shek, 21
children, deaths of. *See* schools, collapsed
Chinese Academy of Social Sciences, 94
Chinese Communist Party (CCP): constitution,
    42; dependence of Chinese people on, 3,
    25–26, 100–102, 140, 148–52; moral
    authority, 12, 21, 151, 152, 155; one-party
    socialist system as superior, 23–24; repressive
    apparatus, 5, 28, 120–21, 151, 153, 161n62;
    reputation, 17–18, 117, 144; Standards on
    Integrity and Self-Restraint, 42. *See also*
    benevolence; discourse; epistemology; glory;
    ideology; legitimacy; mobilizations; Party
    spirit; planning apparatus
Chongqing, 87–88
ci (poetic form), 171n32
civil society, 17, 30, 33, 153, 163n1
class struggle, 57, 61, 159n34, 169n7
coastal provinces, 67; relocation of enterprises,
    69. *See also* partner assistance program
collapse, predictions of, 62, 155
command capitalism, 70–71, 80
Communist Party. *See* Chinese Communist
    Party
communities, 93–103
complaints, 12, 26, 31, 37, 47, 49, 52–54, 72–73,
    96–102, 112, 117, 120, 136, 140, 145, 151,
    155; government handling of, 136–37. *See
    also* protests; psychological trauma; social
    stability; social unrest
Confucius, 7–8, 44; *Analects*, 7, 170n22
construction materials, quality of, 1–2, 12, 47,
    51–53, 78, 95–96, 152–53
consultative authoritarianism, 5, 29–30
consumer consciousness, 99–100, 102, 104
contracts, 78, 88, 90, 111, 113
cooperative organizations, 89
corruption, 42, 58, 76, 87, 95, 118, 134, 142,
    151, 152, 180n20, 191n79
cosmology, 148
countryside. *See* rural areas
County Animal Husbandry and Food Bureau,
    136
crisis discourse, 2, 21, 148–49, 155, 162n2;
    benefits from, 170n20; social problems as,
    157n7

critical reading, 192n6
criticism, 12, 23, 28, 32, 43, 58, 74, 101, 103
Cultural Revolution, 9, 20–21, 56, 60, 171n32;
    repudiation of, 27
cultural stone, 145

Dalai Lama, 37
Davies, Gloria, 162n2
death: and propaganda, 44–48. *See also* schools,
    collapsed
debt, 34, 36, 38, 41, 139, 150
deindustrialization, 109
Deleuze, Gilles, 163n22
deliberative democracy, 29
democracies, electoral, 19, 23, 166n65, 167n90;
    legitimacy, 40, 61; liberal subjects, 147
democratic centralism, 28–31
Dengjiang County, 129
Deng Xiaoping, 187n69; on development, 131,
    137; economic policy, 66; on ideology, 61–62;
    policies, 162n10
Deng Xiaoping Theory, 27
dependence on Chinese Communist Party, 3,
    25–26, 100–102, 140, 148–52
depression, 15, 41, 42, 50–51, 56, 173n72
Derrida, Jacques, 34
development: regional, 64, 66, 76, 92, 109, 126,
    129; subtypes of, 131; sustainable, 69, 128,
    193n17. *See also* economic development;
    reconstruction
Development Research Center (DRC), 24, 78,
    124, 125, 134
Deyang, 82
disabled accessibility, 72
disaster relief, 22, 24, 38–39, 76. *See also*
    reconstruction
disaster zones: allocation of resources, 75–76;
    celebrity, 75–76
discontent, 150–52. *See also* complaints
discourse, 6–11, 13–16, 18–20, 22–24, 28–29,
    32–33, 35–39, 41–42, 48–49, 51, 53, 55, 57,
    59, 60–63, 65, 69–70, 82–82, 84–85, 99, 101,
    103, 105, 121–22, 127, 135–37, 144, 147,
    149–50, 154; discursive rights, 192n6;
    formalism, 31–34; inertia of, 162n7;
    investigation, 26–28; mandatory gratitude,
    34–38; and power, 147, 150, 192n7; Sichuan
    miracle, 18–26; use of term, 6
discursive frames, 146–47
discursive path dependence, 14, 18, 44, 66,
    105, 152
dissidents, 12, 153
domestic demand, increasing, 25, *85*, 100

Donaldson, John, 111
Dongguan Municipal Partnership Reconstruction Team, 75, 110, 114, 119
Donghekou Village, 125, *126*
Dong Yufei, 52–53, 55
DRC. *See* Development Research Center
dreamlike images, 103–7, 115–16
Dujiangyan Municipal Communist Party School, 25, 35, 36, 49, 50, 87, 89, 91, 92, 96, 98, 102
Dujiangyan Municipality, 81–104; bereaved parents, 5; communities, 93–103; industry, 91–93; land, 75, 86–90; new urban citizen construction, 84–86, 93–103; political tensions, 101–2; proximity to Yingxiu, 112; Puyang Industrial Enclave, 91–92; transportation, 83; urban-rural integration, 16, 81–104, 124
Dujiangyan Planning Exhibition Pavilion, 82, *103*, 104
Dujiangyan Village Property-Rights System Reform Leadership Working Small Group, 88

Earthquake Memorial Museum, 110, 117–18
Earthquake Resistant Disaster Reduction International Academic Exchange Center, 110–11
earthquakes: Kobe, Japan, 19; Lisbon, 148; Tangshan, 24, 167n95; Yushu, 77–78, 116. *See also* reconstruction; Sichuan earthquake (2008); victims and survivors
eating bitterness, 9, 48–50, 154
ecological civilization, 16, 127–47; contradictions, 127–30; definitions, 127
economic development, 59–60, 103–4; and environmental protection, 128–29, 135; and ideology, 59–80; increasing domestic demand, 85, 100; metaphors, 65, 176n30; politics and ideology, 59–60, 79–80 (*see also* ideology); and predictions of "coming collapse," 62, 155; pre-earthquake planning, 180n25; and reconstruction, 115. *See also* partner assistance program; reconstruction
economic precariousness, 83, 96, 114–16, 138–40, 182n88, 185n28
economic reform, 10, 63–64; and planning discourse, 15; and post-earthquake reconstruction, 19
economic suffering, 62
Edgerton-Tarpley, Kathryn, 24
Eighteenth Party Congress, 127
electoral democracies, 23; legitimacy, 40, 61

emergencies, 1, 17, 80, 121, 150–51, 193n9; defined, 2; mobilizations, 21–23, 43–44, 48, 57, 66. *See also* crisis discourse; manmade catastrophes; natural disasters; Sichuan earthquake (2008)
Emergency Response Law, 2
emotional distress. *See* parents of earthquake victims; psychological trauma
employment, 16, 25, 38, 69, 74, 83–86, 92–93, 96, 102, 104, 137
entrepreneurship, 67, 74, 100, 102, 112. *See also* businesses
epistemology, 21, 27–28, 63, 105, 129, 133, 147
ethnic minorities, 37, 78–79, 120
ethnographic research, 13–14, 82, 161n64, 178n67
example setting, 8, 41, 44–49, 55, 82, 87–88, 104, 129, 130, 132–33, 135, 143, 169n13. *See also* models of authority
exhaustion, 15, 42, 50, 53, 55–57
expectations, 14–15, 23, 25–26, 34, 37, 41, 44–48, 51, 62, 91, 136, 140. *See also* complaints; gratitude

face projects, 32, 117–19, 140, 142
fairness, 40, 75–77, 136, 139–40
faith, 19–21
fault lines, 140–41
Feng Xiang, 53
feudal past, 20, 24, 26, 37
"Five-in-One Constructions," 127
forest conservation, 16, 126, 130, 146, 188n16
formalism, 31–34, 38, 105–6, 122, 130, 140, 142, 166n77
Foucault, Michel, 192n7
Four Cardinal Principles, 61
fraud, 122, 152
fruitless flowers, 31–34. *See also* formalism
Fujian Province, 78

The Gate of Heavenly Peace (Hinton and Gordon), 12
Geertz, Clifford, 45
generations, 20, 39, 99
gift, discourse of, 34–35, 37, 109, 120
glasnost, 33
global capitalism, 128
global ecological crisis, 127
global financial crisis (2008), 85, 180n17
glory, 15, 22, 41, 43–44, 57, 71, 77, 106, 107, 117, 123, 154
gratitude, 10, 41, 46, 120, 142, 144, 154; expressions of, *3–4*

gratitude education, 3, 9, 34–38, 155
"great leap development," 14, 18, 24–25, 49, 130, 131, 145
Great Leap Forward, 2, 5, 9, 45, 125
green economy, 128, 135
grief, 12, 22–23, 46, 51, 52–53, 153
grievances. *See* complaints
Guangdong Province, 31, 75, 78
Guanghui Village Political Thought Supervision Group, 130
Guangyuan City, 143
Guangyuan Times, 124, 143
Guattari, Felix, 163n22
guilt, 11, 36, 51

Han Fei, 34, 167n95
He Baogang, 29
Heilmann, Sebastian, 18, 64
He Jintang, 110
He Lijun, 74
Hongguang Township, 135–36, 145
Hong Kong, 70
housing: aesthetics, 145–46; empty, 94–95, 115, 144–45; incomplete, 119–20; relocation, 72, 84, 93, 96, 144; temporary, 121–22, 187n69
How to Be a Good Communist (Liu), 43, 57
Hu Angang, 64
Huang Haifeng, 158n23
Huang Qi, 5, 161n62
Huang Shunquan, 47
Huang Yanrong, 110
Hu Jintao, 53
humanitarianism, 79, 153
human nature, 41–43, 49, 169n13; fragility of, 50–53
Hu Ming, 30
Hu Qiaomu, 169n7
Hurricane Katrina (U.S.), 19, 163n14
Hurricane Sandy (U.S.), 151
Hurst, William, 83, 144

ideology, 1, 6–13, 18, 19, 23, 33, 36, 41, 51, 53, 57, 81, 82, 84, 127, 128, 135, 149–50; as backwards, 59–61; and economic development, 59–80; eternity of, 160n58; as vital function of the state, 147. *See also* Mao Zedong
idle proletariat, 86, 97–98, 102–3
industrialization, 16, 85; clusters, 91–93; industrial parks, 69–71, 84, 132
infrastructure, 20, 24, 37, 64, 67, 69, 72, 77–78, 81, 92, 99, 119–20, 125–26; 136, 146; theft of, 114–15

Inner Mongolia, 70
institutional reform, 18, 28
instrumentality, 11, 79
International Academic Exchange Center, 110–11
interpellation, 11–12
interpretive methods, 6, 14, 149–50
intimidation tactics, 144
investigation, 26–28, 31–33, 105, 117
investors, 89, 90

Jiangsu, *67*, *68*, 78
Jiangxi, *67*, *68*, 75
Jiao Yulu, 45–46
Jiuzhaigou nature reserve, 112
Jowitt, Ken, 43

Kang, Yi 17, 117
Kangbashi, 70
Khrushchev, 8
Kleinman, Arthur, 50
Kobe earthquake (Japan), 19
Kuomintang Party (KMT), 21–22

land reform, 86–90; 1947–1952 campaign, 9
landslides, 109, 126, 140–41, 193n9. *See also* mudslides
land-use rights, 75, 83, 85, 87, 89–91
language, 15, 33, 36, 46, 51, 159n34; in Chinese politics, 6–12, 147, 150; Mao on, 1, 5, 8; sacred power of, 9–10, 159n42. *See also* discourse
Lankao County, 45
Laughlin, Charles, 45
leadership inspection visits, 73, 76–77; in Yingxiu, 106–8, 116–23. *See also* investigation
Leadership Reference, 2
Lee, Haiyan, 44
legitimacy, 6–7, 14–15, 17–21, 24–26, 160n49, 161n61; and cadres, 40–42, 50, 57–58, 153–54; and discontent, 150–52; and economic performance, 60–63; in electoral democracies, 40, 61; erosion of, 75, 96, 108, 120, 140; mechanisms for maintaining, 152–55; natural disasters as opportunity for mobilizations, 43–44, 148–49; symbolic forms of, 121. *See also* benevolence; glory
Lei Feng, 104
Lenin, Vladimir, 8, 33, 42
Leninist norms and expectations, 14–15
Lenin's Kisses (Yan), 38–39
Leys, Simon, 6, 81, 170n22

Li, Lianjiang, 160n56

liberal democracies. *See* democracies, electoral

liberal subject, 147

Li Chuncheng, 87, 180n20

Lijiang, Yunnan Province, 113–14

Li Mingjie, 142, 191n79

Lin Chun, 166n65

Li Ruihuan, 45

Lisbon earthquake, 148

Li Shulei, 10, 160n45

Liu Mingxing, 144

Liu Yongdong, 144

Liu Junlin, 87

Liu Qibao, 107, 110

Liu Shaoqi, 2, 43, 57, 58

Liu Tie, 70

Liu Yu, 8–9

Liu Yunshan, 47–48

living conditions, 27, 83, 86, 102, 112, 119–20, 146. *See also* housing

loan repayment, 134, 190n54

Long March (1934), 22

Longmenshan fault line, 157n9

Lu Jun, 193n13

mafia, 144

Ma Hua, 145

Makley, Charlene, 17, 22

mandate of heaven, 60, 148

manmade catastrophes, 1–6, 21, 148–49, 152, 161n61

Mao County, 115, 117, 190n54

Mao's Invisible Hand (Heilmann and Perry), 18

Mao Zedong: compared to Xi, 174n5; on formalism, 31–32; ideology and Communist Party governance, 1–3, 7, 12, 14, 18–29, 56, 58–61, 137, 147 (*see also* ideology); on investigation, 26–27; on language, 1, 5, 8; "Little Red Book," 9–10; "On Practice," 8; "Oppose Stereotyped Party Writing," 27; poems, 171n32; political thought work, 129; "Reform Our Study," 27; on selflessness, 40; on self-regeneration, 68; "Serve the People" speech, 151; "The Foolish Old Man Who Removed the Mountains," 20; "The Role of the Chinese Communist Party in the National War," 27; "The Work Method of Party Committees," 28; "Third Front" campaign, 125

marketization, 70, 85, 91, 132

market risk, 137

Marxist epistemology, 27

mass line, 27, 29, 32, 47

Mass Work Bureau, 47

Mayor's Mailbox, 136–37

Mbembe, Achille, 120

media, 1–3, 10, 12, 13, 17, 43, 62, 75, 76, 110, 116, 127, 136, 151, 153

mediation, 83, 144

Melton, Oliver, 64

Merleau-Ponty, Maurice, 124

methods, 13–14, 161n64; interpretive, 149–50

Mianyang, 51, 82, 161n64

Mianzhu, 25, 67, 82, 115, 144, 161n64

migrant labor, 82, 96–97, 109, 138

Min River, 107, 113

miracle, 18–22, 24–25, 30–31, 66, 83, 109, 147, 149, 153

Mitchell, Timothy, 11, 15, 160n57

mobilizations, 2, 8, 15, 19, 21, 23, 29, 43–44, 48–50, 61, 65–66, 69, 75–76, 129, 148–49

models of authority, 44–48, 133

mourning, 46. *See also* grief

mudslides, 1, 54, 113. *See also* landslides

Mun Young Cho, 175n16

Muslims, 79

Muyu middle school, 47

nail houses, 143–44

National Earthquake Bureau, 66

Nationalist government, 21–22

National Land Bureau, 88

National Public Radio, 116

national self-regeneration, 68–69

natural disasters, 1–6, 12, 21–23, 38, 43–44, 51, 109, 124, 148–49, 152–53

Naughton, Barry, 63

negligence, 121, 151

New Beichuan, 72

New Socialist Village Construction Campaigns, 181n60

New York Times, 130

Ningbo Urban Planning Research Center, 141

Nomenklatura (appointment) system, 106

nonagricultural labor, 16, 25, 83, 85, 139–40, 191n69

nongovernmental organizations (NGOs), 13, 29–31, 82, 94, 102, 116, 120, 153

norms, 14–15, 44–48. *See also* expectations

Norton, Anne, 79

O'Brien, Kevin, 6, 160n56

Olympics (2008 Beijing), 22, 153

One Hundred Flowers Campaign, 32

Orwell, George, 167n90

parents of earthquake victims, 1, 2, 47; emotional distress, 13, 35, 161n63 (*see also* grief); protests by, 1–2, 5, 153, 161n63

participation, 17, 29–31, 123

partner assistance program, 65–80; assisting/receiving partnerships, *67*; blockages between assisting and receiving partners, 71–76; history of, 76–79; industrial parks, 69–71; overview, 66–69; in Qingchuan, 188n13

Party spirit, 14–15, 40–58; definition of, 42, 169n7; discourse of, 42–44; "eating bitterness," 48–50; and fragility of human nature, 50–53; model cadre propaganda, 44–48; and self-care, 53–56

peasants: compliance, 181n60; economic precariousness, 96; employment, 92–93, 96, 102; as idle proletariat, 86, 97–98, 102–3; landless, 90; poverty, 134; relocated to urban settlements, 84, 93, 96; rightful resistance, 160n56; traditional peasant mentality, 101–2. *See also* urban-rural integration; villagers

Pei, I. M., 110

Peng Kaiping, 56

Pengzhou, 82, 91, 145

People's Daily, 18, 31, 119, 130, 162n10, 188n14

People's Liberation Army (PLA), 44

performance legitimacy, 60–63. *See also* legitimacy

Perry, Elizabeth, 18, 181n60

Petition Letter Office, 139

Pi County, 82, 90, 100, 101, 118

Pieke, Frank, 7

Pitkin, Hannah, 63

planning apparatus, 15, 63–66, 71–76, 80, 81, 132, 146. *See also* partner assistance program; urban-rural integration

police behavior, 187n65

political economy, 15, 59–60, 80, 146–47

political violence, 120–21. *See also* repressive apparatus

"Politics and the English Language" (Orwell), 167n90

pollution, 70, 81, 83, 109, 128, 130

Post-Disaster Planning Mutual Support Work Conference, 25

poverty alleviation, 74, 81, 111–12, 124, 135, 175n16, 190n55

power: Communist Party, 20–21, 27, 43–45, 154–55, 161n61; discourse, 6–10, 38, 81, 150, 192n7; dynamics of, 34, 37, 153; hierarchies of, 29, 72–73, 77, 136, 140, 144; ideology, 10–12, 62, 147; of nature, 23, 148; sacredness of, 45; state, 18, 59–60; technological, 18

powerlessness, internalization of, 12

profitability, 32, 34, 64, 70–71, 88–91, 95, 112, 128, 130, 132–33, 135–38, 146–47, 153

proletariat, 90; idle, 86, 97–98, 102–3

propaganda, 1, 2, 6–7, 10, 17, 22, 25, 28, 35–39, 60, 67, 84, 123, 143, 149, 154, 158n23; on model Party cadre, 44–48; as vital function of the state, 147

property rights reform, 87–90

protests, 11, 37, 47, 62, 70, 143–44, 150–52; by parents, 1–2, 5, 153, 161n63; Tiananmen, 12, 45, 60

Provincial Partner Assistance, 65–76, 188n13. *See also* partner assistance program

psychological trauma, 35, 50–53, 154

public opinion, 1–2, 5; approval ratings, 44, 86, 100, 108. *See also* legitimacy

Puyang Industrial Enclave, 91–92

Qiaozhuang, 131, 140–42

Qingcheng Mountain, 83

Qingchuan County, 47, 72–73, 115, 124–47; 11th Five-Year Plan, 131; 12th Five-Year Plan, 128, 131–35; agricultural products, 125, 132–34, 137–39, 188nn13–15; County Seat, 140–45; demolition, 141–44; earthquake damage, 125–26; ecological civilization, 16, 127–47; industrialization, 125, 128, 132; local perspectives on development (villagers), 135–47; parks and struggle over space, 140–46; population growth rate, 125; poverty, 124–25, 134, 190n55; underdevelopment, 124–25; zones, 131–32

Qing Dynasty, 24, 160n42

Qinghai Province, 77, 116

Qing Lidong, 36, 48, 105, 122

Qiu Baoxing, 25

Qiu Jian, 141

Qushan Elementary School, 52

rabbit-raising farms, 135–36, 190n58

A Ray of Sunshine company, 113–14

reciprocity, 34

reconstruction, 12; annual GDP and percent appropriated for, *68*; and corruption, 134; evaluation of, 106; gratitude education campaigns, 35–38; as "great leap development," 14, 18, 24–25, 49; in liberal democracies, 19; as miracle, 18–26, 30, 66, 109, 153; subsidies, 138–39; temporary housing, 55; urban-rural integration, 15,

81–104; wasteful projects, 72–74, 106, 111, 117–22, 140, 142. *See also* blood generation; blood transfusion; economic development; partner assistance program
"Recovering the Memory of Jiao Yulu" (Xi), 45, 171n32
rectification of names, 7–8. *See also* Confucius; Han Fei; Mao Zedong; Xunzi
reflection, 23
reform era, 10, 19, 63. *See also* economic reform; institutional reform; land reform
regional development, 64, 66, 69, 76, 81, 92, 109, 126, 129, 131
relocation, 48, 72, 84, 86, 92–93, 96, 98, 143–44
Ren Zhongping, 18–19, 162n10, 163n14
repressive apparatus, 5, 28, 120–21, 151, 153, 161n62
research sites, 161n64
rightful resistance, 160n56
Rojas, Carlos, 38
Rousseau, Jean-Jacques, 148
rural areas: economic development, 176n29; housing developments, 94; spectralization of, 175n24; underdevelopment, 16, 66, 74, 81. *See also* peasants; urban-rural integration; villagers

safety standards, 141
Saich, Tony, 22
Santner, Eric, 170n16
Sapio, Flora, 42
saving oneself through production, 68
scale: of agricultural production, 84, 86, 88, 126, 133; of commercial operations, 92, 109
Schmidt, Vivien, 6, 162n7
Schoenhals, Michael, 6
schools, collapsed, 1–2, 5, 12, 47, 51–53, 152–53, 161n63; "tofu-dreg schoolhouses," 1, 5, 152, 155
Schurmann, Franz, 159n37, 170n17
Schwartz, Benjamin, 56
Scott, James, 160n57
seek truth from facts, 27, 105
self-criticism, 28, 58, 101
self-reliance, 66–69, 100
self-sacrifice, 12, 15, 23, 41–43, 46–50, 52, 154
Seventeenth Party Congress, 127
Shandong Province, 67, 68, 72
Shanghai Provincial Partnership, 67, 68, 75
Shenzhen, 67, 70
Shifang, 35, 67, 68, 70

Shifang-Beijing Industrial Park, 70
Shuangliu, 91
Shue, Vivienne, 59, 170n19
Shuimo Township, 112, 118, 185n32
Sichuan Academy of Social Sciences (SiASS), 13, 18, 24, 26, 69, 75
Sichuan Communist Party School, 26, 30
Sichuan earthquake (2008): aftermath, 54–55, 57; aftershocks, 1, 49–50, 54, 126; causes of, 157n9; damage, 1, 93, 125–26 (*see also* schools, collapsed); emergency response, 1, 17; epicenter (Yingxiu), 16, 109, 116; impact area map, *xi*; as natural disaster, 152–53; proximity to Beijing Olympics, 22, 153; rupture fronts, 125, 188n8; Xuankou Middle School Earthquake Relics, 110, 112, 114, 118. *See also* victims and survivors
Sichuan Province, 1; map, *xi*
Sichuan Provincial Government, 69, 89, 109–10, 141–42
Slater, Dan, 40
Socialist Education Movement, 9
social stability, 47, 101; threats to, 2, 35–37
social stability maintenance, 47, 63, 78–79, 121, 152
social unrest, 150–52; ethnic minorities, 79
socioeconomic determinism, 62
Soviet Union, 33, 42, 147; revisionism, 8
speaking bitterness, 9
Special Economic Zones (SEZ), 132
Spiritual Civilization General Office, 35
Spring Festival, 119–20
Stalin, Joseph, 42
state capacity, 12, 14, 16, 19, 26, 108
State Council: Development Research Center (DRC), 24, 78, 124, 125, 134; "Notification of the Post-Wenchuan Earthquake Partner Assistance," 66; Post-Wenchuan Earthquake Reconstruction Regulations, 30; "Regulations on Post-Wenchuan Earthquake Restoration and Reconstruction," 66; urban-rural integration, 87
state-owned enterprises (SOEs), 77–78
statistics, 93, 95, 103–4, 142
storefronts, empty, 94–95
stress, 42, 50, 54–56, 101, 154
subsidies, 16, 26, 37, 75, 96, 102, 134–39, 145
success, image of, 105–9
suicide, 42, 50, 52–53, 55–57, 154
Sun Liping, 55, 105
Sun Zhongshan, 68
surplus population, 98

surveillance, 5, 120
sustainable development, 15, 25, 69, 74, 89, 128, 193n17

Tangshan earthquake, 24, 167n95
Tan Zuoren, 5, 158n12
Tao Ran, 144
terrorism, 79
Thaxton, Ralph, 9
The Miracles of Chairman Mao (Urban), 21
Third Front Construction, 125
Thom, Françoise, 33, 167n90
Thornton, Patricia, 157n7, 162n2, 170n20
thought work, 16, 37, 47, 129–30, 133, 146–47
three concentrations, 84, 86–103
Three Gorges Dam, 20, 157n9
Tiananmen protests, 12, 45, 60
Tianjian, 20, 67
Tianjin chemical warehouse explosion, 161n61, 164n36, 193n9
Tibetan Autonomous Region (TAR), 37, 77, 116; partner assistance program, 78–79
tofu-dregs schoolhouses, 1, 5, 152, 155. See also schools, collapsed
Tomba, Luigi, 160n46, 178n2
top-down process, 17, 30, 56, 67, 103, 106, 109
tourism, 16; AAAA status tourist areas, 110–11, 142; market logic, 122; political, 116–22; Qingchuan, 132; Wenchuan County Tourism Bureau, 110–11; Yingxiu Township, 16, 107–16, 122, 124, 130
transparency, 28, 115
transportation, 76, 83, 98–99, 124, 126, 135, 146
truth, 27, 33, 105, 147
Tuan Yi-fu, 99
Typhoon Fitow, 151

Uighurs, 79
unemployment, 38, 86, 102. See also employment
UNESCO world heritage sites, 83
unfairness, 75–77, 139–40. See also fairness
United States, 26; discontent, 150–51; economic suffering, 62; Hurricane Katrina, 19, 163n14; Hurricane Sandy, 151; post-disaster reconstruction, 19
Urban, George, 21
urban areas: cost of living, 98; ghost cities, 94; poverty, 175n16; privileging of, 175n24
Urban Construction Theory Research journal, 92–93
urban-rural integration, 15–16, 81–104; flaws of, 83, 183n109; goal of, 81–82; industry,

91–93; land, 86–90; new urban citizen construction, 84–86, 93–103; Pi County, 183n109; statistics, 103–4; tensions, 101–2; three concentrations, 86–103; urban communities, 93–103
utopianism, 14–15, 18, 107, 110, 123, 130, 178n2. See also utopian urbanism
utopian urbanism, 81–84, 102, 103–5, 107, 110, 123

value systems, 129, 146–47
vanity, 73–74, 105
verification, 28, 71
victims and survivors, 1–2, 12; cadres, 46, 48–53, 154; economic precariousness, 114–16; gratitude education, 35–36; parents, 1–2, 5, 13, 35, 153, 161n63 (see also grief); self-help, 67–68
villagers: income sources, 138; new urban citizen construction, 84–86, 93–103; and property rights reform, 87–90; in Qingchuan, 135–40; relocation, 72, 144; "unruly" habits, 101, 145–46. See also peasants; urban-rural integration
Voltaire, 148

Wang Bin, 54, 109, 122
Wangcang County, 35
Wang Hongxin, 74
Wang Hui, 29
Wang Jihong, 46
Wang Shikun, 47
Wang Yang, 110
Warren, Mark, 29
Weber, Max, 21, 41, 57, 154, 163n26
Wedeen, Lisa, 40
Weibo, 118
Wenchuan County, 1, 4, 109, 115; Du-Wen Highway, 3; Organization Department 2010 End of Year Report, 54; Partner Assistance Program, 31; Party Organization Department, 46; police behavior, 187n65; psychological training classes, 55
Wenchuan County, Yingxiu Township Master Plan Circumstances Report Conference, 110
Wenchuan County Enlarged Working Conference, 109
Wenchuan County Tourism Bureau, 110–11
Wen Jiabao, 18, 22; inspection visits, 118–21
Wenjiang, 91
White Terror, 21
words. See discourse; language

Xiang Cide, 142, 143

Xi'an mist cannon, 130

Xi Jinping, 10, 160n45; anticorruption campaign, 58; on cadre work styles, 27–28, 40–41, 45, 118, 186n50; compared to Mao, 174n5; crackdown on governmental excesses, 118, 186n50; ecological civilization, 127; economic policies, 59, 62; on formalism, 31; on police behavior, 187n65; "Recovering the Memory of Jiao Yulu," 45, 171n32

Xinhua, 111, 119

Xinjiang Autonomous Region, 79

Xuankou Middle School Earthquake Relics, 110, 112, 114, 118

Xu Bin, 17

Xunzi, 169n13

Yang Jie, 37

Yan Guo, 96, 103

Yan Lianke, 38–39

Yan Qianmin, 50

Yaodu township, 137

Yeh, Emily, 37

yiku sitian campaigns, 9

Yingxiu Hotel, 111

Yingxiu Township, 75, *107*, 107–23, *114*, *115*; entertainment facilities, 113; as epicenter of earthquake, 109, 124; leadership inspection visits, 106–8, 116–22; Post-Disaster Reconstruction International Discussion Forum, 110; reconstruction, 109–16; tourism, 16, 107–16, 122, 124, 130

Youth Activity Center, 110

Yunnan Province, 113, 129

Yu Qi, 82

Yurchak, Alexei, 33

Yushu earthquake, 77–78, 116, 161n64

Yushu Prefectural Party School, 77

Yuyao City, 151

Yu Zhaorong, 46

Zhangjiaping Village, 109

Zhao Dingxin, 60

Zhao Hongzhu, 71

Zhao Jianjun, 127

Zhejiang Province, *67*, *68*, 71–73, 133–34, 141, 151, 188n13

Zhengzhou, 193n13

Zhou Dynasty, 60

Zhou Qiang, 79

Zhou Yongkang, 5

Zhu Jiangang, 30

Zhu Rongji, 1

Zhuyuan, 131, 140–41

Zipingpu Dam, 157n9

Žižek, Slavoj, 61

Zuozhuan, 22

CPSIA information can be obtained
at www.ICGtesting.com
Printed in the USA
LVHW08*2039021018
592160LV00012B/218/P